Sydney Goodsir Smith, Poet

# Scottish Cultural Review of Language and Literature

VOLUME 30

The titles published in this series are listed at *brill.com/scrl*

# Sydney Goodsir Smith, Poet

*Essays on His Life and Work*

*Edited by*

Richie McCaffery

BRILL

RODOPI

LEIDEN | BOSTON

Cover illustration: Sydney Goodsir Smith in Milne's Bar 2017 © Alexander Moffat.

Library of Congress Cataloging-in-Publication Data

Names: McCaffery, Richie, editor.
Title: Sydney Goodsir Smith, poet : essays on his life and work / edited by
  Richie McCaffery.
Description: Leiden ; Boston : Brill Rodopi, [2020] | Series: Scottish
  cultural review of language and literature, 1571-0734 ; volume 30 | Includes bibliographical
references and index.
Identifiers: LCCN 2020002409 (print) | LCCN 2020002410 (ebook) | ISBN
  9789004425101 (hardback ; acid-free paper) | ISBN 9789004426498 (ebook)
Subjects: LCSH: Smith, Sydney Goodsir, 1915-1975--Criticism and
  interpretation.
Classification: LCC PR6037.M58 Z86 2020 (print) | LCC PR6037.M58 (ebook)
  | DDC 821/.914 [B]--dc23
LC record available at https://lccn.loc.gov/2020002409
LC ebook record available at https://lccn.loc.gov/2020002410

Typeface for the Latin, Greek, and Cyrillic scripts: "Brill". See and download: brill.com/brill-typeface.

ISSN 1571-0734
ISBN 978-90-04-42510-1 (hardback)
ISBN 978-90-04-42649-8 (e-book)

Printed by Printforce, the Netherlands

*This book is dedicated to the memory of Dr. Margery Palmer McCulloch*

∴

# Contents

# Acknowledgments and a Note on the Poems

Although Sydney Goodsir Smith's *Collected Poems: 1941–1975* (1975) is generally regarded as a flawed text with a number of typographic errors, the decision has been made to follow this book where possible in this edited collection. The reason for this is that the *Collected Poems* is the most readily available and complete of Smith's publications and it contains an extensive glossary of English translations of Scots words, and has yet to be bettered. This present edited collection only contains a selective glossary of the more difficult Scots terms and readers who have any difficulty with Smith's Scots beyond this are advised to use the glossary in *Collected Poems*. Certain poems, such as uncollected translations and those in Smith's first collection *Skail Wind* are not included in *Collected Poems*.

The editor wishes to thank not only those who kindly offered chapters for this book, but also the staff at Brill, particularly Masja Horn, for their interest. The editor also wishes to thank the following people and institutions for their time, knowledge and support: Heather Scott; Tessa Ransford (d.2015); Hugh Mackay; Donald Hall (d.2018); Stefanie Van de Peer; Deirdre Guthrie; Deirdre Grieve; John Manson; Edward Nairn (d. 2013); Roddy Simpson; Robin Fulton; Roderick Watson; James Aitchison; the staff of the Scottish Poetry Library; the staff of Special Collections / National Library of Scotland; the staff of Special Collections / Edinburgh University Library; the staff of Special Collections / University of Glasgow Library and the staff of the Mitchell Library, Glasgow. The editor would also like to particularly thank the artist Alexander Moffat for allowing images of his artworks to be reproduced in this book.

Patrick Crotty's essay 'Sydney Goodsir Smith: A Centenary Appreciation' is a changed and extended version of an article first published as 'Doon Canongate: A centenary appreciation of a Scots makar' in the *Times Literary Supplement* (November 13, 2015, pp. 14–15).

FIGURE 0.1 Poets' Pub (1982)
© ALEXANDER MOFFAT

# Contributors

*Paul Barnaby*
is Scottish Literary Collections Curator at Edinburgh University Library. He previously worked as Editor of the Bibliography of Scottish Literature in Translation (BOSLIT) at the National Library of Scotland and as Post-Doctoral Research Fellow for the Reception of British and Irish Authors in Europe project at the School of Advanced Studies, University of London. He has published essays and given conference papers on French translations of Sir Walter Scott, on the international reception and translation of Scottish literature, on theatrical and juvenile adaptations of Scottish writing, and (drawing on his doctoral research) on the Italian reception of French Naturalism.

*John Corbett*
is presently a CAPES International Fellow and Visiting Professor at the University of Sao Paulo. He was previously a Professor and Head of the English Department at the University of Macau, and before that he was a Professor at Glasgow University, where he served as Head of the Department of English Language. He has published widely on diverse topics, including Scottish literature and the Scots language, literary translation, intercultural language education, and corpus linguistics. He is an Honorary Vice-President of the Association for Scottish Literary Studies and he has twice chaired the MLA Scottish Literature Forum.

*Patrick Crotty*
is emeritus Professor of Irish and Scottish Literature at the University of Aberdeen. He has published widely on Irish, Scottish, Welsh and American poetry has been a regular reviewer for the *Times Literary Supplement* since 1992. His verse translations have featured in many books and periodicals. He edited *Modern Irish Poetry: An Anthology* (1995) and *The Penguin Book of Irish Poetry* (2010.) He has just completed editing the first volume (1908–1930) of the annotated *Complete Collected Poems of Hugh MacDiarmid*.

*Emma Dymock*
achieved her Ph.D. at Edinburgh University in 2008. Her primary research interest is modern Scottish Gaelic poetry. She has worked with the poet and scholar Christopher Whyte, in preparing the collected poems of Sorley MacLean, published in 2011. Her research on 20th century Gaelic poetry has led

her to explore the field of 20th century Scottish literature more widely. She has also attempted to bring the work of Douglas Young more firmly into focus, beginning with the publication of *Naething Dauntit: The Collected Poems of Douglas Young,* in 2016. Emma Dymock's other research interests include Scottish Gaelic drama and 20th Century Irish poetry. She is particularly interested in modern representations of myth, symbolism and socio-political contexts.

### Tom Hubbard

is a writer whose books include the novels *Marie B.* (2008) and *The Lucky Charm of Major Bessop* (2014); the novella collection *Slavonic Dances* (2017); the poetry collections *The Chagall Winnocks* (2011), *Parapets and Labyrinths* (2013), and *The Flechitorium* (2017). Most of his books in recent years concern Scottish connections with mainland Europe, and have appeared from Grace Notes Publications. He has also edited books of essays on Stevenson, Kipling, Baudelaire, Flaubert and Henry James. He was the first Librarian of the Scottish Poetry Library and went on to become a visiting university professor in France, Hungary and the USA. In 2017 he became a Fellow of the Association of Scottish Literary Studies.

### Richie McCaffery

was a Carnegie Trust Caledonian Scholar at the University of Glasgow where his Ph.D. was on the Scottish Poets of World War Two. His academic essays on 20th century Scottish poetry and writing have appeared in places such as *Études écossaises, Scottish Literary Review, Studies in Scottish Literature* and the *International Review of Scottish Studies*. He is the editor of *Finishing the Picture: The Collected Poems of Ian Abbot* and co-editor, with Alistair Peebles, of *The Tiny Talent: Selected Poems by Joan Ure*. He is a poet with two full collections to his name, *Cairn* and *Passport*, both from Nine Arches Press.

### J. Derrick McClure

retired in 2009 after forty years in the English Department of Aberdeen University. Author of *Why Scots Matters, Scots and its Literature, Language, Poetry and Nationhood, Doric: the Dialect of North-East Scotland*, and over 120 refereed articles and conference papers. Editor of the anthology *A Kist o Skinklan Things* and (singly or in collaboration) of several multi-author volumes. Translations include *Sangs tae Eimhir, Ailice's Anters in Ferlielann, The Prince-Bairnie, Scotland o Gael an Lawlander* (translations from four modern Gaelic poets), and numerous individual poems from Gaelic, Italian, German and other languages. In 2002 awarded an M.Litt. for services to Scottish culture.

*Margery Palmer McCulloch*

was Honorary Senior Research Fellow at the University of Glasgow and published widely on Scottish literature. In recent years she focused on Scotland's contribution to international Modernism, with *Modernism and Nationalism* (2004), *Scottish Modernism and its Contexts* (2009), and the co-edited *Edinburgh Companion to Hugh MacDiarmid* and *Scottish and International Modernisms* (both 2011). She was co-editor of *Scottish Literary Review* from 2005–2013. Shortly before her death in late 2019, she completed a joint biography of Edwin and Willa Muir and their Scottish and European contexts, research for which was funded by a Leverhulme Emerita Fellowship.

*Alexander Moffat*

is an artist and teacher. Born in Dunfermline in 1943, he studied painting at Edinburgh College of Art. From 1968 to 1978 he was the Director of the New 57 Gallery in Edinburgh. In 1979 he joined the staff of The Glasgow School of Art where he was Head of Painting from 1992 until his retirement in 2005. His portraits of the major poets of the Scottish Renaissance movement now hang in the Scottish National Portrait Gallery and his paintings are represented in many public and private collections including the Yale Center for British Art, USA and the Pushkin Museum in Moscow.

*Mario Relich*

was born in Zagreb, Croatia, and grew up in Montreal, Canada, where he obtained his MA in English Literature from McGill University. He did his postgraduate studies at Edinburgh University, leading to a Ph.D. thesis on philosophical dialogue during the Enlightenment. He holds dual citizenship, Canadian and British, and has lived in Edinburgh most of his life. He has been an Associate Lecturer in English Literature and Film History at the Open University in Scotland for many years, which led to his involvement as a member of the Open History Society in Scotland, latterly as committee chairman. He has also taught at the Edinburgh College of Art, Napier University, and the University of Ife, Nigeria. A widely published poet, including his collection *Frisky Ducks* (Grace Note, 2014), he is also member of the Scottish PEN Board, and was for nearly twenty years Programme Secretary of the Poetry Association of Scotland.

*Alan Riach*

(b.1957) Poet and Professor of Scottish Literature, Glasgow University. Born in Airdrie, Lanarkshire, studied at Cambridge and Glasgow, worked at the

University of Waikato, New Zealand, 1986–2000, and has been back in Scotland since 2001. Books include poetry: *The Winter Book* (2017), *Homecoming* (2009) and *Wild Blue: Selected Poems* (2014); criticism: *Hugh MacDiarmid's Epic Poetry* (1991), *Representing Scotland* (2005), and co-authored with Alexander Moffat, *Arts of Resistance: Poets, Portraits and Landscapes of Modern Scotland* (2008), described in the *Times Literary Supplement* as 'a landmark book', and *Arts of Independence* (2014). Riach and Moffat are also the co-editors of the annotated edition of J.D. Fergusson's radical manifesto-book *Modern Scottish Painting* (1943; new edition, 2015).

### David Robb

was until his recent retirement a Senior Lecturer in English at the University of Dundee. He has taught and researched modern Scottish Literature since the 1970s. He has published on a variety of 19th and 20th century Scottish authors, with particular emphasis on George MacDonald, Hugh Miller, and Alexander Scott. His work on MacDonald in particular is recognised and valued by specialists throughout the world. His most recent book is on Robert Louis Stevenson (2016). He is currently researching and lecturing on Sir Alexander Gray.

### Stewart Sanderson

is a Glaswegian writer, currently based in the West Midlands. In 2014 and 2016 he was shortlisted for the Edwin Morgan Poetry Award and in 2017 received commendations for the *PN Review* Poetry Prize and the Stephen Spender Prize for Poetry in Translation. He received an Eric Gregory Award in 2015 and a Robert Louis Stevenson Fellowship in 2016. In 2019 he was awarded the Jessie Kesson Fellowship at Moniack Mhor. He completed a Ph.D. at the University of Glasgow, which addressed the role of translation in 20th century Scottish poetry - and has himself contributed to international translation exchange projects involving Frisian, North African and Russian writers. His first pamphlet of poems, *Fios*, was published by Tapsalteerie in 2015. A second pamphlet, *An Offering*, was published in 2018.

### Monika Szuba

is Lecturer in English Literature at the University of Gdańsk. Her research covers 20th and 21st century Scottish and English poetry and prose, with a particular interest in ecocriticism informed by environmental humanities and phenomenological perspectives. She was Bednarowski Trust Fellow at the University of Aberdeen (2015–6). She is co-editor with Julian Wolfreys of *The Poetics and Politics of Space and Place in Scottish Literature* (Palgrave, 2019) and

*Reading Nineteenth-Century Literature: Essays in Honour of J. Hillis Miller* (EUP, 2019). She is the author of *Contemporary Scottish Poetry and the Natural World: Burnside, Jamie, Robertson and White* (EUP, 2019).

### Christopher Whyte

taught at the Sapienza University of Rome from 1977 to 1985, in the English Department at the University of Edinburgh from 1986 to 1989, and in the Scottish Literature Department at the University of Glasgow from 1990 to 2005. He did pioneering work in the application of Carnival theory to Scottish vernacular poetry of the 15th to the 18th centuries in a series of essays entitled 'Bakhtin at Christ's Kirk', as well as using gender and queer theory to mount a critique of more conservative forms of cultural nationalism in 'Defamiliarising "Tam O'Shanter"' and an edited volume of essays *Gendering the Nation* (1995). Between 1995 and 2000 he published four novels in rapid succession. His sixth collection of Gaelic poems *Ceum air cheum/ Step by step*, with facing English translations by Niall O'Gallagher, was published in 2019. An outstanding translator from the Russian of Marina Tsvetaeva, Whyte also edited with commentary two volumes from the Gaelic of Sorley MacLean/Somhairle MacGillEain, *Dàin do Eimhir/Poems to Eimhir* (2002) and *An Cuilithionn 1939/The Cuillin 1939* (2011).

# Introduction

*Richie McCaffery*

As a gifted amateur artist, working mainly in watercolour, and a lively art critic for the *Scotsman* in the 1960s, the poet Sydney Goodsir Smith (1915–1975) might well have appreciated any book attempting to re-evaluate his creative achievement beginning with a discussion of a painting. One of the contributors to this present volume, the artist Alexander Moffat, has kindly allowed one of his portraits of Smith to serve as the cover image, yet it's a much more well-known work by Moffat at which I would like us to have a look. 'Poets' Pub', completed in 1980, is one of Moffat's most recognisable works, having been used as the cover image for the 1981 book *Seven Poets* which was one of the first retrospectives of the major poets of Scottish Renaissance movement. The painting reproduced here is a variation from 1982, and depicts a somewhat idealised and fictionalised image of a cadre of older literary men. Their respective ages put the date implied by the painting at the early 1960s and with the exception of Hugh MacDiarmid (1892–1978), widely recognised as one of the progenitors of the Scottish literary renaissance, all of these men belong, with varying degrees of willingness or reluctance, to the second wave of that movement.

Smith will be the first of this literary corral to die, suffering a heart attack on the 15th of January 1975 outside a newsagents in Dundas Street in his beloved, adopted Edinburgh, not far from his home, a nursery flat at 25 Drummond Place, which he shared with his second wife, schoolteacher Hazel Williamson (1928–2004). He married Williamson in 1967, but had known her since at least the very early 1950s. He had been a chronic asthmatic, as well as a lifelong heavy smoker and drinker. All the other men in this painting with the exception of Edwin Morgan, upon hearing of Smith's death, gathered together in print to publish *For Sydney Goodsir Smith* (1975), a posthumous festschrift for their fallen brother in the muse. The pub setting is a synthesis of period 'howffs' (pubs) from Rose Street in Edinburgh, such as Milne's and, Smith's favourite, the Abbotsford, both of which still exist today. These pubs were transmogrified in Smith's only published novel, *Carotid Cornucopius* (1947) into 'Doddie Mullun's' (Milne's) and 'the Abbotsfork' (the Abbotsford) (Smith: 1964a, 32). In this present book, Richie McCaffery, tackles this particular 'monsterpiece' (Hall: 1984, 15), and we can see already from the mere renaming of pubs that it is an endlessly energetic and inventively neologistic piece of writing, powered by a love affair with both drink and words. As with some of Smith's work, *Carotid Cornucopius* is foremost a spirited *jeu d'esprit* but McCaffery here shines light

on the seriousness and scale of Smith's vision that lies behind it and the need
to look beyond the bluff veneer of his use of humour. In Elegy XXIV of *Under
the Eildon Tree* (1948) Smith's poet speaker admits that he uses humour as a
means of 'self-defence' in difficult times and situations:

> Gin my luve eer should see it, Cynthia,
> And should she comprehend her bard,
>     Her hert, as she did aince…
>                 (Albeid I end thus in mockerie
>                 In sheer sel-defence
>                 Agin the jalous gods' decreets).

SMITH: 1975, 186

If we return to Moffat's 'Poets' Pub' painting, we can see that while Hugh Mac-
Diarmid, in his striking blue suit remains the focal point, Smith sits facing him
with the pose of an acolyte, holding his hand aloft to silence the chatter of the
others so they can all listen to the master's latest pronouncement on whatever
matter. Placing Smith at the heart of the action seems right, as he did act for at
least two decades as a social lynchpin of the literary Edinburgh scene, shaping
many of his days around the opening hours of his favourite pubs. In his mem-
oirs *For the Islands I Sing* (1997), George Mackay Brown remembers Smith's
social graces and kindness in attempting to bring him into the circle of poets in
Edinburgh in the 1950s (Mackay Brown, 122–124), and Robert Garioch wrote
that Smith got Garioch's work into print again and that beneath the Falstaffian
facade, he was 'practical and business-like' (Garioch, 91). This has perhaps also
contributed to his continued neglect as a poet since his death, as he exerted
such a force on people while he was alive. He was a man who seemed to natu-
rally acquire various appellations: wit, raconteur, *bon viveur*, aesthete, editor,
artist, art critic, scholar, playwright and poet and arguably did not like to be
restricted to one narrow identity, preferring instead a synthesis of all the arts.

Maurice Lindsay observed that '[Smith's] ebullient good-nature and ready
wit so filled out his conversation that the impact of his personality perhaps
resulted in an over-favourable assessment of his early books' (Lindsay, 391).
John Herdman has echoed these remarks by questioning whether or not the
poetic work of Smith represents more a triumph of the 'force of his personali-
ty' over achievement, in that he was a 'genius of character' (Herdman, 76).
Looking at the 'Poets' Pub' painting, this might initially seem to be the case,
as the work of every figure within it has been reappraised since their death
with the only exception being Smith, whose name and work has fallen into
relative obscurity, since his *Collected Poems* was rushed into print riddled with

corrigenda in 1975 by John Calder shortly after Smith's death. John Clifford Hall
was perhaps being a little too sanguine when he claimed, in his 1982 PhD thesis
on Smith's work, that the poet's reputation was 'secure' (Hall: 1982, 1). Clifford
Hall's 1982 thesis, followed by Thom Nairn's in 1994, represent the last serious,
substantive attempts to consider Smith's position as a major 20th century Scot-
tish poet. The only work of any real depth to follow from these achievements
in recent years has been Patrick Crotty's 2015 article on Smith's work – 'Doon
Canongate' – which appeared in the *Times Literary Supplement*. An extended
version of this article appears in this book for the first time, with a view to giv-
ing an overview to Smith's achievement and an exhortative case as to why his
work should be read again and reconsidered.

Nowadays Smith is more readily associated with apocryphal drinking anec-
dotes than with his poems, such as going into banks hungover and asking for a
whisky, mistaking it for a pub. His drinking exploits are even immortalised in
the 1968 Norman MacCaig poem, 'The unlikely':

> I dropped a bottle on a stone –
> and the stone broke.
> A friend (drunk) fell from the top box in the theatre
> and landed in the second top one. Impossible.
> MacCaig, 245

This is surely a regrettable fate for one of the most celebrated Scottish poets of
his time. Annalena McAfee's 2017 novel *Hame* is partly set in a fictionalised
Rose Street in Edinburgh in the 1950s and Smith is recounted as a 'degenerate
cherub [...] talking poetry or politics with the men or running after his latest
girlfriend' (McAfee, 235–237). The effect of such writing is to present an histori-
cal figure as a two-dimensional caricature. Smith's philandering is perhaps one
of the major reasons, aside from his highly idiolectal Scots, preventing his work
from being rehabilitated, and it is true that he insidiously divided most of his
life between at least two women so that he always had a steadying, domestic
presence as well as a more spontaneous, vital and inspiring one. In Elegy xv of
*Under the Eildon Tree* the speaker writes of himself as being 'a man between
two lassies' of contrasting temperaments (Smith: 1975, 173). This work is shot
through with a 'Madonna-whore' complex where women are both venerated
and scorned, often in the course of the same elegy, working like a rhetorical
device such as charientism but also revealing the Propertian idea of love's
illogicality. In 1951, to celebrate Hogmanay, Smith privately published, in an
edition of thirty copies, a small collection of poems under the title *The Aipple
and the Hazel*, and dedicated it to 'H.W.   the onlie begetter'. Smith was of

course playing with fire in publicly, though obliquely, dedicating a collection of poems to his secret lover, Hazel Williamson. In a 1952 letter to Alexander Scott, Smith gifted a copy of the pamphlet with the warning 'If you write to me, please don't mention "the Begetter", as I leave my letters all over the place and one does not wish to tempt Providence unnecessarily'.[1]

In a surviving diary entry from the 1949–1950 period, and in an uncharacteristic though private pang of self-pity, Smith wrote about having 'meaningless affairs out of sheer bloody-mindedness' (MS. 26156). In such a context, it is easy to see how he came to write *Under the Eildon Tree* where the Orphean bard is a poet *agonistes* who both sins and is sinned against in 'Luve's arcane delirium' (Smith: 1975, 185). From the late 1940s Smith was having extramarital affairs while still living with his first wife, paediatrician Marion Welsh (1906–1966). This is supported by an anecdote from Peter Main's 2018 biography of the exilic Scottish poet Ruthven Todd, *A Fervent Mind.* In 1948, the year *Under the Eildon Tree* first saw print, Smith was reportedly making attempts to woo Todd's ex-wife Cicely. A party was thrown in her Edinburgh flat and Smith 'might have liked to be present, but was currently *persona non grata*, since as part of his campaign to gain her attention as a suitor, he had on the previous night kicked down to door of Cicely's flat' (Main, 189). When Marion, who had been a devout Catholic, died in 1966, Smith married his 'mistress' Hazel and then embarked on an affair with young artist Stella Cartwright (1938–1985). When this infidelity was discovered in the late 1960s, Smith's relationship with Williamson, who had been effectively working as a school-teacher to provide a home for the both of them, survived after Williamson gave Smith the ultimatum to end his affair with Cartwright. Cartwright was heartbroken and, it is said, never fully recovered, dying in her late 40s from alcoholism. Smith made matters worse by writing secretly after the affair had ended to Cartwright from the Scottish Arts Club, giving her the illusion that matters would blow over soon and he would marry her, which never happened (E96.12). Such behaviour is arguably best understood as part of a thanatic drive, or a pathological compulsion, like Smith's drinking, though this is not to excuse his actions. While the public persona of Smith is most readily remembered as one of ebullience and gregariousness, beneath the surface it is clear that he both suffered and caused those closest to him to suffer as well. For Roderick Watson, the contradictions that lie at the heart of Smith's life and work provide an important dialectic where emotions are continually questioned and problematised, that any joy carries within it a self-destructive element:

---

1   Letter from Smith to Scott, dated 02/03/1952, is from the present author's personal collection of Smith items.

> This ribald, goliardic spirit is constantly qualified by the poet's sense of
> that moment when all the merry music 'turns to sleep' and 'the endmaist
> ultimate white silence faas / Frae whilk for bards is nae retour'. In the
> meantime, as he sees it, there is only love, whose spiritual or carnal de-
> lights bind us to our physical natures and undermine the 'serious' world
> of politics and public affairs.
>
> WATSON: 1984, 420–421

Despite the depth of Smith's aims as an artist, and his political acumen which
became apparent to Sorley MacLean in 1944 in response to the Warsaw Rising
(MacLean: 1970, 11), he was also complicit in his own critical relegation. He of-
ten presented himself as something of a dilettante, in mock heroic and self-
deprecating terms in poems such as Elegy V from *Under the Eildon Tree*:

> Auld Oblomov has nocht on me
> Liggan my lane in bed at nune
> Gantan at gray December haar,
> A cauld, scummie, hauf-drunk cup o' tea
> [...]
> Wi ase on the sheets, ase on the cod,
> And crumbs of toast under my bum,
> Scrievan the last great coronach
> O' the westren flickeran bourgeois world.
>
> SMITH: 1975, 154

It seems unfair that such a poet as Smith, whose reading was wide, varied and
profound and whose poetry, as in *Under the Eildon Tree* shows a vivid intertex-
tuality drawing on a tissue of references, could be dismissed as a dabbler, but
this does seem to be the case. It could be argued that Smith's compulsion to
play the clown, to deflate serious moments in his work with reductive humour
has given off the impression that his poetry is not deeply and sincerely felt.
However, this strikes at perhaps one of the major modernist achievements of
his work of the 1940s and that is its thorough-going interrogation of the nature
of poetry – celebratory, amatory and elegiac, and how all such art is essentially
constructed, and therefore rhetorical: 'Juist sheer damned / Rhetoric!' (Smith:
1975, 185). A poem can be both entirely fictional but also emotionally and intel-
lectually truthful, but it can also operate the other way too. The scale of his vi-
sion is rarely given much credit, although here Christopher Whyte examines
*Under the Eildon Tree* in detail and argues that the poem sequence should be
considered in a postmodern light, as well as harking back to French Decadent

poetry of the 19th century. Hamish Henderson called Smith one of the most successful poets working in the folk idiom to 'heal the gap between song and poetry' (Henderson, 324), and this might sound strange considering his style can be both theatrical and aureate, but he centres his poem in the midst of Scottish folklore with the Thomas the Rhymer myth as well as a classical tradition of the Orpheus and Eurydice myth that is familiar to many, which is also about the fear of being deceived or misled. The curse of Thomas the Rhymer was that he returned from the fairy realm of enchantment with the ambiguous 'gift' of verity, that he could only tell the truth and this silenced him as an artist, 'and he spoke only when some important thing had to be said, and when he did, he startled everybody with his uncanny wisdom' (Scott, 12). Far from being an 'over-bookish' poem as Robert Crawford would have it (Crawford: 2007, 606), this poem is all about accessibility, providing so many registers and narrative frameworks as to speak to all those who read it.

Roderick Watson is right to assert that with Smith there is far more happening than dandyism, 'dialect revival' and 'Scottishness', that he achieves 'a wildly fluid literary voice, a Poundian palimpsest of different cultural references and a Bakhtinian boiling pot of languages and registers with language [...] a deeply unstable, irreverent, intertextual, modernist and even postmodernist reflection on European culture' (Watson: 2011, 15–16). Pound's term for such an effect was 'logopoeia' – 'the dance of the intelligence among words and ideas' (Pound, 57) but with Smith it feels much more immersive, urgent and earthy than this, never forgetting the carnal, mortal body. Like the head of Orpheus, kept to sing after his death, Smith finds modern parallels in the way the work of a poet can still speak to us, long after the death of its creator. This idea that texts have an influence on, and can haunt other texts, even those yet to be written, is one of the great forces of *Under the Eildon Tree* – that fashions and tastes change, but core themes like love and loss are immutable through the ages. T.S. Eliot wrote of the spectral influence of older works on contemporary literature as a form of belatedness in his influential 1919 essay 'Tradition and the Individual Talent' where 'the most individual parts [of a living poet's work] may be those in which the dead poets, his ancestors, assert their immortality most vigorously' (Eliot, 48). The closing lines of Elegy XII of *Under the Eildon Tree* powerfully demonstrate that poetry and thinking, feeling people will always make the same mistakes and turn to important texts to illuminate their condition that are the inalienable property of humankind, like Orpheus looking back on Eurydice in Hades:

> I gang to jyne her in the skuggie airt,
> A convene fou o' dreid for Orpheus' hert.

> Aa this will happen aa again,
> Monie and monie a time [a]gain.
>
> SMITH: 1975, 166

His friends, in private, also often struggled to differentiate between Smith's role-playing and reality, and it is arguable that the overall effect of the persona of boozy-bard that Smith adopted in *Under the Eildon Tree* had an ultimately Pirandellian effect. In a 1941 letter (the year Smith's first collection *Skail Wind* was published) from Sorley MacLean to Douglas Young, MacLean writes:

> I am interested in your new opinion of Sydney. I was never quite sure myself, I have always liked him immensely [...] but he does have a fair amount of what could be called the 'bourgeois-decadent' element.[2]

It could also be argued that Smith's persona was a distraction from the fact that, in Thomas Crawford's opinion, his 'best work [had been] done by the time he was 32' (Crawford: 1976, 18) and his creative energies went into the cultivation of his public image. It is certainly the case that while Smith was always prolific, his poetry did narrow in scope and vision after the late 1940s and many of his love lyrics of the 1950s can strike the reader today as rather formulaic and Parnassian, although longer poems such as 'The Grace of God and the Meth-Drinker' are clearly notable exceptions to this. Tom Hubbard discusses this poem in his chapter on Smith's European translations and adopted image as a 'gangrel' (a wanderer), which also ties him to Russian literature. Stewart Sanderson, in his chapter on Smith's often critically-overlooked translations into Scots, shows how Smith was a crucial contributor to the Scottish Renaissance in its internationalist outlook and scope but that his work also firmly belongs to its time and place, principally the 1940s and 1950s. Smith wrote relatively little poetry going into the 1960s and 1970s and much of his creative energy went into verse drama, such as *The Wallace* (1960) and verse epistle forms such as *Gowdspink in Reekie* (1974) which Mario Relich examines here at length while John Corbett revisits *Kynd Kittock's Land* (1966) which was also televised. Paul Barnaby goes back into Smith's extensive archive at Edinburgh University Library to show us how much of his creative energy in the late 1940s onwards went into writing verse dramas and Barnaby looks in particular at Smith's unpublished play 'Colickie Meg' which was an extension of the novel *Carotid*

---

2   This letter from MacLean to Young, dated 25/09/1941, was offered for sale in 2017 by Edinburgh book dealer John Updike Rare Books (Ian Watson) and featured, partially transcribed, in *Catalogue 51* (item 143, p. 24).

*Cornucopius*. The waning of Smith's poetic powers was something that caused him much anguish. In an entry to his diary in 1949 he writes that he wants nothing more than to 'possess the hizzie again' (Robert Burns's term for poetic inspiration) and that there is no 'compensatory activity' for not being able to write original poetry (MS. 26156). Although highly critical of Smith's work, the poet and critic Robin Fulton has said that in private Smith admitted to him that he should have 'tried harder'.[3] Despite the slow decline of Smith's writing over the years, he was still working at the time of his death, according to Archie Lamont on an anthology of Scottish and Irish poetry (Acc. 10281/1), and as such it seems unjustified to accuse Smith of posturing as a poet, or that his art was mere affectation.

One of the core questions this book sets out to answer is, is Smith's work worthy of our attention now, nearly half a century since his death and are its themes still relevant to us? Almost all of his friends and contemporaries are now dead, and enough time has passed for the memory of his personality to have faded, giving us critical distance. Contributors such as Monika Szuba are much taken up with questions of gender and the treatment of women real and imaginary in this controversially male-dominated scene and era. Should we revisit his work in the same way in which we have revisited the other figures in Moffat's 'Poets' Pub' painting? The only way to do this seems to be to examine his many facets in detail. It is not enough to look at his poetry because this is also bound up with his choice of language and specifically an idiolect, politics, nationalism and his plays such as *The Wallace* (1960), not to mention his art and criticism. These are questions and strands explicitly taken up here by J. Derrick McClure, who discusses Smith's nationalism; David Robb, who explores Smith's nationalism through the lens of his popular play *The Wallace* and Alan Riach and Alexander Moffat who discuss Smith's virtues as a visual artist and art critic for the *Scotsman* in the 1960s. No overarching attempt has been made before to evaluate Smith's work in this way and the criticism that does exist is often either briefly dismissive or excessively hagiographical, having been written by his detractors or friends respectively. Some of Smith's achievements continue to be overlooked. One important aspect of his output as a literary figure was his hard work as a freelance scholar and editor. In keeping with Smith's claim that 'poets generally educate themselves' (Smith: 1966, 7), he also set about trying to educate others with the fruits of his auto-didacticism. Unfortunately there is not sufficient room in this present volume to assess Smith's work as the editor, selector and introducer of half a dozen valuable works on Scottish literature, beginning with the highly accessible 1951 guide *A Short Introduction to Scottish*

---

3   Personal correspondence between Fulton and present author, 2017.

*Literature* and ending with *A Choice of Burns's Poems and Songs* (Faber & Faber, 1966). In this fifteen-year time span, besides his work on Robert Fergusson and Gavin Douglas, Smith had also played a vitally important role in co-editing, with James Barke who died while the book was being produced, an extended version of the long suppressed *The Merry Muses* by Robert Burns. First privately published by M. Macdonald in Edinburgh in 1959, it became publically available in multiple editions in America and the UK in the 1960s, and Barke and Smith's co-edited version remains in print to this day, having been republished in 2009 by Luath Press, with a new introduction and music by Valentina Bold. While this is perhaps Smith's most enduring act of scholarship, this present volume is more akin in outlook, intention and scope to Smith's 1952 edited collection of essays *Robert Fergusson, 1750–1774*. This book was published by Nelson's of Edinburgh to 'commemorate the bicentenary of [Fergusson's] birth' and was an attempt to re-assess the achievement of a poet that Smith himself valued but felt had fallen into a state of critical neglect. Now, the time has come for Smith to receive a similar treatment.

For every accusation of superficiality that could be levelled at Smith, there are counter examples that display a continued commitment to core beliefs. John Manson is correct in observing that Smith 'appears to have been the only Scottish writer who tried to join the International Brigade'[4] and the account of his travails to do so is captured in his letter to Maurice Lindsay (Smith: 1988). For both the Spanish Civil War and World War Two, he was prevented from taking part in both in a combatant capacity because of his poor health and asthma. However, this in turn enabled Smith, who found work in Leven and at Taymouth Castle in Breadalbane teaching English to Polish refugees and soldiers, to become one of the forefront poetic voices of the Homefront experience during the war in Scotland. This work was collected in his third, and widely regarded as his first mature, collection *The Deevil's Waltz* (1946).

Although there is not much substantial extant criticism of Smith's work, saving pieces by his friends such as Thomas Crawford, Norman MacCaig, Alexander Scott and Eric Gold, there are a number of autobiographical truisms that are often repeated about his upbringing. Many people have found it remarkable that he was born in Wellington, New Zealand and educated at some of the most prestigious schools in the UK, mainly Malvern College and later Oriel College, Oxford where, while he was rusticated at least once for drinking and idleness, he still managed to scrape a Third in Modern History, finishing in 1937,

---

4 Personal correspondence between Manson and present author, 2017.

although he was not awarded an M.A. until 1941, according to John Clifford Hall (Hall: 1982, 4). How could a New Zealander, raised in an exalted English tradition, go on to become one of the pre-eminent Scottish 'makars' of his generation? What is often overlooked is the fact that Smith was raised in a household in which Scots was spoken (by his mother Catherine and his nanny) and holidays were often taken in Scotland, but he did not explore Scots as a literary medium until the late 1930s. *Under the Eildon Tree*, widely regarded as his masterpiece, was published in 1948. In little less than a decade, Smith had found the right register and outlet for his literary ambitions and vision. While *Under the Eildon Tree* was his fourth collection, his first two collections are often dismissed out of hand as being uneven and jejune, but Emma Dymock's chapter shows us this is simply not the case. His first, *Skail Wind* (1941), which was published by his friend Robert Garioch and is the only Smith collection to contain any poetry in English, sold 80 copies yet still managed to put Smith on the radar of the socialist 'Pylon school' in London, Louis MacNeice and Stephen Spender both owning review copies, Spender having given the collection his guarded approbation in a review in Cyril Connolly's *Horizon* (Spender, 104). *The Wanderer* (1943), was Smith's second collection marking his complete break from writing in English and was, in his own words, greeted by the public with 'extravagant apathy' (Smith: 1988, 11). However, by this point, Smith had cemented his decision to devote his life to poetry in Scots, as he makes clear in his almost evangelical sounding letter (1 November 1941) to Hugh MacDiarmid:

> I gave up writing English for Scots [...] I myself put it down to the cataclysmic effect of my first reading of *A Drunk Man Looks at the Thistle* [...] I shall never go back to English now, Scots is without any doubt in my opinion the greatest language for poetry in the world.
>
> SMITH qtd. in MANSON, ed., 314

While Smith certainly owed his personal reinvention as a Lallans makar to the discovery of Hugh MacDiarmid's early lyrics and *A Drunk Man Looks at the Thistle*, he did not come across these books himself. During his time in the late 1930s on the pub circuits of Edinburgh he had encountered the Royal High School English teacher and literary panjandrum Hector MacIver (1910–1966). MacIver was sympathetic to the young aspirant poet's search for a voice and put MacDiarmid's most famous long poem into his hands and the effect was quick yet lasting, electric and irrevocable. Smith repaid this gesture in lifelong friendship with Hector and Mary MacIver, and is remembered fondly in their joint 1990 memoirs *Pilgrim Souls*. Although his ascent in Scots poetry was certainly meteoric and raised eyebrows amongst reviewers of the time, it was not arrived at easily or directly. In fact, his formative years were characterised by much disturbance, upheaval, restlessness and many wrong turns. Smith's father was Sir Sydney Smith (1883–1969), a distinguished international pathologist who often worked high-profile murder cases, all recounted in his 1959 autobiography *Mostly Murder*. In 1928 Sydney Smith was made Regius Professor of Forensic Medicine at the University of Edinburgh, and it was this appointment that brought the Smith family to Scotland for good.

However, even before 1928, Sydney Smith's job had meant that his family had stayed in places such as New Zealand and Egypt, and Smith junior and his younger sister Bet were sent to boarding schools in England for long stretches of time. By 1928, Smith was already a teenager and his father was taking an active role in shaping the course of his son's future. His father wanted Smith to follow in his own steps, and once Smith had finished school, arranged to send him to Edinburgh University to study medicine, despite Smith's vehement protests that he wanted instead to go to an art college. What followed was a lost year for Smith in which he came bottom of his classes, became squeamish about blood, learned to drink heavily and disappointed his father, who was often the marker of his son's exam papers. Reluctantly, Sydney Smith allowed his son to pursue a more agreeable course of education, while still firmly refusing his pleas for art school, and sent him to Oriel College, Oxford University. Smith did, however, make a number of lifelong friends during his year at Edinburgh University, such as the artist and future collaborator Denis Peploe and fellow medicine student and New Zealander John Guthrie (d.1986) who went on to become a writer, composer, general practitioner and Edinburgh resident, later settling in Bellapais, North Cyprus. It was John Guthrie's initial incredulity at Smith's adoption of Scots as a literary medium that gave rise to the only anthologised poem from *Skail Wind*, 'Epistle to John Guthrie Who Had Blamed the Poet for Writing in Scots "Which No One Speaks"':

> We've come intil a gey queer time
> Whan scrievin Scots is near a crime,
> "Theres no one speaks like that", they fleer,
> - But wha the deil spoke like King Lear?
>
> And onyways doon Canongate
> I'll tak ye slorpin pints till late,
> Ye'll hear Scots there as raff an slee –
> Its not the point, sae that'll dae.
>> SMITH. 1975, 13

Already in this poem we find Smith's lifelong response to critics of his work, that it is fallacious to expect the language of poetry to faithfully mirror everyday speech, that every poet, like every interlocutor, has their own variation, or idiolect, of a particular language. This line would forcefully surface and reassert itself in 1964 when values Smith stood for as a Scottish poet were targeted by literary critic David Craig as isolating Scottish writing from potential readers and narrowing artistic scope by refusing to write in English. Craig's fear was that modern Scottish literature, in trying to vaunt its distinctive national separateness had become 'neurosed' with an 'over-consciousness of nationality' and cut off from other literatures of the world (Craig, 155). Smith's retort was to write 'Trahison des Clercs, or the Anti Scottish Lobby in Scottish Letters', an impassioned and polemical statement of his artistic intent, to identify a trend he thought he had noticed emerging among academics to dismiss the achievements of the Scottish Renaissance when written in Scots, to 'kill its individuality' (Smith: 1964b, 71). Although both men had reached an impasse in their views, and while Craig was not in any way part of an 'Anti-Scottish' conspiracy, they both nonetheless wanted to see their own vision of Scottish writing flourish, and both clearly cared about their subject but both were also dogmatic. Whether or not Smith was an essentialist and misguided to take the line he did is not the point, but rather that he was willing to defend his right, and the right of others, to write in Scots on whatever subjects of their choosing against the 'ex cathedra' prescriptivism of an academic, which is if anything a pluralist attitude.

However, what Smith's article does reveal is his acceptance that the Scottish Renaissance movement to which he had been a firm card-carrying member was, by 1964, considered 'old hat' (Smith: 1964b, 73). In 1964, discussion about Scottish writing was extremely adversarial and fissiparous, this was a time when the 'Folksong Flytings' had taken place in Scottish newspapers, there were angry debates over Concrete poetry and the American / Beatnik influence on younger Scottish writers in journals such as *Sidewalk*. Although Smith's contemporary in the Scottish Renaissance of the 1940s and 1950s, Edwin Morgan had been able to keep abreast of changes in the literary climate and his protean style had adapted, yet there is a sense that Smith had become, for poets like Morgan, something of a throw-back and an embarrassment to the cause:

> When I saw the 'Wallace' [...] I found it hard to believe that such a talented and sensitive man could write, technically and stylistically, as if the whole of 20th century drama had passed him by [...].
>
> MORGAN: 1974, 174

In private, Morgan would confess to friends in writing about *The Wallace* that, 'you'd think the author had read nothing later than Shakespeare's Chronicle histories. Can dogged, wilful ignorance of what is modern really help any country?' (Morgan, MS. Gen. 519/23). We get a sense of Morgan's disapproval of Smith's drunken singing in support of MacDiarmid during their appearances at the now infamous 1962 Writers Conference in Edinburgh (McGonigal, 151). Also, in his capacity as co-editor of *Scottish Poetry* in the 1960s, Morgan confided to fellow editors Maurice Lindsay and George Bruce that Smith's poetry submissions were 'dreadful stuff surely [...]?' (Acc. 7440/1). What is clear is that by the 1960s, Smith had been identified as an antiquated and largely irrelevant force. It is easier to understand now how, behind the scenes, attempts were made to slowly remove him from the literary landscape, and this downplaying of his achievements and removal from the literary annals of the 1960s and 1970s has largely persisted to this day.

To return to the John Guthrie poem, in it we also see Smith begin to act as an underworld guide to 'Auld Reekie', which would be something he would do throughout his writing, initiating his readers into its pleasures and miseries. It must be stressed, however, that this was no mere affectation, this was a profound choice to dedicate himself to Scots poetry, not easily arrived at. Even before coming down from Oxford in 1937, Smith was at work on many abandoned literary projects, such as a study of Ronald Firbank and Aubrey Beardsley, over which he was in touch with 1890s scholar A.J.A. Symons who invited him to lunch and warned him against eating peacock: 'not really a good table bird' (Acc. 10397). His first completed and major work was his comic undergraduate novel *Bottled Peaches* (MS. 26142). Taking place in the aftermath of Evelyn Waugh's generation of bright young things, the student characters in *Bottled Peaches* are feckless and habitually drunk, all of university life for them is about prolonging a binge and this gets them into plenty of imbroglios. Clearly a *roman-à-clef*, the protagonist is aspiring writer Noel Volpane (a thinly veiled version of Smith) who is renowned for his debauchery and haunted by guilt at wasting his time at university and having to explain himself to his father, 'The Professor'. The book mixes surrealism with the campus novel and is a tragi-comic fictionalisation of Smith's university experience. After the completion of this novel, and its rejection by publishers, a discouraged Smith moved to London in 1937 where he lived in run-down Georgian lodgings in 5 York Buildings, Adelphi, shortly before they were demolished by the City Corporation. He attempted to insinuate himself with limited success into bohemian drinking circles in Fitzrovia and Soho, where 'the poets never write, the composers never compose [...] the painters never paint' (Smith, Acc. 10426/9). Among his only published work of this decade are five deeply neo Romantic and New Apocalyptic poems in English in the little magazine *Seven* in 1938, which show a young poet straining to find his voice and register. He began countless book projects, only to abandon them after the initial research stages. This period is recounted in his 1947 letter to Maurice Lindsay and his surviving diaries make for very sorry reading: he was drinking a lot and writing and eating very little, paralysed by a lack of inspiration and direction, living on a 'breakfast of tea and cigarettes, lunch of beer and wondering how to put in the slow hours of another day' (Acc. 10426/9).

Although Smith and Stella Cartwright's joint friend Hugh Mackay has written disapprovingly of the 'unfortunate and unwarrantable intrusion into matters which are essentially of a private nature'[5] by scholars it is clear that Smith used his own life as raw material for his writing, that pub-going became for him, a form of research or fieldwork. In writing about these difficult years in his unpublished 1938 philosophical prose work *The Wilderness*, Smith began to see himself as an 'Orpheus manqué' and that these years were his time spent trying to navigate the spiritual nadirs and labyrinths of his generation (Acc. 10426/9). *The Wilderness* recounts Smith's early adulthood, from the halcyon days of Oxford where on a whim he would buy 'snuff boxes and Anne candlesticks and Beardsley first editions and Chateau Margaux' through to rustication from university and escaping to the continent to coming back to London and falling into a deep, almost suicidal, depression upon seeing the rise of fascism and the death of the artist, such as the murder of Lorca and the suicide of Ernst Toller. Like his masterwork to follow in a decade, *Under the Eildon Tree*, Smith was going through great trials in his life and relating them back to mythological figures such as Orpheus, pitting his own reality against that of a global backdrop and shoring the fragments of his existence against a nigh-on ineluctable ruin, as he perceived it. As James Kingsley has observed, all experience good or bad is 'grist to the mill of the poet macironical' (Kingsley, 268). His descent into despair and the demise of his ego all play into the Bakhtinian carnivalesque cycle of over-indulgence, obsession and mania, self-destruction leading to symbolic death allowing for spiritual resurrection. Put another way, it is like controversial psychiatrist R.D. Laing's contention that 'madness need not be all breakdown. It may also be break-through' (Laing, 110). This is what happens in *Under the Eildon Tree* and it is clear that this also happened in Smith's early adulthood, towards the end of the 1930s. This is why it is important to look at this underexplored period in Smith's life, that his subsequent socialist values, political awareness and disdain for middle-class respectability and the mores of the Establishment are a reaction against his early life.

---

5   Personal correspondence with the present author, 2017.

In Elegy VI of *Under the Eildon Tree* Smith's speaker observes that 'I was born excessive' and that 'The middle airt, the Gowden Mean, / Has little recommendan it' (Smith: 1975, 157). This can also be seen in his writing of the play *The Wallace* which Stanley Roger Green suggested was in a way an act of revenge against a don at Oxford who refused Smith's proposal to write a thesis on the Clearances because he intended to argue they were a 'bad thing' (Green, 26).

Writing to his friend 'Scomo' (the dramatist George Scott Montcrieff) in 1939, Smith had been back home in Edinburgh for a year or so, living both with his parents and his new wife, Marion, nine years his senior – a marriage that had caused great controversy in the Smith household. He confessed that he was still in an existential 'muddle' and 'desperately seeking roots' in Scotland which was the only country where he had felt at home (MS. 26144/1–11). At this point he had already sent another batch of poems to Hugh MacDiarmid for consideration for *The Voice of Scotland* and although they would be rejected, it would spark a correspondence and friendship that lasted until Smith's death in 1975. It is Smith's friendship with MacDiarmid and the elder poet's influence on Smith's writing that is the focus of Margery Palmer McCulloch's chapter in this book. In effect, the copy of *A Drunk Man Looks at the Thistle* given to him one day in the pub by Hector MacIver, offers him the opportunity of a new home and a new identity and sense of belonging. His intensely personal, eccentric and idiolectal Scots which might present a barrier to new readers of his work who do not like any form of linguistic challenge, is much more than some sort of clever, artificial confection. Smith argues that he could no longer write poetry in English because it had become standardised and divorced from any specific community. As a young man casting around for a place to attach himself to, he discovered the literary Scots of the Scottish Renaissance and in John Guthrie's words 'his life's course was set' (Guthrie, 2).

Scots poetry offered Smith friendships and a community with which to belong. He described his bardic protagonist of *Under the Eildon Tree* as 'the makar macironical' which nods towards William Dunbar's 'macaronic' technique of creating a multi-layered poetry of different registers from the basilect and acrolect, allowing for multiple, often contradictory viewpoints or interpretations. This dualism surfaces conceptually in G. Gregory Smith's oft-quoted *Scottish Literature: Character and Influence* (1919) which was a key theoretical book of MacDiarmid's conception of the Scottish Renaissance. Gregory Smith's contention, and later developed by David Daiches in *The Paradox of Scottish Culture* (1964), was that the Anglicisation of Scottish culture after the Union of 1707 had given the nation an identity complex, where Scots and Gaelic was suppressed and English was encouraged. This ultimately caused a split in the national character and gave the Scottish mind-set the ability to use but also

subvert the prestige language while also celebrating the use of forbidden, de-
motic forms of expression. The present-day viability of this theory is not here
up for discussion, but for Smith, the existence of the 'Caledonian Anti-Syzygy'
was undeniable (Smith: 1919, 4). In his own annotated copy of the first edition
of Gregory Smith's book, he writes in 1940 of the opening chapter 'Two Moods':
'The best general description of the literature yet written'.[6] However, you will
see that Smith deliberately spells it 'macironical', to emphasise the fact that he
was also using irony. His use of irony is perhaps not stressed enough, but much
of his work is suffused with it, take for instance the bedroom scene in 'Elegy V'
in *Under the Eildon Tree* where the speaker lies in the bed, lighting a cigarette.
For some, Smith's language will come with a politically-incorrect cringe, but it
must be understood not simply as humour, but highly critical irony, as an at-
tack on the state of affairs in the world, colonialism, imperialism and exploita-
tion, the same way he criticises Robert Burns for his potential involvement in
slavery:

> Luntan Virginian fags
> – The New World thus I haud in fief
> And levie kyndlie tribute. Black men slave
> Aneath a distant sun to mak for me
> Cheroots at hauf-a-croun the box.
>
> SMITH: 1975, 154

One conceit used by Smith in *Under the Eildon Tree* that has been criticised as
inappropriate is his contention that love can be as destructive as 'Hiroshima'
(Smith: 1975, 151). Looking over the fact that the entire poem is almost a treatise
on rhetoric and its concomitant techniques such as hyperbole, this remark
does not show insensitivity so much as a desire to plant the event firmly in the
head of the reader. Not many poets writing in 1947–1948 would have been bold
enough to mention it and its presence in Smith's poem shows that he was not
insular or blind to what was happening around him, even in the depths of his
own obsessions.

     Throughout his life, Smith upheld an interest in the largely niche and un-
fashionable poets of the 'Yellow Decade', the 1890s. Writing in 1946 to celebrate
the shady life and works of publisher Leonard Smithers, Smith described the
era as 'A remote, almost forgotten period labelled artificial, superficial and es-
capist, and on those counts now relegated to a limbo' (Smith: 1946, 219). The

---

6  Quotation from the present author's personal collection of books, ex-libris Sydney Goodsir
   Smith.

imagery Smith uses here is in itself Orphean and it could easily be applied to his own writing now, and the attempts over the years to dismiss or ignore it. The Lallans revival was also attacked as artificial and irrelevant, but poetry in Scots is still being written to this day, and it is difficult to account for why Smith's work is not more widely read and appreciated, even if his highly idiosyncratic style is taken into consideration. When confronted with such a challenge as coming to grips with Smith's style for the first time, it is worth remembering Hugh MacDiarmid's half-facetious response to his wife Valda when she claimed not to know anything about 'Victorian epic poetry': 'Well, you've nothing but laziness and ignorance to conquer!'(Riach, 10). This book of essays by both early-career and established academics is an attempt not only to restore Sydney Goodsir Smith's place to Alexander Moffat's 'Poets' Pub' painting but also to re-orientate his position on the critical map, to bring him out of his Tartarean realm and shine a light on his work, to show that it offers us more than mere period-pieces and caricature and that as a cultural figure he was much more than a monocled eccentric offering some local colour to an erstwhile literary movement.

## Bibliography

Brown, George Mackay, *For the Islands I Sing: An Autobiography* (London: John Murray, 1997).

Carrell, Christopher, ed., *Seven Poets* (Glasgow: Third Eye Centre Ltd, 1981).

Craig, David, 'A National Literature? Recent Scottish Writing' in *Studies in Scottish Literature* Vol. 1 / Iss. 3 (1964), pp. 151–169.

Crawford, Robert, *Scotland's Books: The Penguin History of Scottish Literature* (London: Penguin, 2007).

Crawford, Thomas, 'Goodsir Smith: The Auk of the Mandrake Hert', in *The Scottish Review: Arts and the Environment* Vol. 1 / No. 2 (spring), pp. 17–22.

Eliot, T.S., 'Tradition and the Individual Talent' in *The Sacred Wood: Essays on Poetry and Criticism*, 7th edn. (London: Methuen, 1977), pp. 47–59.

Garioch, Robert, Letter dated 12 October 1980 to Alastair Mackie, in Robin Fulton, ed. *A Garioch Miscellany* (Edinburgh: Macdonald Publishers, 1986), p. 91.

Green, Stanley Roger, *A Clanjamfray of Poets: A Tale of Literary Edinburgh* (Edinburgh: Saltire Society, 2008).

Guthrie, John, 'Sydney Goodsir Smith' in *Scotia Review* No. 10 (August 1975), pp. 2–4.

Hall, John. C., 'Sydney Goodsir Smith' in *Lines Review* 88 (March 1984), pp. 15–19.

Hall, John C., 'The Writings of Sydney Goodsir Smith', a PhD thesis submitted to the University of Aberdeen, September 1982. Accessed online (June 2018): http://ethos.bl.uk/OrderDetails.do?uin=uk.bl.ethos.330725.

Henderson, Hamish, 'The Poet Speaks' in *Alias MacAlias: Writings on Songs, Folk and Literature*(Edinburgh: Polygon, 1992), pp. 321–325.

Herdman, John, *Another Country: An Era in Scottish Politics and Letters* (Edinburgh: Thirsty Books, 2013).

Kingsley, James, *Scottish Poetry: A Critical Survey* (London: Cassell & Company Ltd, 1955).

Laing, R.D., *Politics of Experience* (London: Penguin, 1967).

Lindsay, Maurice, *History of Scottish Literature* (London: Robert Hale, 1977).

McAfee, Annalena, *Hame* (London: Harvill Secker, 2017).

MacCaig, Norman, 'The unlikely' in *The Poems of Norman MacCaig* (Edinburgh: Polygon, 2005), p. 245.

MacCaig, Norman, ed., *For Sydney Goodsir Smith* (Loanhead: M. Macdonald, 1975).

McGonigal, James, *Beyond the Last Dragon: A Life of Edwin Morgan* (Dingwall: Sandstone Press, 2010).

MacIver, Mary & Hector, *Pilgrim Souls* (Aberdeen: Aberdeen University Press, 1990).

MacLean, Sorley, Letter dated 25 January 1941 to Douglas Young in Ian Watson / John Updike Rare Books, *Catalogue 51* (Edinburgh, 2017), p. 24 / item 143.

MacLean, Sorley, 'Poetry, Passion and Political Consciousness' in *Scottish International* 10 (May 1970), pp. 10–16.

Main, Peter, *A Fervent Mind: The Life of Ruthven Todd* (Stirling: Lomax Press, 2018).

Morgan, Edwin, 'The Beatnik in the Kailyard' in *Essays* (Cheadle: Carcanet Press, 1974), pp. 166–176.

Morgan, Edwin, Letter to Maurice Lindsay and George Bruce, dated 11 May 1969, in Acc. 7440/1, National Library of Scotland.

Morgan, Edwin, Letter to Meic Stephens, dated 'Xmas 1969', in MS. Gen. 519/23, Glasgow University Library.

Pound, Ezra, 'Others' [review] in *The Little Review* Vol. V / No. 11 (March 1918), pp. 56–58.

Riach, Alan, 'Serious Characters' in *Scottish Review of Books* Vol. 3 / No. 2 (2007), pp. 10–12.

Scott, Tom & Heather, *True Thomas the Rhymer and other tales of Lowland Scots* (London, Oxford University Press, 1971).

Smith, G. Gregory, *Scottish Literature: Character and Influence* (London: Macmillan & Co., 1919).

Smith, Sydney Goodsir, *The Aipple and the Hazel* (Glasgow: Caledonian Press, 1951).

Smith, Sydney Goodsir, Assorted letters access in National Library of Scotland: MS. 26156; Acc. 10281/1; Acc. 10397; MS. 26144/ 1–11.

Smith, Sydney Goodsir, 'Bottled Peaches' typescript, MS. 26142, National Library of Scotland.

Smith, Sydney Goodsir, *Carotid Cornucopius*, 2nd edn. (Edinburgh: M. Macdonald, 1964a).

Smith, Sydney Goodsir, *Collected Poems: 1941–1975* (London: John Calder, 1975).

Smith, Sydney Goodsir, 'Introduction' to *A Choice of Burns's Poems and Songs* (London: Faber & Faber, 1966), pp. 7–13.

Smith, Sydney Goodsir, Letters to Stella Cartwright, E96.12, Edinburgh University Library.

Smith, Sydney Goodsir, Letter dated 1 November 1941 to Hugh MacDiarmid in John Manson, ed., *Dear Grieve: Letters to Hugh MacDiarmid [C.M. Grieve]* (Glasgow: Kennedy & Boyd, 2011), p. 314.

Smith, Sydney Goodsir, 'A Publisher of the Nineties' in John Singer, ed., *The Holiday Book* (Glasgow: William MacLellan, 1946), pp. 219–228.

Smith, Sydney Goodsir, *Saltire Self-Portraits 3: A letter written to Maurice Lindsay in 1947* (Edinburgh: The Saltire Society, 1988).

Smith, Sydney Goodsir, 'Trahison des Clercs or the Anti Scottish Lobby in Scottish Letters' in *Studies in Scottish Literature* Vol. 2 / Iss. 2 (1964b), pp. 71–86.

Smith, Sydney Goodsir, 'The Wilderness' manuscript, Acc. 10462/9, National Library of Scotland.

Smith, Sir Sydney, *Mostly Murder, etc.: An Autobiography* (London: George G. Harrap & Co., 1959).

Spender, Stephen, 'Poetry in 1941' in *Horizon: A Review of Literature and Art* Vol. V / No. 26 (February 1942), pp. 96–111.

Watson, Roderick, *The Literature of Scotland* (London: Macmillan Publishers, 1984).

Watson, Roderick, 'Scotland and Modernisms' in Emma Dymock & Margery Palmer McCulloch, eds., *Scottish & International Modernisms: Relationships & Reconfigurations* (Glasgow: ASLS, 2011), pp. 8–19.

# CHAPTER 1

# Sydney Goodsir Smith: A Centenary Appreciation

*Patrick Crotty*

## Abstract

This chapter reworks a short centenary assessment of Smith's achievements published in the *Times Literary Supplement* in November 2015. Locating Smith in the Scottish tradition of the divided literary self, it explores the paradoxical emergence of an English-educated upper-middle class New Zealander as a Scots language poet with a flair for evoking the street life of a far from genteel Edinburgh. It notes the co-existence in Smith's work of, on the one hand, broad democratic sympathy and breezy conviviality, and, on the other, an austere classicism and high modernist tendency towards literary allusiveness. The essay laments the obscurity into which the work of an engaging, bracing, endlessly entertaining poet has fallen.

## Keywords

Centenary – Scotland – Poetry – Scottish Literary Renaissance – Biography – *Under the Eildon Tree* – Scots language poetry – Lallans – Hugh MacDiarmid – Edinburgh

A 1981 entry in the *Dictionary of National Biography* noted that the forensic scientist Sir Sydney Alfred Smith (1883–1969) 'had one son and a daughter who became a doctor'. The profession of the son, already six years dead in 1981, might have merited mention if only he'd had the good sense to stick with his medical studies at Edinburgh. As it turned out, though, the younger Sydney Smith went south after a year to read modern history at Oriel College, Oxford. His prospects went south, too – he managed to get himself suspended for indiscipline, eventually graduating with a third in 1941. The poor scholar later professed amusement at the fact that his surname marked him from birth as a 'makar' (i.e. maker), the Scots term for poet; within little more than a decade of his graduation he had confounded the uncertainty of his setting forth by forging in the smithy of the old tongue of the Lowlands many of the wittiest and most elegant Scottish poems of the 20th century.

Scottish literary history is full of improbable transformations – of the poetaster James Macpherson into the lionised 'translator' of Ossian, of the cowherd James Hogg into the *magister ludi* of *Private Memoirs and Confessions of a Justified Sinner*, of the anti dialect campaigner C.M. Grieve into Hugh MacDiarmid – but for sheer unlikelihood none can match the makeover of the New Zealand-born, English-educated Sydney Goodsir Smith into the foremost Scots-language poet born in the last hundred years. Smith first saw the light of day on 26 October 1915 in Wellington. His father was a native of Otago who had worked his way up from pharmacist's assistant on the South Island to public medical officer in the capital via a scholarship to Edinburgh University. By the time the newly qualified doctor returned to the southern hemisphere in 1914 he had met and married the poet's Scottish mother, Catherine Goodsir Gelenick. When, after an itinerant decade, the family finally settled in Scotland on Sydney Alfred's 1928 appointment to the Regius Chair of Forensic Medicine at Edinburgh, Sydney Goodsir was despatched to Malvern College to continue an education hitherto conducted mainly at a Dorset prep school. For the rest of his life he spoke in what to Scottish ears was an upper-class English accent.

As a young man Smith was intoxicated by the strangeness of the speech he heard all round him in Edinburgh and its environs, and by his discovery of the poetry of Hugh MacDiarmid, then 'spleet-new frae the mint' (MacDiarmid, 98). In psychology, politics and phonology, MacDiarmid's verse was founded on a faith in the significance of the distinctiveness of the language used in the south-eastern half of Scotland. Scots is Teutonic rather than Celtic in origin, and retains many Middle English elements long lost from its sister-tongue south of the border. The unabashed vigour of the various subdialects that survive from Galloway to the Moray Firth (where Scots is known as 'the Doric') can still take visitors by surprise and leave them lost for comprehension. That Scots is also the medium of a rich and varied poetic tradition that came to full flower in the 15th century and underwent energetic renewal in the 18th bequeaths it a cultural freight unparalleled by any other 'dialect of English' (a designation dismissed as 'facetious' by Smith and still frequently contested north of the Tweed).

While much of the wider world's resistance to 20th century attempts to use it for serious writing may be said to derive from misapprehensions with regard to the nature and unfinished history of Scots, scepticism cannot entirely be put down to prejudice. Suspicion was an understandable response to the terminology deployed in justification of their efforts by the new makars. How were 'ootlands' ('foreigners', Smith's joking name for readers who need a glossary) to know that 'Lallans' simply means 'Lowlands'? The label might have seemed less baffling and exotic if tendered in that southern form, not least in view of the fact that propaganda for Scots was (and is) conducted more or less exclusively in English. 'Synthetic Scots', a phrase coined in 1923 by the French academic Denis Saurat, one of MacDiarmid's early patrons, acknowledged that the new poetry drew its lexis from many areas of Scots (as Burns had done a hundred and fifty years earlier). Unfortunately, however, it also gave the impression that the language of the Scottish modernists was a concoction to be contrasted on grounds of artificiality to the somehow more natural, 'organic' idioms of, say, Yeats and Eliot. Smith was nonetheless comfortable with Saurat's formulation, arguing in his *A Short Introduction to Scottish Literature* (1951) that the language of ambitious poetry is necessarily synthetic: 'The literary leid transcends the vernacular as a cathedral transcends a cottage [...] the basic materials are the same, in one case words, in the other stones' (Smith: 1951, 14).

He began writing poems at Malvern and was still doing so solely in English at the end of the 1930s when he became friends with Robert Garioch (1909–1981) and Sorley MacLean (1911–1996), poets respectively in Scots and Gaelic. (He was already a MacDiarmid enthusiast). The sizeable quantity of English material in *Skail Wind* (1941) was subsequently suppressed by the author, and that debut volume is now remembered chiefly for its breezy apologia for Smith's ultimate choice of the northern over the southern tongue:

> We've come intil a gey queer time
> Whan scrievin Scots is near a crime,
> "Theres no one speaks like that", they fleer,
> – But wha the deil spoke like King Lear?
>
> And onyways doon Canongate
> I'll tak ye slorpin pints till late,
> Ye'll hear Scots there as raff an slee –
> It's no the point, sae that'll dae.
>
> ...
>
> Did Johnnie Keats whan he was drouth
> Ask "A beaker full o the warm South"?
> Fegs no, he leaned acrost the bar
> An called for "A point o bitter. Ma!"
>
> But the Suddron's noo a sick man's leid,
> Alang the flattest plains it stots;

> Tae reach the hills his fantice needs
> This bard maun tak the wings o Scots.
>           'Epistle to John Guthrie' SMITH: 1975, 13

The wings of Scots carried the poetry associated with the Scottish Renaissance movement in many different directions in the inter-War years and later. If Mac-Diarmid's work was the most electrifying and unpredictable, it was unusual in its relative lack of continuity with tradition. Exploiting the coincidence of the familiar and the strange in a language that was at once the speech of the poet's childhood and the object of his excited discovery/recovery in dictionaries a quarter of a century later, it effected a series of startling lyrical illuminations that in retrospect can be understood as half-deliberate, half-intuitive elaborations of the Uncanny as defined in Freud's 1919 essay of that name. Quieter and less rhythmically vibrant than MacDiarmid's, the best poems of William Soutar (1898–1943) found contemporary interpersonal contexts for the eerie fatalism of the ballads. Robert Garioch used a speech based, self-consciously inner-city Scots to address across-the-ages banter to his eighteenth-century Edinburgh forerunner Robert Fergusson and the Renaissance Latin humanist George Buchanan. He also revived verse forms that had been staples of the Scots tradition until Burns's time, even dusting down the pre-Reformation car-nivalesque of 'Peblis to the Play' to serve as model for 'Embro to the Ploy', his good humoured caricature of the annual shenanigans surrounding the Edin-burgh Festival.

Smith reached further back than any of his fellow revivalists, enriching his vocabulary with words that had not featured in verse since before the Battle of Flodden and redeploying William Dunbar's satanic villain Mahoun as an embodiment of the militaristic 'diablerie' that brought about the World War Two. Much of Smith's most obviously medieval collection *The Deevil's Waltz* (1946) was written at the height of that terrifyingly modern conflict. The book includes elegies for the British dead of the North African campaign and po-ems about the suffering of civilians and Red Army soldiers on the Eastern Front. (A non-conscriptable asthmatic, the poet contributed to the war ef-fort by inducting Polish servicemen into what he termed 'the mysteries of the English language'). While a formalism that owes something to the exam-ple of Dunbar is in evidence at many points in *The Deevil's Waltz*, here and there out-of-date modes of figuration lead to mere attitudinising. The lump-ing together of industrialists and unionists along with murderers and fascists as 'mongers' who 'aye need masks for cheatrie' (Smith: 1975, 46), for instance, reveals more about the ardour than the perspicacity of the young author's politics.

After the war, Smith turned his attention to more private themes. The influence of the medieval poets persisted, in stylistic terms at least, in the lyrics collected in *So Late into the Night* (1952) and *Figs and Thistles* (1959). These cultivate sound patterns modelled on the 'enamilit' or aureate manner of Gavin Douglas's Scots version of the *Aeneid* (completed in 1513) and the statelier among Dunbar's poems. They do so, often very cleverly, in the service of modern and urban subject matter. Thus the sophisticated vowel music of 'The Grace of God and the Meth-Drinker' highlights by contrast the shambolic indelicacy of the protagonist:

> Hidderie-hetterie stouteran in a dozie dwaum
> O' ramsh reid-biddie – Christ!
> > The stink
> O' jake ahint him, a mephitic
> Rouk o miserie, like some unco exotic
> Perfume o the Orient no juist sae easilie tholit
> By the bleak barbarians o the Wast
> But subtil, acrid, jaggan the nebstrous
> Wi 'n owrehailan ugsome guff, maist delicat,
> Like in scent til the streel o a randie gib ...
> > *O-hone-a-ree!.*
> > > SMITH: 1975, 94–95

In general, Smith's individual poems of the later 1940s and 50s are marked by a faintly dandyish intricacy. At their purest they exhibit a directness and economy that can be seen as characteristic of Scottish verse from Henryson and the ballads to Gaelic song (and even perhaps to the late work of W.S. Graham). Read in bulk they have a tendency towards the formulaic, particularly in their treatment of amatory subjects. The extent to which Smith's love lyrics borrow from the muse theories of Robert Graves remains unclear, but they provoke similar questions about male presumption and the recruitment of the feminine for complacent mythologising:

> Luve was the first was struck
> By the goddess mune
> The luve she gied she took –
> The tides aye rin.
>
> Celebrate the seasons
> And the hours that pass

> She that rocks the tides
> Rocks ye at last.
>
> 'Credo' SMITH: 1975, 88

Nevertheless, Smith's strongest claim on posterity's attention rests on his achievement as a love poet. Memorable though his incidental lyrics are, they nowhere match the energy and inventiveness of the series of twenty-four Propertian elegies he composed over a ten-week period from December 1946 and assembled for publication in 1948 as *Under the Eildon Tree* (second edition, 1954). These raffish, tender, learned and ironic meditations are so skilfully interconnected and so powerful in their cumulative in effect that they deserve to be thought of as a long poem rather than a mere grouping or sequence. Whatever its final taxonomical status, *Under the Eildon Tree* can fairly be described as the most polished extended exercise in Scots verse since Burns's 'Tam o' Shanter', and the most ambitious since MacDiarmid's *A Drunk Man Looks at the Thistle* (1926). In British poetry more widely, perhaps only Basil Bunting's *Briggflatts* absorbs the example of pre-*Cantos* Ezra Pound with comparable verve. Smith finds a way of being serious (and seriously funny) about the sexual subject matter that can make for affectation elsewhere in his work.

In *Under the Eildon Tree* affectation gives way to obsession, and love is presented as simultaneously – or successively – enabling and disabling, as the power that makes poetry possible and destroys poets. Personal experience is measured against the witness of the literature of the past: Ronsard, Villon, Burns, the Scottish balladeers and the poets of classical antiquity are evoked in a rueful pageant of the exhilarations and abasements of erotic passion. Taking his title and the third of his three epigraphs from the Ballad of Thomas the Rhymer (Child 37), Smith frames proceedings in the traditional story of the 'glamouring' of True Thomas by the Queen of Elfland:

> 'Betide me weill, betide me wae,
>     That weird sall never daunton me'.
> Syne he has kisst her rosie lips
>     All underneath the Eildon Tree.
>
> SMITH: 1954, 10[1]

---

1   These epigraphs which appear on page 10 of the 'second edition revised' version of *Under the Eildon Tree* (Serif Books, 1954) were not reproduced alongside the poem in *Collected Poems* (John Calder, 1975).

There is a risk of portentousness in the identification of the 20th century poet/speaker with the soothsaying thirteenth-century True Thomas, but it is forestalled by humour:

> Here I ligg, Sydney Slugabed Godless Smith,
> The Smith, the Faber, ποιητής and Makar

> •••

> Wi ase on the sheets, ase on the cod,
> And crumbs o toast under my bum,
> Scrievan the last great coronach
> O' the westren flickeran bourgeois world.
>> SMITH: 1975, 154

The wide circulation in anthologies of Elegy V, from which these lines are taken, can lead readers unfamiliar with the whole work to suspect that *Under the Eildon Tree* amounts to little more than an exercise in high-end blokeish entertainment. The overall impact of Smith's masterpiece is, rather, to expose of the power of sexual obsession to overwhelm judgement and eviscerate happiness. Though the boisterous authorial personality of V recurs here and there, it is refused admission to the book's finest passages. Thus Orpheus's retelling in Elegy XII of how he finally lost Eurydice stylises male tenderness at its most desperate. Elegy X, by contrast, is alert to the ways sentimental versions of masculinity can cloak brutality. That the wearer of the mask of sentiment in this instance is Robert Burns, who recounts his affair with Highland Mary, shows that Smith was not intimidated by the cultural pieties of his adopted nation.

Flexibility of register is one of the strengths of *Under the Eildon Tree*. Bacchanalia, bawdry, lyrics of love (VII, the exquisite 'New Hyne') and death (XVIII, 'Strumpet Daith') co-exist with bravura rhetorical performances like XX, in which Tristram's heartbroken recollection of Iseult pays glittering homage to Alexander Scott (*c*.1520-*c*.1583) and Alexander Montgomerie (1550?-1598), last of the old makars. The account of Dido's desolation in XVI shares something of the dignity of its ultimate source in Virgil:

> She grat. And greitan turned, her wemen
> Round her speakless, aa the midnicht glorie o' her hair
> About her face hung doun like wedow's weeds;
> Back til the tuim palace, tuim the great haas
> Whar Æneas walked, whar Æneas drank and leuch,
> Whar Æneas tellt his silken leman's talk,

Whar Æneas took her bodie and her hert,
Took aa her luve and gied back bonnie aiths and vows,
Tuim, tae, the chaumer and the bed o' luve,
Tuim Dido's hert of aa but wanhopc's plcnishings.
SMITH: 1975, 176

The book's most vivid exploration of the duality of sexual impulse occurs in Elegy XIII, the longest in the book, where a drunken encounter between the comically grandiloquent narrator and a teenage Edinburgh prostitute is backlit by a chaste classical moon's transmogrification of the seedy capital:

– And Dian's siller chastitie
Muved owre the reikan lums,
Biggan a ferlie toun of jet and ivorie
That was but blackened stane. [...].
SMITH: 1975, 170

To 21st century sensibilities, it must be said, the narrative comes across as troublingly untroubled by the power imbalance between the middle-aged, middle-class speaker and Sandra, his 'princess-leman o' a nicht o' lust' (Smith: 1975, 171).

The testosterone-heavy, beery ethos of post-War Scotland similarly vitiates the most energetic of Smith's non-poetic productions, the prose extravaganza *Carotid Cornucopius* (privately printed, 1947; revised and extended, 1964). This novel (if that's what it is) has been described as a Scots *Finnegans Wake*, but its indefatigable punning serves a succession of dirty jokes and unlikely stories about Edinburgh lowlife rather than a Joycean vision of human history. *Carotid* introduces the author (or 'auktor') by his literary nickname, the Auk (glossed as 'an extinct bard'). The extended version is embellished by superb Rendell Wells cartoons of Smith in avian guise (sometimes accompanied by an owlish MacDiarmid). A lengthy subtitle describes the protagonist as 'Caird of the Cannon Gait and Voyeur of the Outlook Touer'.

The imperfect distinction between auktor and hero in *Carotid* justifies a pause over the implications of Smith's persistent punning on the Scots noun 'caird' ('gypsy' or 'vagrant') with the etymologically unrelated English 'card' ('sly or knowing person') and – more dubiously – 'cad'. Smith, who liked to wear a monocle and whose drunken patrician wheezes regularly disrupted Edinburgh literary gatherings in the 1960s and 70s, appears to have been torn in life as well as art between the conditions of 'gangrel' (a Scots term for 'vagabond' that recurs throughout his work) and privileged rake. Little is known of his relationship with his distinguished father, who lived in the same small city for much the greater part of the poet's adulthood, other than that Sydney

Alfred obstructed his son's youthful ambition to be a painter. (The ambition persisted: Smith never gave up painting and drawing, and worked for years as art critic for the *Scotsman*. A large format selection of his drawings was published in 1998). The tramp and the cad in SGS (his preferred signature) so sustained their combined assault on respectability that an unresolved quarrel with the values of his brilliant but establishmentarian progenitor may be thought to lie behind his art in its many forms.

It was certainly no knight of the realm who wrote the plays. Easily the best known of them is the five-act *The Wallace: A Triumph*, a hit in 1960 at the Edinburgh Festival, where it was revived twenty-five years later. Though it too palpably manipulates the historical record in the interests of a rousing nationalist climax – Smith, like many incomers, was baffled by the popular Scottish attachment to the Union – *The Wallace* vividly stylises in linguistic terms the differing perspectives of its Scottish and English characters. (The contrast between the speech styles of the warring Chroniclers is particularly well worked). The Scots of Smith's plays has a tough colloquial quality that can come as a surprise to readers familiar only with the bookish and at times merely orthographical Scots of the poems. The free verse radio play *The Stick-Up* (1961) brings an O'Casey-like realism to its portrayal of slum life in Glasgow. Once again, the dialogue exhibits a knarled authenticity; the plot, however, is melodramatic almost to the point of hysteria. (Robin Orr nevertheless took the text as his libretto for *Full Circle*, presented in Perth in April 1968 by Scottish Opera). The scarcely actable comedy *Colickie Meg*, a spin-off of *Carotid Cornucopius*, was published piecemeal in magazines in the 1950s and was due to be published in book form by John Calder in 1999 but fell through.

Smith's work features such stylistic as well as generic range that some of his surest poems risk slipping through the net of a summative account of his achievement. 'The Twal' (from *Figs and Thistles*) offers an appropriately rasping Scots version of 'Dvenadtsat', Alexander Blok's famous twelve-section portrayal of a march through Petrograd by a dozen rowdy, unsettlingly apostle-like Bolsheviks. 'The Twa Brigs' fulfils the requirements of a public commission (by the BBC, to celebrate the opening of the Forth Road Bridge in 1964) while gleefully satirising the impatience of motorists and the pomposity of councillors as it meanders towards its climactic demand for drink for a bard who has too long contemplated the salty waters of the Firth. Drink features also in 'The Riggins o' Chelsea', which describes the ejection of Robert Garioch and the auktor from a well-known London pub for laughing, one of the few activities that *were* permitted in the taverns of puritanical mid-century Edinburgh ('The Riggins' is mysteriously absent from *Collected Poems*, 1975).

Friendship was one of Smith's gifts. In 1959 he founded the 200 Burns Club along with MacDiarmid and Norman MacCaig, two poets from whom his lifelong pal Garioch maintained a distrustful distance. He shared a house in the late 1940s with the recently married Sorley and Renee MacLean. (It is likely that MacLean's at that stage only partially published *Dàin do Eimhir* provided a model for the blend of autobiography and legend in *Under the Eildon Tree*. In his later work Smith, who had sparse knowledge of the language, uses the Gaelic phrase *Ni Chaltuinn* – 'Daughter of the Hazel' – as a code for his second wife, Hazel Williamson). For decades after his death, the antics of 'Sydney' were affectionately recounted by acquaintances from across Edinburgh's social classes: his hungover mistaking of a bank – for a bar-counter, his falling from a top tier theatre balcony to land in the balcony below, saved by the looseness of drunken limb that had caused the fall in the first instance, and so on.

There is little doubt that Smith was an alcoholic. He was also, despite his asthma, a heavy smoker. He had so manifest an ability to combine chaotic living with steady production (across a range of artistic media and as critic and then columnist for the *Scotsman*) that he deserves to be remembered as disciplined as well as dissolute. The extravagance of the art and self-destructiveness of the life that came to an abrupt end on January 15, 1975 when the poet collapsed outside a newsagent's shop in Dundas Street suggest an uneasiness of spirit no high jinks could disguise. Forty years after his death and a hundred after his birth, there remains much to admire in his verse and its informing belief that poetry should and can be learned as well as funny, passionate as well as inventive. The fact that Smith's work – so admired by MacDiarmid, MacCaig, Iain Crichton Smith, Kurt Wittig, David Murison and other poets and scholars – has fallen comprehensively from view since the immediately posthumous publication of *Collected Poems* is a matter of dismay. Even while he lived, the portents were not good: Smith's last collection, *Fifteen Poems and a Play* (1969), was published by subscription. 'Tailpiece', the Sapphic fragment that brought the volume to a close, might have been designed as his epitaph:

> The howffs are shut langsyne
> The late snugs tae
> It is the how-dumb-deid, the whures
> Are aa abed – and the Auk his lane.

> Pissed, of course.
>
> SMITH: 1969, 64[2]

---

2   'Tailpiece' as it appeared in *Fifteen Poems and a Play* (Southside, 1969) was later reprinted in *Collected Poems* (John Calder, 1975) as 'Another Version' of 'Sappho' and dedicated to Hector MacIver (see Smith: 1975, 109).

## Bibliography

MacDiarmid, Hugh, 'A Drunk Man Looks at the Thistle', in *Complete Poems of Hugh MacDiarmid: Volume I* (London: Martin Brian & O'Keefe, 1978), pp. 80–167.

Smith, Sydney Goodsir, *Collected Poems 1941–1975* (London: John Calder, 1975).

Smith, Sydney Goodsir, *Fifteen Poems and a Play* (Edinburgh: Southside, 1969).

Smith, Sydney Goodsir, *A Short Introduction to Scottish Literature* (Edinburgh: Serif Books, 1951).

Smith, Sydney Goodsir, *Under the Eildon Tree* (Edinburgh: Serif Books, 1954).

# CHAPTER 2

# Skail Winds and Scattered Personalities: The Formation of Identity in Sydney Goodsir Smith's Early Poetry

*Emma Dymock*

## Abstract

Douglas Young's review, in *The New Alliance*, of Smith's first poetry collection, *Skail Wind* (1941) is rather scathing. Young writes 'Here is a sign of the times, another epiphenomenon of English cultural decay. To find his mode of expression, a globe-trotting English speaker, of Antipodean provenience, has recourse to Lallans, which moreover he wields not worse than many autochthonous North Britons'. He goes on to accuse 'the makar' of trailing 'relics of the English Thirties' and comments that 'the rhythm also is too often slack, and interminable spavined lines schauchle [shamble] over the excellent paper'. In a letter to Sorley MacLean, Young is concerned that he has gone too far and caused offence. To examine the relationship between these three men is to journey to the heart of the later Scottish Renaissance with its lively debates on language and politics. As such, this chapter examines the part that Smith played in this Scottish literary circle of the late 1930s and early 1940s, placing his first collection into a wider literary context and exploring his (sometimes fraught) search for an authentic poetic voice at a time when the markers of Scottish literature were being redefined and refined.

## Keywords

*Skail Wind* – Smith's first collection – contemporary reception – Douglas Young – Sorley MacLean – Scottish Literary Renaissance – 1930s/1940s – Lallans – Hugh MacDiarmid – poetry

Sydney Goodsir Smith's first poetry did not have the impact on the Scottish literary scene that much of his later work garnered. Unlike, for example, his friend, Sorley MacLean's first major publication, *Dàin do Eimhir*, which was published a few years later in 1943, there was not the feeling that *Skail Wind* had changed the direction of a language or literary culture; Smith's first iconic or defining moment would come later in the 1940s with his *Under The Eildon Tree*.[1] While *Skail Wind* appears to have had two editions, any perceived popularity relating to the book is ill-founded; the 'second edition' was actually the first edition with 'second edition' stamped on it – the book certainly did not sell as well as Smith or the publisher, The Chalmers Press, would have hoped. For this and other reasons, it is easy to downplay the role that *Skail Wind* played in Smith's development as a poet and, more particularly, in the development of his identity as a Scots poet. Smith was born in New Zealand (his mother, Catherine Goodsir Gelenick was of Scottish origin) and educated in England. Scots was not his native language but he absorbed the language and culture when he stayed with his prep school teacher in Heriot, and his sister's nanny in Moniaive. One of the main factors that makes Smith's story so fascinating in the context of the latter part of the Scottish Literary Renaissance is his adoption of Scots as a poetic medium. Richie McCaffery has noted the 'rather steep learning curve of only a few years' that the poems in *Skail Wind* exhibit (McCaffery, 25), while Norman MacCaig encapsulates the dramatic nature of this experience when he writes:

> With the suddenness of a conversion he seceded from English, adopted Scots, and never wrote a poem in English from then on [...] an extraordinary fact which is worth recording only because in that at first almost foreign tongue he went on to write poetry in Scots of a quality hardly equalled in this century.
>
> MacCaig, 7

This chapter will investigate *Skail Wind* from a number of perspectives. Rather than taking the acknowledged stance that Smith's collection was a disappointment – a piece of work that should be played down and criticised for its weaknesses – the wider context of *Skail Wind* will be examined from the perspective of Smith's formation of literary and cultural identity. This was significant rite of passage, not only for Smith but for many of his friends, including Douglas Young, Sorley MacLean and William Soutar, who shared the literary scene in Edinburgh with him in the early 1940s. *Skail Wind* will be examined as the first fruits of Smith's identity shift, but also as the vehicle with which he began to achieve it. While the collection may be less than fully-formed in its

---

1  All following references to *Skail Wind* relate to: Smith, Sydney [Goodsir], *Skail Wind* (Edinburgh: The Chalmers Press, 1941). Note: only fourteen of the poems included in *Skail Wind* are reprinted in: Smith, Sydney Goodsir, *Collected Poems: 1941–1975* (London: John Calder, 1975).

literary vision, it is, nevertheless, an invaluable addition to the Scottish Literary Renaissance canon and the way it was received and discussed by Smith's literary peers will also be scrutinised in order to more fully understand the literary climate from which this collection emerged. While a poetry collection such as *Skail Wind* is undoubtedly the poet's own personal creation, the effect of the environment produced by the collective interests of the Scottish Literary Renaissance writers should not be underestimated in relation to the evolution of identity, particularly for a writer, like Smith, in his formative years. For this reason, much attention will be given to published reviews of the book and personal correspondence from Smith and others, in order to analyse both the overt and latent strands which accentuate Smith's sometimes fraught search for an authentic poetic voice.

1      The Gangrel Visions of *Skail Wind*

While one of the criticisms levelled at *Skail Wind* has been that the poems in the collection are dislocated and lack a central theme, this evaluation seems to be rather unjust.[2] The collection reveals the temporary and disquieting effects of an individual and a community experiencing war by exploring its influence in relation to the personal and the political. There are several obvious 'war poems' ('The Refugees', 'Lament in the Second Winter of War', 'A Day Apart') as well as poems addressed or dedicated to specific individuals who, at this transitory point in Smith's life, were influential in allowing Smith to work out his place in the world ('Epistle to John Guthrie', 'Letter to Hector MacIver', 'Ode to Hector Berlioz', 'For Denis Peploe'). Other poems appear to have been dated to the time before Smith's transition to the Scots language in his poetry and thus show where he has come from, both physically and figuratively in relation to poetic language ('June Afternoon', 'The Vision of Love', 'To John Guthrie in Gratitude'). There are also poems which explore where Smith is heading; his vision as an artist, his hopes for Scotland and its culture ('The Weird o Scotland is the Makar's too', 'Odin's Boat', 'The Dark Days are by'), as well as examples of his exploration into different Scots styles and themes (love songs, lullabies etc.).

---

2   See, for example, John Clifford Hall's comments 'The problem with most of the influences at work on Smith in his first volume is that too often they are completely unassimilated. He tries out various styles, wearing them like successive layers of ill-fitting clothing and, like ill-fitting clothes, they give us little idea of the true shape of the poet buried beneath' (62).

All of this achieves the effect of a poet in transition, which is exactly the position Smith was in in the early 1940s. When Smith's early poems and his biographical writing are considered together, the impression is that of Smith as something of a bohemian or a wandering artist. Interestingly, he was living in Oxford at the same time as both Douglas Young and George Campbell Hay and, in a letter to Maurice Lindsay he plays up his shiftless bohemian image somewhat, explaining that he was expelled from Oriel College for 'drunkenness and idleness' and that, while he never knew Young at this stage, '[Young] used to visit some friends of his who lived in my digs and evidently they often told him of their strange and disorderly neighbour' (Smith: 1988, 7). He paints a picture of himself to Lindsay as a drifter, who travelled around France, Germany and Italy, and eventually ended up in London, attempting to become serious about 'literature and life' (Smith: 1988, 8). However, 'the pressure in Soho, Bloomsbury etc. of obviously quite bogus poseurs of the various arts sickened my soul'. (Smith: 1988, 8). While at first casting himself as a sort of Orwellian figure straight from the pages of *Down and Out in Paris and London*, Smith seems to have navigated himself to Scotland and, if *Skail Wind* is any sort of testimony, Smith effectively swaps one sort of Bohemianism for another, of a more Scottish variety. The 'gangrel' – the outcast, wanderer or neer-do-weel (64) – is a potent image in *Skail Wind* and one which Smith returns to again and again as a self-identified rebel character for his poetic vision. In 'Odin's Boat' he is 'the gangrel pilot lashed tae a yelling wheel' who 'strains aye tae glimpse thro the drifting wrack/ The antrin licht he seeks' (19). He returns to this idea in 'Sonnet in the Small Hours' – while 'Embro sleeps ootby i the yirdit nicht o Europe' he knows that 'in ilka lan theres ither watchers wait a trubly dawn' (55). In 'The Refugees', Smith aligns the displaced peoples of Europe with his own cause, railing against conformity and the Establishment – 'For you are rebels by your suffering as makars by their act/ Wha 'gin the massed conformity build inner keeps tae haud their hated dreams' (62). Smith has found for himself a place of belonging in the Scottish literary tradition and, while the way of the gangrel poet at first appears to be a lonely road, Smith is actually celebrating a whole community of gangrels, brought together by circumstance (war) or by choice (art and culture).

It is possible that Smith's choice of poems was more considered than he has been given credit for, and that the sense of fragmentation for which he has been criticised was actually a deliberate attempt to 'show his working' as a poet who was in the midst of political and personal turmoil. When viewed through this specific lens, the symbols in many of the poems make more sense. The wild and extreme weather in *Skail Wind*, which plays the role of scatterer and fragmenter as well as awakener and cleanser (with the new dawn/new hope that comes after the storm has subsided), mirrors the effect of Smith's continuing evolution of identity, which could not have been plain sailing and also resulted in a 'scattering' of which he had to gather the different aspects of his poetic voice and persona in order to reform himself anew. The assured poet of *Under the Eildon Tree* could not have existed without first weathering the storms of *Skail Wind*.

The first poem in the collection, 'Lament in the Second Winter of War', effectively sets the scene and the tone for much of what is to come; composed in January 1940, Smith paints a bleak picture of chilly weather and the figurative spaces made cold by the absence of his friends.

> Yir een maun watch the slaughtrous stramash, booted doom
> Fae sleep wheer aa ligs broun as the snug deep howe o the womb
> And oorie truth returns to ache lik snaw i the teeth
> And naethin but crottled despair beneath. (9)

Smith's feelings are understandable; due to chronic asthma he was turned down for active service (he went on to work with the War Office and taught English to Polish troops) and thus he found himself in the unenviable situation in which he was left in Edinburgh at a time when many of his circle were conscripted and had left the city. The desolate winter season mirrors his own experience and his friends and the natural environment intermingle:

> All, all are gane, aa my prood yins; blin me that an ye can!
> Aa the bricht sterns o ma darklin lyft 're awa –
> Auld Embro's bluid is thin, the bars 're toom
> An cauld is her fierce iren heart, her black banes
> Rigid wi cauld, [...]. (9)

While Smith is mourning the loss of 'the haill clanjamphrey' (9) to the war, it is clear that Edinburgh is also a main character, personified as a woman whose health has suffered due to the change in her environment. Smith casts himself as a lone figure – 'An the gangrel left, the skalrag; here lik Iain Lom, I'm left alane' (9). This is an interesting comparison, given Smith's obvious frustration at not being able to participate in active service in the War. The Gaelic poet, Iain Lom (c1624–c.1710) was thought to have been slightly disabled, walking with a limp, and, as a traditional poet, he catalogued the actions of his clan in poems such as 'Là Inbhir Lochaidh' ('Day of Inverlochy'). It is said that when

Alasdair Mac Colla offered him a sword at the Battle of Inverlochy in 1645, he declined saying 'Cathaichibh sibhse 's innse mise' ('You fight and I'll narrate') (MacKenzie, xxxviii). While not necessarily self-imposed, this seems to have been Smith's view of himself in relation to his present circumstances. After finding himself among kindred spirits in Edinburgh, after a long time in Oxford attempting to forge a bohemian existence as a writer, it is not difficult to imagine Smith's frustration as his friends are scattered and his way of life is drastically altered. Douglas Young recounts a similar experience of drastic and unwanted change from a scholarly perspective on the eve of war in Europe in his poem, 'After Lunch, Ekali' (Dymock, 18–19). However, despite the harshness of weather and circumstance, the poem finishes on a different note, reminiscent of the resilience of nature after the worst of the winter weather – acknowledging 'dochter daith', Smith reveals ambitions which hint at much more to come beyond *Skail Wind* – 'Na, na, my quean; ye'll hae to bide a ween,/ I've vengeance yet tae verse afore ye ding thir een' (9).

Similar allusions to wild weather and stunted nature ('wreisted roots', 'the hail an yowdendrift', 'goustrous haar', 'elritch darkness'), emerge in the July 1940 poem, 'Shall Brithers Be for a' that' (10–11), which calls for a recognition of common humanity amid the chaos of war. If the autumn and winter winds have scattered his friends to far-flung places, it is also possible to interpret the natural elements which are woven throughout these poems as a catalyst for change. In 'The Samphire Gatherers', inspired by a verse from *King Lear*, a wind-whipped, barren landscape is evoked –

> And here this gaunt dry tree broods bent abune a stricken cliff
> Wheer the last few crazy samphire gatherers cling
> In wunds' wild boistery neth a torn balck lyft,
> An tossed gulls owre the roarin daze of foam
> Dip screichin lik sea trolls, vultures for carrion come –
> An the fingers o the searchin madmen caulder grow, grow numb. (35)

The poet may be 'deemed mad or wind-drunk' but he views himself as 'wiser than the warld, awake while reason sleeps' (35).

While Smith's way of life has been changed by the violent events across Europe (just as, if the metaphor can be stretched still further, weather can impact locations hundreds of miles away), there is a sense in *Skail Wind* that harsh winds will not last and can also have a cleansing effect, ridding one of the detritus of life and blowing in new experiences and new times. In 'A Dawn was glimpsed at Stormy Midnight' the poetic voice is akin to a parent softly comforting a child who is suffering a restless night's sleep –

> No, never heed, childe, whit the wunds micht tell ye,
> They greit their passion tae sleep wi wailin,
> Dark tae the farthest cave o grief they cry [...]. (14)

The poet achieves a calmness in the midst of the storm at the end of the poem –

> Their eyes refuse the burning surf, the boulders screichin i the spate,
> Nor glimpse the dawn I watch now i this how-dumb-deid o nicht;
> No, let them dree their ain, you've auld an drumlier skaiths tae richt. (14)

This emphasis on destiny and future aspirations, in the face of old wounds, is significant. There can be no doubt that Smith's personal visions are bound up with a collective literary vision for Scotland, first imagined by the likes of Hugh MacDiarmid in the 1920s. It is worth noting that the poems in *Skail Wind* which deal with storms, turbulent times and subsequent rebirth and renewal, particularly in relation to the poet's craft and the direction of Scotland's literature are all written in Scots. It is here that we glimpse Smith's new-found commitment and his creed. In 'The Quickening No.1' it is difficult not to read the last stanza in connection with the Scottish Literary Renaissance and Smith's own awakening to the Scots language.

> Bend yir heid tae the beating fields, childe; lay your han
> On the warmth o flooers efter hayr –
> For the winter o stealth is deid, a green lan
> Waves in its thoughtless youth. Weep nae mair. (45)

In 'Epistle to John Guthrie' his approach to the Scots language in poetry is more pronounced – 'Tae reach the hills his fantice needs/ This bard maun tak the wings o Scots' (50) – and his chosen mechanisms are laid bare:

> But mind, nae poet eer writes "common speech",
> Ye'll fin eneuch o yon in prose;
> His realm is heich abune its reach –
> Jeez! wha'd use ale for Athol Brose? (51)

At this point, Smith was perhaps blissfully unaware of the controversy that such an approach to writing in Scots would provoke among his own community of 'gangrels' and the subsequent stormy exchanges that were to come.

## 2        The Reception of *Skail Wind*

A great deal can be gleaned about Smith from correspondence between his friends, Sorley MacLean and Douglas Young. It is clear that he was a trusted and valued member of their circle; this trust is manifested in MacLean's willingness to leave his own unpublished poems with Smith when he left for military training at Catterick Camp – MacLean wrote to Young on 1st October 1940 that 'I left a Gaelic copy of most of my stuff with Sydney Smith, and sent another home, one to you and a Skye schoolmaster has a third, so they are fairly well scattered' (Acc. 6419, Box 38b). During World War II, with so many of his friends dispersed, Smith also seems to have been the glue that held them together when they did make it back to Edinburgh; his home appears to have been a meeting place during a time when location was uncertain and military leave could be sudden and fleeting. The reading and commenting on each other's poems is also evident in the correspondence from this time and it is clear that the poems that would become Smith's *Skail Wind* were being circulated among his friends. On 22 August 1941 MacLean wrote to Young that 'On Thursday morning I saw Sydney Smith who mentioned that you might be in Edinburgh on the weekend. He also showed me his poems to be published but I had no time to go into them' (Acc. 6419, Box 38b). He elaborated further on 9 November regarding *Skail Wind*:

> Sydney sent me the proofs of his book but I have not been able to find the time for reading it thoroughly as yet, and it takes pretty long for me to digest Sydney's earlier stuff at any rate – and I find it difficult to assess his poetry. Indeed I find it difficult to read anything exacting at present and, though I was never more full of poetic ideas myself than I am now, I cannot concentrate on them nor even allow them the opportunity of simmering, and Sydney's poetry requires close reading. (Acc. 6419, Box 38b)

This last line is revealing; Smith's friends, for all the warmth and encouragement found in the Edinburgh Rose Street scene, could nevertheless be his harshest critics and one may wonder if the reason for MacLean's need for concentration over Smith's work was at least partly due to 'his being badly dyed with the Eliot-Auden-Spender humbug out of which he is trying to grow', a comment made by MacLean in another letter dated 25 May 1941 (Acc. 6419, Box

SKAIL WINDS AND SCATTERED PERSONALITIES

38b). MacLean also wrote along similar lines to Hugh MacDiarmid on 23 February 1942:

> I have read Sydney's book *Skail Wind* and have been much attracted by
> his more recent pieces in Scots and some of his shorter things in English
> or Scots-tipped English. I thought they marked a very great advance on
> his earlier stuff which was so influenced by the contemptible verse of the
> Auden clique and the (to me) unsuccessful aspirations of Dylan Thomas
> and his followers of the surrealist or near-surrealist type.
>
> MANSON, 318

This was obviously a later letter and by this point, MacLean seems to be hinting that Smith has moved on from *Skail Wind*. However, this letter, while indicative of the opinion of Smith's friends, perhaps reveals more about MacLean himself. MacLean's own fears of being influenced by the 'Auden clique' has been well-documented in his own autobiographical prose and his aversion to the English war poets is as much bound up with his political stance as it is with his poetic sentiments.[3] Smith's struggle in shedding the influence of modern English poets is an experience which is perhaps very close to the bone for MacLean and hints at a common challenge for the modern Scottish poets in the 1930s and 1940s that goes beyond Smith himself. This considered, criticism of Smith must be viewed within the wider context of his own circle's biases and insecurities.

Smith's fellow writers were as aware of his poetic journey from English to Scots as, no doubt, he was himself and this 'difference' (if it can be called that), which set him apart a little from his peers, came back to haunt him on the publication of *Skail Wind*. On 4th January 1941 MacLean wrote to Young that 'When you see Sydney give him my best wishes and tell him that this time a collection of post earlier than I expected has prevented me from writing to him fully and giving him my impressions of his book which I have read and re-read very carefully' (Acc. 6419, Box 38b). There is no way of knowing what MacLean's impressions of Smith's collection were in this instance, but Young's own opinions made it into *The New Alliance* in the form of a rather scathing review. Young informs MacLean that 'Sydney was peeved at my review [...] but we mollified him' (MS. 29540). Smith's feelings were understandable because

---

3   See MacLean's comments in his essay, 'My Relationship with the Muse' – 'Only in very rare
    moments, and never at all during the years 1936 to 1945, did I think of the poet primarily or
    secondarily as a virtuoso or craftsman, no has my practice implied that he should be a "com-
    mitted" propagandist even in the very best sense. If "committed" the poetry must be in some
    way confessional if it is to be true to the perpetual dilemma of the "Existentialist" choice [...]
    I could not have been an Iain Lom at Inverlochy or an Auden in America in 1939' (12).

Young, intentionally or not, seems to have focussed mostly on the area of Smith's poetic identity which was newly emerging and of which Smith was perhaps most self-conscious. Young begins with a rather backhanded compliment regarding Smith's use of the Scots language, writing that

> Here is a sign of the times, another epiphenomenon of English cultural decay. To find his mode of expression a globe-trotting English speaker, of Antipodean provenience, has recourse to Lallans, which moreover he wields not worse than many autochthonous North Britons.
>
> YOUNG: 1942, 10–11

He goes on to accuse 'the makar' of trailing 'relics of the English Thirties' and comments that 'the rhythm also is too often slack, and interminable spavined lines schauchle over the excellent paper' (Young: 1942, 10–11). It says much about Smith's good nature and resilience (and perhaps a little about Young's tenacious confidence in his own judgement) that by May 1942 Young was reporting to MacLean, who was stationed in the Middle East, that '[Sydney] is putting out a new book. We made up our quarrel; his fault' (MS. 29540). Young was not alone in his views on *Skail Wind*. W.D. MacColl, the Gaelic enthusiast and nationalist, described it – in conversation rather than in print – as 'turgid muttering of loose thought' (Acc. 6419, Box 38b). A short review in *Scots Independent* in March 1942 judged Smith's use of Scots as being of the tradition of MacDiarmid's 'Synthetic Scots', which achieved 'some eerie and goustie effects' (G.H.K., 2). However, the reviewer's conclusion borders on patronising; 'it is a language of richer resources, as this promising poet will discover when he broadens and deepens his theme' (G.H.K., 2). William Soutar's review in *The Free Man* was negative enough to garner criticism, which resulted in him defending his position in a letter to the editor in a later volume. While apologising for remarks concerning false information about Smith's background (this preoccupation with Smith's lack of Scots heritage appears to have dogged the poet for some time), he nevertheless remained resolute in his opinion of Smith's use of Scots in *Skail Wind*; 'many of Mr. Smith's verses come under no category of Scots – artificial, provincial or synthetic' (Soutar, 4).

Interestingly, it was Hugh MacDiarmid, a writer well-known for his own caustic remarks, who was the most prominent figure to defend *Skail Wind*. In an article in *The Free Man*, he gave his seal of approval to Smith's use of Scots in the poems, praising 'his experimentism and the rich synthetic vocabulary he employs' (MacDiarmid, 4). He reproached both Soutar and Young for their comments regarding Smith's 'alleged unScottishness' and went to great lengths to caution against what he seems to have viewed as a growing sense of exclusionary behaviour among his fellow Scots writers.

> Even if Sydney Smith were not half Scottish by birth, and domiciled in
> Scotland, and deeply involved in the Scottish Literary Movement, his de-
> votion to the Scots language would be very welcome, as a rare kind of
> compliment indeed for any non Scot to pay to thc Scots tongue. Save us
> from any "little Scotlandism" in this connection.
>
>           MacDiarmid, 4

His words are significant, particularly in the context from which Smith arises;
if much of these negative opinions were even slightly coloured by prior knowl-
edge that Smith was not a native speaker of Scots, with very little previous
personal background in Scots literature and, until recently, with more than a
passing connection to the influence of the Bloomsbury group and New Apoca-
lypse writing, it seems that MacDiarmid was keen to foster an air of inclusive-
ness in relation to those writers who were drawn to Lallans, the Scottish Liter-
ary Renaissance and MacDiarmid's own cultural programme. It is clear that
MacDiarmid viewed Smith as one of his own; Smith could not have hoped for
a better welcome into the fold than MacDiarmid's proposal to Hogarth Press of
a publication which would include his own work alongside poems by Sorley
MacLean, George Campbell Hay, William Soutar and Hugh MacDiarmid him-
self (Manson, 282). MacDiarmid's keenness to defend Smith's work may also
have been personal by this stage. The two men had already had their first meet-
ing by the time MacDiarmid's letter was published in *The Free Man* in August
1942. Sorley MacLean reports in a letter to Young later in 1942 that 'Sydney
spoke enthusiastically of his first meeting with Grieve at Easter. They had
"many pints at the Cafe Royal"' (Acc. 6419, Box 38b). However, MacDiarmid's
support of Smith dates back to much earlier than this. In Smith's invaluable
1947 autobiographical letter to Maurice Lindsay, he goes into detail regarding
some of his early poems. In the late 1930s Smith had sent MacDiarmid 'some
English verses of mine, which later appeared in *Skail Wind*. He was very kind
about them and I was grateful' (Smith: 1988, 9). Note that these were English as
opposed to Scots verses; it may be that MacDiarmid was perceptive enough to
notice Smith's conversion from an English poet into a more fully-fledged Scots
poet, which had occurred in a very short space of time and was keen to nurture
Smith's development rather than discourage his first attempt. Smith's letter to
MacDiarmid on 1 November 1941 provides detailed evidence that Smith was
not only shaken by the *New Alliance* comments of Douglas Young but was also,
rather poignantly, keen to prove his credentials to MacDiarmid.

> Anent the recent correspondence in the *New Alliance* I might mention
> that though born in New Zealand of a Scottish mother and a New Zea-
> land (English descent) father the first words I remember being spoken

to me were 'Haud yir wheesht' by my mother. Praps that is why I gave
up English for Scots in my poetry; though I myself put it down to the
cataclysmic effect of my first reading of *A Drunk Man Looks at the Thistle*,
an effect similar to my discovery of the existence of poetry at the age of 13
with *Childe Harold*. I shall never go back to English now, Scots is without
any doubt in my opinion the greatest language for poetry in the world.

MANSON, 314

Smith, in his opinion of MacDiarmid's poetry, echoes Sorley MacLean, who has
written similarly of its transformative effect (in MacLean's case this was in rela-
tion to poetic impact rather than language, since MacDiarmid did not alter the
course MacLean had set himself in relation to the Gaelic language) (MacLean:
1985, 11). However, this observation aside, Smith's words make uncomfortable
reading if viewed from the a 21st century literary perspective. Smith's language
choices and subsequent need to defend and explain his background in the face
of criticism, much of it coming from his own circle, would be noticeably ab-
sent in present literary discourse, with the threat of accusations of unsavoury
nationalism or even racism dissuading writers from taking this sort of route.
The 1940s writers did not have such qualms but it is tempting to see in Smith,
a prototype of the writers who came after him whose first languages were not
Scots or Gaelic, and who chose to write in these languages without need to
prove a 'native' connection to these traditions.

Identity lies at the crux of the matter. It is important to be aware of these
personal opinions and more public reviews of a collection such as *Skail Wind*
because they say as much about the critics as they do about Smith himself.
Many of these writers – Douglas Young, Sorley MacLean, William Soutar –
were undergoing their own transformations and attempting to find their own
literary places in the early 1940s. Identity, whether self-professed or bestowed
by peers, was important. Smith was not the only poet of this period to 'come
out' in favour of one language over another or to argue the case for its usage.
The formation of Sorley MacLean's own poetic identity was every bit as dra-
matic in its genesis. By his own admission he destroyed all of the poetry that he
had written in English once he had made the decision that he would be a 'Gael-
ic poet' who would write only in the Gaelic language. Only one English poem,
'East Wind' published by the English Literature Society of Edinburgh Univer-
sity in 1933 pamphlet entitled *Private Business* remains (Hendry, 14) and there
is a startling resemblance in both theme and atmosphere between it and some
of the poems in *Skail Wind*; this may be another reason for the harshness of
MacLean's criticism of Smith during this period – it is likely that he saw some-
thing of his 'English' self in Smith's book. Parallels can be drawn between

MacLean and Smith in relation to their struggle with English-language poetry. Like Smith, who was aware of the strength of influence exercised upon him by the likes of T.S. Eliot et al., MacLean felt that his English poetry was too greatly influenced by English language poets, and it was only with the use of Gaelic that he could step out of the shadow cast by these writers.[4] However, Gaelic was MacLean's native language while Scots was not Smith's. Perhaps Douglas Young's poetic journey has more in common with Smith's own experience, particularly in relation to publication record. In Young's first collection, *Auntran Blads*, published in 1943, English and Scots poems comfortably co-exist and there does not seem to have been a favoured language choice; clearly certain poems called for specific language in the mind of Young and, unlike Smith, Young does not seem to have been publicly criticised for this or felt the need to explain himself in any definite way. Perhaps his confidence as a polyglot allowed him this freedom but it is worth noting that by the time his next publication, *A Braird o Thristles*, was published in 1947, the number of Scots poems had greatly increased while only a few English language ones remained, and the Scots glossaries for each of the poems in this collection were noticeably expanded and afforded more detail than they were in *Auntran Blads*. It is likely that Young's own identity as a nationalist with his interests definitively centred on Scotland had grown in significance by this time, especially with his high-profile anti-conscription trial. Thus, there is the possibility that the transformation achieved by Smith in one collection was actually undertaken by other writers such as Young across two or more publications, and may have been less jarring for this reason. Smith's only error, if it can, indeed, be viewed as such, appears to have been the honesty with which he embraced Scots as his authentic poetic voice and went on to reveal this so openly in *Skail Wind*; no other poet in Scotland in the 1940s seems to have left himself open to criticism by conducting the formation of poetic identity through Scots poetry in such an overt way. Despite a rather difficult road, the 'gangrel' had come home.

Sydney Goodsir Smith's *Skail Wind* is proof that a poet can choose an identity and cultivate it until it becomes an integral part of his self; while the collection can never be viewed as the finished product of Smith's conversion into a primarily 'Scots poet', it is certainly evidence of Smith's poetic process which was well underway in the early 1940s. When scrutinising its genesis and its later reception once published, *Skail Wind* really tells two separate stories. Firstly, it shows Smith's early poetic visions – his feelings about the nature of the poet and his craft, as well as his wider concerns for Europe at a time of war and the

---

4   MacLean writes in 'My Relationship with the Muse', 'My English verse could try to follow Donne, Eliot and Pound because I could not follow Blake and Shelley' (10).

fate of humanity in general. It is also a testament to his convivial and gener-
ous nature, with its themes of friendship and 'conversations' with specific
individuals. On a secondary level, *Skail Wind* also offers a glimpse into the wid-
er Scottish Literary Renaissance. While it is clear that this circle of poets nur-
tured strong friendships, it is also rather surprising how harsh they could be
about each other in print. With *Skail Wind*, Smith perhaps uncovered a num-
ber of insecurities shared by some of those attached to the Scottish Literary
Renaissance in relation to language choice, identity and the deliberate shed-
ding of the legacy and influence of English writers at a time when poets in
Scotland were situating themselves firmly within the orbit of the Scots and
Gaelic languages. *Skail Wind* was the product of Smith's early poetic transition
but equally, the critics of *Skail Wind* were a product of their own time too.

## Bibliography

G.H.K., 'Review of *Skail Wind*' in *Scots Independent*, No. 178 (March 1942), p. 2.

Hall, John Clifford, *The Writings of Sydney Goodsir Smith*. PhD Thesis. (University of
    Aberdeen, 1982).

Hendry, Joy, 'Sorley MacLean: the Man and his Work' in Joy Hendry & Raymond J. Ross
    (eds.), *Sorley MacLean: Critical Essays* (Edinburgh: Scottish Academic Press, 1986),
    pp. 9–38.

Lom, Iain, *Orain Iain Luim; the Songs of John MacDonald, bard of Keppoch*. Edited by
    Annie M. Mackenzie (Edinburgh: Scottish Gaelic Texts Society, 1964).

MacCaig, Norman, 'Introductory Note' in Norman MacCaig (ed.) *For Sydney Goodsir
    Smith* (Loanhead: M. Macdonald, 1975), pp. 7–10.

MacDiarmid, Hugh, '*Skail Wind* Review: Another point of View' in *The Free Man agus
    Alba Nuadh*, Vol 5 / No. 12 (1942), p. 4.

MacGill-Eain, Somhairle (Sorley MacLean), *Dàin do Eimhir agus Dàin Eile* (Glasgow:
    William MacLellan, 1943).

MacLean, Sorley, *Letters from Sorley MacLean to Douglas Young*, Acc. 6419, Box 38b,
    Special Collections, National Library of Scotland.

MacLean, Sorley, 'My Relationship with the Muse' in William Gillies (ed.) *Ris a'
    Bhruthaich: The Criticism and Prose Writings of Sorley MacLean* (Stornoway: Acair,
    1985), pp. 6–14.

Manson, John (ed.), *Dear Grieve: Letters to Hugh MacDiarmid* (*C.M. Grieve*) (Glasgow:
    Kennedy and Boyd, 2011).

McCaffery, Richie, 'Sydney Goodsir Smith's *Skail Wind*' in Walter Perrie (ed.) *Fras* 22,
    (2015), pp. 25–32.

Smith, Sydney [Goodsir], *Skail Wind* (Edinburgh: The Chalmers Press, 1941).

Smith, Sydney Goodsir, *A Letter Written to Maurice Lindsay in 1947* (Edinburgh: The Saltire Society, 1988).

Soutar, William ('The Reviewer'), 'Letter to the Editor concerning *Skail Wind*' in *The Free Man agus Alba Nuadh*, Vol. V / No. 11 (1942), p. 4.

Young, Douglas, 'Review of Skail Wind' in *The New Alliance*, Vol. III / No. 1 (1942), pp. 10–11.

Young, Douglas, *Auntran Blads: an outwale o verses* (Glasgow: William MacLellan, 1943).

Young, Douglas, *A Braird o Thristles: Scots Poems* (Glasgow: William MacLellan, 1947).

Young, Douglas, *Letters from Douglas Young to Sorley MacLean 1940–1968*, MS. 29540, Special Collections, National Library of Scotland.

Young, Douglas, *Naething Dauntit: The Collected Poems of Douglas Young*. Edited with an introduction and notes by Emma Dymock (Edinburgh: Humming Earth, 2016).

# CHAPTER 3

# 'My Elder Brother in the Muse': Sydney Goodsir Smith and Hugh MacDiarmid

*Margery Palmer McCulloch*

### Abstract

This chapter discusses the inspiration MacDiarmid's new Scots-language poetry pro-
vided for Smith, although the New Zealand-born poet had had no previous contact
with Scots-language culture. Nevertheless, Smith became a prominent Scots-language
member of the second phase of the Scottish Renaissance poetry revival. The chapter
explores the similarities and differences between Smith's and MacDiarmid's approach-
es to the Scots language as, for example, in Smith's involvement in the attempt to de-
velop a standard of Scots for poetry purposes as opposed to MacDiarmid's more hap-
hazard 'apostrophe' activity. The chapter also explores differences in the thematic
nature of their poetry. 'Back to Dunbar' did not have the same meaning for Smith as it
had for MacDiarmid. The influence of the Classics in Smith's writing will be discussed
as will Smith's visual imagination in relation to MacDiarmid's emphasis on the 'soon',
no' sense, that faddoms the herts o' men'. In conclusion, the chapter considers whether
the reputation of both poets has been unfairly restricted by their decision to write a
modern(ist) poetry in Scots.

### Keywords

Hugh MacDiarmid – mentor – Scots poetry – Scottish Literary Renaissance – second
wave – modernism – *A Drunk Man Looks at the Thistle* – *Sangschaw* – *Penny Wheep* –
influence – makar

By the end of the 1930s Hugh MacDiarmid's ambitious post-1918 attempt to cre-
ate a modern Scottish literature led by poetry in a revitalised Scots language
had become increasingly fragile. MacDiarmid himself had spent most of the
1930s in a kind of self-imposed – or self-accepted – exile on the small Shetland
island of Whalsay after a disastrous venture to London to act as editor for
Compton Mackenzie's short-lived *Vox* magazine: a venture that ended not only

in the failure of the magazine but also the failure of MacDiarmid's subsequent attempts to find employment in England and finally in the collapse of his marriage and his retreat north to the alcohol-free Whalsay. Although in 1933 the London *Spectator* magazine had announced a new editorial policy of regular coverage of Scottish affairs because 'the cultivation of Gaelic and the conscious development of a modern Scottish literature are movements demanding not only observation but discussion' (Spectator: 1933, 434), the new literature as envisaged by MacDiarmid a decade earlier, and in particular the new poetry characterised by a modernist, literary use of the Scots language, had not developed to any significant extent beyond his own use of that revitalised language in his ballad collections *Sangschaw* and *Penny Wheep* and his long dramatic monologue *A Drunk Man Looks at the Thistle*. In England the 1930s had become the political decade, with middle-class, left-wing poets such as Day Lewis, Spender and Auden taking up themes of socialist commitment and the celebration of technological innovation; and although he would attack these English poets in the late 1930s in his new magazine *Voice of Scotland*, MacDiarmid too turned to contemporary political themes in the thirties, with his first two *Hymns to Lenin*, written in Scots, published in 1931 and 1932 (the latter in Eliot's *Criterion*), and the third *Hymn*, written in English around the mid-1930s, first published in his own *Voice of Scotland* in 1955. Themes of political commitment do not lend themselves easily to innovative and imagistic language, and so MacDiarmid's discursive poetry of the 1930s took him further away from his literary Scots of the 1920s and eventually to an increasing use of English. Ironically, his serious breakdown in relations with Edwin Muir, whom in the mid-1920s he had hailed as 'a critic incontestably in the first flight of contemporary critics of *welt-literatur*' (MacDiarmid: 1926, 108), and who had been one of the few critics to write with both appreciation and understanding of his Scots-language early lyrics and *A Drunk Man*, came as a result of Muir's opinion in his 1936 book *Scott and Scotland* that the Scottish writer who wished to find a readership for his work would have to write in English. For Muir, the problem was not only one of language but also one of the absence of 'a faith among the people themselves that a Scottish literature is possible or desirable'; and following on from that, the problem of no opportunity 'of making a livelihood by his work' (Muir: 1982, 4). This was indeed MacDiarmid's own situation in the mid-1930s, a time when he himself was increasingly moving to the use of English, but his anger at Muir's putting the problem into the public domain caused a breach which even in later years MacDiarmid refused to heal.

This precarious outlook for the future of a literary revival led by poetry in Scots was the prevailing situation when the New Zealand-born Sydney Goodsir Smith settled in Edinburgh in the late 1930s and discovered MacDiarmid's

*A Drunk Man Looks at the Thistle.* Smith himself had had a somewhat uneasy passage to adulthood. Born in New Zealand in 1915, he and his family seemed to be regularly on the move when he was a child as a result of the war and his father's position in the Royal Army Medical Corps in Egypt where Smith spent much of his early childhood. His father was appointed Professor of Forensic Medicine at Edinburgh University in 1928, but previous to that move Sydney had been sent at the age of six to prep school in Swanage in England where he remained until he entered Malvern College in Worcestershire at the age of thirteen. Although he pleaded with his parents to be allowed to study art when he left school, this was not a course of action acceptable to his father who insisted that he should follow the family medical tradition and study medicine in Edinburgh. Perhaps unsurprisingly, this move was not a success academically, although Smith wrote later that it provided him with 'one crowded *year* of glorious life'. It was followed by similar 'three or four crowded years of glorious life' at Oxford, from which he eventually graduated with a not so glorious degree after expulsion for a short period for 'drunkenness and idleness' (Smith: 1988, 6–7). A few years in London where his irregular lifestyle continued, accompanied this time by more serious thoughts about the possibility of a literary career, eventually ended in a retreat to his home in Edinburgh in the late 1930s where he fell out with his family, married, and became associated with some of the literary people in the city who were supporters of MacDiarmid's attempt to create a new poetry in Scots. When one of these supporters, Hector MacIver, sent him a copy of *A Drunk Man Looks at the Thistle*, Smith's response was that until reading MacDiarmid's long poem he 'hadn't been born' (Smith: 1988, 9). He very soon became a significant contributor to the second wave of the Scots-language poetry revival which, like poetry more generally, found new impetus with the outbreak of World War Two in 1939.

Smith would appear to have sent MacDiarmid some poems in English shortly before he read *A Drunk Man*, and MacDiarmid would appear to have responded 'kindly' to him about them (Smith: 1988, 9). These may have included 'The Last Dusk' and 'A Day Apart', later published in his first collection *Skail Wind* of 1941, and dated respectively '1 September 1939', and 'September 1939'. The former, a poem apparently dealing with some form of mental distress – 'They stalk across with great insane feet,/The sombre beasts that walk the mind's grey corridor' – is written in an artificial style akin to that of English poets such as Spender and MacNeice as they described pylons stalking the landscape or other technological innovations changing city and countryside. 'A Day Apart' is directly related to the everyday life of its time of writing as its speaker, on a visit to Anstruther in Fife, cannot escape from the memory of the sounds of aeroplanes operating from Leuchars airport further up the coast and the thought of the air-raids these sounds imply, despite the quietness of his present location: 'Here is no tumult nor horror nor evening editions thick as rumour, /Only sun and winds [...] And yet, and yet, I cannot sleep' (Smith: 1975, 3). This English language poem is more formally akin to the personally-felt or experienced poems in Scots that would shortly follow, whether about the ongoing war in Europe or about the speaker's own conflicting emotions. MacDiarmid was later quick to notice and support Smith's potential in Scots-language poetry, although his use of that language for literary purposes was different from his own. As early as May 1940, for example, MacDiarmid was writing to William Soutar to tell him that Hogarth Press was willing to consider for publication a selection of poems made by himself and titled 'Six Scottish Poets' for inclusion in their *Poets of Tomorrow* series. The poets he had chosen were, in addition to Soutar and himself, George Campbell Hay, Douglas Young, Somhairle MacGill-Eain (Sorley MacLean), and the new poet in the group, Sydney Goodsir Smith. Later, after the publication of Smith's first collection, *Skail Wind*, in 1941, MacDiarmid would write a long letter to the *Free Man* magazine criticising reviews of Smith's poems both by Soutar in the *Free Man* and Douglas Young in *New Alliance* which had argued that Smith's use of the Scots language was 'unScottish'. MacDiarmid attacked the 'little Scotlandism' of both critics and emphasised his own approval of Smith's 'experimentalism and the rich synthetic vocabulary he employs'; adding that 'so far as poetic quality goes I regard him as by far the best young poet writing in Scots who has emerged in our midst for over twenty years'. For MacDiarmid, whom Smith himself would readily acknowledge as his 'elder brother in the muse',[1] this new Scots-language poet's first collection 'deserves every encouragement' not 'cold water dribbled on it' by 'some of his dyspeptic seniors' (MacDiarmid: 1940 & 1942 / MacDiarmid: 1984, 172–173 & 783).

MacDiarmid was in the right about the *Skail Wind* collection, for despite a sense that in many of its poems the poet is still finding his own identity formally and in relation to the use of Scots (which was to Smith, schooled in England, in the nature of a foreign language), the ambition of his themes in poems such as 'Lament in the Second Winter of War', 'The Refugees: A Complaynt' (with its epigraph from *King Lear*), 'Ode to Hector Berlioz', and the assured ironic comedy in defence of the Scots language in 'Epistle to John Guthrie' points to an important recruit to Scots-language poetry. Smith was fortunate also in that his discovery of MacDiarmid's poetry and his own capacity to use

---

1   The 'elder brother in the muse' quotation is from Robert Burns' poem on Fergusson (untitled), *Burns Poems and Songs*, ed, James Kinsley (Oxford: Oxford University Press, 1969), p. 258.

the Scots language for a new poetry of his own coincided with the appearance of a number of new poetry magazines in the early 1940s including *Poetry Scotland* and *Scottish Art and Letters*, supported by the Glasgow publisher William MacLellan who also published Sorley MacLean's *Dàin do Eimhir* in 1943 and MacDiarmid's *In Memoriam James Joyce* in 1955. *Poetry Scotland* was edited from the war front by Maurice Lindsay and many of its contributors sent their poems from the front also. While Lindsay had initially emphasised that he did not intend his new magazine to be particularly devoted to poems in Scots, or even to poems from Scotland, his contributors and readers soon established *Poetry Scotland*'s identity as an important supporter of a new Scottish poetry, including a resurgence of poetry in Scots. For health reasons, Smith himself was not a combatant, but, unlike MacDiarmid in relation to both the first and second World War, several of his early poems relate explicitly to the ongoing war, especially to the destruction experienced in Poland and the fate of Polish airmen serving in the Allied forces, to some of whom he acted as an English-language teacher in Perthshire in the early years of the war. Apart from 'The Refugees' from his first collection, *Skail Wind*, most of these war poems were collected in *The Deevil's Waltz* of 1946, including 'October 1941' with its opening reference to Tchaikovski's (Smith's spelling) 'Waltz o' Flouers' and its haunting closing line in each verse: 'An the leaves o wud October, man, are sworlan owre the warld' (Smith: 1975, 52). 'On Readan the Polish Buik o the Nazi Terror', also from *The Deevil's Waltz*, was surprisingly left out of the *Collected Poems* prepared by Smith himself, but fortunately restored by its substitute editor, Tom Scott, after Smith's unexpected death shortly before the book's publication. This is a forceful, emotional poem that opens with the sending of Scotland's sympathy and support to the suffering people of Poland: 'Poland, the warld is greitan as they read,/ O Polska martyr, raxed on a wreistit rood,/ Frae Scotland tak oor tears, oor blinnd an burnan dule'. Its use of language such as in the alliterative 'raxed on a wreistit rood' seems to speak also of older times and older conflicts and that continuity of war in human history which would itself become a theme in Edwin Muir's English-language poetry of the 1940s; and this is openly continued in the poem's reference to Scotland's own historical awareness of conflict and death: 'We ken the Black Rider, ken him weel'. Yet the poem ends with the belief that the undying positive human spirit will in the end overcome: 'We'se drink thegither yet, lang tho the onwyte be,/ The dear tint wine o libertie!' (Smith: 1975, 250–251). While these World War Two poems are not typical in theme or form of the poetry now most associated with Smith, they are important not only for themselves but also for the insight they give into his development as poet and into the emotions of the man behind a poetry that would later become more complex to situate in its seemingly personal terms.

As his writing quickly developed in maturity, it became clear that Smith's poetry, thematically and in his use of Scots, was very different from that of the elder poet MacDiarmid who had inspired him. In the early years of the post-1918 Scots-language poetry revival – and at times even today – MacDiarmid was frequently criticised for his battle-cry: 'Not Burns, Dunbar!', which was taken to mean that he wanted poets writing in Scots to follow the language of the late medieval Scottish Makars in their attempt to create a new Scottish poetry. This was something that MacDiarmid himself was clearly *not* doing in his own modernist-influenced Scots-language poetry which was based in his own experience of spoken Scots, mostly from rural areas of the country, enlarged by his exploration in Scots-language dictionaries for forgotten words and expressions, and inspired formally by Pound's Imagism and the poetry of French symbolists such as Mallarmé and Valéry as well as by the verse form of the Scottish ballads. It was, however, not the language forms of the Makars that interested MacDiarmid, but their independent spirit and their belief that there could be a discrete Scottish poetry with its own identity, different from the English Chaucerian tradition, as Gavin Douglas's ambitious translation into Scots of Virgil's *Eneados* had shown. MacDiarmid was interested also in a revival of a Scots language that was available for literature, a literary use of Scots as in the example afforded by the practice of the Makars as opposed to the spoken Scots revival supported by the London Burns Club in the early 1920s which planned to offer prizes in schools for speaking in Scots. Smith did not have this dual dilemma when he encountered MacDiarmid's *A Drunk Man*. Scots, literary or spoken, was a foreign language to him and he went back to the Makars and to the 18th century Fergusson and Burns to trace its history and to develop a literary form appropriate for his 20th century themes: themes which included the experience of the city, absent, as a result of historical time-scale, from the poetry of the Makars, largely absent from the poetry of the country-born MacDiarmid and mostly unsuccessful when attempted, but very much the poetic territory of the 18th century Fergusson from whom Smith also learned the skill of direct approach to his themes.

Smith also differed from MacDiarmid in relation to the thematic range of his poetry which early focussed on the theme of human love and sexuality. In contrast, MacDiarmid, who wrote little, if any, direct love poetry, ranged widely in his poetic interests, being essentially an explorer into the nature and meaning of human life: what Edwin Muir called in his autobiography the three mysteries of 'where we came from, where we are going, and, since we are not alone, but members of a countless family, how we should live with one another'. Muir's own poetry, and especially his mature late poetry from the 1940s onwards, is largely occupied with that third mystery of how we should live with one another in a 'single, disunited world' (Muir: 1980, 56 & 194). MacDiarmid's poetry covers this aspect of human life also, especially in his overtly political poetry and in a poem such as the metaphorical 'Lo! A Child is Born' which contrasts the united human atmosphere in a household waiting for a child to be born with the disunited history and uncertain future of humanity as a whole. He is primarily concerned, however, whatever the thematic or stylistic form chosen in which to explore it, with the theme of the *mystery* of human existence and of the natural world in which we humans live our lives. This is the overarching theme of his long dramatic monologue *A Drunk Man Looks at the Thistle* as it is also of the later English-language long philosophical poem 'On a Raised Beach', and it is the ground bass of many poems of varying surface topics and lengths throughout his poetic career. In contrast, Smith's poetry, like that of the 18th century Burns, as opposed to Fergusson, is situated primarily in the theme of human love and sexuality, although this theme can also interact with other elements of human life and experience.

This sexual love between two human beings, and the emptiness engendered by its absence, makes an immediate appearance in *The Deevil's Waltz* collection of 1946 through the five-part 'Reasoun and the Hert: A Sang-Quair for John Guthrie's music'. In the first 'song', 'The Lane Hills', the absence of the loved one is communicated through reference to elements in the world of nature which pattern the pain and emptiness felt by the solitary partner: 'Lane as the hills/ Ma saul the nou,/ The gray wund's shrill/ Wi the want o you'. The use of nature imagery here is not the Pathetic Fallacy trope of the Romantic period, where the natural world is described as mourning or rejoicing with the emotions of the lover. Instead, the speaker of the poem borrows qualities of the landscape and of the creatures which inhabit it in order to communicate feelings of isolation and pain: the solitariness of the hills, the searing sharpness of the wind, the desolate crying of the curlew on the moor. In contrast, in song IV: 'Whan the Hert is Licht' the speaker's 'thochts are whiddan owre the hills', his 'hert's abune wi a laverock flicht,/ A blye burd daft wi luve'; and the final verse ends: 'A lowsit bird maun seek his nest/ And I ma ain white doo' (Smith: 1975, 27–28). It is probable that the love poems in this collection, both poems of absence and despair and the joyful ones of reunion, derive at least in part from Smith's own troubles with his family over his wish to marry the 'Marion' to whom several of the love poems are dedicated. But as often in Smith's writing about love relationships, a poem, although apparently direct and deeply personal, can also have a wider resonance in relation to human life as in the final lines of 'Sang: Lenta La Neve Fiocca, Fiocca, Fiocca' where the lover's imagination captures at one and the same time through the falling snow flakes 'twa dark een/ Saft an deep with kennin' and a contrasting landscape 'Eastlins horror-reid wi war' (Smith: 1975, 34).

The focus of the sequence 'Five Blye Sangs for Marion' is principally on the happiness of togetherness with just a fleeting mention in the first song 'Sweet Womankind' that without his lover the drinking lover is 'a tuim glass'. In the second poem, the poet celebrates the colour green, as does the young traveller in Schubert's *Schöne Müllerin* in the early happy days of his love for the miller's daughter: 'O green's the spring, ma hinny,/ Alowe in ilka tree,/ Green as the luve has burst atween/ Ma hinny burd an me'. But he is equally happy when he sits with his love 'in a lamplit bar/ Braw on a wuiden stool,/ Her knees cocked up and her neb doun/ Slorpan a pint o yill'. The last song in the series returns to the happiness of the colour green which had supplanted the lover's earlier wintry feelings of loss, this time via 'Words for the Tune of Greensleeves' (words which perfectly fit the tune): 'A green burd flew intil ma airms,/ O ma winter lassie O,/ In ma hert she'll tak nae hairm,/ Greensleeves O ma dearie O' (Smith: 1975, 34–36). The final love poem in this 1946 collection as a whole, 'Hymn of Luve til Venus Queen', is very different in nature from the personalised poems of human love which have preceded it. The formal and declamatory tone of its speaker, as he presents this poem to Venus, Queen of Love, on behalf of the historical lovers 'Naoise and Deirdre / Cleopatra, Antony', and the 20th century 'Marion an Sydney' (Smith: 1975, 38) makes it a fit prelude to the dramatic *Under the Eldon Tree* series of love poems which would follow shortly in 1948.

Smith's early love lyrics which brought him to public attention as a new Scots-language poet might be compared with the similar functioning of MacDiarmid's Scots lyrics in *Sangschaw* and *Penny Wheep* in the mid-1920s, although the thematic and formal nature of the lyrics themselves is very different in each poet. Similarly, but with the same caveat, Smith's *Under the Eldon Tree* might be seen as occupying the place in his oeuvre taken by *A Drunk Man Looks at the Thistle* in the work of the elder poet. Both poems have as their principal protagonist a character who – while he has a dramatic life of his own – also shares character qualities and interests with his poet creator. And both poets entice readers into their lengthy poetic journeyings by their deliberately exaggerated opening appeals to that potential readership: MacDiarmid's protagonist through his claiming drinking companionship with 'Cruivie and Gilsanquhar and the like' before taking his readers 'by visible degrees/ To heichts whereo' the fules ha'e never recked' (MacDiarmid: 1978, 83); Smith's 'luve-doitit bard' by paying his exaggerated homage to the Queen of Love, aware that there will be many who share his 'afflictioun' and so will be open to following his forthcoming 'Spectacle of Follie' (Smith: 1975, 151–153). These long poems are also essentially different in nature, with MacDiarmid's *A Drunk Man* being both a poem about the condition of Scotland, 'a scene/ O Scottish life

A.D. one-nine-two-five', and simultaneously a philosophical exploration of the nature of human existence itself. Smith, too, is interested in an exploration of the human, but with his focus primarily on love and sexuality: 'You are my subject anerlie, there is nae ither/ Fills my musardrie,/ Nae word by your name in my dictionarie' (Smith: 1975, 150). Both poems, however different, were central to their respective author's recognition and lasting reputation. MacDiarmid wrote of Smith's poem in the year of its first publication that *Under the Eldon Tree* 'will hold a permanent place in our literary annals', showing itself to be an 'important substantive achievement in the development of our current literary movement' (MacDiarmid: 1984, 26–27). As with his immediate support of Smith's early lyrics in Scots in the late 1930s, there was no sense of rivalry in MacDiarmid's critique of this new poetry, only strong support for this new recruit to the recovery of Scots as a literary language.

The several poems in *Under the Eldon Tree* are often referred to as 'Love Elegies', probably because of the introductory poem 'Bards Hae Sung' which intimates that this will be the 'dune bard's' final love testament before 'his music turns to sleep'; and the closing 'Fareweill' poem which takes a final leave of the goddesses of love he has so long worshipped. His closing 'Guidnicht, leddies!', on the other hand, has more the friendly tone of a temporary farewell and the accompanying reference to Thomas the Rhymer's release from his seven years captivity by the Queen of the Faeries might be interpreted as bringing the possibility of a new beginning (Smith: 1975, 149 & 187). The principal love poems are also not 'elegiac' in the usual sense of the word. Dido is certainly betrayed by the false Aeneas who weakly sails hurriedly away without explanation or formal farewell. But it is the splendid visual image of Dido's burning palace – 'The orange, scarlet, gowden lowes/ Her ae wild protest till the centuries' – that captures the imagination of the reader and restores Dido's control of her reputation: 'Queen Dido burned and burnan tashed/ Æneas' name for aye wi scelartrie' (Smith: 1975, 176). Other love stories from the past are also presented in new perspectives. While Orpheus certainly loses Eurydice as in the classical scenario, it is Eurydice, usually the subordinate character in the myth and used in the concluding moralitas of Henryson's rewriting of the story to signify lustful human desire, who gains sympathetic attention in Smith's poem. Here, Orpheus admits his own neglect which first resulted in her death and passage to the underworld, and then his second moment of carelessness when he forgets the instruction not to look back at her when he hears her stumble and cry out. As used in Smith's context, the stark, painful quotation from the earlier Henryson's rewriting of the story: '"Quhar art thou gane, my luf Euridices!"' (Bawcutt & Riddy, eds., 71) tells a human story of love and careless but unintended neglect. Similarly, the poem 'Hieland Mary' rewrites the rumoured accounts of

Burns's relationship with Mary Campbell by having the poet, like Orpheus, admit his part in her neglect and untimely death, while insisting that in contrast to the various attempts by later critics to play down this relationship, 'There's me kens/ And Mary kens' what that relationship meant to each of them (Smith: 1975, 162). Such references from individual poems point to the fact that more generally throughout this sequence of love poems, as in the individual love poems of earlier collections, there is a 'modern' recognition by the male speakers in the poems of the separate identity of their various female lovers; these women have their own integrity of action apart from their temporary or more lasting relationship with their male partners. And this is as true of the portrait of Sandra in the Cowgate as it is in regard to the various speakers' more 'upmarket' female relationships.

*Under the Eldon Tree* will be explored more fully in Christopher Whyte's chapter in this volume, but in this present discussion of Smith's relationship to his predecessor MacDiarmid brief mention should be made of its fifth poem, titled 'Slugabed'. This is the kind of poem which most obviously points to Smith's difference from MacDiarmid. MacDiarmid's attempts at clever humour in *A Drunk Man* are mostly of a heavy-handed nature such as the lines relating to a Scottish soldier 'in a sham fecht' who 'louped a dyke and landed on a thistle./ He'd naething on ava aneth his kilt,/ Schönberg has nae notation for his whistle' (MacDiarmid: 1978, 96). There are also many serious as well as humorous attacks on the Burns Club movement in the poem, mostly well deserved. However, one of the early ones, unpleasant at any time, would certainly cause racial discrimination problems in present-day society: 'You canna gang to a Burns supper even/ Wi'oot some wizened scrunt o' a knock-knee/ Chinee turns roon to say, "Him Haggis – velly goot!"'; and the Drunk Man adds for good measure (although he probably would get away with this one): 'And ten to wan the piper is a Cockney' (MacDiarmid: 1978, 84). Smith's literary humour is of a different nature. He himself was a *bon viveur*, and despite the painful beauty of his early love lyrics, he proves himself equally compelling when it comes to creating literary comedy out of his complex and disorganised lifestyle. His fictional namesake in the poem 'Sydney Slugabed Godless Smith' takes as his mentor (although he claims to surpass him) the character Oblomov from the novel of that name by the Russian writer Goncharov. He too would appear to have spent his time 'Liggan my lane in bed at nune' with or without Slugabed's 'cauld, scummie, hauf-drunk cup o' tea' at his bedside or 'luntan Virginian fags'. There is also a splendid mingling of language registers and rhythmic movement as the comic but ironic opening section of the poem careers to its end: 'Wi ase on the sheets, ase on the cod,/ And crumbs of toast under my bum,/ Scrievan the last great coronach/ O' the western flickerin bourgeois world', and this coronach's ironic Latin lament or blessing is placed divergently on the page as if to imitate the rhythm of a priest's enunciation and scattering of holy water:

> Eheu fugaces!
> > Lacrimæ rerum!
> Nil nisi et cætera ex cathedra
> > Requiescat up your jumper.
> > > SMITH: 1975, 154

The following sections of the poem are no less cleverly compelling as they make ironic comedy out of Stalin's Communism and the 'far-famed Aist-West-Synthesis!/ Beluved by Hugh that's beluved by me' (Smith: 1975, 154–155).

*Under the Eldon Tree* had been preceded in 1947 by 'The First Quart' of Smith's Joycean prose work *Carotid Cornucopius*, published by the Caledonian Press, which may have influenced the comedy of his Slugabed Smith poem. Several collections of verse and dramatic works followed, together with critical works such as *A Short Introduction to Scottish Literature* (1951), the editing of a collection of essays on Robert Fergusson (1952) and co-editing of a festschrift for Hugh MacDiarmid (1962), and a selection of the poetry of Gavin Douglas (1959). This critical work again points to the way in which Smith differed from the elder MacDiarmid. MacDiarmid's skills as a journalist were essential in the creation and continuation of the small magazines that supported the literary revival of the 1920s, but in later years, as his own life and work became more difficult to sustain, he too often relied on quotation from the publications of others for his critical opinions. And even in his early days, a *mis*understanding of the European movements and poets who inspired him could be the fertile source of his own innovations. Smith was very different in this respect. His Introduction to his selection of poems by Gavin Douglas shows a commentator who has studied Douglas at first hand, comparing his use of Scots with that of Henryson and Dunbar and singling out his early innovative use of nature imagery in his Prologues to the *Eneados*. Douglas, in Smith's view, 'was at least 200 years *ahead* of his time in writing pure Nature poetry, *i.e.* poetry in which Nature is the *subject per se* and not merely introduced as the background to set a scene or adorn a tale' (Smith: 1959, 10). Similarly his Introductory essay to the collection of essays he edited on the eighteenth-century poet Robert Fergusson provides a well-structured argument for the revisiting of Fergusson's place in the canon of Scottish poetry, pointing to his 'richer and fuller' Scots language than that of Burns, and speculating as to how different the future course of Scottish poetry might have been had the city-based Fergusson come after

Burns as opposed to preceding him. For Smith, who learned much from Fergusson, 'he was a far greater and more prophetic figure in Scottish letters than the mere pace-maker for Burns that he has generally been made out to be' (Smith: 1952, 12 & 15). As critic, Smith also wrote meaningfully about the contemporary MacDiarmid who had inspired his own writing, although he joined with others in attempting to develop a form of writing that would banish the apostrophes that pepper the older poet's poetry. Although he himself was not political in his poetry, he wrote with understanding of MacDiarmid's three Hymns to Lenin, considering his poetry generally to be 'didactic, political, almost all the time' (Smith: 1962, 76). A view, however, which perhaps underestimates the ontological searching in MacDiarmid's work.

In the American journal *Studies in Scottish Literature* of October 1964, Smith contributed a substantial critique of the current Scottish literary scene titled 'Trahison des Clercs or The Anti-Scottish Lobby in Scottish Letters', after having been invited by the editor to make a response to David Craig's derogatory article 'A National Literature?' in the previous issue. Smith made a strong response in support of a literature in which the Scots language plays its part, yet five years later, in the same journal, the literary scholar Thomas Crawford found himself complaining about the lack of recognition in Scotland 'that poems of real merit have been produced by the second generation of the Scottish Renaissance', placing the blame for this firmly on 'Scots critics both inside and outside the universities' (Crawford, 40). Not much has changed today, almost fifty years later, with Burns and other safe antiquarian studies continuing to be well-financed and promoted while those like MacDiarmid and Smith lie on the shelf without modern editions or critiques of their works. Critics 'hae sung o' lesser luves/ Than I o' thee' (Smith: 1975, 149). It's time to stop taking the more challenging elements in our literary heritage 'to avizandum' (MacDiarmid: 1978, 166).

## Bibliography

Bawcutt, Priscilla & Riddy, Felicity, eds., *Selected Poems of Henryson and Dunbar* (Edinburgh: Scottish Academic Press, 1992).

Burns, Robert, Untitled poem on Fergusson, in James Kingsley, ed., *Burns Poems and Songs* (Oxford: Oxford University Press, 1969).

Crawford, Thomas, 'The Poetry of Sydney Smith', in *Studies in Scottish Literature*, Vol. VII, (July 1969–April 1970), pp. 40–59.

Grieve, C.M. (Hugh MacDiarmid), 'Edwin Muir' in *Contemporary Scottish Studies* (London: Leonard Parsons, 1926), pp. 108–119.

MacDiarmid, Hugh, *A Drunk Man Looks at the Thistle* (1926) in *Hugh MacDiarmid: Complete Poems 1920–1976* Vol.1 (London: Martin Brian & O'Keeffe), pp. 81–167.

MacDiarmid, Hugh, 'Editorial', in *Voice of Scotland*, Vol. 5 / No.2 (1948), pp. 26–27.

MacDiarmid, Hugh, Letter to William Soutar 8 May, 1940 and letter to *Free Man,* 8 August 1942, in Alan Bold, ed., *The Letters of Hugh MacDiarmid* (Athens, Georgia: University of Georgia Press, 1984), pp. 172–173 & 783.

Muir, Edwin, *An Autobiography* ([1954] London: Hogarth Press, 1980).

Muir, Edwin, *Scott and Scotland* ([1936] Edinburgh: Polygon, 1982).

Smith, Sydney Goodsir, *Collected Poems* (London: John Calder, 1975).

Smith, Sydney Goodsir, 'Introduction', in *Gavin Douglas* (Edinburgh: Oliver & Boyd, 1959), pp. 7–14.

Smith, Sydney Goodsir, 'Introductory' in *Robert Fergusson 1750–1774* (Edinburgh and London: Nelson, 1952), pp. 11–50.

Smith, Sydney Goodsir, 'Letter to Maurice Lindsay in 1947', *Saltire Self-Portraits* (Edinburgh: Saltire Society, 1988).

Smith, Sydney Goodsir, 'MacDiarmid's Three Hymns to Lenin', in K.D. Duval & Sydney Goodsir Smith, eds., *Hugh MacDiarmid: A Festschrift* (Edinburgh: K.D. Duval, 1962), pp. 73–86.

# CHAPTER 4

# Refraction, Intertexts and Diegesis in Sydney Goodsir Smith's *Under the Eildon Tree*

*Christopher Whyte*

## Abstract

The essay distinguishes two narratives in Smith's sequence. The first concerns the love affair which ostensibly forms its subject matter, the second the writing of the sequence itself, in the course of which they interact and interweave, even if there is no chronological overlap. Whyte discerns a repeated intervention, mirroring and refraction of competing voices, indicative of Smith's difficulty in attaining unmediated, frank utterance, as well as of his 'lastness', his link to the French Decadent poets and to a tradition reaching back to the Scottish Makars and beyond. The 'lastness' also implies a vivacious polemic with the leftist political commitment of fellow poets Somhairle MacGill-Eain / Sorley MacLean and Hugh MacDiarmid, from which Smith takes pains to distance himself.

## Keywords

modernism – diegesis – intertextuality – Hugh MacDiarmid – Scottish Renaissance – Scottish makars – *Under the Eildon Tree* – Sorley MacLean – French Decadent poets (19th century)

Irony creates its own implicit form of intertextuality. If we fail to realise that what is being said does not correspond to what is meant, we are in danger of seriously misinterpreting what we are reading or listening to. What happens is that we are prompted, or invited, to construct step by step a second, hypothetical text corresponding to what the speaker actually thinks or means. Otherwise we will miss the point of whatever is being put across. While Smith's *Under the Eildon Tree* sequence[1] stresses its links to the traditional love lyric, with

---

[1]   The text of the sequence is quoted from the second, revised edition: Sydney Goodsir Smith, *Under the Eildon Tree: A Poem in XXIV Elegies* (Edinburgh: Serif Books, 1954). Alternatively, the poem can be found in: Sydney Goodsir Smith, *Collected Poems: 1941–1975* (London: John Calder, 1975), pp. 147–187.

a forlorn, obsessed poetic 'I' in the spotlight who combines the roles of besotted lover and poet, it repeatedly offers a spectrum of different voices which alternate, interrupt and comment on one another. Often the intervention of a new voice or attitude undercuts what has previously been said with devastating bathos. Only occasionally does the 'I' shed his mask, or shield, and attempt to convey what he thinks or feels without mediation. Even these rather more straightforward passages are destabilised by the possibility, almost the expectation, of being suddenly undermined, as happens so regularly elsewhere.

When, as in the celebrated 'Slugabed' elegy (v), the speaker offers a 'no warts' portrait of himself, apparently supplying useful background information for the narrative which underpins the elegies, its 'diegesis',[2] ironic distance increases rather than collapsing. Here we can observe a species of 'triangulation', involving the reader and two distinct manifestations of the supposed author/narrator. One is the self-portrait he offers us,

> Liggan my lane in bed at nune
> Gantan at gray December haar,
> A cauld, scummie, hauf-drunk cup o tea
>     At my bed-side,
>     Luntan Virginian fags. (v, 19, ll.5–9)

The other is a critical 'alter ego' whose self-deprecation is, however, so riddled with implied irony that it is difficult to take at face value.

The sequence owes perhaps its most magical moment of all to just such an alternation of voices and registers. The speaker gives us his own inimitable definition of the erstwhile capital city fallen on leaner times which is the setting for his narrative, personified as a prostitute who never gets to take a day off:

> My bonie Edinburrie,
>     Auld Skulduggerie!
> Flat on her back sevin nichts o the week,
> Earnan her breid wi her hurdies' sweit. (XIII, 41, ll. 148–151)

---

2   Gérard Genette uses this term, taken from film theory, to indicate the supposed, chronologically ordered and preceding series of events which forms the basis of a written narrative. See 'Discours du récit' in his *Figures III* (Paris: Éditions du Seuil, 1972).

Upon which he moves without transition to a stunning evocation of the same
place transfigured by moonshine, traversed by characters from four centuries
back whose spectres continue to haunt it:

> - And Dian's siller chastitie
> Muved owre the reikan lums,
> Biggan a ferlie toun o jet and ivorie
> That was but blackened stane,
> Whar Bothwell rade and Huntly
> And fair Montrose and aa the lave
> Wi silken leddies doun till the grave.
>     - The hoofs strak siller on the causie!
>     And I myself in cramasie! (XIII, 19, ll. 152–160)

At the close the speaker himself becomes a character in the pageant, as if a
time machine could transport him back to this legendary past and make him a
participant in it.

Smith, or his proxy, insists on the parallels with what happens in a whole
series of pre-existent texts dealing with doomed, compulsive love, including
Douglas and Henryson, writing shortly in advance of the tragic life of Mary
Queen of Scots, and reaching back as far as Sextus Propertius and the Rome of
the Emperor Augustus. These texts, and the characters they contain, come to
life again and again as the sequence progresses. They people its pages. Their
stories and personality traits are instances the speaker's own can bounce off,
returning to us at a changed angle like refracted light from carefully positioned
mirrors, or else ricocheting on and on, like a bullet whose trajectory never
ends, without however threatening to shatter any of the surfaces deflecting it
as it proceeds on its way.

In the passage just quoted, from the close of section IV of elegy XIII, both
voices or registers are crucial. One does not supersede the other or cancel it
out. Whatever overall effect or conclusion is being aimed for, whatever unified
message the sequence carries must emerge from the interaction, the oscilla-
tion between different modes and tonalities of discourse.

Five major set pieces do not, strictly speaking, form part of the underlying
narrative of the sequence. Yet they inevitably interact with and deepen it,
thanks to their placing, to the obvious parallels with the speaker's own experi-
ence, and to an undeniable confusion of voices, evident, for example, at the
start of X, where the reader receives no clear warning that this is a monologue
by none other than Robert Burns, rather than a continuation of the speaker's

self-narrative from the preceding elegy. The 'set pieces' concern Burns and Mary Campbell (x), Orpheus and Eurydice (xII), Cuchulainn, Fann and Eimhir (xv), Aeneas and Dido (xvI) and Tristram and Iseult (xx).

Most puzzling and intriguing of all is a further 'set piece' whose inclusion in the sequence can at first seem difficult to justify, and is even stressed by the central position assigned to it. xIII concerns a young woman, almost certainly a prostitute, whom the speaker picks up in a Leith pub called the 'Black Bull o Norroway' and whom he christens, for present purposes, Sandra. It is paradoxical that, given the plethora of naming the speaker indulges in elsewhere, Sandra to all intents remains anonymous. When he invokes the addressee of the sequence as 'Ward o black-maned Artemis,/ The Huntress, Slayer, White Unmortal Queyne' (IV, ll. 11–12), or as 'My ain Perdita, Phryne, Cynthia' (IV, l. 10) whose tale deserves to stand alongside those of 'Helen, Cleopatra, Lesbia,/ Wi Morfydd, Dido, Heloise/ And Marie o the whitest blee – ' (IV, ll. 5–7) we can make a shrewd guess that the woman's name is perfectly familiar to the speaker, but is withheld for reasons of discretion, given that the underlying narrative is set specifically in the here and now of the time of narrating. With Sandra, he has simply forgotten what she was called. Her name emerges as the consequence of one of the bathetic descents so characteristic of these poems:

> I tine her name the nou, and cognomen for that –
> Aiblins it was Deirdre, Ariadne, Calliope,
> Gaby, Jacquette, Katerina, Sandra
>    Or sunkots. (xIII, 37, ll. 8–11)

We can posit two narrative threads which combine to give the sequence its onward thrust. Diegesis A would be 'what happened/ is happening between you and me', with 'you' the addressee of the cycle, and 'me' the speaker, identified with the writer of the text. Diegesis B would be 'how these poems got/ are getting written', the story of the text's coming into being. B, so to speak, unfolds as we read, there being no indication to contradict the notion of the poems being written down in the order in which we come upon them. A, on the other hand, has reached its end before the poems start, so that its 'time of happening' does not coincide with our 'time of reading'. The concluding elegy, xxIV, rather neatly ties together the two 'diegeses', with the start of B a consequence of the finishing of A:

> The door was steekit, neither was there answer
>    Til my urgent summons;
>    There was nae licht i the house,
>    Tuim it was, fremmit and desertit.

> Dowilie I turnit back the road I'd come...
> And syne dounsat and made this nobil leid
>    O' the spulyies o luve. (XXIV, 63, ll. 9–15)

The closed door and the window without a light refer back to the last but one episode in the self-narration, where the speaker fervently hopes to be conceded one more night of love – or should we say, one more night of sex? – despite the fact he realises things are over:

> And whan I come til the street I ken
> Grant me a licht i the winnock leaman
>    And the door ajee... (XIX, 54, ll. 61–63)

Again rather neatly, Smith has the last elegy end with the opening lines of the first, reproducing a device frequent in manuscript anthologies aimed at ensuring no spurious matter would be added at the end of a text:

> Bards hae sung o lesser luves
>    Than I o thee,
> O, my great follie and my granderie. (XXIV, 64, ll. 47–49 & I, 11, ll. 1–3)

The love sequence has concluded, which means it can actually get properly started in a different sense. Diegesis A in fact begins with V, the first poem to take us into the 'now' of a narrative that is happening as we read. The brief flash forward, or forecast, in IV is more an indication of how the story is shaped, what happens in it, than the opening of the story itself:

> Och weill, it was your richt, I ken,
> To gie, syne to withhaud again,
> My grail I got and it was taen –
> Was it no yours to tak again? (IV, 17, ll. 22–25)

This means that the first four elegies, rather than concerning themselves with the story, are a prolonged metatextual reflection about the poem we are going to read, which will be the 'final testament/ Infrangible as adamant' of a 'dune bard' (I, ll. 14–16), the 'ultimate great sang' which 'Rounds aff the lustrum' (III, ll. 4–5), 'this last testament', 'this endmaist coronach' (IV, l. 4 & 27).

Smith's obsession with what I will call 'lastness', but could easily be described as 'afterness', is a recurrent element in the cycle. It forms part of his aggressively Decadent stance, linked in literary terms to his reading of the

French 'poètes maudits'. It is no accident that he translated Tristan Corbière, or that the episode with Sandra provokes an unapologetic revelling in 'la belle nostalgie de la boue' (xiii, l. 182). Where else but to French literature in the latter part of the 19th century and at the start of the 20th, but not only then, could Smith look for treatment of the interaction between a poet and a prostitute? The three concluding names he finds for the woman he christens Sandra are all French: 'O, Manon! Marguerite! Camille!' (xiii, l. 201). This predicament of 'lastness' is a feature of the exasperated intertextuality that characterises the sequence, which comes at 'the end of a michtie line,/ 'Dunbar till Smith the Slugabed' (v, l. 50–51). The Orpheus elegy is pervaded by a sense of repetition. The singing god refers directly to the fact that he is telling his listeners a story they already know: 'Ye ken the tale' (xii, l. 58). Its conclusion extends this intertextuality or overlapping indefinitely into the future. What lies ahead is condemned not to produce any new elements, but simply offer a repetition of what we have already witnessed:

> Aa this will happen aa again,
> Monie and monie a time again. (xii, 36, ll. 131–132)

The perceived impossibility of any kind of renewal is a source of frustration. Whatever one may write risks turning into an interminable cliché. This is, in fact, a reproach the writer makes to himself at the close of elegy iv:

> (Cliché!
>      Echo answers Clichy!
> Whar the debtors went in gay Paree!
> O, God!
>      O, Montrachet!
>           O, Arthur's Seat!) (18, ll. 33–39)

Echo as a concept is peculiarly appropriate, and useful, to the issue of intervening and undercutting voices, as if one were moving away from the original discourse at a series of angles, getting further and further (See for example vi, 5 ff. and 42 ff.). Here the reminiscence is significantly of 19th century Paris, which one suspects was best known to Smith, who had a lively interest in the visual arts, through the paintings of the Impressionists. A plea to God, which may merely be an expression of impatience, leads to a plea to the well-known white Chardonnay from Burgundy. That, in turn, provokes the reference to Arthur's Seat, another 'Mont – ', in Smith's own city. Where MacLean's linking of the

Fairy Bridge in Skye with the River Volga aimed at a fully-fledged internation-alisation of issues affecting the Gaelic community, here the return home to Scotland is bathetic (MacLean / MacGill-Eain, 354–355).

The concentrated inventiveness of Smith's play on words is evident in a much-quoted epithet, used as the title of this very book, which the speaker applies to himself at XXIII, l. 19, 'The Makar macironical!' Here 'makar' evokes the trio of so-called post-Chaucerian poets writing in 'inglis', Robert Henryson, William Dunbar and Gavin Douglas. 'Macironical' looks like the poet's surname, with the ubiquitous Gaelic 'son' prefix, while also suggesting that irony is such an intrinsic part of his nature as to dictate his surname and define his ancestry. But of course the word also indicates his mixing of languages and registers of language, while setting up a skilful echo with the preceding word, as if this one could also be written 'makaronical'.

Fears that whatever one writes is doomed to coincide with the words of a predecessor evoke, notwithstanding the radically different tone, the opening of the 'First Dedication' to the Russian poet Anna Akhmatova's *Poem without a Hero*, specifically dated to 27 December 1940:

> and because I don't have enough paper,
> I am writing on your first draft.
> And here a strange word shows through
> and, like that snowflake on my hand long ago,
> melts trustingly, with no reproach.
>
> AKHMATOVA, II, 403

The predicament in Akhmatova's case is supposedly a consequence of acute material shortages, which were a feature of not only wartime life in Soviet Russia. There will always already be material there, the product of other hands in other ages, and this material will show through no matter what the current poet does. In Akhmatova's case, the conceit is also a warning to the reader that hers is a coded text, in which what is not said, what does not show through, may be almost as important as what is shown. It is no accident that in Part II of *Poem without a Hero* certain lines and stanzas are replaced by dots, standing in for what cannot be written, in this case due to censorship. It would be unfair, despite the far less drastic political situation, to behave as if in Smith's case intertextuality were any the less subtle and complex a phenomenon, or to imagine that he, differently from Akhmatova, can permit himself the luxury of saying exactly what he means without mediation, or without coinciding in his discourse with preceding poets. However humorously presented, no matter how much Smith exults in the richness of echoes, quotes and asides which constellate his text, he, too, grapples with the impossibility of direct, unmediated, 'pure' and 'fresh' discourse.

Smith's 'lastness' also possesses a contemporary, political aspect. Imminent catastrophe could easily take the form of a nuclear war ('the doundingin o the Westren Emperie/ Or the jurmumblement o baith the hemispheres/ In a holocaust o scientific glamor') (XXII, ll. 32–35). V, where we see the speaker in bed perhaps writing down the very lines we are reading, 'the last great coronach/ O' the western flickeran bourgeois world', presents the predicament of 'lastness' as characterising a class and an imperial enterprise doomed to collapse in a postwar reality marked by the emergence of new Marxist regimes following the example (and enforced by the troops) of 'michtie Stalin i the Aist' (V, l. 22). This particular elegy, an explicit rejection of political engagement, can also be read as a sly and astute denunciation of the totalitarian politics which were in the process of gaining the upper hand in so many European countries. It is one of the points where we cannot help remembering Smith's physical closeness in the years immediately following the war with the Gaelic poet Sorley MacLean. For eighteen months the two poets and their wives shared accommodation. Smith translated items from the *Dàin do Eimhir* sequence into Scots, including an excellent version of the sequence's effective conclusion (poem LVII), a complex philosophical meditation on perception and the ephemeral nature of experience which is also the moment at which MacLean the politically engaged communist sympathiser definitively throws in the towel in favour of the obsessed lover.

MacLean wrote that it was the information Smith picked up, from the Polish exile soldiers he was teaching in Edinburgh, about the failure of the Red Army to intervene in the 1944 Warsaw Uprising being savagely suppressed by the Nazi forces on the other side of the Vistula, that finally disenchanted him with the political ideology he backed so eloquently in 'An Cuilithionn' (MacLean / MacGill-Eain, ll. 478–479). In elegy V, the speaker, in distancing himself implicitly from MacLean's earlier stance, and explicitly from the ongoing communist commitment of MacDiarmid and his 'Aist-West Synthesis' (V, l. 41), also rejects the whole Scottish tradition of 'leftism', support for radical changes to the social order brought about by violent means on the basis of an interpretation of Marx's writings. Perhaps the most direct evocation of MacLean's love sequence comes in the last paragraph of VI, which recycles the terminology of *Dàin do Eimhir* IV: 'Tho Scotland's saul is brairan/ As the saul of Europe crynes (VI, ll. 66–67)'. The evocation is all the more haunting because placed after the explicit disavowal of radical left-wing politics in elegy V.

The first four elegies are almost entirely concerned with the kind of poem we are in the process of reading. II considers in turn other contemporary poets who might in theory deal with diegesis A, other women who could potentially be the heroines of such a sequence, and other subjects which are at least in theory more deserving of having time and effort devoted to them. It is characteristically disconcerting that the speaker, at the very moment when he affirms with verve his commitment to his chosen subject, indulges in typical undercutting bathos, in a dropping of tone which lands us unceremoniously in the contemporary and the vernacular:

As weill gie me the wale o skillie or drambuie
As screive a leid o politics or thee!
You are my subject anerlie, there is nae ither
    Fills my musardrie,
Nae word but your name in my dictionarie,
The heidlines i the news mean nocht til me
    For your name isna there,
    The faces i the streets
Micht aa be walkan neaps or tattie-bogles,
Or aiblins a new race descendit frae the mune. (II, 13, ll. 39–48)

The fifth section of II offers one of the most interesting formulations of how the sequence can be viewed. It is a scientific experiment 'Whas happie confluence in some divine laboratorie/ Concocts a new untolerable catalyst', 'Like a bombardment o the saul's uranium, / [...] Sae that e'en the experts are bumbazed and speakless/ For the first time on record' (II, 14, .ll 69–70, 73, 75–76). There follows a marvellous description of how the lovers themselves are set apart, in their exalted state, from ordinary mortals, which leads to one of Smith's recurrent Shakespearean reminiscences:

Whan thegither, whiles, a skimmeran licht,
    Men say, plays round our heids,
Our hands become electric til the touch
And the causie brunt and smouchteran ahint our feet.
    A divinitie doth hedge a king,
But our aureolie is surelie frae the pit. (II, 14, ll. 78–83)

The experiment looks set to bring about mass destruction on a thoroughly contemporary scale, being nothing other than 'Luve's Hiróshima' (II, l. 86).

   Diegesis A does not truly get going until elegy VIII. After the presentation of 'Sydney Slugabed Godless Smith' in V, VI turns again to the issue of an appropriate choice of subject matter. The risks of redundancy and repetition are indisputable, and the speaker asks: 'Hae ye no had a thrave o sangs/ Frae me ere nou?' and again 'Hae ye no had a haill buke-fu/ O' sangs frae me?' In a resumption and amplification of elegy V, politics and political leaders undergo a more detailed debunking, after which the self-portrait is extended. This continues to be a discussion of poetics in so far as the character of the speaker is likely to dictate the character of the poems we will be reading:

> For I was born excessive, Scorpio,
> In aathing and in luve;
> Eneuch's no near as guid's a feast til me,
> The middle airt, the Gowden Mean,
> Has little recommandan it
> As far as I can see. (VI, 22, ll. 54–59)

VII again evokes the 'Nirvana Oblomovian' of V, and restates reservations about the possible senselessness of the whole undertaking of writing the sequence: 'What havers is this?' (VII, l. 20).

   It may be worth trying to tease out the structure of diegesis A, the supposed doomed love affair which the sequence is ostensibly 'about'. Perhaps we should not be surprised that some of the items devoted to diegesis A stand out for their simplicity, for the absence of abrupt changes in tone, perspective and register which are so endemic in the sequence. VIII is a retrospective account with the setting at the edge of the sea which comes back again and again in *Under the Eildon Tree*. It presents a moment of reciprocity and convergence where both lovers are moved to tears by the beauty of sunset on the waves, with a single boat setting out from the pier that attentively prefigures Aeneas's boat leaving for Italy as a distraught Dido watches in XVI. Both are reduced to silence by the intensity of their shared emotions. IX is in the present tense, with the world effectively reduced to the area of grass covered by the lovers' bodies. XIII, perhaps the most powerful single item in the sequence, has no obvious connection to diegesis A, unless as an example of the attempts to forget its addressee in the arms of other women which XIV describes as doomed to failure. XVII comes at a crucial juncture. The speaker has abandoned the beloved, has been taken back, and has then abandoned her again, upon which she appears to propose they should be merely friends. It is a moment where one almost gets the impression of hearing her voice entering the fabric of the poem: '- Sae we'd be friens! Friens! We!' (XVII, l. 13). An emphatic rejection is based on the tendency to excess referred to in VI:

> It's aa or nocht – and maun be aa –
> There's fient a gowden mediatioun
> In this luve's damned, compund equatioun. (XVII, 50, ll. 18–20)

She, however, refuses to countenance his repeated infidelities, and breaks off all contact. This is basically where diegesis A concludes, though there are two epilogues. XIX contains the plea for one more night of love. XXI is another, peculiarly moving 'insert', not organically connected to the main narrative, or to the poetics of diegesis B. It is couched in a straightforward first person and all the more effective for that simplicity, for lacking a specific addressee. The window motif recurs from XIX. Passing by in the street, the speaker raises his head on hearing the lovelorn song of a girl who is sitting at the window. Their eyes meet in a brief moment of understanding. It is noteworthy that commiseration here crosses boundaries of gender.

The speaker's self-presentation as, in the end, a victim serves to demasculinise him in the world of the poem. Intriguingly, the climax of the night spent with Sandra concerns the acute pleasure she experiences during the act of love. Conventionally and superficially, as the client is paying, one would expect the pleasure he obtains to be the point of the whole transaction. Whether or not the prostitute derives satisfaction would be irrelevant. Not so in Smith's elegy, where the pleasure is mutual, and may even have been more intense on Sandra's part than on his. Unless, of course, one cynically concludes that what matters, for the client's pleasure, is getting the illusion of having procured huge enjoyment for his partner:

> My Helen douce as aipple-jack
> That cack't the bed in exstasie! (XIII, 42)

Generally speaking, the cycle makes nonsense of Bakhtin's concept of lyrical poetry as intrinsically monologic. A reading in terms of Bakhtin's approach to prose, which highlighted the jostling competition of different voices and points of view within and between elegies, would seem far more appropriate (Bakhtin: 1984). Sandra dirtying the bed sheets as she reaches orgasm, however, demands to be viewed according to Bakhtin's understanding of the body in terms of carnival ideology (Bakhtin: 2009). All its excrescences, faeces in particular, are endowed with enormous value. The practice in the 1970s and 1980s of referring to cannabis and other drugs as 'shit' is one instance of how carnival ideology continues to inform and inspire language use today. One is tempted to add that the last minute bathos at the end of elegy XIII as the narrator contemplates the possible consequence of a night of passion he paid for, 'And maybe, tae, the pox', resembles, as elsewhere in the sequence, a 'fart' or a 'raspberry' in response to particularly elevated or ennobled discourse. This would be a further reference to the carnival conception of the body, to those apertures whose noises and excrescences played such a crucial role in carnival ideology. One could also argue that 'the pox' is an instance of a 'joyful malady' along the lines of gout, the consequence of determined indulgence in carnal pleasures.

The effective conclusion of diegesis A in XVII is followed by the introduction of a new 'character' in XVIII, which presents one of the most charged images in the whole cycle. This is Death not as a skeleton carrying a sickle which he uses to reap the fields of the living, but 'Strumpet Daith', a prostitute whose clients we all must become sooner or later, whether we choose to or not:

> Nane ever flees her, nane
> Escapes, no ever ane,
> And she can byde, byde three
> Score year and ten
> And mair gif there need be –
> I' the end we aa gae doun
> The bricht and fleeran anes,
> The runklit and forworn,
> Aa i the end maun gratifie
> Her deidlie aye-unstecht desire,
> Clipped til her pyson-drappan paps
> O' cauld, cauld alabaister. (XVIII, 52, ll. 22–33)

Dying is figured as the ultimate sexual act, compulsory rather than pleasurable, in a manner reminiscent of the Elizabethans' understanding of orgasm as a species of death. Rather than a woman who is used and exploited, the prostitute becomes an all-powerful figure, herself subject to no limitations of ageing or time, fixing in turn on the chosen client. Encountering her means his life is at an end. She has been prefigured when, at the close of XI, which resumes the notion of the love affair as an experiment on the speaker, carefully planned and set up by detached, even sadistic gods 'For demonstration purposes/ And for his ain torment' (XI, ll. 32–33). His heart will be preserved as a rather disgusting exhibit for future generations. The speaker ironically turns to 'Advocatus Mei' (XI, l. 37), presumably his lawyer, before introducing the 'divine white chirurgeon' (XI, l. 40) who is to carry out the autopsy, clad in a mask and gloves more suitable for a tournament than a hospital operation. She is already well known to him, 'My maistress wi the satin smile' (XI, l. 43). Her name is 'Mors!' and she is the addressee of the closing paragraph of this elegy.

In his book-length study of the work of Nobel Prize-winning Russian poet Joseph Brodsky, Jens Herlth has this to say:

> The 'mask' of ironic speech, however, seen in a wider context, is a cultural strategy deployed in the interests of nonconformist writing. With Brodsky, and with Soviet counterculture in the second half of the 1960s, irony is more than a straightforward literary technique. Where any form of utopia is impossible, it amounts to a cultural *statement*.
>
> HERLTH, 134[3]

The poem of Brodsky's which Herlth is discussing is a love poem from 1967 couched in ironic mode, 'Farewell, Mademoiselle Veronica'. We know it was addressed to Véronique Schultz, an art historian who was also responsible for translating a series of Russian literary texts into French, including Brodsky's own poems. Hands will be thrown up in horror immediately, at the incongruity of comparing a poet writing in Scotland immediately after World War II to a poet writing in the admittedly post-Stalinist Soviet Union. How could one possibly draw parallels between a situation where freedom of speech was assured and one where it was so egregiously denied? The fact is that, rather than about 'freedom of speech', it would be appropriate to talk about 'constraints on discourse', which always exist, in every conceivable kind of social interaction. At the simplest level, this is a matter of the topics and language which are considered appropriate for discussion, with general avoidance of 'bad language' and sexually explicit topics (such as Sandra 'cackin' the bed').

Poetry as 'loud speech', whether in Scotland or in the Soviet Union, characteristically highlights constraints on discourse, on what can and cannot be said. Where the basic units of prose discourse tend to be ideas or plot elements, poetry interacts directly with the facts conditioning language use, most notably in the tendency to turn on its head the Saussurian principle of the arbitrary nature of the link between 'signifier' and 'signified'. Poetry is that which could not have been said in any other way, that which can only be paraphrased in part and with a major loss to the range of meanings. As such it enters into a Foucauldian relation with power manifested as constraints on discourse. By challenging those, poetry inevitably empowers itself, and therefore provokes a destabilising of prevailing power relations.

Constraints on discourse are effectively masked in any discourse which reproduces them. No less today than at the time when Smith wrote *Under the*

---

3  Translation from German to English by Christopher Whyte.

*Eildon Tree*, writing in Scots was an 'unnatural', 'artificial' choice, always to be assessed within the context of the available options which, of course, included writing in Standard English. The tragically misguided conclusions Edwin Muir draws from his famous (infamous?) analysis in *Scott and Scotland* (1936) are the consequence of reproducing prevailing constraints on discourse rather than examining or questioning them. Instead, they are treated as inevitable and axiomatic:

> [...] a Scottish writer who wishes to achieve some approximation to completeness has no choice except to absorb the English tradition ... if he thoroughly does so his work belongs not merely to Scottish literature but to English literature as well [...] All these things are part of a single problem which [...] cannot be solved by writing poems in Scots.
>
>          MUIR, 4–5

The power relations specifically challenged by the choice of Scots as a poetic language can be identified in the suffocating domination of the English cultural project, one obvious manifestation of which is obligatory general education delivered exclusively in that language, imposed on a population the majority of whom use a different language in their daily intercourse. It is a paradox of Scottish cultural history throughout the 20th century that, whereas a striking portion of poets, writing in any of Scotland's three languages, were nationalists, in the sense of being committed to facilitating Scottish independence, nationalism as a political discourse was marginalised and consistently minimalised.

Smith's choice of Scots – eclectic, impure, with a disconcerting mixing and alternation of registers and historical usages – aggressively flags its 'artificial', 'unnatural', arbitrary nature, in a manner that is no less politically explosive than Brodsky's ironic discourse in a love lyric from a quarter of a century later, even if the penalties the Scottish poet risked incurring were nothing compared to the trial and sentence the Russian poet eventually faced, on the part of a regime that was only too well aware of the subversive nature of such apparently apolitical discourse.

A fascinating element in the poet's relationship to Sandra is that the language he autocratically claims as his own is, so to speak, hers by right. A dialectal form of Scots is the only speech form of which she has an adequate command. This gives her an everyday, unquestioning relationship to the language which Smith, with his public school education at Malvern and the years spent at Oxford, could never hope to match. It would be easy to imagine Sandra or, even more, her mother, delivering aloud several of the devastatingly undermining asides which pepper Smith's sequence: 'The sheer bress neck o the man!' (VII, l. 25), 'He was his ain worst enemie' (XIV, l. 48), 'Rhetoric!/Juist sheer damncd/ Rhctoric!' (XXII, ll. 63–65). This is one further instance of the ongoing, fruitful interaction between the subject matter of the sequence and its politicised choice of language. Of course, Sandra's use of Scots can very rarely be a political act in the way Smith's espousal of the language, coming from his very different, bourgeois stance, is.

One last point to be considered is the historical placing of *Under the Eildon Tree*. Every poem creates its own historical collocation through links, explicit and implicit, established with earlier and, in some cases, with future texts. This means that two poems written in the same calendar year, even notionally in the same month, can have radically different historical collocations. On the one hand, Smith's sequence flags a connection to turn of the century Decadentism with its debt to Baudelaire and the French poets who succeeded him, as well as to the modernism of Pound and Eliot, to a certain extent inspired and sparked off when poets using English at last caught up with what had been happening in French over the last half century. A triumph of Smith's cycle is the way it consistently avoids the intermittent primness of tone and the pervasive intellectual one-upmanship which threaten to mar the credibility of the speaking voice in Pound's *Homage to Sextus Propertius*. On the other hand, rather than celebrating a modernist breach with a tradition no longer perceived as valid, in part due to the historical catastrophe of the First World War, and therefore redefining the literary canon in a manner which undermines the common understanding between a poet and his or her readers (implicitly disenabling the latter) *Under the Eildon Tree* struggles to re-establish a continuity with earlier texts, to make them relive in its lines, which could justifiably be termed postmodernist. The sense of writing on the brink of the imminent catastrophe of a nuclear conflagration, rather than in the wake of a catastrophe that has already taken place, is also postmodernist rather than modernist. All of which suggests that assigning the sequence to a specific historical period and placing is an extremely complex matter.

Proving indisputably the literary rank and quality of a text, in near objective terms, is close to an impossibility. Nevertheless it can be hoped that the preceding discussion has served to reveal a subtlety and complexity in Smith's sequence, in terms of plot structures, intertextuality, shifting speech situations, alternations of linguistic register and, last but not least, interlinguistic and intercultural politics, to demonstrate that, as the 21st century proceeds upon its way, the work will continue to demand, and reward, very close scrutiny indeed.

Bibliography

Akhmatova, Anna (Hemschemeyer, Judith, trans. & Reeder, Roberta ed.), *The Complete Poems of Anna Akhmatova* (Somerville, Massachusetts: Zephyr Press, 1990).

Bakhtin, Mikhail (Emerson, Cary ed. & trans.), *Problems of Dostoevsky's Poetics* (Minneapolis: University of Minnesota Press, 1984).

Bakhtin, Mikhail (Iswolsky, Helene trans.), *Rabelais and His World* (Bloomington: Indiana University Press, new edition, 2009).

Genette, Gérard, *Figures III* (Paris: Éditions du Seuil, 1972).

Herlth, Jens, *Ein Sänger gebrochenere Linien. Iosif Brodskijs dichterische Selbstschöpfung* (Cologne Weimar Vienna: Böhlau Verlag, 2004).

MacLean, Sorley / MacGill-Eain, Somhairle (Dymock, Emma & Whyte, Christopher, eds.), 'An Cuilithionn' (1989) / 'The Cuillin' (1989) in *Caoir Gheal Leumraich / White Leaping Flame Collected Poems* (Edinburgh: Birlinn, 2011).

Muir, Edwin, *Scott and Scotland: The Predicament of the Scottish Writer* (Edinburgh: Polygon, 1982).

Smith, Sydney Goodsir, *Under the Eildon Tree: A Poem in XXIV Elegies* (Edinburgh: Serif Books, 1954).

CHAPTER 5

# Nationalism in the Poetry of Sydney Goodsir Smith

*J. Derrick McClure*

## Abstract

This chapter discusses the ways in which Smith, ostensibly an outsider to Scottish culture at the start of his writing life, embraced the internationalist ideals of the Scottish Literary Renaissance. His use of the Scots tongue and of Scotland (especially Edinburgh) as the setting of many poems are relatively superficial aspects of his literary nationalism: much more important are his frequent references to earlier Scottish literature, emphasising the scope and the unity of the national literary achievement, and his association of heroic figures from Scottish history with comparable freedom-fighters from other countries, emphasising Scotland's traditionally international outlook.

## Keywords

nationalism – unionism – internationalism – Scots language – Scots poetry – Scottish Literary Renaissance – Scottish history – freedom fighters – Caledonian antisyzygy – G. Gregory Smith

Since the issue of Scottish independence re-established itself as a political force in the late 19th century, 'Scottish nationalism' has been the recognised term for the principle that Scotland should resume its place as an autonomous member of the world comity of nations. Yet 'nationalism', and it would be as well to confront the fact at the outset, is potentially a dubious word. At the time of writing Scottish independence is a realistic prospect as (we can say with hindsight) it was not during Smith's lifetime, and the continuously active and often passionate debates on the issue sometimes take unedifying forms: a particularly base and contemptible ploy of Unionists is the attempt to associate the word 'nationalism' in its Scottish context with the overtones which it has acquired elsewhere. This is in direct contradiction to the stated and practised policy of the Scottish government that the forthcoming independent

Scotland will continue to be, as the country is at present, an inclusive multi-ethnic and multi-cultural community. I assume that readers of the present book are aware of this, and use the word freely on this understanding.

Scottish nationalism was among the key forces effecting and shaping the Scottish Renaissance of the 20th century, one of the most remarkable instances of a national cultural recovery in recent European history. Integral to the entire movement was an awareness that a great national literature which had once existed was in eclipse, if not actually moribund; and that this decline was intimately linked to a steadily growing confusion – leading, as it developed, to increasingly desperate attempts to turn away from the entire issue – surrounding Scotland's very identity. In Sydney Goodsir Smith's *A Short Introduction to Scottish Literature*, to which we will return, the chapter on the Stewart period is headed 'The Golden Age'; and in discussing the end of this golden age he summarises the common perception of the reasons for its disappearance: 'We had no Renaissance, for the end of the Gothic period,[1] and the end of Scotland as a separate kingdom and culture, and the end of the Scots language as an official and standard vehicle, all occurred disastrously at the same moment. The triple blow was almost mortal' (Smith: 1951, 10).[2]

To counter this pathological state of Scottish national consciousness, a dynamic effort was made to revive Scotland's literary culture as it had existed in the past; and, as an integral part of this project, the Scots language in which much of it had been written. Scots was deliberately promoted, in fact, to a status which it had not held even for Allan Ramsay or Robert Burns: they and their contemporaries had assuredly been aware that in using Scots as their medium (when they did, because of course they could and did use English too when it suited them) they were overtly defying the fashionable assumption that only English was suited for serious literary or intellectual endeavour. But now the

---

1   An idiosyncratic term. 'In the middle ages the whole culture of Western Europe was what we may call Gothic – except, of course, for the Celtic cultures which in any case have closer psychological affinities with the Gothic spirit than either of them have [*sic*] with the Classical tradition of Greece and Rome. This Gothic culture was the product of the international systems of Catholic Christianity and feudalism'. (Smith: 1951, 9).

2   This assessment of the cultural history of Scotland in the 16th and 17th centuries has long ago been recognised as a radical over-simplification: in particular, the statement that 'we had no Renaissance' (and cf. the chapter heading 'What should have been our Renaissance' in Mackenzie, Agnes Mure, *An Historical Survey of Scottish Literature to 1714*) (London: Maclehose, 1933) would be firmly rejected now by most scholars in the field. Nonetheless, the gradual assimilation of the written language from the Scots of (for example) Sir David Lyndsay to the grammatical and orthographic practices of metropolitan English, and its deliberate revival in the 18th century as a gesture of cultural nationalism which 20th century poets proceeded to emulate, are real enough.

use of Scots, and not merely the *use* of it but the energetic development of it for the cutting-edge literary experimentation which characterised the period, was to be virtually a patriotic duty, and part of an overall plan of action designed to lead eventually to full political independence. The principal figure in this deliberately-planned regeneration of the Scots language was of course Hugh MacDiarmid; though it should not be forgotten that such achievements as the North-Eastern dialect poetry of Charles Murray, the lyrics, traditional in their language but memorably expressive, of Violet Jacob, Marion Angus and (slightly later) Helen Cruickshank, the sonnets in quasi-archaic Scots of Lewis Spence and the vigorous rhymes in realistic vernacular of Pittendrigh MacGillivray had already been visible as very substantial straws in the wind.

In the truly extraordinary company of poets who wrote in MacDiarmid's wake, Sydney Goodsir Smith holds a central place. As with many of the others, his use of the Scots tongue is one aspect, and one illustration, of his cultural nationalism. His initial attempts at writing Scots show a headlong and undisciplined experimentation resulting often in near-chaos;[3] but his delight in the opulence and the sheer expressive power of the Scots vocabulary is manifest; and the inventive and highly distinctive use of the Scots tongue in his mature poetry, seamlessly combining realistic colloquialisms with polished and erudite aureation, is one of the high-water marks in the modern literary development of Scots.

As another feature which his poetry shares with that of his fellow makars, Scotland itself, from first to last (from *Skail Wind* in 1941 to *Gowdspink in Reekie* in 1974), is a recurring theme in his work. His first collection is geographically anchored in Scotland by frequent local references and vivid evocations of Scottish landscapes and weather:

> Drear an dreich the grey flats steich of Dali's Sound
> Wheer Solway casts this airm intil the rain-dim land
> They ca the Mote Merk: tummlin past Rough Island, pounding Castle Ness
> Wi a last tired scunner, conquered noo bi the driving mist...
>> 'Hornie wi the Green Ee', 5[4]

---

3  For discussion see Murison, David, 'The Language of Sydney Goodsir Smith' in Norman MacCaig (ed.) *For Sydney Goodsir Smith* (Loanhead: MacDonald, 1975), pp. 23–29, and the present writer's *Language, Poetry and Nationhood* (East Linton: Tuckwell, 2000), pp. 122–132.
4  All following page references to Smith's poems relate to: Smith, Sydney Goodsir, *Collected Poems. 1941–1975* (London: John Calder, 1975).

It is observable that the names here are not those of exceptionally famous or iconic places, and are not themselves of the familiar type of emotive and phonaesthetically distinctive Gaelic-derived Scottish toponyms (unlike the practice of, as an almost random example, Flora Garry in 'Bennygoak');[5] nor is Smith concerned to mention a particular locality for its historical or traditional associations (unlike, say, Violet Jacob in *Songs of Angus*). The Scottish setting is not being assertively emphasised but is simply a given: a subtle sign of confidence in an autonomous national identity. Another such example from the same collection is 'Kinnoul Hill' (4–5), a poem in ballad metre[6] of love-longing in winter: the hill referred to has no particular status among Scotland's thousands of medium-sized elevations with fine views. In these poems the 'drear and dreich' surroundings are an appropriate counterpart to the evocation of personal grief, with in the case of 'Hornie' a deeper note being struck by the reference to the War in the final line: by contrast, the suggestion of springtime and renewing life conveyed in the bounding anapaests of 'The Dark Days are By' (8–9) arouses a mood of exultant optimism for both the natural world and the spirit of Scotland. In 'Ballant: The Wraith o Johnny Calvin' the evocative powers of characteristic Scottish flora are put to effective use:

> O, broun the bracken burns on the brae
> And reid the rowan tree...
> Her mou was reid as the gean, and broun
> As a tink, as a nut, was she. (78)

And carefully-chosen Scots vocabulary adds vividness to the forbidding atmosphere of 'The War in Fife':

> Gurlie and grey the snell Fife shore,
> Frae the peat-green sea the cauld haar drives [...]. (56)

A wartime poem which includes the bitter lines:

> Twa hunner years o Union's bled
> The veins mair white nor ony war.

---

5   I look far ower tae Ythanside,
      To Fyvie's laich, lythe lan's,
      To Auchterless an Bennachie
      An the mist-blue Grampians. (Garry, 7)

6   Oddly, in each of the four verses the metre requires the name to be mispronounced with an accent on the first syllable.

Edinburgh is omnipresent in his poetry: in *Skail Wind* he evokes the gloomy mood of a capital city bereft by the War of its lively society:

> Auld Embro's bluid is thin, the bars 're toom
> An cauld is her fierce iren hert, her black banes
> Rigid wi cauld, the bluid's fell thin aneth the snaw.
> Aye, my prood yins 're taen, the hail clanjamphrey noo, [...]
> For the drouthy lech o war can neer be slaukit [...]
> > 'Lament in the Second Winter of War', 4[7]

At the other end of his life *Gowdspink in Reekie* is a riotous satirical harangue, suggestive like MacDiarmid's poem of a drunk man's uncontrollable verbosity, in which Edinburgh's social, intellectual and convivial life are sent up in explosions of mingled laughter and fury. One of his very finest poems, 'King and Queen o the Fowr Airts' (65), juxtaposes an Edinburgh setting with exotic places and personages and presents the whole through an exuberantly fantastic imagination:

> The Dean Brig lowpt a Hieland Fling
> Our regal whim to gratifie,
> Schir Wattie sclimmed his steeple's tap
> The better to view sic majestie.

Smith's use of Scottish references, like his use of the Scots language, is a simple aspect of his proclaimed identity as a Scottish poet, as is the case with many of his contemporaries: in a country possessed of full cultural and intellectual autonomy, such as Scotland has still not completely attained, such devices would not even be worthy of remark.

Smith, however, explores the issue of cultural 'Scottishness' in more individual ways, and incorporates the result of his investigations into his poetry. In his *A Short Introduction to Scottish Literature* he summarises his perception of the essential features, rooted in the national character, which give Scottish literature its 'Scottishness'. These are, first, a democratic spirit developed to an

---

7   Cf. the mood evoked in the opening stanza of Allan Ramsay's 'Elegy on Lucky Wood':
> O Canigate! Poor elritch hole,
> What loss, what crosses does thou thole!
> London and death gars thee look droll
> > And hing thy heid,
> Wow! But thou has e'en a cauld coal
> > To blaw, Indeed. (Ramsay, 18–19)

extreme degree: '[...] almost all national movements in Scotland have failed, because each individual Scot is apt to form a one-man party disastrous to any unity' (Smith: 1951, 7); second, an intensely *popular* quality: this '[...] has meant that the best folk literature in Europe is the Border balladry, and that our national poet is a truly popular figure, unlike Shakespeare in England, or Goethe in Germany, Pushkin in Russia, and so on. There is no other national poet in Europe who is so truly and quite unaffectedly *beloved* by his countrymen at large [...] as Burns' (Smith: 1951, 8); thirdly, a continuity of tradition: even after the long eclipse of the great Stewart literary culture, Burns emerged as 'the culmination of the old folk-song and ballad tradition of pre-Renaissance, pre-Reformation and pre-Union times' (Smith: 1951, 11); and finally the 'Caledonian Antisyzygy' or 'combination at once of two or more seemingly irreconcilable qualities' (ibid.). Searching his work for illustrations of these traits provides clearer demonstration of his cultural nationalism.

The 'Caledonian antisyzygy' is, in the last analysis, perhaps the least serious or credible of these manifestations of 'Scottishness'. First concocted by G. Gregory Smith[8] to refer to 'the contrasts which the Scot shows at every turn, in his political and ecclesiastical history, in his polemical restlessness [...]' and enthusiastically taken up by Hugh MacDiarmid, it has an unquestionable and very understandable appeal; but the concept is too general and elusive to be of real value as a technical term of criticism. Nonetheless, if the use of abrupt contrasts in tone and mood as a stylistic device qualifies as a sample of Caledonian antisyzygy, it is certainly to be found in Smith's poetry. Edinburgh as a centre of learning and culture is simultaneously exalted and mocked in *Gowdspink in Reekie*. The Dunbar-like phantasmagoria 'Prolegomenon' (29–31) evokes a world engulfed in madness with terrifying intensity; but what are jokey references to the price and quality of drink – the two lines containing them being the only ones in the poem marked with exclamation points – doing in this context? The sequence 'Armageddon in Albyn' (53–57) opens with the bleak vision, in dignified slow-march rhythm, of 'El Alamein' and maintains this sombre and tragic tone steadily through the next four poems and deceptively into the opening of 'Mars and Venus at Hogmanay':

> The nicht is deep,
> The snaw liggs crisp wi rime,

---

8  The passage is accessible in McCulloch, Margery Palmer (ed.), *Modernism and Nationalism: Literature and Society in Scotland 1918–1939* (Glasgow: Association for Scottish Literary Studies, 2004), pp. 6–7.

> Black an cauld the leafless trees;
> Midnicht, but nae bells chime.

– only to demolish it with:

> Throu the tuim white sleepan street
> Mars an Venus shauchle past,
> A drucken jock wi a drucken hure
> Rairan "The Ball o Kirriemuir"!

and resume it as if uninterrupted in the final poem in the sequence, 'The War in Fife'. And in *Under the Eildon Tree*, no negligible contribution to the effect of a tempest of irreconcilable emotions is made by the parenthetical comments printed in italics: (*A maist reprehensible estate / O' affairs, I maun admit*) – (*The sheer bress neck o the man!*) – (*Rhetoric! / Juist sheer damned / Rhetoric!*); though the section in 'The Black Bull o Norroway' in which the timeless trope of the beloved's body as a world to be explored is first expounded with parodic exaggeration and then dynamited with

> My Helen douce as aipple-jack
> That cack't the bed in exstasie! (171)

bears the gree for a poetic instance of 'whaur extremes meet'. A search for such instances in Smith's poetry is undeniably rewarding, but hardly provides any underpinning of his qualifications as a Scottish poet.

Again not entirely seriously, it could be argued that the frequent references to pubs and drink which abound with cheerful persistence in Smith's poetry are an aspect of his determination to maintain the popular and populist aspect which he saw as an essential trait of Scottish literature. In the course of his work, indeed, he makes a cumulative and very convincing attempt to do for Edinburgh something of what Joyce did for Dublin, by celebrating, sometimes in extravagantly experimental language, the city's exuberant, anarchic, disreputable but aboundingly vital tavern culture. The comparison with Joyce was deliberately invited by Smith, most notably in his prose work *Carotid Cornucopius* and this is explored in Richie McCaffery's chapter on the novel in this book but also in such lines as the following from *Gowdspink in Reekie* (the addressee is Oliver Goldsmith, on whose sojourn in Edinburgh the poem is pegged). For a fuller discussion of *Gowdspink in Reekie* refer to Mario Relich's chapter:

But tell me nou, in your ain perembrodrouthie
Possage through mine ain romantick toun
Did ye find, I ferlie, when your wealth
Decumulatit hour by fluid hour
That man was thereby grandified?
Objectively, I mean —
  For I ken as weill as you
  The splendant spurious granderie o' booze,
  But ye cannae traivel on this line
  Wi yon auld punched and clipt tyke-luggit
  Ragment o' a bastart bit
  O' synthetical, subjective exsqueeze
  For a ticket-o'-leave on the beat-up broke-doun
  Escape route that ye think ye're on...
  Ye maun rise dooms early at the skreak-o'-daw
  To win a hurl on yon ghaist trolley-bus route
  Wi the Shennachie Smith as clippie, Gowdspink,
  I can tell ye. (221)

The poetic association of 'Scottishness' with pubs and drink is by no means a mere joke. The poems of Ramsay, Fergusson, Burns and the lesser lights of the 18th century Vernacular Revival abound in references to the culture of convivial drinking. Burns, in particular though not uniquely, associated drinking with exultant freedom and defiance of authority:

Freedom and whisky gang thegither —
  Tak aff your dram!

and in the 20th century Milne's Bar in Edinburgh, and other pubs such as the Abbotsford, acquired a place in literary history to match those of Chaucer's Tabard and Shakespeare's Mermaid as the haunt of vociferous and argumentative men of letters. (A 'literary pub tour' of Edinburgh is one of the delights offered to visitors, particularly at Festival time.) In a late masterpiece, *Kynd Kittock's Land* (1965), Smith evokes the association of poets and pubs:

Grieve and Garioch aye tuim their pints,
Mackie wheezes, Scott aye propheseezes
Frae his lofty riggin tree
While lean MacCaig stauns snuffin the Western seas
And Brown leads wi his Viking chin
And winna be rebukit. (210)

Lines which name six of the finest poets of the 20th century.[9]

A much more important aspect of Smith's nationalist persona is the strongly-emphasised continuity with the Scottish literary tradition. In their verse forms as well as their themes, several poems in the earlier collections recall the love-lyrics of Alexander Scott and Alexander Montgomerie in what James VI called 'cuttit and brokin verse [that is, verse in which the lines are of varying length], quhairof new formes are daylie inuentit according to the Poets pleasour' (James VI, 82) genre poems in their time, but representing a genre which in Scotland, after its splendid development in the 16th century, fell largely into eclipse: examples are 'Hymn of Luve til Venus Queen', 'Exile', 'Say ye Sae?'. The quasi-mediaeval aureate diction which is part of Smith's stock-in-trade appears with particular appropriateness in such poems. In the 'Orpheus' section of *Under the Eildon Tree* the refrain line from Henryson's *Orpheus and Eurydice*, 'Quhar art thou gane, my luf Euridices?', is quoted; and by revising Dunbar's line (from a Latin hymn) *Timor mortis conturbat me* to *Timor mortis non conturbat me* as the refrain of 'In Time of Deepest Wanhope' (32–33), he makes an equally unmistakable reference, but this time a subversive one, to a great mediaeval makar. Later in *Under the Eildon Tree* he places himself and Dunbar in ironic juxtaposition:

> Thus are the michty faaen,
> Thus the end o' a michtie line,
> Dunbar til Smith the Slugabed [...]. (155)

*Kynd Kittock's Land* recognisably takes its name from a character in a medieval comic fantasy who died of thirst and now passes eternity in an alehouse on the road to Heaven. The word *solsequium* ('marigold') is a keyword in a poem by Montgomerie 'Lyk as the dum Solsequium [...]', but never appeared again in Scottish literature until Smith brought it into 'The Years of the Crocodile' (104–105).[10] A more subtle and elusive reminiscence of earlier poetry is the use of the word 'rossignel' in the title of a poem (23) and again in *Under the Eildon Tree* (159): this form of the word, with –*el* instead of the usual –*ol*, is attested only in Middle Scots, and rarely even there.

---

9    Four of the poets are visible in Sandy Moffat's painting 'Poets' Pub' (1980), as is Smith himself. Norman MacCaig's pose in the picture suggests that the artist had this line in mind.

10    Montgomerie's line is the only quote for the word in *A Dictionary of the Older Scottish Tongue* (DOST); it does not appear in *The Scottish National Dictionary* (SND). Interestingly enough, none of the instances quoted in *The Middle English Dictionary* (MED) is of a *poetic* use of the word.

More recent poetry is also recalled by specific references. One of his Edinburgh poems, 'To Li Po in the Delectable Mountains of Tien-Mu' (101–104) in which the action is located by mentions of the city's landmarks, is 'in memoriam Robert Fergusson', author of one of the greatest poetic evocations of Edinburgh, or any city, in Scottish literature. MacDiarmid is apostrophised in 'Perpetual Opposition' (99); 'Octopus' (92–93), with its peculiar opening line 'The makar's mynd an octopus', was surely suggested by the section so entitled in *A Drunk Man Looks at the Thistle*. (MacDiarmid, 30–33). The title of the poem 'Reason Speaks at Howe-Dumb-Deid' likewise brings to mind a lyric ('The Eemis Stane') by MacDiarmid, and Smith is by no means the only one of his disciples to use the compound in deliberate reminiscence of the master; but it is now a double harkening back, for MacDiarmid's line 'I' the howe-dumb-deid o' the cauld hairst nicht' is from a story in an 1820 number of *Blackwood's Magazine*, quoted in Jamieson, and is one of many cases where he set a fashion for weaving quotations from earlier writings into his work (or *renewed* the fashion, for verbal reminiscences of Ramsay and Fergusson are not hard to find in Burns).

More overt statements of political nationalism illustrate Smith's upholding of the democratic principle, another of his criteria of 'Scottishness'. As one example, 'The Arbroath Declaration, April 6th, 1320' proclaims not only Scottish independence but, much more importantly, the fact that the cause won its support from the grass-roots of society:

> In Thirteen-twanty Scotland tauld
> The warld in the words o raucle men
> She humbled neck til King nor State
> -The commontie was soverain! (57)

In 'The Shade of Yeats'[11] he vigorously counters the Irish poet's 'feudalistic glaumerie' by predicting the independence of the downtrodden classes:

> We luik till the kenless dawn[12] aheid
> As the few richt Scots aye did luik,
> Indomitable yet the breed
> O' Burns an Maclean as the Irish fowk;
> An sure we'se yet prove ye wrang,

---

11    One thing in favour of the *Collected Poems* is the inclusion of some poems rejected – undeservedly in several cases – by the author, this being one.

12    'Drawn' in the text is an obvious misprint; far from the only one in the book.

The outlan wants nae lord's dictate,
This skalrag land in shackles lang
Taks the free man's richt tae gang's ain gate. (250)

And in 'El Alamein' the conflict is presented as a struggle for not only freedom but, by implication, Scotland's freedom in particular:

[...] That this was for Alba
Maun we mak siccar!
It wasna for thraldom
Ye ligg there deid,
Gin we should fail ye
The rocks wad bleed! (53)

*The Wanderer* (1943) opens with two poems inspired by the gipsy fiddler Peter Morrison: in the first he is presented as an archetypal figure of independence recalling the characters in Burns' 'The Jolly Beggars':

Sae he poached his meat an fiddled his sangs
An drank like a cod an a drouthie drain,
A skalrag saul he waifed alang
An cursed the Mongers in howff an hame. (21)

In the second his indomitable struggle against oppression is compared to that of Scotland. In the collection of wartime poems *The Deevil's Waltz* (1946), the first set in which Smith proved beyond question his status as a major poet, the poems range over such themes as freedom, patriotism and the fight against tyranny, finding icons of those timeless forces in Scotland's history, mythology and contemporary life. But as an admirable illustration of the principle that Scottish nationalism is truly *internationalism* – that the goal of independence is to end Scotland's enforced marginalisation in the world and enable the country to participate again in the cross-currents of international affairs,[13] a principle strongly and overtly upheld in both its cultural and its political aspects from the first stirrings of the Scottish Renaissance to the present day – a keynote of this collection is his celebration of patriots through the ages, and

---

13    Cf. the slogan 'Stop the world, Scotland wants to get on!', coined by Winnie Ewing at the time of her landmark election as a Westminster MP in 1967 and used ubiquitously ever since.

emphasis on the spiritual kinship binding those who fought for Scotland's freedom with their co-idealists in other places and other historical periods.

'Prometheus' opens 'Nou freedom fails in field an wynd [...]', and imagines the tormented Titan looking from his rock over the downfall of heroic figures like William Wallace, Thomas Muir and John Maclean. A poem commemorating the last-mentioned of these great Scottish radicals, 'John Maclean Martyr', is followed by 'Ballant o' John Maclean' in which his name is linked with those of other revolutionaries:

> Muir an Wallace his prison mates,
> Lenin an Connolly
> Nane ither ever was his maik
> But ithers there wull be. (45)

In 'Agin Black Spats' (46–48) the poet shows his colours at the very outset:

> On Kenmore Brig that Geordie made
> Wi Jacobite fines I staun [...].

and proceeds to cite the Declaration of Arbroath before meditating on 'great rebels':

> Thae that fell
> In ilka land
> For freedom's cause
> Nor widna bend
> Til unricht laws
> Nor a tyrant's will.

If some of his examples are dubious (to take the most blatant example, Villon as a man is scarcely a moral exemplum for anything), the point is forcefully made; and the stanza concludes with a gibe (the same one is made more than once by MacDiarmid) at the professed admirers of a poet whose bold radicalism is even now all too often misrepresented or ignored:

> An Rabbie's leid gies text to clods
> That prate o Freedom
> An practise feedom.

In the next poem in the sequence, 'The Pricks' (from the expression 'kick against the pricks': 'kick' is a keyword in the poem) Barbour's line 'Fredome is ane nobil thing' is quoted, and Burns, [Thomas] Muir and Maclean are linked with the first great poet of the Scots tongue as inspirational upholders of the principle. A similar selection of names appears in 'Vox Humana' (96–97):

> I am aa men that raised a cry,
> Will ne'er be still again' man's tyrannie.

Poland, a country whose historic ties with Scotland were strengthened by the War, is present in *The Deevil's Waltz*, associating Scotland's long struggle for independence with that of the Poles.[14] 'On Readan the Polish Buik o the Nazi Terror' evokes the sufferings of both countries and ends defiantly:

> We'se drink thegither yet, lang tho the onwyte be,
> The dear tint wine o libertie! (251)

The practice of enriching the Scots tongue and widening its range by means of Scots translations of poetry from other literatures is an integral part of the Scottish Renaissance; and in this collection Smith, unusually,[15] includes versions of two poems by the Polish aviator Stefan Borsukiewicz, 'Ma Brither' and 'Ballad of the Defence of Warsaw 1939'. The mastery of the Scots leid which Smith had by then achieved is visible in these translations, evoking the death-throes of the city with unsparing vividness:

> Oor breith was hechlan as the air
> Thickened lik a wuid,
> On the kirk's larach mortars bloomed
> Lik roses roun a loch o bluid. (50)[16]

---

14  Cf. Agnes Mure Mackenzie, writing in 1939: 'She [Scotland] fights shoulder to shoulder now with her old friend, with her sometime enemy, and with a third nation whose long heroic stand for nationhood can give lessons of will and endurance even to Scotland'. Mackenzie, Agnes Mure, *The Kingdom of Scotland: A Short History* (Edinburgh: Chambers, 1940), p.373.

15  Unusually because, first, translations do not form a major part of Smith's oeuvre as they do for several of his confrères (George Campbell Hay, Douglas Young, Alasdair Mackie, Robert Garioch); and second, except for the special case of translations from Gaelic *contemporary* poets at this stage in the Renaissance rarely provided Scots translators with models.

16  Borsukiewicz died in 1942 when his parachute failed to open, and his only book of poems was published in the year of his death. The Independent Parachute Brigade, the regiment in which he served, was based for a time in Scotland, and Smith's wartime service consisted in part of teaching English to Polish soldiers: I know of no record that the two men actually met, but since Borsukiewicz's poetry can hardly have become internationally

In 'Ye Mongers Aye Need Masks for Cheatrie' (46), Delacroix' portrait of Chopin, whose ardent Polish patriotism was an integral part of his personal and artistic identity —

> His rasch face sterk wi pouer an daith
> An aa the agonie o Poland's skaith

becomes an analogy for the future liberating realisation of the true state of Scotland:

> Ye mak a myth o a cheated land
> As Chopin's made a lilly man;
> But truth wull screich an Scotland rid
> Ye mongers as the Irish did;
> The bluid ye drave til ilka airt
> Shall feed its ain reid sleepan hert.

Chopin, interestingly enough, is one of several composers whom Smith extols as great human spirits and icons in the universal struggle for freedom. 'Ode to Hector Berlioz, 1803–1869' (6–8), in its torrent of disjointed phrases and clauses, unrelated ideas and images and wildly assorted Scots words, is one of the worst results of Smith's early experimentation with language; but as an exaltation of the composer, and by implication of the power of his music to stir and inspire, it impresses by its sheer vigour. Beethoven (43) is hailed as a 'shackle-brakkan saul',[17] and in 'October 1941' (52) the music of Tchaikovski (Smith's spelling) is set in sad and ironic counterpoint to the desolation of Eastern Europe in the nadir of the war. It may not be accidental that those four musical giants are all from different countries. Nationalism in Scotland has from the beginning been cosmopolitan in outlook. The abundant use of wide-ranging literary, historical and geographical references as a means of restoring Scotland to its former and rightful place as a nation among nations was a central aim of the entire Scottish Renaissance movement (it could be said, not too fancifully, to mesh fittingly with the love of learning which is itself a traditionally Scottish characteristic); and it is an integral part of Smith's method throughout his work.

---

famous by the time Smith was writing the poems compiled in *The Deevil's Waltz*, it is surely likely that he was prompted to make these translations and incorporate them in his book by a personal encounter.

17    Cf. *Co-Chur*, no. XXIII of Sorley MacLean's *Dàin do Eimhir* (MacLean, 126–129).

It is manifested with power, if with none of the control or discipline of expression which he was shortly to attain, in the last and most substantial poem in *Skail Wind*: 'The Refugees: A Complaynt' (14–18), in which impassioned laments for the dispossessed peoples of the world lead in the final section to the victims of the Highland clearances; and the finest development is undoubtedly his acknowledged masterpiece *Under the Eildon Tree*, a poetic celebration of love in its diversity and intensity unique in Scottish literature, in which archetypal lovers from history and mythology appear in procession.

In the Scottish literary canon love poetry is more remarkable for quality than for quantity, at least in the work of the canonical 'art' poets (it goes without saying that love is and always has been a ubiquitous theme in folk-songs and ballads). Given the scope and variety of 15th and early 16th century literature there is, if anything, a notable paucity of poems on the theme of love (*The Kingis Quair* being a monumental exception), and no identifiable figure prior to Alexander Scott who can be described as primarily a love poet. Gavin Douglas, in the Prologue to Book IV of the *Eneados*, uses the Dido story as a peg on which to hang a stern poetic denunciation of the dangerous temptations of love; and another of Smith's direct quotations from his Scottish literary predecessors is a couplet from this prologue:

O luif, quhidder ar yow joy or fulichnes
That makis folk so glaid of thair distress?

(In its context in *Under the Eildon Tree* the passage is applied directly and straightforwardly to the emotional state evoked by Smith at this point in the poem. But as Douglas overtly counters Chaucer by weighting the moral balance, in his translation as well as his arguments in this Prologue, in favour of Aeneas and against Dido,[18] is Smith in his turn implying a confrontation with Douglas in *his* presentation of Dido in *Under the Eildon Tree*, which is magnificently weighted in the other direction?). The accomplished sonneteers of James VI's court, including the King, made of Scotland a leading participant in the exuberantly cosmopolitan poetic culture of the time, in which love was a topic of abounding interest; but in the Vernacular Revival period it sank again to an inconspicuous place: love is a motivating factor in the plot of Ramsay's *The Gentle Shepherd* but is scarcely examined or displayed with passionate intensity; it is the mainspring of Alexander Ross's *Helenore* but is given an ironic gloss by the unexpected 'double inconstance' which leads to the happy ending;

---

18     For discussion see my 'The Dido episode in Gavin Douglas's translation of the *Aeneid*', in *The European English Messenger* 19.1 (Spring 2010), pp. 47–58.

it is virtually absent as a theme in Fergusson. In this context Burns, who would under any circumstances have an unchallenged place among the world's great love poets, stands out as a mighty exception; and it is in this context that Smith's poem-sequence should be assessed: he is inviting comparison with, not a fine abundance of good or very good poets, but a few outstanding ones; a challenge which he accepts with aplomb. In a verse from early in the sequence:

> I luve doitit bard o' the Westren Warld
>        That saw but couldna win
> The Fortunate Isles ayont the westren sun
>        Forge this last testament to stand
> Heroic wi the tale o' Helen, Cleopatra, Lesbia,
>        Wi Morfydd, Dido, Heloise
>        And Marie o' the whitest blee —
> As Rab his Mary, Hugh his Jean,
>        Sae I nou sing o' thee,
> My ain Perdita, Phryne, Cynthia. (153)

he places himself alongside Burns and MacDiarmid, and the loves celebrated in their poetry and his own alongside the beloved women commemorated in the greatest of literature: an audacious step, but one which he takes with re-sounding success.

The list in this verse of women who are either fatal objects or tragic victims of love would be sufficient in itself to demonstrate the wide-ranging erudition which Smith applies in the cause of Scottish cultural nationalism and interna-tionalism. Such lists are a familiar literary device (Tom Scott in 1953, shortly after *Under the Eildon Tree,* would remind Scottish readers again of the tradi-tion by including 'Ballade des Dames du Temps Jadis' in his *Seevin Poems o Maister Francis Villon Made Ower intil Scots*) but Smith adds some pointedly Scottish touches: Gaelic as well as Greek mythology is evoked by the opening reference to the Fortunate Isles, and the identity of 'Marie o' the whitest blee' does not require to be guessed at. Throughout the sequence, a galaxy of liter-ary, historical and mythological references (and an abundance of actual quota-tions) serves to place the Scottish poet's love, and by extension the language and the literary tradition in which it is evoked, in a universal context, and by that means proclaims the universal status of the Scots language and its poetic achievement.

All the features which Smith saw as archetypically Scottish can be found in his poetry. By any standards a major poet, his work is among the most impressive of modern literary embodiments of Scottish nationalism at its finest, and of the internationalism which inseparably complements it.

### Bibliography

Garry, Flora, 'Bennygoak' in *Bennygoak and Other Poems* 3rd edn. (Aberdeen: Rainbow Books, 1975), pp. 7–8.

James VI, 'Reulis and Cautelis' in J. Craigie (ed.), *The Poems of James VI of Scotland,* Vol. I (Edinburgh & London: Scottish Text Society, 1955), p. 82.

MacDiarmid, Hugh (Kenneth Buthlay ed.), *A Drunk Man Looks at the Thistle: Annotated Edition* (Edinburgh: Scottish Academic Press 1987).

Mackenzie, Agnes Mure, *An Historical Survey of Scottish Literature to 1714* (London: A. Maclehose, 1933).

Mackenzie, Agnes Mure, *The Kingdom of Scotland: A Short History* (Edinburgh: Chambers, 1940).

MacLean, Sorley (MacGill-Eain, Somhairle), 'XXIII' from 'Dàin do Eimhir' in Emma Dymock & Christopher Whyte (eds.), *Collected Poems in Gaelic with English Translations* (Edinburgh: Polygon, 2011), pp. 126–129.

McClure, J. Derrick, *Language, Poetry and Nationhood* (East Linton: Tuckwell Press, 2000).

McClure, J. Derrick, 'The Dido episode in Gavin Douglas's translation of the *Aeneid*' in *The European English Messenger* 19:1 (Spring 2010), pp. 47–56.

McCulloch, Margery Palmer (ed.), *Modernism and Nationalism: Literature and Society in Scotland 1918–1939* (Glasgow: Association for Scottish Literary Studies, 2004).

Murison, David, 'The Language of Sydney Goodsir Smith' in Norman MacCaig (ed.) *For Sydney Goodsir Smith* (Loanhead: MacDonald, 1975), pp. 23–29.

Ramsay, Allan, 'Elegy on Lucky Wood' in *Poems* (London: A. Millar & W. Johnston, 1751), pp. 18–21.

Smith, G. Gregory, *Scottish Literature; Character and Influence* (London: Macmillan & Co., 1919).

Smith, Sydney Goodsir (Scott Tom ed.), *Collected Poems: 1941–1975* (London: John Calder, 1975).

Smith, Sydney Goodsir, *A Short Introduction to Scottish Literature* (Edinburgh: Serif Books, 1951).

CHAPTER 6

# 'Huntress, Slayer, White Unmortal Queyne': Women in the Work of Sydney Goodsir Smith

*Monika Szuba*

### Abstract

The chapter explores the diverse poetic vision and the representations of femininity in Sydney Goodsir Smith's poetry. The discussion focuses on the ways in which Smith romanticises and idealises female figures, drawing from the hoard of myth and legend, which includes the Moon goddess, the witch, Eurydice, Dido, and the Queen of the Fairies, appearing recurrently in his poetry. It attempts to examine the central position given to the Muse who acts as the moving force behind the poetic and argues that by placing the feminine *Thou* at the forefront of his poetry, Smith stresses the totality of the female other. Finally, the chapter aims to demonstrate how, by employing traditional poetic forms such as the sonnet, the song, the ballad, the elegy and writing in Scots, Smith revisits, revises and challenges lyrical conventions.

### Keywords

Classicism – femininity – feminism – gender – myth – Scots – *Under the Eildon Tree* – 'Thomas the Rhymer' – *The White Goddess* (Robert Graves)

The above title comes from the poem opening Sydney Goodsir Smith's sequence *Under the Eildon Tree* (1948).[1] These three epithets – 'Huntress, Slayer, White Unmortal Queyne' – are just a few of the female incarnations present in his poetry, which demonstrate a diverse poetic vision and the polymorphous nature of femininity. Female figures abound in Smith's work: from a nameless 'thee', who occupies a central position in so many poems, to the Muse, the Moon goddess, the witch, Eurydice, Dido, and the Queen of the Fairies, to mention just a few. In his poems, women are idealised, romanticised, mythicised:

---

1   For the purposes of this chapter, the version of this poem in Sydney Goodsir Smith, *Collected Poems: 1941–1975* (London: John Calder, 1975), pp. 147–187, has been used.

fierce and fearless, generous and merciless, they fill the poet's writing life in a total and totalising manner. Frequently it is the women – either embodied, imagined or mythical – who constitute the moving force behind Smith's verse. The Muse appears under many guises: a muse and a witch, she is the prime mover, in charge of inspiration, which she gives but also takes away. Thus Smith refers to traditional female roles and at the same time redefines the image of women, offering images of female figures who are highly polyvalent as well as ambivalent. I wish to argue in this chapter that through the use of traditional poetic forms such as the sonnet, the song, the ballad, the elegy and the employment of lyrical conventions of the love lyric and courtly love, all of them expressed in Scots, Smith both upholds a male tradition of idealising the female and attempts to modernise some of the traditional poetic images of women. Given the special significance of language and tradition in Smith's work, before turning to female visions and re-visions in his poetry, I wish to examine his approach to poetic expression and the use of literary forms.

Considered to be an 'outstanding new late modernist writer in Scots' (McCulloch, 8), Smith made it one of his major preoccupations to revive and revitalise the Scottish language in literature. As Margery Palmer McCulloch argues, he is among the poets who 'drew on the legacy of MacDiarmid's revitalisation of Scots as a modern literary language [...] although experimenting with these influences in new ways' (8). His aim was to create a new, distinct poetic language. Not being a native Scots speaker, he acquainted himself with the work of the late 15th and 16th century Makars, and based on that, he developed a modern Scots literary language (McCulloch, 209). This careful, conscious creation of a poetic language was systematised in the 1947 'Style Sheet' published in *The New Alliance and Scots Review*, which managed to 'give his poetry the appearance of a distinctive literary language, related to English, but having its own identity and forms, and without the distraction for the reader of the apologetic apostrophes' (McCulloch, 209). As Christopher Whyte notes, reinventing the language unscrupulously in terms of a strongly personal idiolect, one which bore little relation to cultural or social realities, Smith accommodated himself to creating a place in the heritage of the Renaissance Movement (Whyte, 53). The leading voice of the Renaissance Movement, Hugh MacDiarmid wrote that Smith found in Scots 'and in our demotic language generally – qualities to which his whole nature responded and which he could not find in official English at all' (MacDiarmid, xi). Smith's passion for language led some critics to believe that '[s]ometimes he seems to be more interested in the special effects of the Scots language than in the subjects he writes of' (Gifford et al., 742). His is indeed poetry conscious of, or even flaunting the sound or words and their rhythm; but he remains faithful to the major preoccupations of his work. As I shall argue, Smith combines linguistic innovation with an inventive exploration of universal themes, particularly the theme of love, loss and poetic inspiration through the role and image of the female, exploding familiar images and imbuing them with the spirit of creativity. His keen interest in renewing and reinventing language pushes him to seek a refreshed vision of women figures which take an essential place in this writing.

Through frequent allusions to earlier Scottish poets, Smith's work proposes a continuation of a long tradition as 'the choice of Scottishness involved a profound osmosis with the work of poets writing in different languages or in a different age' (Whyte, 209). As MacDiarmid argues, Smith 'takes his place alongside not only Burns but Dunbar and Alexander MacDonald' (MacDiarmid, xii). Ian Brown and Alan Riach highlight the responsibility that Smith shared with other authors of the Renaissance Movement in 'rediscovering and revitalising Scotland's cultural history', which revealed itself in 'his scholarly work on Burns and Fergusson' (Brown & Riach, 7). Kurt Wittig cited by MacDiarmid, extends the literary affinities beyond the Old Makars, comparing Smith to Charles Baudelaire, Jean Baptiste Racine, Aristophanes, Juvenal, Ezra Pound, and T.S. Eliot (MacDiarmid, xi). Drawing from various traditions, Smith 'gains his perspective by bringing the Scots outlook into relationship with classical and Celtic mythology' (Wittig qtd in MacDiarmid, xi). The fusion of traditions in his work is also visible in the use of fixed metrical forms such as sonnets, as well as traditional ballads and songs. Throughout his writing career, he continued the exploration of traditional poetic forms, making references to the bardic tradition, recurrently exploring major themes.

Critics agree that Smith's principal theme is love. As Douglas Gifford argues, '[m]uch of his poetry is lyrical and centres on the general and ancient themes of lyric poetry: love and death' (Gifford et al., 742). McCulloch aptly points out, 'this apparently limited subject matter provides the route to a full experience of life as we live it' (McCulloch, 210). From his first collection of poems, *Skail Wind*, published when he was twenty-six, Smith tests the limits of the love lyric. Two songs from that collection, 'Song: The Dark Days are by' (Smith: 1975, 8–9) and 'Song: The Steeple Bar, Perth' (Smith: 1975, 12), are punctuated by a returning refrain 'my luve'. This is a common, recurrent address in Smith's poems which are directed towards a nameless woman dear to the speaker. This iterative rhetorical gesture is an important one as, by referring to the object of feelings as 'my luve', Smith refuses to fix the character and avoids pinning it down, thus leaving it open and free. He continues to use this convention throughout his work, equating female figures with an ever-expanding love and making the beloved woman the addressee of his poems.

Returning in many poems, the theme of the loss of love occupies a central place in *Under the Eildon Tree: A Poem in XXIV Elegies* (1948), '[a]n outstanding sequence of love poems' (McCulloch, 210). Smith's poetic survey of the theme of love culminates in these twenty-four variations on the subject of love, which Moira Burgess calls one of the 'landmarks in Scottish poetry' (Burgess, 106). Gifford considers *Under the Eildon Tree* Smith's 'greatest poetic achievement', 'where individual elegies [...] range over a wide variety of moods of love like a medieval love-allegory or Renaissance sonnet-sequence. This love has universal qualities but works itself out in Smith's beloved Edinburgh' (Gifford et al., 744). The poems present a powerful weaving of the theme and language with the grand themes of love and loss, which constantly nourish Smith's poetic vision, focused around the mystery of the intertwining of beauty and pain, love and terror.

The sequence takes its title from the Scottish folk ballad of Thomas the Rhymer 'who was carried off by the Queen of the Fairies' (McCulloch, 210), or True Thomas, 'the poet who made love to a magical creature' (Scott, 15) and was spirited away to the underworld only to return seven years later unable to tell a lie ever again. Thus in *Under the Eildon Tree*, Smith assumes the role of a modern Thomas the Rhymer as he too 'served his mistress seven years' (Scott, 15) and his function is 'to tell the truth, the whole truth and nothing but the truth about that service' (Scott, 15). Comparing the sequence with MacDiarmid's *Drunk Man Looks at the Thistle*, McCulloch argues that for the 'protagonist sexual relationships are at the heart of his creativity and sense of self' (McCulloch, 210). The elegies present women as highly ambivalent figures: tormenting the poet and lover, providing inspiration, and suffering themselves. Reimagining the stories of Dido, Queen of Carthage and Aeneas, Orpheus and Eurydice, Burns and Highland Mary, Smith foregrounds the entwining of love and death, two grand, universal themes of literature, which highlights his immersion in literary traditions mentioned above. In the first stanza of the elegy IV 'I, Luve-Doitit bard' (Smith: 1975, 153–154), Smith lists women figures across just three lines: Helen, Cleopatra, Lesbia, Morfydd, Dido, Heloise, Mary. These are women from ancient Greek and Roman myths, Arthurian legends, historical characters, heroines of enduring love and tragic romantic entanglements. This enumeration serves to highlight the importance of the speaker's loved woman who combines all the features which the mentioned female characters possess, while at the same time stressing the singularity of the beloved by addressing her directly. The poem concludes with the following words: 'Sae I nou sing o thee, / My ain Perdita, Phryne, Cynthia' (Smith: 1975, 153), where the reference to Cynthia, sometimes associated with Selene, the Greek personification of the moon, suggests an allusion to the moon goddess who constitutes a central female figure in Smith's lyric. Some critics have noted that Smith relies completely on the use of 'the stock figures' from history (Robin Fulton qtd in Scott, 14), yet, as Scott points out, the poet's 'use of cliché there is deliberately designed to blow the gaff on his own tendency towards self-dramatisation'(Scott, 14), adding that '[n]o modern Scottish poet has had fewer illusions about himself than Smith, and none has shown more genial humour in exposing to the reader those all-too-human weaknesses which were inextricably interwoven with the power of his passion' (Scott, 14). I shall return to the *Eildon Tree* sequence at the end of this chapter.

Smith continues to explore the theme of enduring love through the use of myth in the dramatic poem *Orpheus and Eurydice*, which was broadcast by the BBC Scottish Service in 1949 with music by Cedric Thorpe Davie, and published six years later. In it he delves into the ancient story of two lovers, separated and briefly reunited, only to be parted forever. The figures of Orpheus and Eurydice return in Smith's writing and link it with the early Scottish poetic tradition, appearing in *Under the Eildon Tree*, where Smith cites a line from Henryson: 'Quhar art thou gane, my luf Euridices!' (Smith: 1975, 166) in an attempt to make significant a chiefly folkloric, bardic and oral culture in classical terms that challenges Anglo-Saxon primacy. Composed of six parts, bracketed by the prologue and epilogue, *Orpheus and Eurydice*, recreates the myth of Orpheus descent into Hades to bring Eurydice back. The model poet, Orpheus's creation entranced trees and rocks. Playing a mourning song, he was torn to pieces but his head kept singing thus foregrounding the immortal, death-defying power of poetry. Eurydice is an idealised woman, as the frequent references to whiteness indicate; for example, 'my white lass' (Smith: 1955, 24), 'my white Euridicie' (26), 'my fair' (20), 'my dear luve Euridicie/ That was the fairest blume i the fields o men' (16), highlight the idealised features of the beloved such as purity and goodness. Eurydice was 'the Queen o Orpheus' hert' (Smith: 1955, 11), without her his life was devoid of mystery, 'weirdless', worthless, all his activities – '[s]ingin, dancin, waunerin' – have lost their meaning. As Orpheus confesses, she was 'mair nor life itsel to me' (Smith: 1955, 11). This seemingly clichéd expression verbalises Orpheus profound feelings for the beloved Eurydice: being a poet, he does not search for original ways to express his grief but in a moment of crisis he recurs to commonly used phrases which demonstrate his lack of pretence and the sincerity of his feelings towards Eurydice. He frequently addresses her 'hert o my hert, Euridicie' (Smith: 1955, 20). The expression returns when he pleads with gods to give him back his heart's own heart, 'my hert's ain hert' (Smith: 1955, 12). This repeated phrase foregrounds Orpheus's and Eurydice's inextricable connection, which binds them emotionally as well as corporeally. This is revealed in Orpheus's language when he addresses Eurydice as 'my hert' (22), '[m]y hert o herts', 'my saul' (24), '[s]aul o my saul' (20). The repeated possessives culminate in the phrase 'my ain' (my own) ending the line '[m]y hert o herts, my luve, my ain' (21). This gesture of gathering the beloved into himself, making her an essential part of his own body suggests that he is aware of the fact that the only possibility to accomplish the whole in himself is by being with his love. Yet it also sublimates the woman to a use function of the male poet, consuming her into his body and craft.

Smith returns time and again to the theme of love, navigating stereotypical representations of women – at times embracing, at other times challenging them. Women remain. A poem about 'the persistence of love' (Gifford et al., 744), 'Cokkils' (Smith: 1975, 135) from the collection published in 1953, bearing the same title, highlights the enduring power of feelings for a woman by setting it aside constant elements of the world such as the ocean and the 'rain o' cokkils' on the seabed. The eponymous 'cokkils', or shells, stand for the deep time, which formed, a slow accretion of layer upon layer, building up '[s]lawlie through millenia'. In this brief poem, the word 'continuallie', repeated four times together with the word 'continual', and such expressions as 'the ceaseless on-ding'(the ceaseless downpour) and '[w]i nae devall' (without cease), repeated twice, stress the enduring love to a woman, whom the poet calls 'my true-luve'. The preposition 'throu', which appears four times, foregrounds the sense of movement, which continues in time and space. In a performative manner, these repetitions strengthen the effect of the endurance of feeling, which transcends temporality. The rhythm of thought is rendered in the recurring lines as the woman appears continually in the poet's mind. The downward movement of shells falling onto the seabed and the thought of the loved one in the speaker's mind underlines the profundity of his feelings. The whole poem's reliance on an extended simile strengthens the effect that the combination of brittleness and endurance created by the references to the seashells evokes the image of the beloved woman, the speaker's 'true love'.

The spell-bound poet – 'beglaumert' as in '"Go to Bed, Sweet Muse"' (Smith: 1975, 131) – frequently writes about the muse and the witch as one who affects him profoundly. The figure of the witch returns in many other poems, invariably mesmerising the poet, holding him in thrall to his emotions and managing his creative forces. At times the muse, the witch, transmogrifies into the priestess, which perhaps recalls Edmund Spenser's *The Faerie Queene* (1590). For instance, in 'The Aipple and the Hazel' (Smith: 1975, 129–130), the two lovers are fused, '[p]riestess and bard as ane'. Smith evokes an image, where two lovers occupy a room – 'My luve and I / in a wee room lain' – echoes the line from John Donne's poem 'The Good Morrow'. 'one little room an everywhere'

(Donne, 661). Smith's line echoes the image but also makes it ordinary (perhaps one might risk a statement that it is part of his project of Scotticisation: to make the everyday the metaphysical). For Donne, the lovers make a room the universe, infinity, in Smith's poem, the room is a little room in which the lovers lay. Perhaps this is the polemic in the appropriation and re-inscription in Scots. In this poem, the beloved woman is described by the use of many terms: she is the Muse, the goddess, the Queen, the priestess, the witch. This multiplicity of names is suggestive of the woman's polymorphous nature, impossible to be fixed in one place. The season of mellow ripeness is represented by two trees: the hazel, which stands for song and love, and apple tree, symbolising immortality, both under the reign of muses, 'are as ane'.[2] Thus Smith underlines the intertwining of poetry, love and timelessness. The motif of oneness and wholeness returns in his other love poems. In 'The Mune May' (Smith: 1975, 130), the bard 'convenes' with the witch, who has him 'bewitcht'. The use of the verb 'convene', or to come together in a body, presents an image of the two as one. Her power over the speaker is overwhelming: holding him spellbound, she leaves him transfixed, unable to 'flee' as she has 'bunden' him even though she is but 'a wee thing'. The poet also calls her '[t]his nymph o the mune', suggesting that her existence is entwined with moonlight and lunar rhythms. The bard remains under her powerful spell, being at the mercy of the witch who affects him magically. The alchemy of creation comes about through witchcraft, the witch being the higher power, her magical skills ending in a composition of the poem.

In the poem 'Credo' from the 1959 collection *Figs and Thistles* (Smith: 1975, 87), Smith states firmly the importance of the Muse in his writing. As Gifford affirms, '[t]he muse of his poetry must be awaited in all her fickleness. Equally fickle and inconstant is love, influenced by the moon, which will bring pain and betrayal into the poet's life' (Gifford et al., 743). In this poem, the bard sings '[i]n the goddess' name' but he has to be patient, waiting for her to appear, '[n] e'er seek her out'. The poet is subject to the goddess' wishes, he is in the Muse's hands: it is up to her whether she appears, he must be ready, entirely at her mercy, lying in wait in his boat for her to approach him. This presents a reversal of the stereotypical images of female passivity and male activity. The brief

---

2   It is worth noting that 'Hazel' in the context of Smith's poems not only refers to the genus of tree, but also his second wife, Hazel Williamson (1928–2004), who was the coded dedicatee ('the onlie begetter') of many of Smith's poems from the 1950s. Smith was having an affair with Williamson while still married to his first wife, Marion, who died in 1966, thereby allowing Smith to marry Williamson. The grave Smith shares with Williamson in the Dean Cemetery in Edinburgh carries the following epitaph, taken from Smith's poem 'The Aipple and the Hazel': 'And the aipple and the hazel are as ane'.

refrain, an appeal '[c]elebrate the seasons', appearing at the beginning, in the middle and the end of the poem which foregrounds temporality and tran- sience, expressing a readiness to accept the ephemerality of things. The Muse's association with the moon and the tide rhythms is stressed by the regular rhymes. She is the Moon-goddess who inspires poetic myths, but is also the Love-goddess and the Underworld-goddess, responsible for love and death, giving and taking, the man's life and fate in her hands. She is the goddess who has the power to 'gie', but also to take: what she gave she took. Thus the poem as well as other poems inspired by her, becomes the gift of the Muse who gives when she pleases. The Muse breathes life into the poet's creation. As the dic- tionary of etymology tells us, in the Middle Ages, inspiration meant the 'im- mediate influence of God or a god', from Latin *inspirare*: 'blow into, breathe upon'. For Smith it is not a god but a goddess who endows the poet with inspi- ration, breathing upon and pushing the poet's pen forward.

The power of the Moon-goddess is expressed in a potent, renewed poetic language. As was stated at the beginning of this chapter, a renewal of poetic language in Smith's writing occupies a central position, but as he keeps re- minding us, for him creation is heavily dependent on the Muse. Smith's ap- proach to literary creation resembles the ideas of Robert Graves, who argues in *The White Goddess* that:

> the language of poetic myth anciently current in the Mediterranean and Northern Europe was a magical language bound up with popular reli- gious ceremonies in honour of the Moon-goddess, or Muse, some of them dating from the Old Stone Age, and that this remains the language of true poetry— "true" in the nostalgic modern sense of "the unimprov- able original, not a synthetic substitute".
>
> GRAVES, 9–10

Thus by celebrating the Moon-goddess, Smith maintains 'the language of true poetry', following a matriarchal religion before all religions, preserved by poets in verse, a poetic re-imagination of an enduring myth. A conviction of a god- dess inspires by adding breath and nourishing Smith's poetry. His constant re- turn to the 'White Unmortal Queyne; (inevitably bringing to mind Una from *The Faerie Queene*), an eternal symbol of femininity, suggests what David Con- stantine writes about *The White Goddess*, 'the experience of beauty – beauty being the form in which this access to mythic life takes place – actually brings home, to the poet at least, his own immortality' (Constantine, 82). It appears that Smith, like Robert Graves 'came to believe that the poet's chief, or even sole, responsibility was to keep telling, in its different manifestations, the 'one story and one story only' whose prime mover is the White Goddess. In any number of incarnations, in countless myths, she appears as the goddess, muse and woman whom the poet must love and at whose hands he is bound to suffer' (Constantine, 82).

Before concluding this chapter, I wish to return to *Under the Eildon Tree* in an attempt to argue that Smith's poetry explores the singular within the universal: the singularity of a woman within the universal subject of love. In the third poem from the sequence, the speaker announces that even if there exist other subjects 'for a makar's pen' (Smith: 1975, 150), which are '[m]aist wechtie and profund' (Smith: 1975, 150), for him it is the beloved who remains at the centre of his poems. The beloved is the whole world, eclipsing other people and things. 'I see but you' (Smith: 1975, 150), the poet declares. If, as Luce Irigaray argues, 'the *Thou* of certain philosophers or a theology that forgets that this is you (*tu*) is generally a *he*' (Irigaray, 48), in Smith's love poetry it is invariably a singular you, or *she*. In the third poem from the sequence, the poet confesses, 'You are my subject anerlie, there is nae ither / Fills my musardie, / Nae word but your name in my dictionarie, / The heidlines in the news mean nocht til me/ For your name isna there' (Smith: 1975, 150). The beloved woman's name is unmentioned in the poems, indicating that she cannot be contained, making her divine. In this she resembles God whose name cannot be uttered or comprehended as it would fix and contain him. The poet has no other subject before the beloved as the following lines indicate:

> And scrievin sangs o' ye
> Is aa my haill activitie,
> The occupation o' my waukan days,
> The dwaums that thrang my restless nichts,
> The bouk in clouds,
> The figures i' the reik,
> The ferlies i' the gleid
> And in the trunks o' auldern treen
> 　　　　Is aye the face
> 　　　　O' my dear lass.
> SMITH: 1975, 151

The poet's 'dear lass' occupies the whole of his days and nights, her sight 'aye', always, fills the landscape. The key word in the above lines is 'haill', or whole, which constitutes the essence of Smith's creative process. The man and the woman are made whole only when they joined together as one.

In response to a question posed by Robert Graves in *The White Goddess*, 'What is the use or function of poetry nowadays?' David Constantine writes: 'The function of poetry is religious invocation of the Muse; its use is the experience of mixed exaltation and horror that her presence excites' (Constantine, 14). Celebrating numerous other impersonations of women, Smith's poetry invokes the Muse with a religious reverence, and by doing that, it inscribes itself in the male convention of idealising and romanticising the woman. His representations of female figures combine traditional poetic forms and familiar tropes with the use of a renewed language, which offers Smith a chance to renew images of femininity, constituting the heart of his poetic work. He puts the feminine *Thou* at the forefront of his writing thus stressing the totality of the female other. For Smith, women are not the object of his love lyric but present a profound expression of love: being one with the poet, they make him whole.

## Bibliography

Brown, Ian, & Alan Riach (eds.), 'Introduction' in *The Edinburgh Companion to Twentieth-Century Scottish Literature* (Edinburgh: Edinburgh University Press, 2009), pp. 1–14.

Burgess, Moira, 'Arcades: The 1940s and 1950s' in Ian Brown & Alan Riach (eds.), *The Edinburgh Companion to Twentieth-Century Scottish Literature* (Edinburgh: Edinburgh University Press, 2009), pp. 103–111.

Burns, Robert. *A Choice of Burns's Poems and Songs*. Selected with an Introduction by Sydney Goodsir Smith (London: Faber and Faber, 1966).

Constantine, David. '"A Grace it had, devouring..." Apparitions of Beauty, Love, and Terror in the Poetry of Robert Graves' in Monika Szuba & Tomasz Wiśniewski (eds.), *Poets of the Past. Poets of the Present. Between. Pomiędzy* Series vol. 4. (Gdańsk/Sopot: University of Gdańsk Press, 2013).

Donne, John. *The Complete Poems of John Donne*. (London and New York: Routledge, 2013).

Gifford, Douglas et al., *Scottish Literature* (Edinburgh: Edinburgh University Press, 2002).

Graves, Robert, *The White Goddess: A Historical Grammar of Poetic Myth* (New York: Farrar, Straus, & Giroux, 1966).

Irigaray, Luce, *I Love to You: Sketch for a Felicity within History*. Trans. Alison Martin. (New York & London: Routledge, 1996).

MacDiarmid, Hugh, 'Introduction' in Sydney Goodsir Smith, *Collected Poems: 1941–1975* (London: John Calder, 1975).

Marsack, Robyn, 'The Seven Poets Generation' in Ian Brown & Alan Riach (eds.), *The Edinburgh Companion to Twentieth Century Scottish Literature* (Edinburgh: Edinburgh University Press, 2009), pp. 156–167.

Palmer McCulloch, Margery, *Scottish Modernism and its Contexts 1918–1959: Literature, National Identity and Cultural Exchange* (Edinburgh: Edinburgh University Press, 2009).

Riach, Alan, *Representing Scotland in Literature, Popular Culture and Iconography: The Masks of the Modern Nation* (Houndmills, Basingstoke: Palgrave, 2005).

Scott, Alexander. '*Under the Eildon Tree*' in Norman MacCaig (ed.), *For Sydney Goodsir Smith*. (Edinburgh: Macdonald, 1975), pp. 11–22.

Smith, Sydney Goodsir, *Collected Poems: 1941–1975* (London: John Calder, 1975).

Smith, Sydney Goodsir, *Orpheus and Eurydice: A Dramatic Poem* (Edinburgh: Macdonald, 1955).

Whyte, Christopher, *Modern Scottish Poetry* (Edinburgh: Edinburgh University Press, 2004).

Wittig, Kurt, *The Scottish Tradition in Literature* (Edinburgh: Oliver and Boyd, 1958).

# CHAPTER 7

# 'Order and Adventure': Sydney Goodsir Smith's Translations

*Stewart Sanderson*

## Abstract

The reference in the title of this chapter is to one of the writer's versions of Apollinaire, and provides a fitting lens through which to read his use of foreign poets – on the one hand to order his own Scottish experience as regards its international setting, on the other to stravaig adventurously through the wider poetic world. This chapter looks at Smith's translations of the following poets: Guillaume Apollinaire, Alexander Blok, Stefan Borsukiewicz, Tristan Corbière, Ivan Jelinek, Sorley MacLean, Sappho and François Villon. It takes a broad view of Smith's work as a translator from Gaelic, French, Czech, Polish, Ancient Greek and Russian. In each case it explores the reasons for his being drawn to translate particular poets and what he hoped to achieve by doing so, linking his work in this area to the wider Scottish Renaissance project of translation as part of an effort to internationalise Scottish letters.

## Keywords

translation – internationalism – Scots language – Guillaume Apollinaire – Alexander Blok – Stefan Borsukiewicz – Tristan Corbière – Ivan Jelinek – Sorley MacLean – Sappho – François Villon – Gaelic – French – Czech – Polish – Ancient Greek – Russian

As with many of his Scottish contemporaries, verse translation into the Scots language was central to Sydney Goodsir Smith's practice as a writer. His versions of poems in a number of languages – Gaelic, Greek, French, Polish, Czech and Russian – constitute a key part of his oeuvre. They are a potentially unifying presence in a remarkably diverse body of work, combining poetry, art criticism, drama, song and experimental prose – not to mention his achievement as a passionate amateur watercolourist, documented in the 1998 volume *The Drawings of Sydney Goodsir Smith*. They are, moreover, important texts for critics trying to come to terms with the complex mixture of nationalism and internationalism which might be taken as the defining characteristic of the post-MacDiarmid generation of Scots language poets. Nonetheless, as with his writing more generally, Smith's translations have been sorely neglected by scholarship. This essay will therefore provide a much-needed overview of his work in this area, situating the translations in the context of Smith's individual collections and broader project as a writer, as well as in their wider literary and cultural context.

One of Smith's earliest extant translations is from the Gaelic of his close friend (and sometime housemate) Sorley MacLean (Wilson, 7). Working from the Gaelic 'An Trom-laighe' /, 'The Nightmare' (MacLean, 181–183), Smith writes a Scots poem entitled 'The Widdreme' (literally 'the mad dream'). The Gaelic title carries associations of heavy lying and weighted sleep, rewarding etymo-logical dissection. Similarly, the Scots title rewards speculation into its various potential components – 'wid-' could be interpreted as hinting at the potential 'would' or the darkened 'wood' of visions and dream states, as well as the meta-phorically wooden heaviness of a disturbed mind:

> Ae nicht o thae twa year
> Whan I thought ma luve
> Was strak wi a skaith as dure
> As wumman's had sen Eve,
> We ware thegither in a dwaum
> By the stane dyke that stauns
> Atween the loons' an lassies' yards
> O' ma first schuil.
> 　　　　　　　　　Ma airms
> Ware round her an ma lips
> Seekan her mou
> Whan the laithlie gorgon's heid stuid up
> On a sidden frae hint the waa,
> An the lang mirk ugsome fingers graipt
> Ma craig wi a sidden grup –
> And then the words o weirdless dule:
> "Owre blate, ye fuil!"
> 　　SMITH: 1975, 249

Smith's translation is included in his *Collected Poems* (1975) in the section of poems deleted from *The Deevil's Waltz* (1946) and *So Late into the Night* (1952). However, it originally appeared in the former collection, which comprises Smith's poetic response to the World War Two.

'The Widdreme' comes towards the start of Smith's career as a translator. Part of the complex nexus of Scots-Gaelic interaction in the 1940s, emblematised by the translation of MacLean and, to a lesser extent, George Campbell Hay, this text shows the poet attempting to come to terms with the plurality of Scotland's languages. The 'stane dyke' of 'The Widdreme'/ 'An Trom-laighe' refers on one level to material things. On another, it is the wall between languages, complementary modes of expression separated by difference. Smith's translation, from one marginal form into another, seeks to surmount that difference, while preserving its integrity. This is valuable, despite the gorgon's pronouncement of lateness – indicative of language loss as much as erotic despair.

The second translation in *The Deevil's Waltz* is from the French of François Villon, a text omitted from the *Collected Poems* – an omission rendered doubly baffling by Smith's posthumous editor, Tom Scott's, own distinguished translations of Villon, published in the 1950s. Unlike Scott, Smith does not translate from one of the French poet's celebrated ballades, instead making a Scots version of *Le Lais*, stanzas 2–4. The Scots translation, given alongside the French, begins as follows:

> At this time, as I have tauld
> Roun Christmas, the deid hin-enn
> Whan wolves eat the wund an the cauld
> Hayr gars aa fowk keep ben
> Huddered roun the bleezan gleid,
> There cam on me a wull tae brak
> Frae the loosum jail I lang hae dreed,
> That aye ma hert does rack.
>
> SMITH: 1946, 22

> En ce temps que j'ay dit devant
> Sur le Noel, morte saison,
> Que les loups se vivent de vent
> Et qu'on se tient en sa maison
> Pour le frimas, pres du tison,
> Me vint ung vouloir de brisier
> La tres amoureuse prison
> Qui souloit mon cuer debrisier.
>
> VILLON, 16

Smith employs a light touch in his rendering of Villon's octosyllables. In the eighth line, he foreshortens by one beat, concluding his first stanza with a trimeter. This deviation will not be repeated, though the Scots poet consistenly departs from Villon's tight a-b-a-b-b-c-b-c. As regards the sense of the translation, Smith has stayed fairly close to his original, finding equivalents – sometimes fairly loose ones, but equivalents nonetheless – for most of what is going on in the French poem.

On the page facing the translation from *Le Lais*, Smith's translation 'Ae Shouer o Hail an Three o Rain', from the Czech poet Ivan Jelinek (1909–2002), provides a complementary perspective. A note, appended below the poem, reveals that the poet (also translated into English by Edwin Muir)[1] was 'Born 1912; Czech Armoured Brigade; Author of *Basne* 1938–1944' (Smith: 1946, 23). Among other things, then, this poem is a reminder that the Anglophone translation of Eastern European poets as part of a wider project of political sympathy predates the reception of Czech and Polish writers like Miłosz, Herbert, Holub and Szymborska in the 1960s. Turning to the text itself, which follows the Scots translation of *Le Lais* 2–4, one finds the four following ballad-like quatrains:

> Throu a shouer o hail an three o rain
> We twa gang – and no alane;
> Gin the tyke I had wi me is ane,
> Wha's by me then?

> Efter ilk rain the sun's bleezan;
> I' the efternuin
> The hail's dingan –. Cauld are yir hauns
> And wha may kiss them?

> Leaf o the aik, did ye luik in her een?
> Ower the brig juist lean,
> Let faa yir tears i the burn
> Frae luve alane.

> Ye can greit in sang anerlie
> Until the Dee,
> Ahint the hous, spates owre the land
> For the blytheness o yee.
>           SMITH: 1946, 23

---

1   See Jelinek, Ivan, 'To the Czech Language', trans. by Edwin Muir, *Modern Poetry in Translation*, No.17 (2001), p. 167.

This translation is interesting not simply because of the cultural sympathies which it encapsulates, but also because of the degree to which it reveals Smith's language as a perpetual work in progress. The probable typo in the first line – 'Throu *a* shoucr', not *ac* shoucr – is indicative of a wider flux and mutability of spelling convention and syntax, predicated on the ideal but also unreal concept of a fully realised synthetic Scots. This is to emphasise the point that, while one reading of Smith and his contemporaries' MacDiarmidian project would focus on its preoccupation with the past of the Scots language, another might seek to foreground its investment in a never fully tangible future, destabilising conventions of spelling and grammar towards this end.

Moving now to the final pair of translations collected in *The Deevil's Waltz*, from the Polish of Stefan Borsukiewicz, the reader finds the following biographical footnote, similar to the one appended to the Jelinek translation: 'Stefan Borsukiewicz, born 1914, died 1941. Polish Parachute Brigade in Scotland. Author of *Kontrasty* 1941 (Kolin, London)' (Smith: 1946, 44). For Douglas Young, conscientious objection was a politically urgent, morally justified action, even if it meant going to prison. Smith found a greater moral urgency in the fight against Fascism, despite being unable to take part in it as a combat soldier. Teaching English – a language towards whose imperial pretensions he was deeply critical – to Polish soldiers in Perthshire, Smith perhaps sought to balance the scales in favour of minority speech by translating Borsukiewicz into Scots.

Smith's familiarity with Polish and other Eastern European literature was considerable. Writing to Young, he asks him for help locating English translations of the Polish Romantic poet Slowacki, whom he had come across in Madame Pilsudski's memoirs. He also writes that he has recently read Adam Mickiewicz's *Pan Tadeusz*. Possibly inspired by Mickiewicz, he is presently working on a heroic poetic drama.[2] Whether or not this is a reference to an early incarnation of *The Wallace*, it is clear that Smith was open to the whole Polish tradition – not just those parts of it rendered topical by recent events. With this said, there is certainly a topical element to the inclusion of the Borsukiewicz translations in *The Deevil's Waltz* – coming through very clearly in the latter's 'Ballad o the Defence o Warsaw, 1939':

> The nicht was reid wi whorlan munes
> (It neer wald faa again),
> Ootwith the toun the suburbs clung
> In fear lik a drunkart's wean.

---

2   See Acc. 6419/38b in the National Library of Scotland (Young papers).

Warsaw, o steermen brave as gyte,
On rifles ye piped a hymn,
A feylike sang o the saikless lyft
Whaes licht nae cloud wald dim.

SMITH: 1975, 50

Smith, transfiguring Borsukiewicz, elegises Warsaw, arguing in effect that, whatever tragedies followed the Poles' inability to hold back the Germans, the example of their sacrifice endures. In this, an important detail seems to be the choice of image, in the second line of the second quatrain: the city playing a hymn on its citizens' rifles, as though they were the stops and keys of a great organ. This image is reminiscent of the Russian Futurist Vladimir Mayakovsky, memorably translated into Scots by Edwin Morgan, who urged his readers to play on drainpipes as though they were flutes (Morgan: 2016, 19).[3]

In *The Deevil's Waltz* Smith used translations to add nuance and texture to a heterogeneous, but still carefully structured collection. The strict elegiac series of his next major book, *Under the Eildon Tree*, left little room for such a strategy. Nevertheless, in the same year, 1948, Smith published a pair of translations in MacDiarmid's periodical *The Voice of Scotland*. Both were from modern French *avant-garde* poets – Guillaume Apollinaire (1880–1918) and Paul Éluard (1895–1952). Never subsequently collected, these texts are of clear interest as regards his poetic affinities with modernism and attempt – as seen in *Under the Eildon Tree* – to compose new kinds of Scots poetry.

'La Jolie Rousse' is the last poem in Apollinaire's 1918 collection, *Calligrammes*, published just a few months before his death. His editors Marcel Adéma and Michel Décaudin describe it as 'le testament poétique d'Apollinaire' (Apollinaire, 1104). 'La Jolie Rousse' is among the more conventional poems in the volume, employing a relatively straightforward unpunctuated *vers libre*, to which Smith adds full stops. In the opening strophe the poet describes himself, emphasising his war service and that 'l'effroyable lutte' has killed his best friends (Apollinare, 313–314). Smith renders 'l'effroyable lutte' as 'the gastrous stour', (Smith: 1948, 28) suggesting the dusty, muddy chaos of the fighting, as well as the gas used as a weapon for the first time in the World War One. The strophe concludes as follows:

I ken new and auld as weill as ae bodie can
And wiout fashan myself wi war the-day

---

3   See: Edwin Morgan, *Wi the Haill Voice: 25 Poems by Vladimir Mayakovsky* (Oxford: Carcanet, 1972; 2016), p. 19.

Atween and for wirsels, my fieres
I judicate the lang tulyie atween tradition and invention
  Atween Order and Adventure.

*Je sais d'ancien et de nouveau autant qu'un homme seul pourrait des deux*
*savoir*
*Et sans m'inquiéter aujourd'hui de cette guerre*
*Entre nous et pour nous mes amis*
*Je juge cette longue querelle de la tradition et de l'invention*
  *De l'Ordre et de l'Aventure.*

From the life of the artist and critic in wartime, Apollinaire turns to the conflict of successive aesthetics – old and new, tradition and invention, order and adventure. Smith's 'new and auld' is a fair match for 'd'ancien et de nouveau', though the line is shortened considerably in his translation. His 'lang tulyie' for 'longue querelle' is a neat Scots equivalent. He keeps tradition, invention, order and adventure much as they are in Apollinaire.

While there are certainly continuities, Apollinaire is a slightly more traditional poet than proponents of surrealism (a movement whose name he coined) such as Éluard. In Smith's version of the latter's poem 'Grand Air', the reader finds a much more challenging text in both Scots and French. Shorter than 'La Jolie Rousse', the version of 'Grand Air' is in some ways a more intractable work than the Apollinaire translation – which, though it presents the reader with some conceptual difficulties, is a comparatively straightforward poem. The poem was first published in Éluard's 1936 volume *Les Yeux Fertiles*. In their notes to the *Oeuvres Complètes*, Éluard's editors Dumas and Scheler write that the fruitful eyes are Picasso's (Éluard, 1476). The first stanza of Smith's 'Open-Air' reads as follows:

The shore the hands trummlan afluther o fareweill
Cam doun under the rain
A stair o haars
Reid-naukit ye outgaed
Like breathan marble
The hue o a rosie-fingert daw
Treisure gairdit by the muckle beasts
That gairdit the sun-lassies neth their wings,
For thee
Beasts that ye kent but didna see.
  SMITH. 1948, 29

From the French:

> La rive les mains tremblantes
> Descendait sous la pluie
> Un escalier de brumes
> Tu sortais toute nue
> Faux marbre palpitant
> Teint de bon matin
> Trésor gardé par des bêtes immenses
> Qui gardaient elles du soleil sous leurs ailes
> Pour toi
> Des bêtes que nous connaissions sans les voir.
>
> ELUARD, 509

It is possible to extract some sort of a narrative sequence from the poem; whether this is the best way to read it is a moot point. In terms of the political implications of Smith's writing, one remembers that the surrealist approach to reality involved a radical rejection of what its practitioners perceived as the tyranny of self-proclaimed rationalism. The estranging effect of the Scots, in the context of surrealism, strengthens this feeling of difficulty (once again Smith adds full stops in his translation, domesticating slightly). Nonetheless, together with 'The Bonnie Reidheid', the poem is an important piece of evidence as to Smith's literary preoccupations around the time he was working on *Under the Eildon Tree*, highlighting his interest – also evident in the translations from Gaelic, Czech and Polish – in introducing new types of writing into Scots and so expanding the tongue's poetic possibilities.

*Figs and Thistles* (1959), was the first Smith collection in thirteen years to contain translations. Reviewing the book for *Poetry* (*Chicago*), Norman Mac-Caig described the translations as 'tours de force', concluding that 'These poems belong to no school: any two lines are immediately recognizable [sic] as Smith's and that is because they are idiosyncratic, not eccentric. Sometimes they fall into typically Scottish faults of sentimentality and rhetoric, but these faults are the excesses of its virtues. For this is a poetry of the passions, not the intellect' (MacCaig, 321–322). There are three poems in translation: 'Sappho', 'The Twal' and 'The Gangrel Rymour and the Pairdon o Sanct Anne', placed in this order at the end of the collection.

'Sappho', dedicated to Edith Sitwell, is not explicitly identified as a translation (save for the reader proficient in Ancient Greek). However, it is clearly an adaptation of Sapphic fragment 168B, the first of whose four lines Smith includes as an epigraph. The Scots poem, in its entirety, reads as follows:

> Dwynit is the mune awa
> And the Pleiades, the nicht
> Is at her mid, the hours flee, and I
> – My lane I ligg.
> SMITH: 1975, 109

After the minimalism of 'Sappho' comes Smith's much longer version of the Russian Symbolist poet Alexander Blok's 'The Twelve' ('The Twal'). The version is preceded by a title page giving the poem's title in Scots and Russian, the year of its first appearance (1918) and its source 'Frae the Russian of Alexander Blok'. There is also a dedication 'Til' C.M. Grieve (Smith: 1959, 53). This information and separate dedication (not given below the title and immediately below the poem as usual) sets 'The Twal' apart from the rest of the book, indicating its importance.

Blok (1880–1921) is one of early 20th century Russia's iconic poets. While not a Bolshevik or Communist himself, his work is nevertheless essentially a product of the cultural prehistory and fallout of the 1917 Revolution, which event he responds to in 'The Twelve'. MacDiarmid had already included a Scots version of Blok's 'The Stranger' in *A Drunk Man Looks at the Thistle*. In light of its dedication, Smith's version of Blok's most famous poem can be read in continuity with the Scots echoes of the Russian poet MacDiarmid wove into *A Drunk Man* (MacDiarmid, 89). Interestingly, this translation was the subject of a BBC Third Programme in the 1950s. Produced by the North East poet George Bruce, the dramatic reading of the poem was preceded by a brief introduction from Smith, in which the poet makes clear his fondness for Blok – whom he argues is the greatest modern Russian poet.[4]

Reading 'The Twal' itself, one finds a much more ambitious translation than Smith had hitherto attempted, requiring him to mingle verse forms and sustain tension and interest throughout the poem's various sections. His version begins as follows:

> Mirk the nicht,
> White the snaw,
> The snell wind blaws,
> Ca'an aa fowk doun –
> The snell wind blaws
> Through aa God's mappamound.

---

4   See Acc. 10397/20, National Library of Scotland.

Frae the white grund
The yowden-drift
Blaws in lacy wreithes,
Under the snaw is ice –
Slidder and glaizie...
Aabodie skites around
And doun they faa
Puir craturs aa!.
SMITH: 1975, 109–110

Jon Stallworthy and Peter France translate these two stanzas thus:

Darkness – and white
snow hurled
by the wind. The wind!
You cannot stand upright
for the wind: the wind
scouring God's world.

The wind ruffles
the white snow, pulls
that treacherous
wool over the wicked ice.
Everyone out walking
slips. Look – poor thing!
BLOK, 94

In the English the distinction between the darkness of the night and the whiteness of the snow is more pronounced than in the Scots poem, where the unfamiliarity of the 'mirk' and the 'grund' pulls the reader towards an aural experience of the poem at the expense of the English version's imagistic visual familiarity. The Scots poem achieves, certainly, a far greater level of semantic complexity, encouraging the reader to unpick the various linguistic layers and elemental gestures Smith uses to set the scene. Symbolically speaking, the language of Smith's poetry, which is a cluttered assemblage of words from many times and places, could be understood as mirroring the poet's understanding of the various Scottish historical periods from which these words sprang. Smith's language is alienated from itself, presenting the reader with the paradoxical vision of a Scotland in which a plethora of diffuse lexical terms, neologisms and multifarious intertextual references could inhabit the same space on the page.

The Blok translation enabled Smith to engage with aspects of 20th century radical art and history which clearly attracted him. The dedication to MacDiarmid highlights this – the older poet presumably representing the strongest Scottish incarnation of the spirit of 1917. The third and final translation in *Figs and Thistles*, from the Francophone Breton poet Tristan Corbière (1845–1875) pushes the volume in another direction. Like Blok, Corbière is a key figure in the strand of symbolism leading towards literary modernism.

Dedicated to Norman MacCaig, Smith's version of Corbière's 'La Rapsode Foraine et le Pardon de Sainte-Anne' ('The Gangrel Rymour and the Pairdon of Sanct Anne') is a second *tour de force* to set beside 'The Twal'. The dedication to MacCaig is indicative of the collection's background in the linguistically brackish milieu of the later Scottish Renaissance; it is also a reminder that the next decade would see a swerve away from the more idealistic formulations of Scots and Scottish poetry prevalent at this time. With this in mind, and despite the various collections Smith published over the next decade and a half, it is tempting to see a book like *Figs and Thistles* as in a sense the swansong of the Scottish Renaissance project, at least in terms of its more overtly MacDiarmidian inclinations. The translation begins as follows:

> Sainit is the fouthless shore
> Whar, like the sea, aa is nude,
> Hailie is the fremmit kirk
> O' Sanct Anne-de-la-Palud,
>
> O' the Guidwife Sanct Anne,
> Guid-Auntie til the bairnie Jesus,
> In the rotten wuid o her soutane
> Rich, mair rich nor Croesus.
>
> By her, the shelpit wee Virgin,
> A spindle, onwytes the *Angelus*;
> Joseph, wi his candle, skouks in a neuk,
> Nane nou to fête his sanctliness.
>
> SMITH: 1975, 119

From the French original:

> Bénite est l'infertile plage
> Où, comme la mer, tout est nud.
> Sainte est la chapelle sauvage

De Sainte-Anne-de-la-Palud....
De la Bonne Femme Sainte Anne,
Grand'tante du petit Jesus,
En bois pourri dans sa soutane
Riche ... plus riche que Crésus!

Contre elle la petit Vierge,
Fuseau frêle, attend l'Angelus;
Au coin, Joseph tenant son cierge,
Niche, en saint qu'on ne fête plus...

CORBIÈRE, 128

Smith's translation, like the French, is written in loose tetrameters, sticking closely to the meaning and linear structure of Corbière's poem. By doing so, he writes a translation which, through its close adherence to the Breton poet's curious blend of liminal and littoral imagery, infuses his Scots poem with a doubled strangeness. In the first line, Corbière describes the shoreline near the chapel of Saint Anne as 'bénite', that is to say, consecrated or blessed. He develops this description in the second line, informing the reader that everything on this wild Atlantic shore is 'nud', bare. By translating 'bénite' as 'sainit' and 'nud' as 'nude', Smith sets the poem firstly in an archaising and domestic field of reference, where, as in medieval Scottish religion, blessed things are 'sainit'. The word nude, as opposed to bare, adds a pathetic fallacy to the description of the Scots 'fouthless shore' – which is not simply an empty space, but one in which the nakedness of the human before a Godless creation becomes apparent.

The poem concludes with the image of the ragged rhapsodist of the title – an old woman 'cried Miserie' in Smith's version, 'Misère' in Corbière's original. She wanders the country singing ballads for a half-farthing – '*L'Istoyre de la Magdaleyne, | Du Juif-Errant* ou d'*Abaylar*' (Corbière, 135), tales Smith translates as '*The Ballant o the Vagabone Yid,| Abelard,* or *The Magdalen*' (Smith: 1975, 125). The archaic spelling of 'histoire' ('ballant' is an appropriate equivalent) is significant, given the strongly medieval overtones of the whole poem.

With her trove of medieval ballads, 'La Rapsode' is explicitly identified as a tradition bearer, providing a strong symbol for Smith's cultural and linguistic preoccupations. In this context one might recall Iain Crichton Smith's cognate preoccupation with the old woman on the margins of the community. Though very different in tone to Corbière's poem, the Socratic dialogue *Ion* investigates the nature of the eponymous rhapsodist's skill, concluding that it is not learnt or acquired, but ultimately divine in origin (Plato, 47–65). Not himself a poet, Ion is presented as having a very limited understanding of the Homeric material he has memorised and performs. There is, moreover, a slightly mocking aspect to the urbane manner in which Socrates leads the rhapsodist towards an admission of his own lack of independent skill. Smith would, no doubt, have disagreed profoundly with this view of the folk tradition, feeling that figures like his 'gangrel rymour' are on the contrary in possession of extremely valuable skills of memory and performance, sustaining aspects of the tradition which would otherwise pass out of existence.

Translation was a very important aspect of Smith's writing, allowing him to make links with other cultural moments and voices with whom he was in sympathy. As well as extending his poetry into new areas, his translations can be read in terms of a desire to resist a narrowly provincial nationalism in favour of a more cosmopolitan approach – an adventurous re-ordering of Scottish literature which sought to bring the Scots language into closer contact with other tongues and traditions. In *Figs and Thistles* one also sees him using translations, dedicated to Sitwell, MacCaig and MacDiarmid, as a means of publicly identifying himself not just with foreign writers, but with a community of Scottish (and in Sitwell's case English) poets. This practice of using translation to public signal identification with a gifted contemporary is also evident in the MacLean translation.

In *The Translator's Invisibility*, his polemical history of translation into English from the Renaissance to the 1990s, Lawrence Venuti argues that, since at least the early 17th century, Anglophone translation has been dominated by what might be described as ideals of fluency and domestication (Venuti, 2). Domesticating the source, 'a fluent translation masquerades as true semantic equivalence [...] reducing if not simply excluding the very difference that translation is called upon to convey' (Venuti, 21). In the face of such fluent strategies, Venuti advocates a resistant, foreignising approach which 'seeks to restrain the ethnocentric violence of translation' by somehow recreating the otherness of the source text in the target language.

In Venuti's terms, Smith's Scots translations could be viewed as foreignising, re-imagining the source in a partially synthetic language, whose orthography and vocabulary distinguish it from Standard English. On the other hand, for a native Scots speaker, such a text might well be experienced as domesticating, whereas Standard English would be the foreignising medium. As John Corbett writes: 'The choice of Scots – and particularly the choice of literary Scots, or Lallans – allows the Scottish writer a medium of translation that is simultaneously foreignising and domesticating' (Corbett, 185). It is also interesting to note that for some 20th century poets, fluency within the Scots language was itself a highly desirable, if perhaps only partially achievable goal – the goal of translation into a semi-synthetic form of the language being in part to extend the range of spoken Scots.

The famous binary between domestication and foreignisation is, one might conclude, a theory of translation which, while useful, has certain inbuilt limitations. Appropriately enough then, Smith seems to have had a strong sense of the limits of the translator's art, as well as its more expansive possibilities. He touches upon this subject in a letter to Young sent sometime in March 1943, returning the latter's version of MacLean's 'An Cuilithionn' with praise, but also tentatively suggesting that Young do a little more work on the text. Smith discusses the way in which his own recent experience of translation from the Polish has taught him how difficult it can be to adequately render another author's work into one's own language – unless the translator feels so strongly in spiritual and mental sympathy with the foreign writer that the poem slips seamlessly into their oeuvre. In the latter case he feels that the translation often renders the foreign text less faithfully, but on the other hand achieves a greater degree of aesthetic excitement.[5] Drawing a clear distinction between freedom and fidelity, Smith finds a tension between the wishes of the reader – whom he feels will be happiest with a relatively smooth, domesticating translation which purports to provide comparatively unmediated access to the original – and the poet's own wishes, which in his case tend more towards foreignising creative imitation. Smith goes on to suggest that, while MacLean manages to escape the worst of this due to the difference in situation as regards Gaelic, Anglophone or Scots translators have to be careful with his work lest they fall into the trap of easy sentimentality and *faux*-vatic furore.

In light of these comments and the small, carefully curated body of works collected in his various volumes, it would be possible to detect a certain diffidence in Smith's critical presentation of his translations – even a doubt as to the ultimate value of his work in this area. The dearth of Smith translations post-1959 can also be seen in relation to the movement of MacDiarmid-inspired synthetic Scots away from the centre of Scottish poetry in the 1960s. Nevertheless, Smith's translations constitute an important intervention in the twentieth-century Scottish cultural landscape – and one which ought to be foregrounded in the context of this volume's timely attempt to redress the deep neglect into which his writing has fallen.

### Bibliography

Apollinaire, Guillaume, 'La Jolie Rousse' in Marcel Adéma & Michel Décaudin (eds.), *Oeuvres Poétiques* (Paris: Gallimard, 1956), p. 1104. See also pp. 313–314.

---

5    See Acc. 6419/38b, National Library of Scotland.

Begg, Ian & Hendry, Joy (eds.), *The Drawings of Sydney Goodsir Smith* (Edinburgh: Chapman for The New Auk Society, 1998).

Blok, Aleksandr, 'The Twelve' in Jon Stallworthy & Peter France, trans., *Selected Poems* (Manchester: Carcanet, 2000), p. 94.

Corbett, John, *Written in the Language of the Scottish Nation: A History of Literary Translation into Scots* (Clevedon: Multilingual Matters, 1999).

Corbière, Tristan, *Les Amours Jaunes* (Paris: Gallimard, 1953).

Dumas, Marcelle & Lucien Scheler (eds.) Éluard, Paul, *Oeuvres Complètes*, Vol. I (Paris: Gallimard, 1968).

Grieve, Michael & W.R. Aitken (eds.) *The Complete Poems of Hugh MacDiarmid* (Harmondsworth: Penguin, 1985).

Jelinek, Ivan, 'To the Czech Language', Edwin Muir, trans., *Modern Poetry in Translation*, No. 17 (2001), p. 167.

MacCaig, Norman, 'A Living Poetry', *Poetry (Chicago)*, Vol. 96 / No. 5 (August), pp. 320–322.

MacLean, Sorley (MacGill-Eain, Somhairle), 'An Trom-laighe' / 'The Nightmare' in Emma Dymock & Christopher Whyte (eds.), *Caoir Gheal Leumraich / White Leaping Flame: Collected Poems* (Edinburgh: Polygon, 2011), pp. 181–183.

Morgan Edwin, *Wi the Haill Voice: 25 Poems by Vladimir Mayakovsky* (Manchester: Carcanet, 1972; 2016), p. 19.

Plato, *Early Socratic Dialogues*, Trevor J. Saunders, ed. & trans. (Harmondsworth: Penguin, 1987).

Smith, Sydney Goodsir 'The Bonnie Reidheid' & 'Open-Air' in *The Voice of Scotland*, Vol.5, No.1 (September 1948), pp. 28–29.

Smith, Sydney Goodsir, *Collected Poems: 1941–1975* (London: John Calder, 1975).

Smith, Sydney Goodsir, *The Deevil's Waltz* (Glasgow: William Maclellan, 1946).

Smith, Sydney Goodsir *Figs and Thistles* (Edinburgh and London: Oliver and Boyd, 1959).

Smith, Sydney Goodsir, *Under the Eildon Tree: a poem in XXIV elegies* (Edinburgh: Serif, 1948; 2nd revised edition 1954).

Smith, Sydney Goodsir, Manuscript material consulted: Acc. 10397/20 (Smith's introduction to BBC Third Programme feature on Alexander Blok) in the National Library of Scotland.

Venuti, Lawrence, *The Translator's Invisibility: A History of Translation* (London: Routledge, 1995).

Villon, François, *Poems*, French text with translations by Peter Dale (London: Anvil, 2001).

Wilson, Susan R., ed., *The Correspondence Between Hugh MacDiarmid and Sorley MacLean* (Edinburgh: Edinburgh University Press, 2010).

Young, Douglas, Manuscript material consulted: Acc. 6419/38b (letters from various correspondents incl. Smith) in the National Library of Scotland.

# CHAPTER 8

# Sydney Goodsir Smith: Gangrel Rymour, European Scot

*Tom Hubbard*

## Abstract

Sydney Goodsir Smith fused an acquired mastery of Scots with a mainland-European cultural sophistication. The pedigree of his notion of the 'gangrel buddie' is traced briefly in Hugh MacDiarmid and in Russian literature, as in Dostoevsky's archetype of the 'undergound man' and in Pushkin's and Goncharov's 'superfluous man', as well as in Garcia Lorca, the subject of a poem by Smith. He also finds an affinity with French poetry, especially in the vagabond mode, e.g. Tristan Corbière, translated into Scots by Smith. This chapter goes on to argue, against charges of his supposed dilettantism that Smith's deep social conscience led him to identify with those from wartime Europe (especially from Poland) who suffered from displacement and exile. Like his contemporary Edwin Muir, Smith wrote poetry about refugees; both he and Muir had witnessed, in Germany and Austria, the early trappings of fascism and anti-semitism.

## Keywords

Europe – internationalism – translation – Scottish Renaissance – Russian literature – Dostoevsky – Pushkin – Goncharov – French poetry – Tristan Corbière – World War II – fascism

Certain European mythical archetypes, and explicitly those considered by Søren Kierkegaard to be prominent ones, are invoked in Smith's 'more-than-novel' *Carotid Cornucopius*. The closing paragraphs of this essay argue that, as in his novel, the poem-sequence *Under the Eildon Tree* 'offers us a grand tour of European cultural landmarks – by way of the Black Bull howff (pub) at the top of Leith Walk'.

> The wan leafs shak' atour us like the snaw.
> Here is the cavaburd in which Earth's tint.

> There's naebody but Oblivion and us,
> Puir gangrel buddies, waunderin' hameless in't.
>> MACDIARMID: 1987, 160

The scene is a snowstorm, and a drunken Scotsman is trying to find his way home. He addresses his companion, who is no less a personage than Fyodor Dostoevsky. These two poor lost souls cannot even communicate satisfactorily with each other – the wind rises and separates them. The drunk man tries to address his eminent friend through weather that is typically Russian and typically Scottish. 'I ken nae Russian and ye ken nae Scots' [I know no Russian and you know no Scots] (MacDiarmid: 1987, 160). The drunk man could almost be talking about our own times, about the enormous gap in experience between the Far West and the Far East of Europe.

Yet this point in Hugh MacDiarmid's masterpiece, *A Drunk Man Looks at the Thistle* (1926), needs to be set beside the poet's lifelong strategy of bringing diverse cultures together: this could be viewed both sympathetically and mockingly by his friend and fellow-makar Sydney Goodsir Smith in his own key-work, *Under the Eildon Tree* (1948/1954): 'And sae we come by a route maist devious / Til the far-famed Aist-West Synthesis! / Beluved by Hugh that's beluved by me' (Smith: 1975, 155).

A major MacDiarmid scholar, Kenneth Buthlay, has commented on the stanza quoted above. He relates MacDiarmid's 'gangrel buddies' – meaning, roughly, vagabond persons – to Dostoyevsky's 'skitalets'. 'Skitalets' is an intellectual wanderer, without a home, as described by Dostoyevsky in his Pushkin speech of 1880; here, Dostoevsky refers specifically to Pushkin's *Eugene Onegin*:

> [...] in the remote heart of his motherland he is in exile, not at home. He knows not what to undertake, and feels as if he were a guest in his own home. Later, when he roams, seized with anguish for his own land, in foreign countries and among strangers, as an unquestionably clever and sincere man he feels even more a stranger to himself. True, he, too, loves his country, but he does not trust it. Of course, he has heard about its ideals but he has no faith in them. He merely believes in an utter impossibility of any kind of work in his native land, and he looks upon the few – now as heretofore – who believe in this possibility with a sad smile.
>> DOESTOEVSKY, 971

We could earlier meet MacDiarmid's 'gangrel buddies' in Robert Burns's cantata *The Jolly Beggars*. Here are the rejected, the outcasts, the drinkers and vagabonds who rail at and mock the blandness, the oppressiveness, the

respectability of the Establishment. They're considerably less elegant and ur-
bane, than Eugene Onegin. They've got more in common with Dostoyevsky's
own characters, like the Underground Man in his short novel *Notes from the
Underground* (1864). That most archetypal of wandering Scots, Robert Louis
Stevenson, knew such people from his rebellious days in the labyrinth of Edin-
burgh's Old Town: Mr. Hyde challenging Dr. Jekyll.

Sydney Goodsir Smith was born in New Zealand, but came to Scotland as a
child, when his father was appointed Professor of Medicine at Edinburgh Uni-
versity. The son became a kind of latter-day Robert Louis Stevenson. He com-
bined a cultured, aristocratic manner with a dark, earthy Scots idiom; the stars
reflected in the gutter. A gangrel Onegin, or, rather, another figure from Russian
literature: Oblomov. Smith comically identified himself with Oblomov, the ex-
ample of the 'superfluous man' archetype in Goncharov's novel. Note again
that line in the MacDiarmid stanza: 'There's naebody but Oblivion and us' –
Oblivion, Oblomov: the word-play could not be more resonant. Here is Smith,
addressing one of the alcoholic denizens of Edinburgh's Grassmarket, in 'The
Grace of God and the Meth-Drinker':

> There ye gang, ye daft
> And doitit dotterel, ye saft
> Crazed outland skalrag saul
> In your bits and ends o winnockie duds
> Your fyled and fozie-fousome clouts
> As fou 's a fish, crackt and craftie-drunk
> Wi bleerit reid-rimmed
> Ee and slaveran crozie mou
> Dwaiblan owre the causie like a ship [...]
>                                                        There
> - But for the undeemous glorie and grace
> O' a mercifu omnipotent majestic God
> Superne eterne and sceptred in the firmament [...]
> But for the 'bunesaid unsocht grace,
>     unprayed-for,
> Undeserved
>             Gangs,
>                 Unregenerate,
>                         Me.

SMITH: 1975, 94–95

So there's distance from, as well as identification with, the meth drinker: a curi-
ous contradiction.

As a privileged product of the upper middle-classes, Smith was naturally drawn to those on the fringes of, or outside, the society in which he had been raised, such as those in the travelling community. The tinks, gypsies, travelling people – they have many names, those they give themselves and those conferred upon them, and they have their own oral culture that Hamish Henderson and his colleagues have documented in the School of Scottish Studies at Edinburgh University. It is fitting that Smith wrote a Scots lament for the tragic Spanish poet Federico Garcia Lorca – 'Ye bard o the tinks, o gipsy Spain, / Frae Granada, frae Granada, / Aa the gangrel folk that scorn chains – O wae for Garcia Lorca!' (Smith: 2017, 82).

A wandering Scot? The irony is that Smith chose to root himself and his poetry in Edinburgh, a relationship as deep in its way as that of Lorca to Andalusia. Smith's physical wandering from his native New Zealand ended in Edinburgh. Spiritually, however, he was always the gangrel: his poetry has a European range of cultural reference. A left-wing nationalist, he would still have been a rebel even if his ideals were realised – he has a poem called 'Perpetual Opposition' (Smith 1975: 99). Against the po-faced conformists, his poetry is an irreverent blend of melancholy and merriment; he is a Scottish Arlecchino (the original *commedia dell'arte* version of the harlequin), a one-man carnival of the north.

During the closing years of the 19th century, the pomposities of established poetic diction were increasingly challenged by those who were alert to the speech of the common folk. In France, a number of poets were discovering the power of *argot*, notably the Breton-born poet Tristan Corbière (1845–75), Jehan Rictus (1867–1933) and Robert Louis Stevenson's pen-pal Marcel Schwob (1867–1905). From his Leith Walk peregrinations Smith would surely have found a fellow-spirit in the speaker of Rictus's 'La Charlotte prie Notre-Dame durant la nuit du Réveillon':

> J'suis là, Saint'-Vierge, à mon coin d'rue
> ou d'pis l'apéro, j'bats la semelle;
> j'suis qu'eune ordur', qu'eun fill' perdue,
> c'est la Charlotte qu'on m'appelle.
>      RICTUS, 96[1]

In Corbière's long poem 'La Rapsode foraine et le pardon de Sainte Anne' Smith found a blend of popular Catholic piety and rough-tongued irony. I suspect

---

1 Trans. by present author: 'I'm there, Holy Mother of God, at my street corner / where the worse for drink, / I wear out my sole[s] / I'm just a turd, a fallen woman, / They call me Charlotte'.

that he must have found this a relief from Scots Presbyterian couthieness. Cor-
bière's poem, like Rictus's, doesn't address the saint with the stockbroking unc-
tuosity of 'Whatever Lord we give to thee / Repaid a thousandfold shall be', but
on terms of near-equality, a weird blend of respect and cheek, of the affection-
ate and the gallus (bold). This spirit belongs also to Smith's version of Corbière:

> O, Mither hackit frae hairt o aik,
> Dour and guid, wi dunts o an axe,
> Aneath the gowd o her robe she derns
> Luve in the likeness o Breton francs!
>
> —Auld Greenie wi the face worn
> Like a stane wi the fluid,
> Runkelt wi the tears o luve,
> Crynit wi the greit o bluid!
> > SMITH: 1975, 120

Smith transcreates the title as 'The Gangrel Rymour and the Pairdon of Sanct
Anne' so that we are more aware of gangrels (vagabonds) than of sancts (saints).
During a 1995 talk to the Robert Henryson Society at the Abbot House, Dun-
fermline, the poet, and a contemporary of Smith's, George Bruce emphasised
the compassion, and the sense of community, which distinguishes the creator
of *The Testament of Cresseid* and his successors in the Scots tradition. Smith is
a true heir of Henryson and the makars; his Corbière bears witness to that:

> *Hae ruth for the mither-lassie*
> *And the bairn at the roadside...*
> *Gin onie cast a stane*
> *Gar it cheynge intil breid!* [...]
>
> Efter vespers, amang the lave
> Sprent wi hailie water, a cadaver
> Thrives, livan by leprosie,
> —Memento o some crusader... [...]
>
> Gin ye should meet wi her, makar,
> Wi her auld sodjer's poke:
> It's our sister ... gie her — it's holidays —
> A bit baccy, for a smoke!
> > SMITH: 1975, 121, 123 & 125

Henryson had presented his Cresseid, the beauty turned prostitute turned leper, with neither self-righteousness nor patronage but with love. In *Axel's Castle* (1931), the American critic Edmund Wilson portrays Corbière the man: 'In Paris, he slept all day and spent the nights in the cafés or at his verses, greeting at dawn the Paris harlots as they emerged from the station house or the hotel with the same half-harsh, harsh-tender fellow-feeling for the exile from conventional society [...] Melancholy, with a feverishly active mind, full of groanings and vulgar jokes, he used to amuse himself by going about in convict's clothes and firing guns and revolvers out the window in protest against the singing of the village choir; and on one occasion, on a visit to Rome, he appeared in the streets in evening dress, with a mitre on his head and two eyes painted on his forehead, leading a pig decorated with ribbons' (Wilson, 94).

It is little wonder that Smith warmed to Corbière; and readers who have French are warmly urged to explore this further in Christopher Whyte's excellently argued and documented essay, 'Corbière, Laforgue et Goodsir Smith' (Whyte, 61–90). If Whyte links Smith to poets of late 19th century decadence, he is not the first to do so, as Hugh MacDiarmid a quarter-century earlier had observed that his friend's idiomatic Scots possessed 'transpontine inclusions from the vocabulary of the English poets of the 'nineties' (MacDiarmid: 1975, xi). Above all there are Smith's ubiquitous echoes of Ernest Dowson (1867–1900), notably of the latter's best-known poem, the widely anthologised 'Non sum qualis eram bonae sum regus Cynarae'. Smith deploys the much-quoted 'gone with the wind' as well as familiar points elsewhere in his poems such as 'Made when Boskie' with its refrain 'Yestreen, ah yesternicht' (Smith: 1975, 132). One recognises Smith's affinity with Dowson, that most cosmopolitan of 'nineties poets after Oscar Wilde, and a translator of yet another French 'gangrel rymour', Paul Verlaine.

It is not surprising, then, that Smith himself risks being labelled a decadent, a self-indulgent poseur, deliberately and wearily out of kilter with his times. This is not far off the stern judgment of Smith's fellow makar Tom Scott (1918–95), who was otherwise an admirer. Here, though, the assumed milieu is not 1890s Paris, but somewhere nearer home and of a more distant era: 'Sentimentality is the soft underbelly of Smith's work, failing it ultimately (so far) of major achievement. He lacks a grasp of certain basic social and spiritual realities, and has been infected by the Edinbourgeois vice of pretending to live in the 18th century, all conviviality and snuff-mulls, instead of the Age of Horror, all murderous warfare and man's inhumanity to man' (Scott, 52). I would argue, rather, that Smith's 'gangrel rymour' persona (as distinct from the masks of decadence) actually sustains and informs his deep social conscience. We have seen that already, latent in his transcreation of Corbière; beyond that, we have very strong evidence that he was far from indifferent to his own times. As someone born in 1915, he was a thinking and feeling adult in the 1930s and 1940s, and in his early life as man and artist eloquently alert to 'man's inhumanity to man' in Europe at so many points east of his Edinburgh base.

> They join thon fell grey press, the listless trail
> Alang the roads o Europe oozing a' these years, a bad flux -
>
> Across the drouth of Polska's steppes a black sun burned ye,
> Mows o brick gouped arid neth a brazen lyft,
> In winter rashed wi cavaburd, snaw-dinged tae deid white tumles [...]
>       SMITH: 1975, 15

These lines are from Smith's long poem 'The Refugees: a Complaynt', significantly dated October/November 1940. For such an early work, the Scots is not yet assured, but that is hardly the main point. Note, in particular, the image of the Polish steppes: the poet was not a combatant in the War, but he played his noble part in the war effort, as a teacher of English to Polish troops and refugees stationed in Scotland. He made Scots versions of two poems (one of which concerned the defence of Warsaw in 1939) by Stefan Borsukiewicz, who was killed during a training exercise near Manchester with the Polish parachute brigade (Smith: 1975, 49–50). Interestingly, another Borsukiewicz poem was translated into English by the Scottish poet Burns Singer (1928–64), who was of Polish and Jewish descent and who also admired the work of Smith (Peterkiewicz & Singer, 104). Note, too, the word 'cavaburd' (blizzard) which is also a natural threat to the 'puir gangrel buddies' in MacDiarmid's *A Drunk Man Looks at the Thistle*, as quoted at the beginning of this chapter.

Smith's poem can also be linked thematically to Edwin Muir's similarly titled poem 'The Refugees': 'We saw the homeless waiting in the street / Year after year, / The always homeless, / Nationless and nameless, / To whose bare roof-trees never come / Peace and the house martin to make a home' (Muir: 1963, 95). As a visual artist, Smith was witness to the pre-war Nazi presence, while travelling in southern Germany during 1936: these drawings still have the power to shock, with their depictions of everyday life – the dancing and the drinking – all underway beneath the swastika flags and portraits of Hitler (Begg & Hendry, 80–89). He was not the only Scottish writer to document such incongruities. Edwin Muir, again, was an alert recorder of 1930s Austria, while visiting 'that lovely provincial town' of Salzburg: 'In a *café* we came across a little local paper called *Der Eiserne Besen*, the Iron Broom. It contained nothing but libelous charges against local Jews, set down with great rancour' (Muir: 1964, 214). Clearly Smith was writing at a time when the concept of 'gangrel buddies', far from referring to frivolous decadence, could potentially acquire a darkly ironic meaning as vast numbers of civilians were on the move across Europe, in fear for their lives. Indeed, he was in the company of those Scottish 'gangrel rymours', as it were, who have left us their own witness of the war years – Smith's close friends Sorley MacLean, Robert Garioch, Hamish Henderson, who all saw action in North Africa. As for Muir, he would return to central Europe and be on the spot when Stalinism took hold of post-war Czechoslovakia.

In 1976 Raymond Williams brought out a book, *Keywords*, which interrogated various terms that that had entered social and political discourse. It may be that 'exile' was considered too nebulous for inclusion, but together with its French cognate 'exil' it became a buzzword throughout the 19th and 20th centuries, not least in literary usage. For the French poet Charles Baudelaire, to whom Smith alludes frequently in his writings, the artist was an 'exil' in a materialistic, philistine society, and his image of the noble albatross, mocked by crass sailors, was piously and explicitly intended as an objective correlative for just that. In literary descent from Baudelaire is Verlaine, who in his *Poèmes saturniens* (1866) is even more emphatic, even defensive-aggressive, against bourgeois society's contempt for the 'Chanteurs': 'Le monde, que troublait leur parole profonde, / Les exile. A leur tour ils exilent le monde!' (Verlaine, 6).[2] It is a short step from this to James Joyce, himself steeped in a post-Baudelairean, Symbolist-elitist aesthetic, though in his case the tone is a subtle blend of approval and mockery of such – as when he wears his Stephen Dedalus mask, famously, regarding the artist's need for 'silence, exile, and cunning'. Joyce's only play is actually titled *Exiles* (1918), in which the writer Richard Rowan pronounces portentously: 'There is an economic exile and there is a spiritual exile' – as if there were an equivalence between desperate migrancy and the alienation of the 'Chanteurs' (Joyce, 129). For a number of personae in the fiction of Joseph Conrad, whose father fought Tsarist oppression in Poland, the prospect of leaving one's homeland is not one to be taken lightly; Yanko Goorall, the displaced central-European character in his short story 'Amy Foster' (1901) finds himself cast up among the mainly non-empathetic inhabitants of a southern English coastal village: 'It is indeed hard upon a man to find himself

---

2   Trans. by current author: 'The World, which their profound word[s] have troubled / Exiles / banishes them. In their turn, they exile / banish the World.

a lost stranger, helpless, incomprehensible, and of a mysterious origin, in some obscure corner of the earth' (Conrad, 113).

Although Smith has a poem with the title 'Exile', and its lovelorn persona suggests the 'spiritual' rather than the 'economic' or political sense, the point is hardly laboured in what is after all a minor piece in the poet's œuvre; far more pertinent is his application of the word to the politically persecuted, such as the great Scottish socialist activist John Maclean (see 'The Pricks' – Smith: 1975, 48–49 – for instance). Smith is generally closer to the 'Conrad' than to the 'Baudelaire-Verlaine-Joyce' end of the spectrum (despite his affinity with Joyce in the wordplay of his only published novel *Carotid Cornucopius* (1964), which is surely the Scottish *Finnegans Wake* and is discussed at length in the present volume by Richie McCaffery). Smith was never an 'exile' in any serious sense, and thus does not quite fit the Dostoevskian 'skitalets' model of a homeless alien even in his own homeland. Edinburgh was very much his lifetime milieu, the New Zealand birth apart. Certainly he was the resident sceptic, the eloquently gravel-voiced rebel, hilarious at the expense of the exploitative 'mongers' and the buttoned-up bourgeoisie of his city, though with an edginess that prevented him becoming the court jester. He resists being patronised as the wrong-headed yet lovable 'character' of Auld Reekie: his left-wing, pro-Scottish independence sympathies would be anathema to the reactionaries, 'the dour douce folk' (Smith: 1975, 21). As a cultured cosmopolitan he did not so much bring Edinburgh to Europe as bring Europe to Edinburgh, and in this he is not far off the original ethos of city's International Festival (EIF), which was an initiative of the phoenix-like mood of the post-war years. Smith possessed a deep and wide appreciation of classical music, as part of his vast knowledge of the continent's artistic riches, and his 1940 'Ode to Hector Berlioz, 1803–1869' (Smith: 1975, 6–8) anticipates the historic staging of that composer's *Les Troyens*, co-produced by Scottish Opera at the 1969 EIF. His friend the Scottish composer Ronald Stevenson (1928–2015), a man of similar European and international culture, once remarked to me (half in jest) that he dared not pick up Smith's *Collected Poems* as he would not be able to stop himself from setting one piece after another to music.

*Carotid Cornucopius*, Smith's more-than-novel, is a labyrinth of allusion to *Weltliteratur*, leading the reader hither and thither by means of endlessly suggestive macaronic (and Mac-Ironical!) wordplay deriving from his stream-of-consciousness of the howff (pub). In 'Caput Fowr or Quart Fitt', the Danish philosopher and father of existentialism, Søren Kierkegaard, is invoked for his citation of three great European archetypes – Don Juan / Giovanni, Ahasuerus the Wandering Jew, and Faust (Smith: 1964, 88). In a sense Smith contained this trinity within himself, as lover, stravaiger (wanderer across Europe in the 1930s), and as restless scholar (*Carotid Cornucopius* is prefaced with the lines 'By Geck and by Goak / I'll be Faust in this Boke') (Smith: 1964, 9). We noted earlier his comical identification, via Oblomov, with the Russian archetype of the 'superfluous man', which itself is an Eastern counterpart to the Baude-lairean *flâneur*, and Smith didn't need to travel further than the Edinburgh howffs in order to fulfil that role. 'The crowd is his element', wrote Baudelaire in his essay 'The Painter of Modern Life', 'as the air is that of birds and water of fishes. His passion and his profession are to become one flesh with the crowd. For the perfect *flâneur*, for the passionate spectator, it is an immense joy to set up house in the heart of the multitude, amid the ebb and flow of movement, in the midst of the fugitive and the infinite' (Baudelaire, 9).

The poem-sequence *Under the Eildon Tree* is more than a *Carotid-Cornuco-pius*-in-verse, but it also offers us a grand tour of European cultural landmarks – by way of the Black Bull howff at the top of Leith Walk. The stravaiger always returns to the Scottish capital; not absinthe, but whisky, is his liquid music, even if this Scots poem here and there serves up a cocktail of other languages.

One cultural marker in *Under the Eildon Tree* deserves special attention in the present context: that of the legendary stravaiger between paganism and piety, Tannhäuser. He is best known to us by means of Wagner's eponymous opera, and in 19th century literature the tradition of his long séjour in the Ve-nusberg (aka Hörselberg or Mons Veneris) was taken up by the likes of Alger-non Swinburne, John Davidson and Aubrey Beardsley. It is Smith, however, who significantly juxtaposes this with Scotland's own seven-year visitor to his own country's Borders equivalent to the Venusberg:

> [...] True Tammas
>   Neth the Eildons steers again;
>  As the sand rins in the gless, aince mair
>    Tannhäuser, blae and wan as sin –
>    As I, depairts frae Horselberg,
>  Lane and weirdless [...].
>      SMITH: 1975, 185

As ever, Smith draws a direct line between Scotland and the rest of Europe.

The poet and verse dramatist Bill Dunlop (1951–2017) was a true heir to Smith, rooted in his beloved Edinburgh and committed to the fusion of Euro-pean lore and Scots expression. Dunlop's *Klytemnestra's Bairns*, his version of Aeschylus, won plaudits in 1990 on the performance of its first act at the

Edinburgh Festival Fringe. At his funeral in November 2017, *Chapman* editor Joy Hendry's moving eulogy quoted Dunlop's 'Afterword' to the published text of the play: he had concluded this with a remark on 'our potentially limitless capacity for what we too often choose to believe lies beyond our capabilities – understanding and compassion' (Dunlop, 57). These qualities belonged to Smith, a man and artist both loved and admired, the possessor of a roguish wisdom grown from his empathetic experience of peoples and cultures dispossessed, both in Scotland and beyond.

## Bibliography

Baudelaire, Charles, *The Painter of Modern Life and Other Essays*, Jonathan Mayne, trans. & ed. (London: Phaidon, 1995).

Begg, Ian & Hendry, Joy (eds.), *The Drawings of Sydney Goodsir Smith, Poet* (Edinburgh & East Linton: Chapman Publishing for the New Auk Society, 1998).

Conrad, Joseph, *Typhoon and Other Stories* (London: Heinemann, 1903).

Dostoevsky, Fyodor, *The Diary of a Writer*, Boris Brasol, trans. & ed. (New York: Braziller, 1954).

Dunlop, Bill, *Klytemnestra's Bairns* (Edinburgh: diehard, 1993).

Joyce, James, *Exiles* (London: NEL Signet Modern Classics, 1968).

MacDiarmid, Hugh, *A Drunk Man Looks at the Thistle: Annotated Edition by Kenneth Buthlay* (Edinburgh: Scottish Academic Press, 1987).

MacDiarmid, Hugh, 'Introduction' in Sydney Goodsir Smith, *Collected Poems* (London: John Calder, 1975), pp. xi–xiv.

Muir, Edwin, *An Autobiography* (London: Methuen, 1964).

Muir, Edwin, 'The Refugees' in *The Collected Poems* (London: Faber and Faber, 1963), p. 95.

Peterkiewicz, Jerzy & Singer, Burns, eds. & trans., *Five Centuries of Polish Poetry* (London: Oxford University Press, 1970).

Rictus, Jehan, 'La Charlotte prie Notre-Dame Durant la nuit du Réveillon' in *Le Cœur populaire* (Var: Editions d'Aujourd'hui, 1981), p. 96.

Scott, Tom (ed.), 'Introduction' to *The Penguin Book of Scottish Verse* (London: Penguin Books / Allen Lane, 1970), pp. 27–56.

Smith, Sydney Goodsir, *Carotid Cornucopius* (Edinburgh: Macdonald, 1964).

Smith, Sydney Goodsir, *Collected Poems 1941–1975* (London: John Calder, 1975).

Smith, Sydney Goodsir, 'In Granada, In Granada' in J. Derrick McClure (ed.), *A Kist o Skinklan Things: An Anthology of Scots Poetry from the First and Second Waves of the Scottish Renaissance* (Glasgow: Association for Scottish Literary Studies, 2017), p. 82.

Verlaine, Paul, 'Chanteurs' in *Oeuvres completes Vol. 1* (Paris: Vanier, 1900), p. 6.

Whyte, Christopher, 'Corbière, Laforgue et Goodsir Smith' in David Kinloch & Richard Price (eds.), *La nouvelle alliance: influences francophones sur la littérature moderne* (Grenoble: ELLUG, 2000), pp. 61–90.

Wilson, Edmund, *Axel's Castle: A Study in the Imaginative Literature of 1870–1930* (New York: Charles Scribner's Sons, 1931).

# CHAPTER 9

# Unreal Edinburgh: From Li Po to Kynd Kittock

*John Corbett*

### Abstract

Smith returns repeatedly to the subject of Edinburgh. In poems such as 'To Li Po in the Delectable Mountains of Tien-Mu', 'Gowdspink in Reekie' and, 'Kynd Kittock's Land' (a poem for television on which he collaborated with the photographer Alan Daiches), he attempts a synthesis of the 'unreal', contemporary city of modernist poetry and the historical capital whose vibrant representation in literature stretches back through Fergusson and Burns in the 18th century, to Dunbar and his fellow mediaeval makars. This synthesis involves an integration of opposites, not least the alienation of High modernism versus the sociability of the Enlightenment, and the demands of elite versus popular culture. This chapter considers how Smith resolves, or at least balances, these contradictions.

### Keywords

Edinburgh – *Kynd Kittock's Land* – *Gowdspink in Reekie* – modernism – Robert Fergusson – television – photography – Enlightenment

Sydney Goodsir Smith is often described as a poet of Edinburgh. In this respect, he is an heir of two apparently dissonant traditions. On the one hand, he inherits the sociable tradition typified by the 18th century vernacular revivalist, Robert Fergusson, a selection of whose poems Smith edited and who appears as the dedicatee of the first of three poems that might all be described as a spectral pub crawls around the capital city. The spirit of Fergusson's poetry haunts all three poems. On the other hand, Smith inhabits the role of the alienated modernist poet observing the 'unreal city', as does Eliot in 'The Waste Land', Hart Crane in 'The Bridge' and William Carlos Williams in 'Paterson'. 'To Li Po in the Delectable Mountains of Tien-Mu' (1950) can be seen as initiating a three poem sequence that continues with 'Gowdspink in Reekie' (first published in 1955, and republished with minor changes in 1974, this poem recalls the titles of Fergusson's 'Ode to the Gowdspink' and 'Auld Reekie'), and culminates in 'Kynd Kittock's Land'. A short version of the last of these poems was commissioned for and broadcast in a BBC television series entitled 'Poets' Places' in 1965 before an extended version was published later that year in book form. Each of these poems follows Fergusson's 'Auld Reekie' in giving a picaresque view of Edinburgh, but each also conforms to and adapts a set of conventions that were firmly established in the first wave of high modernist literature from the early 20th century onwards. By the time Smith was writing, and certainly by 1965, these tropes had lost their innovatory edge – the subversively modernist had become the canonically familiar. Nevertheless, as Christopher Whyte observes in a discussion of Smith's poetry, the adoptive Scot's work, even in the 1950s and 1960s, owes as much to the earlier poetry of Ezra Pound and T.S. Eliot, published four decades beforehand, as to those of his friends and Scottish contemporaries, Hugh MacDiarmid and Robert Garioch (Whyte, 109–117). This chapter focuses on 'To Li Po in the Delectable Mountains of Tien-Mu', 'Gowdspink in Reekie' (1974 version), and, in particular, 'Kynd Kittock's Land',[1] to flesh out the high modernist framework that largely informs Smith's oeuvre, and to suggest ways in which he domesticates the, by then familiar, tropes of early modernism by drawing on the neo-Horatian ethos of the 18th century vernacular revival in Scots poetry. The chapter concludes by reflecting on possible reasons why this poet continued to mine high modernist poetics almost half a century after Pound and Eliot had burst onto the literary scene.

The extended apostrophe, 'To Li Po in the Delectable Mountains of Tien-Mu' (hereafter 'To Li Po') immediately signals Smith's fascination with the roots of modernism, through its allusion to the poems contained in Ezra Pound's *Cathay* (1915). The publication of this slim anthology of free translations, mainly of classical Chinese poetry by Li Po (or 'Rihaku' in the Japanese form that Pound used), was one of the founding events of Western literary modernism. Li Po (AD 701–762) was one of the most venerated poets of the Tang dynasty (AD 618–907), a swashbuckling figure whose poems often celebrate the virtuous effects of wine. One poem attributed to him, 'Drinking alone in the moonlight', which is cited by Smith, late in 'To Li Po', in the line, 'Wildly drinkan alane by munelicht' (104), describes the merging of the moon, the speaker and his shadow during a night of solitary indulgence – the poem is clearly related to the legend that Li Po drowned on a boat trip, after drunkenly attempting to embrace the reflection of the moon in the water.

---

1   The page numbers in this chapter refer to the versions of the poems reprinted in Sydney Goodsir Smith, *Collected Poems* (London: John Calder, 1975).

For the reader of Scottish modernist poetry, the image also evokes the speaker's extended dialogues with the moonlight in MacDiarmid's *A Drunk Man Looks at the Thistle.* In addressing the poem to the shade of Li Po (a footnote tells us that the mountains of Tien Mu represent paradise; the Chinese character 天 'tian' means 'sky' or 'heaven'), Smith is foregrounding his modernist credentials. However, by dedicating the poem to Robert Fergusson, noted as being, like Li Po, 'in the Blythfu' Fields' of paradise, Smith also establishes a parallel, or even an equivalence, between classical Chinese poetry, the 18th century Scottish vernacular revival, Anglo-American modernism and Scots Renaissance verse from the time of MacDiarmid onwards. Smith brings Fergusson, Li Po and himself together in a hallucinatory moment towards the close of the poem (104), acknowledging that time differences have been elided in their nocturnal crawl around Edinburgh's pubs: 'Guidsakes, and I thocht, a moment, we three/ Were on the bash thegither!' The trope of co-opting historical figures in an ecstatic, ruminative odyssey around Edinburgh's bars and dives is repeated in 'Gowdspink in Reekie' (see, elsewhere in the present volume, Mario Relich's chapter on the influence on Smith of the Irish novelist, poet and playwright, Oliver Goldsmith, who is associated with the eponymous 'gowdspink', or 'goldfinch') and once again in 'Kynd Kittock's Land'. The domestic odyssey is itself, of course, a modernist conceit that has its greatest exponent in Joyce (for a discussion of Smith's Joycean fiction, *Carotid Cornucopius*, see Richie McCaffery's chapter in the present volume).

In these three poems, then, Smith plays variations on a, by then well-worn but still productive, theme, which has been described by commentators as 'the tradition of return'.[2] Jewel Spears Brooker observes that by 1965, the year in which 'Kynd Kittock's Land' was broadcast and published, literary modernism had 'run its course' and major critics such as Richard Ellmann, Charles Feidelson and Frank Kermode were beginning the business of defining the term, and charting its various undercurrents (Brooker, 58). While members of early or 'high' modernism were often at loggerheads – Crane and Williams' poems are in some respects critical response to Eliot's *The Waste Land*, and Virginia Woolf's dismissal, in her diary, of sections of James Joyce's *Ulysses* as 'the work of a queasy undergraduate scratching his pimples' is one of the more quotable moments of the contest for the soul of early modernism, although she also allowed that the work displayed 'genius' (Woolf, 57). Despite their quarrels, many

---

2    See, for example, Jeffrey M. Perl, *Tradition of Return: The Implicit History of Modern Literature.*
     (Princeton, NJ: Princeton University Press, 1984) and Jewel Spears Brooker, 'Transcendence
     and Return: T.S. Eliot and the Dialectic of Modernism' in *South Atlantic Review* 59.2 (1994),
     pp. 53–74.

prominent members of the first wave of high modernists shared what Brooker terms 'a defining characteristic [...], namely, the tendency to move forward by spiralling back and refiguring the past' (Brooker, 54). It is one of modernism's ironies that in order to 'make it new', in Pound's terms, the high modernist poets ransacked literary history and peppered their work with quotations or allusions to ancient Chinese poetry, Anglo-Saxon and Provençal troubadour verse, and poets such as Homer, Dante, Chaucer, Marvell and Shakespeare.[3] A corollary to the desire to 'move forward by spiralling back' is 'dispensationalism', the idea that civilisations are born, rise, mature and decay in stages, and that these stages are cyclical. If to progress is to return to an earlier period in history, then time zones can be elided, since, as Eliot argues in *Four Quartets*, the future is contained in the past, and all is eternally present. Brooker further observes:

> In *Heart of Darkness*, Conrad had provided an aerial view linking the most civilized – geographically, politically, psychologically, ethically, spiritually – with the most primitive. In *Les Demoiselles d'Avignon*, Picasso had invented cubism by combining primitive and modern in a single face, and in 'The Love Song of J. Alfred Prufrock', Eliot introduced an intellectual who was nauseated by culture, who identified more with crabs scuttling across the floors of silent seas than with refined ladies strolling across the floors of drawing rooms in Harvard.
>
> BROOKER, 58

Following firmly in the steps of the early high modernists, then, Smith, in each of the three poems considered in this chapter, effects a journey through an urban landscape that conflates historical periods whose traces are still present in the architecture of the Old Town. In 'To Li Po', the speaker and his drinking companions begin at the foot of the Canongate, in a pub opposite Queen Mary's Bathtub, by the Palace of Holyroodhouse, and continue up the Royal Mile on a drunken carouse until the company reaches home. History is continually evoked (102), as in the comparison between the drinkers' golden whisky and the fine embroidery of a displayed waistcoat, supposedly owned by Lord Darnley, consort to Mary, Queen of Scots:

---

3  Pound possibly took the phrase 'make it new' from the Scottish sinologist James Legge's account of 'a historical anecdote concerning Ch'eng T'ang [...] first king of the Shang dynasty (1766–1753 BC), who was said to have had a washbasin inscribed with this inspirational slogan'. See Michael North, 'The Making of 'Making it New'' *Guernica* (15 August 2013). Online at http://www.guernicamag.com/the-making-of-making-it-new/.

Ay, a crousie companie, a cheerie howff
And the whiskie was liquid ingots,
Dauds o the purest gowd!
– Like Darnley's broiderit wallicoat
There hingan on the waa.

In 'Gowdspink in Reekie' an address to the late Irish writer, Oliver Goldsmith blends into Smith's imagining him on a pub crawl around Edinburgh (a 'perembrodrouthie/ Possage through mine ain romantick toun'; 221), before the poets join together on a drinking spree that, it is implied, has happened before and will happen again (226):

Ay, says Ollie the bauld boyo when I tellt him,
I've heard it all before, and shall again
Doubtless – and ordered anither round.

In 'Kynd Kittock's Land' the mediaeval innkeeper, Kynd Kittock, a character from a poem sometimes attributed to William Dunbar, is a constant presence on another circuit around Edinburgh. In all three poems, then, there is movement forward by a return to earlier eras: Smith and his contemporary Scottish Renaissance companions can, appropriately, be imagined to be the likes of Li Po, Robert Fergusson and Oliver Goldsmith reborn. The idea of mid-20th century Edinburgh being a 'Historic throwgang o' the Modren Athens' might be dismissed as 'a lauch!' (221), but high modernist poetry still yearns for a return to earlier civilisations. Smith's literary medium itself is, as commentators have often noted, a self-consciously literary amalgam of older and contemporary Scots features. For example, Derrick McClure observes that Smith's 'mature verse shows an abundant skill in combining, or modulating between, an aureate register adorned with authentic or invented Middle Scots words, and a register approximating to expressive colloquial demotic' (McClure, 191). The resulting linguistic hybrid not only gives the reader or listener the impression of moving in and out of different time periods; it is an expression of faith that in returning Scots to its mediaeval past, the poet will release its potential for renewal.

If Stephen Dedalus speaks for all high modernists when he complains that 'history is a nightmare from which I am trying to awake' (Joyce, 40) then one might argue that, for Smith, history was a nightmare which he was drinking to forget. The particular means by which he attempts to erase historical difference in these poems is only in part by evoking spirits of the illustrious dead to join and his contemporary drinking companions ('Aa/ "Scholards an'

gennemen, beGode!'"; 101). The very acts of imbibing alcoholic spirits and en-
gaging in boisterous camaraderie and sexual adventure serve as a bulwark
against the mood of desolation conventionally prompted by the modernist
poet's acute sensitivity to the decay of society. In this respect, Smith departs
from at least some of his high modernist predecessors and draws instead on
the ethos of the poetry of the Scottish Enlightenment. He counters modernist
angst with the comfort of neo-Horatian clubability, the continuing legacy of
the homosocial ambience found in 18th century taverns where the bards of the
Scottish vernacular revival tried out their new rhymes and songs, and pro-
pounded Enlightenment ideas before a live audience of largely male compan-
ions, both critical and appreciative.

Smith invites the reader into the circle of 'scholards and gennemen' by fre-
quent apostrophe, and by referring to his companions, living and departed,
only obliquely, as if the reader is well-acquainted with them: in 'To Li Po' we
read of 'the Gowden Horde/ O' Hippogriphs, Hughs, Seceders and Hectors,/
Rab the Ranter and Rab Sir Precentor,/ Clunie and the Hunter Bard' as well as
William Dunbar (102–3). The identity of members of this motley crew can be
in part recovered: the two 'Rabs' are no doubt Burns and Fergusson; the 'Hunt-
er Bard' is likely to be Duncan Ban MacIntyre, the 18th century Gaelic poet who
lies buried in Edinburgh; at least one of the 'Hughs' must be Hugh MacDiarmid
and one of the 'Hectors' is likely to be Hector MacIver, a teacher at Edinburgh's
Royal High School and one of Smith's mentors; and 'Clunie' might be a refer-
ence to James Crichton of Clunie, known as 'the Admirable Crichton', a 16th
century polymath whose exploits were commemorated by one of Smith's fa-
vourite writers, Sir Thomas Urquhart of Cromarty.[4] In 'Gowdspink in Reekie'
the speaker drinks not only with 'Ollie' Goldsmith, or 'Gowdie', but also, at one
point, with Albert Einstein (227); and in 'Kynd Kittock's Land', the ghost of the
eponymous tavern keeper is joined by Robert Burns, Allan Ramsay, Robert
Fergusson, James Hogg ('the ghaist o' the Electric Shepherd'), their shades con-
jured by pub names, and several living members of the Scottish Renaissance –
Denis Peploe, Hugh MacDiarmid again ('Grieve'), Robert Garioch, Norman
MacCaig, Albert Mackie, Tom Scott and George Mackay Brown – as well as the
poem's readers ('you'). These characters are typically referred to by forename
or surname alone, or by nickname (Smith, of course, being the 'Auk', a flightless
bird, significantly extinct, which appears in a variety of literary works, from
Charles Kingsley's *The Water Babies* to Joyce's *Ulysses*). The effect of this is ei-
ther to exclude the reader from the intimate society of male drinkers, or, more

---

4 I am indebted to Richie McCaffery for suggestions as to the identity of some of these
figures.

generously, to include him (and the reader position is typically male and heterosexual, a point to which we shall return). Even so, the relative obscurity of the references is the probable reason why, in the televised version of 'Kynd Kittock's Land' the lines referring to the drinkers by name were largely excised, leaving only a brief mention of 'our friend the Resident' alongside a close-up of Tom Scott as a verbal and visual trace of the literary clique (Corbett, 272–275).

The effect of being immersed in an exclusive milieu, with its nicknames, secret language and arcane knowledge, is intensified by the high modernist poet's characteristic strategy of quotation. The three poems feature a collage of citations and near citations that – like Eliot's *The Waste Land* and Pound's *Cantos* – range widely over erudite and popular culture. In 'To Li Po' there is the aforementioned reference to Fergusson's 'Auld Reekie' alongside classical Chinese poetry via Pound's *Cathay*. Further citations in the text allude to Burns' song 'Is there for honest poverty'; William Dunbar's poem 'The Dance of the Seven Deadly Sins'; a mediaeval Scots ballad (Child 275, 'Get up and bar the door', also popularised by Burns as 'Johnie Blunt'); the *Rubáiyát of Omar Khayyám* by Edward Fitzgerald, which features 'Saki', a cup-bearer (102); and a parody of the popular music hall song, 'Abdul Abulbul Ameer', the original of which was written by Percy French in 1877. The version alluded to by Smith (102) probably refers to a bawdy parody that was popular with rugby fans. The Islamic, and specifically Turkish, references occur in a dreamlike section in which a mosque is superimposed on the Edinburgh skyline, complete with muezzin calling the faithful to prayer. The reference prompts a welter of references to 'the Terrible Turk', 'Bulbul Ameer' and the 'Gowden Horde'. The Golden Horde was originally a Turkicised khanate stretching from Eastern Europe to Siberia, but in the poem the phrase refers to the 'shennachies' who accompany Li Po and Smith on their crawl around the city. Smith might also be referring to a Hollywood epic, *The Golden Horde* (1951) in which a swashbuckling crusader unites with 'Princess Shalimar' (Ann Blyth) to defeat Genghis Khan's Tartars. The name 'Shalimar' also occurs in 'Kynd Kittock's Land', in an apostrophe to 'Black Rose of Shalimar' (211). It is perhaps no coincidence that *The Black Rose* (1950) was another swashbuckling movie in which Cecile Aubrey played the titular heroine in a similar mediaeval romp with an eastern setting: in this film, Tyrone Power plays a young, Saxon scholar who leaves England and joins the army of Kublai Khan on a campaign to conquer China.[5] Any reader, then, who recognises some or all of these the references is implicitly invited to become an insider, a knowing member of Smith's 'touzie tregallion o tykes', a

---

5   Both films are discussed in Jeffrey Richards, *Swordsmen of the Screen: From Douglas Fairbanks to Michael York.* (London: Routledge, 2014).

barbarian gang that is bent on assaulting the decencies of douce Edinburgh folk. Familiarity with the animalistic nicknames (such as 'Auk', and 'Toad'),[6] facility in the secret codes, and recognition of the arcane references give the reader permission to join these noble savages who are in league with 'Mahoun'/ Mohammed, the mediaeval Scots synonym for the devil.

A similar strategy of co-option of the reader into an exclusive club of boisterous male drinkers by inviting them to recognise and respond to a collage of citations is evident in 'Gowdspink in Reekie' and 'Kynd Kittock's Land'. In 'Gowdspink in Reekie', there are allusions, obviously, to Oliver Goldsmith's work, but also (implicitly, and ironically) to Ezra Pound's *The ABC of Economics,* and to Robert Fergusson's 'The Daft Days' ('As lang's there's pith into the barrel/ We'll drink and gree', 220); while the Joycean wordplay throughout the poem (in coinages such as 'cansoterations', 'sobredient', 'verbobesitie', 'perembrodrouthie') alludes more generally to the poem's high modernist antecedents. In 'Kynd Kittock's Land', an entire television audience is expected to recognise and respond to the mosaic of arguably more accessible citations and allusions, from the mediaeval poem from which the titular character is taken (which Smith explains in some detail); from Burns again ('The man o' independent mind', 'auld lang syne', 207; and a reference to 'Sylvander''s relationship with 'Clarinda', 210); from Shakespeare's 'Scottish play' ('signifying naething', 207; 'cry a halt! [...]/ And drouth tak him that first cries Haud enuff!' 211); and from Kipling's 'The Ladies' ('Judie O'Grady and the Colonel's Lady'; 209). Section III of the poem (211) is an extended parody of the Song of Solomon in which the allusions are multi-layered: there is an allusion to the 'Black Rose of Shalimar' which, as noted above, as well as being a reference to the royal gardens of the Mughal empire, might also be a conflation of two Hollywood swashbucklers of the early 1950s: the titular heroine of *The Black Rose* and 'Princess Shalimar' from *The Golden Horde*. There is a quotation from the traditional song 'On Tintock Tap', and a closing reference to 'Venus Merrytricks', a pun on 'Venus meretrix', which degrades the goddess of love by identifying her with one of the 'meretrices', or registered prostitutes in ancient Rome. However, 'Venus meretrix' is also a type of edible saltwater clam, and so here Smith may also be slyly alluding to Fergusson's poem celebrating fresh Scots seafood, 'Caller Oysters'. Later in the poem there are references to another 18th century popular song, 'My mistress that's pretty' ('The frolic and the gay', 212) but the crescendo of intertextual references peaks in the third section and lessens as the poem draws to a close.

---

6   Richie McCaffery (personal correspondence) notes that 'Toad' was Hazel Williamson's private nickname for Smith, used in love letters, such as MS. 26152 in the NLS.

The technique of proceeding by a collage of citations is a familiar trope from earlier high modernist poems, and, as we have argued, it has a consistent function in these three poems: the reader who appreciates the abruptly juxtaposed quotations, or who at least is open to the echoic quality of the verse, meets the criteria for adoption into an elite group with a shared ethos – here a merry band of drinking companions. And it is in the outcome of the interpellation, and in the character of the elite group that 'hails' the reader and enjoins him to share its values, that provide the means by which Smith distances himself to some extent from his high modernist models, Eliot and Pound, and establishes his own voice. If Pound, a totemic figure in high modernism who espoused eccentric economic beliefs, is an implicit target for the anti-economics satire of 'Gowdspink in Reekie', then he and Eliot and Joyce are conspicuously absent from the roistering band of sexually charged drunkards on a spree. Why are Li Po and Goldsmith present while Pound is absent? Why are Tom Eliot and James Joyce not found drinking in a corner with Tom Scott and Christopher Grieve? The high modernists whose work informs the structure and poetics of the three poems here considered are also curiously absent from the tissue of citations that permeates each one of them. After all, MacDiarmid famously cites Eliot's *The Waste Land* in *A Drunk Man Looks at the Thistle*, only a few years after the publication of Eliot's poem. The absence of Pound, Eliot and Joyce from the merry rabble of drinkers who inhabit Smith's poems is perhaps understandable: Joyce might have made a good drinking companion, but by the 1950s Pound's extreme politics had put him beyond the pale of clubbable society while Eliot's apparent astringency would no doubt have rendered him something of a wet blanket. The characters in the London pub in the 'A Game of Chess' section of Eliot's *The Waste Land*, however sympathetically they might be portrayed, are observed by a timeless narrator from an external perspective, while Smith's pub scenes are always shown from a bibulous insider's viewpoint. Smith's poetic antecedents in this respect were another trio whose work is continually cited in the three poems considered here: Ramsay, Fergusson and Burns. Their verses celebrating the pleasures of male society, drink, discussion and song – poems such as Ramsay's domestication of Horace's 'Ode No. IX', 'Look up to Pentland's tow'ring taps', Robert Fergusson's 'Verses on Visiting Dumfries', in which he remembers Horace 'that pleasant sinner/ Wha luv'd gude wine to synd his dinner', and Burns' 'The Jolly Beggars', to name but a few – are the lineal ancestors of a strain of convivial verse that continued into the 19th century with poems such as those of the 'Harum Scarum Club':

> It has been said, that Love inspires
> Ilk ane to sing wha feels his fires;
> Yet some we see just humph and ha,

Sae blate, can neither sing nor say;
But rightly to display your passion,
Frae Port and Claret seek expression.
For moral, dry, didactive verse,
With style sententious, quaint, and terse,
Frae Whitbread's brew-house waught a bicker –
There's sterling sense in good malt liquor.

*Edinburgh Magazine*, 189

Far from breaking with tradition, then, Smith is, even in his late modernist poetry, uncritically extending an ethos that extends from Ramsay's Easy Club in the 18th century to the Rose Street poets, a contemporary milieu and mythology to which Smith's poems explicitly contribute. There is, as noted earlier, a dissonance between the confident, urbane, neo-Horatian celebration of conviviality and the alienation that characterises high modernist poetry. This dissonance is preserved in Smith's poems where the intimacy of drink and debate is counterpoised against the harshness of a winter that in turn serves as a metaphor for the bleakness of modernity, as in 'To Li Po' (103):

The nicht was ourie richt eneuch;
But nocht we felt the drowie rouk
Bane-cauld, or the weet – or ocht
Ither, as I can mynd –
Hamewith mirrilie up the brae
Wi a hauf-mutchkin and hip-pint,
And screwtap chasers clinkum-clankum
In tune wi our maist important bletherin,
Our maist significant piss-and-wind...
  – While the world in its daith-dance,
  Skuddert and spun
  In the haar and wind o space and time...

Smith, then, opposes an ironic neo-Horatian celebration of 'maist significant piss-and-wind' against the speaker's awareness of the 'daith-dance' of modernity. In the downward of this generation's cyclic spiral towards destruction, the only recourse of the poetic soul is to drink, blether and sexual adventure, while he waits in a 'cheerie howff' for a new dispensation that may never come ('To Li Po', 103):

"The saul of Scotland, sleepan sound!"
– Aiblins. Maybe. Ye could be richt;

I wadna ken, at that...
But hae my douts.

Given the role of unreconstructed Horatian urbanity in erecting a bulwark against the wretchedness of modernity, the representation of women in Smith's poems is, consequently, largely confined to their traditional literary and social roles, as the muses and objects of sexual desire who populate what in 'Gowdspink in Reekie' he calls 'the trollopie toun' (221). The imagined professor in 'To Li Po' is an expert in either the Scots tongue or 'cute wee hures' while the pub crawlers stream forth from their tavern with at least the voiced intent of ravishing the daughters of 'douce burgesses' (102). In 'Gowdspink in Reekie' the speaker enjoins his muse to 'Kilt your coats, lassockie, shake-a the hips/ And ben the bar wi me, hen,/ Ben the bar wi' me.../ For a wee' (220), while later, in an extended sequence, the speaker and Goldsmith discuss the significance of her evanescent appearance as 'a lassie frae the mune direct' (225) while the speaker was in a characteristic state of inebriation. More substantial roles are given to women in 'Kynd Kittock's Land' but even here their portrayal seldom extends beyond the kind of earthy muses that Burns describes in 'The Vision', and Fergusson in 'Leith Races', or the objects of sexual attraction – the attentive barmaids and serving girls – who are omnipresent in Ramsay, Fergusson and, of course, Burns' verse. Kynd Kittock herself, however, in Smith's poem, performs the not inconsiderable role that Eliot's Tiresias plays in *The Waste Land*. The mediaeval tavern-keeper is introduced to the television viewers and readers 'Humped in a doorway stinko as a Bacchic maid' (208) before they are told that she died of thirst half a millennium previously. Nevertheless, her presence remains in Edinburgh, keeping a 'cantie howff' (the phrase is repeated from 'To Li Po') for a company of drinkers extending from the Old Testament to the present day. Kynd Kittock is the patron saint of the other women in the poem, the 'dochters [who] ply the trade/ And dream of film stars' (209); the child who will be 'beauty-queen o' Portibellie withoot doubt/ – And mither o' five' (209); the barmaids and serving-women who double as the speaker's muses in Section III (211): the 'dochter o' Sharon', 'Salome', 'Hebe', 'Black Rose of Shalimar' and 'Venus Merrytricks'; and the 'floosies' of fond remembrance in Section IV (211). However, in this poem, the last words are given to this female figure: it is Kynd Kittock who rebukes the maudlin speaker, as he regrets the dawning of day and the end of 'diversion', by restating her durability and confirming the speaker's ignorance: 'Wretched, tae, ye cried us, ach, young man,/ Ye ken nocht aboot it – as ye said yersel' (215). It is the figure of Kynd Kittock, not the speaker or his drinking companions, who represents both

Edinburgh itself, and the promise of 'return' that characterises high modernist poetry. The movement forward by recovering an idealised past is evident in the lines (215):

> Times aye cheynge and this auld runt
> Will flouer again (Heh! Heh! Yon's me!)
> And hae nae cheynge ava – we're aye the same,
> The desperate and the deid, the livin raucle yins,
> D'ye ken? Ay, though, and sae it is,
> Auld Reekie through the keekin glass
> Looks fine, and sae it does.
>     And the morning and the evenin
>     Were anither age gane by...

Kynd Kittock provides a rousing affirmation at the end of this poem – and this series of poems – that the enduring spirit of the city lies not with the decent burghers, the museum keepers or the gaping tourists, but with the 'auld companie' of drinkers and carousers who frequent its low dives. It is as if Eliot had returned, at the end of *The Waste Land* to the cockney pub where his women are discussing good ham and abortion, and confirmed that (*pace* Shakespeare, Chaucer and Dante, or even Li Po, Fergusson and Goldsmith), it is they who represent the abiding value of civilisation. In this respect, Smith departs from his high modernist forbears and makes new his solution to the high modernist's dilemma.

If Smith in 'Kynd Kittock's Land' plays an original variation on a well-worn theme, then the medium in which it was first exposed as an unfamiliar one for high modernist poetry. If Eliot published *The Waste Land* for 'fit audience, though few' in 1922, the same year as the birth of BBC radio, 'Kynd Kittock's Land' was commissioned, as noted above, for a BBC Scotland television series 43 years later. I have detailed elsewhere the collaboration between Smith and the photographer Alan Daiches in the process of composing the poem (Corbett, ibid.). Daiches recalled to me, when he was reconstructing the broadcast from the surviving negatives and his copy of the shooting script, all now digitally preserved by the Scottish Cultural Resources Access Network (SCRAN), that he and Smith toured the city and planned the poem together. The broadcast version of the poem was considerably shorter than the one later published (the sections about 'flux and floosies', and, as already noted, the section naming fellow poets such as Tom Scott and Albert Mackie are among the omissions), but ideally the lines in the poem that survive in the broadcast version should be read in conjunction with the photographs to which they refer.[7] The introduction of Kynd Kittock, quoted above, for example, is linked to a visual of a woman walking into the actual World's End Close in Edinburgh, her head already disappearing in the shadows. Her 'lineal descendant' is shown pulling pints in a bar (see Figures 9.1–9.3 below).

One of the consequences of viewing 'Kynd Kittock's Land' alongside the images that inspired it is that the timeless poem is nevertheless anchored in time, the faces and places particularised. The photograph of a 'man and dray' (Caption 57) that leads up to the textual reference to 'milk-cairts cloppering by' (the 'Sanct Cuthberts' in the published version is excised in the script, presumably to avoid advertising) is one of a sequence of still images that memorialise one particular dawn. Another consequence is that some of the more rhetorically florid passages, such as the apostrophe to 'dochter o Sharon' are ironised and humanised by being counterpointed against affectionate images of elderly couples.

If the television format dilutes the elitist interpellation associated with the high modernist genre, then, as we have noted, it also broadens the cultural references (Shakespeare and Burns are cited more frequently than, say, classical Chinese poetry and Fergusson), and it dissipates some of the intimacy that the oblique references to specific individuals creates in 'To Li Po', 'Gowdspink in Reekie', and in the published version of 'Kynd Kittock's Land'. Even who Kynd Kittock was has to be spelled out to the television audience in a way that Li Po and Oliver Goldsmith do not in their poems, the speaker having to resort to the patronising explanation that 'She dee'd o' drouth five hunder year sinsyne/ (But ye'll no ken o' this)' (208). Even if the popular medium resists the kind of elitist interpellation that characterises high modernist poetics, the broadcast, with the others in the series, remains a testament to an attempt to use television to engage an, admittedly relatively limited, mass audience in the kind of poetry that had been considered, earlier in the century, to be in the 'difficult' avant garde.

Ironically, of course, this kind of poetry had fallen relatively out of favour by the time 'Kynd Kittock's Land' was broadcast. The long, high modernist poem flourished between the wars, when writers like Pound and Eliot seemed almost to yearn for a cataclysmic period of destruction, so that a new renaissance, a

---

7  SCRAN (www.scran.ac.uk) makes available online all the surviving photographs Daiches took for this project, plus a copy of the shooting script. Thirty-five years after the original broadcast (which no longer survives), in my presence, Daiches matched up those photographs that he recalled being used in the broadcast with those indicated in his copy of the shooting script. While there is always the possibility of his misremembering some of the vaguer directions in the script, his recall seemed sure and reliable.

(21) (Cam. 2) (World'sEnd Close) Look down there now and see –

                PUSH IN to Close     See! Down the close at the World's End

    MIX
22.  CAM. 3                          Kynd Kittock

                CAPTION 21
                CU on Woman      Haein fun as usual in her ain sweet way

                             Stinko as a Bacchic maid

                           – She dee'd o' drouth five hunder year
                                     sinsyne, but ye'll no ken o'this

                PULL OUT
                to reveal Close    She couldna thole the bourgeois joys of
                                      Paradise

                           Whar they sent her, Christian buddies,

                           And by a special dispensation o' the Court

                           Now keeps a cantie howff outby the Gowden Yetta

                           For drouthie tinks like Peter, Noah,

23.  CAM. 1               Auld Methusalem/– and you.

                CAPTION 22
                Woman in pub      Her lineal descendant's makkin siccar

24.  CAM. 2               Yon awfae fate shall never hap again. /

                CAPTION 23
                Gp. of women

                          —— Och, terrible, says the Bylie's wife,

                         There should be a law. Ay, and sae there is, man.

                         It's jungle law. Eh? Terrible?

25.  CAM. 3               Awa wi ye! – See there! /

                CAPTION 24
                2 old men        An auld ane sittin on a bink

                PUSH IN
                on bearded one    His medals popped or m" hingin proodly

                         Like a banner on the wall

26.  CAM. 1               Abune his empty grate in some foosty single-end/

                CAPTION 25
                House & stairs    Whar's dochters ply the trade

                BEGIN ON R.WINDOW
                PAN L. to girl    And dream of film stars

                         But for wee-er fees, I fear –

                         The game's the same, though, efter an,

27.  CAM. 2               For Judie O'Grady and the Colonel's lady. /

                CAPTION 26: Old men with cigarette
      (3 next)               – 4 –

FIGURE 9.1  Shooting script, p. 4

FIGURE 9.2 'See! Doun the close at the World's End...'
        © ALAN DAICHES

reborn civilisation that would be more attuned to artists than bourgeois capi-
talism was perceived to be, could be born from the ashes. When their yearning
was answered by the horrors of World War II, many poets changed. Pound fell
silent after his release from St. Elizabeth's sanatorium in the end Eliot turned
from poetry to the more popular form of the theatre, albeit marrying the
themes of Greek tragedy with drawing room drama. While American poets of
the 1940s to the 1960s, writers such as Robert Lowell and Theodore Roethke,
continued to find inspiration in the poetry of early high modernism, their own
verse grew less bardic, more intimately confessional as they matured. As this
chapter has demonstrated, while excluding the Anglophone modernists from
his exclusive coterie of drinking companions, Smith continued to write poetry
that in its techniques and concerns, was strongly informed by the early work of
Eliot and Pound. Its relative populism and its unreconstructed nostalgia for the
sociability of 18th century verse distinguishes Smith's oeuvre from that of his
predecessors, but it can still usefully be asked why he continued to mine this

FIGURE 9.3  'Her lineal descendant...'
          © ALAN DAICHES

particular – arguably politically discredited – literary tradition. Some answers might lie in the peripheral nature of much of Scottish literature in the 1950s and 1960s and in the long shadow of Hugh MacDiarmid, who was still the central figure in Smith's circle of literati. A decade after 'Kynd Kittock's Land' was broadcast, in 1976, MacDiarmid was still, in an interview with Scottish school pupils expressing the kind of desire for a new dispensation that characterised the modernist poets of the 1930s. When asked, 'Do you still stand by your statement in 'Hymn to Lenin' – 'What maitters't wha we kill?" MacDiarmid responded in a way that echoes the excitable extremism of the younger Pound:

> Yes. I still stand by that statement. Progress demands that recalcitrant or reactionary elements must be swept away. This has always happened throughout history. The USSR, under Stalin, is no exception and indeed in sacrifice of life compares favourably with the USA or UK'.
>
> MACDIARMID, 2010

Smith's poems, 'To Li Po', 'Gowdspink in Reekie' and 'Kynd Kittock's Land' display none of the high modernists' appetite for bloodshed as a means of precipitating the new dispensation. The living and the dead who populate these poems are content to wait out the current arid phase of modernity in a 'cantie howff', taking solace in drink, debauchery and debate. The resisting reader or viewer may worry that even by the time that 'To Li Po' was written, the high tide of modernism had long receded, and that Smith's recourse to 18th century clubbability remains reactionary in its portrayal of gender relations. Yet, largely thanks to Smith's endlessly inventive and idiosyncratic handling of his rich Scots literary medium, and his blending of apparently incommensurate perspectives – a paradoxical neo-Horatian modernism – he invigorates familiar tropes with fresh energy and he draws the willing reader, and even willing television viewers, into a timeless, yet concrete and particular, social ambience.

## Bibliography

Anon., 'The Harum Scarum Club' in *The Edinburgh Magazine and Literary Miscellany* Vol. 92, (1823), p. 189.

Brooker, Jewel Spears, 'Transcendence and Return: T.S. Eliot and the Dialectic of Modernism' in *South Atlantic Review* 59.2 (1994), pp. 53–74.

Corbett, John, 'Photographing Lallans: Alan Daiches, Alexander Scott and Sydney Goodsir Smith's Poems for Television', in Eleanor Bell and Linda Gunn (eds.), *The Scottish Sixties: Reading, Rebellion, Revolution?* (Amsterdam: Rodopi, 2013), pp. 272-5.

Joyce, James, *Ulysses* (Harmondsworth: Penguin Modern Classics, 1971).

MacDiarmid, Hugh, 'Hugh MacDiarmid: The Lost Interview' in *Scottish Review of Books* November 18th (2016). Accessible at http://www.scottishreviewofbooks.org/2016/11/hugh-macdiarmid-the-l''ost-interview/.

McClure, J. Derrick (ed.), *A Kist o Skinklan Things: An Anthology of Scots Poetry from the First and Second Waves of the Scottish Renaissance* (Glasgow: Association for Scottish Literary Studies, 2017).

North, Michael, 'The Making of "Making it New"' *Guernica* (August 15, 2013). Online at http://www.guernicamag.com/the-making-of-making-it-new/.

Perl, Jeffrey M., *Tradition of Return: The Implicit History of Modern Literature* (Princeton, NJ: Princeton University Press, 1984).

Richards, Jeffrey, *Swordsmen of the Screen: From Douglas Fairbanks to Michael York* (London: Routledge, 2014).

Smith, Sydney Goodsir, *Collected Poems: 1941–1975* (London: John Calder, 1975).

Whyte, Christopher, *Modern Scottish Poetry* (Edinburgh: Edinburgh University Press, 2004), pp. 109–117.

Woolf, Virginia, *The Diary of Virginia Woolf 1920–1924*. Vol. 2. Ed. by Anne Olivier Bell (New York Harcourt, 1978).

# CHAPTER 10

# Reveries of a 'Gangrel Scriever': *Gowdspink in Reekie* and Oliver Goldsmith

*Mario Relich*

## Abstract

This chapter examines why, in one of his final poems, Smith looked to Oliver Goldsmith as something of an alter-ego. It is the epistolary aspects of Smith's poem that are of interest here: why is it addressed to the Irish, but London-based Goldsmith rather than for example Robert Fergusson, although the title of his poem alludes to one of Fergusson's most popular poems, 'Ode to the Gowdspink'. Smith focuses primarily on Goldsmith's *The Deserted Village*, and aspects of the eighteenth-century poet's 'gangrel' life.

## Keywords

Irish literature – Oliver Goldsmith – Edinburgh – *The Deserted Village* – *Gowdspink in Reekie* – alter-ego – epistolarity – Robert Fergusson – 18th century

Sydney Goodsir Smith wrote his sequence of poems 'Gowdsmith in Reekie' for *The Saltire Review* in 1955. Nearly twenty later, in 1974, he published pretty much the same sequence as a separate pamphlet, with the title changed to *Gowdspink in Reekie*.[1] It turned out to be his last published poem-sequence, but the first version preceded his 1965 poem-sequence, *Kynd Kittock's Land*. In a way, 'Gowdsmith in Reekie' seems like a trial-run for the later sequence, which explores various aspects of the High Street, or 'Royal Mile', but it is his revision, with the title slightly changed, that turned out to be the poet's last major work.

---

1   All following page references in this chapter, unless otherwise stated, relate to: Smith, Sydney Goodsir, *Gowdspink in Reekie* (Loanhead: Macdonald Publishers, 1974). Alternatively, this poem sequence can be found in its entirety in Smith, Sydney Goodsir, *Collected Poems: 1941–1975* (London: John Calder, 1975), pp. 217–229.

The poem – in both versions – is very much a fantastical 'reverie' about Oliver Goldsmith as the Edinburgh poet's imagined boon-companion. Goldsmith himself wrote what he called 'reveries' in his periodical essays. The most relevant in relation to Smith is 'A Reverie at the Boar's Head Tavern in Eastcheap' (Goldsmith: 1966, 97–112). It is an essay in which he imagines a scene with Falstaff, Mistress Quickly, and others at the Boar's Head. As it happens, Goldsmith was familiar with this pub, as it still existed in the 18th century. Smith's 'reverie' is more intimate, but equally fantastical, as he imagines himself to be hob-nobbing with the Irish Augustan, who as a young medical student had also prowled the pubs of the Lawnmarket and elsewhere in the Royal Mile.

While formally *Gowdspink in Reekie* has more in common with Goldsmith's prose 'reveries', his poem-sequence *The Deserted Village* has stronger intertextual links with Smith's poem. For a start, Smith chose as his epigraph to both versions one of the most famous of Goldsmith's lines: 'Where wealth accumulates and men decay'. As will be seen, Smith applies this observation to more personal circumstances. Goldsmith and Smith do diverge radically in how they structured their respective poem-sequences. T.S. Eliot particularly valued Goldsmith's poem for its structure:

> I place *The Deserted Village* higher than any poem by Johnson or by Gray. In Goldsmith's poem the art of transition is exemplified in perfection. If you examine it paragraph by paragraph, you will find always a shift just at the right moment, from the descriptive to the meditative again, [...] These parts are properly proportioned.
>
> ELIOT, 181[2]

Smith's poem-sequence, on the other hand, is structured completely differently. About his way of structuring poems, the scholar and critic Thomas Crawford had this to say: 'Smith has shown again and again that he can create serial forms with the shape of a chain rather than of a building, so that the metaphor of structure is peculiarly inappropriate to his work' (Crawford: 1969, 46). Crawford's observation is certainly applicable to *Gowdspink in Reekie*, but Smith manages the transitions between one section and another with considerable panache, and possibly in a more compact way than in his more celebrated

---

2  Comparing Johnson and Goldsmith as poets, Eliot also observes that Goldsmith is 'more original and also prophetic', reinforcing his point by quoting two lines from *The Deserted Village*: '*Ill fares the land, to hastening ills a prey,/ Where wealth accumulates, and men decay*'. Smith chose the second line (l 52) as his epigraph to *Gowdspink in Reekie*.

poem-sequences *Under the Eildon Tree* and *Kynd Kittock's Land*, and in this in-direct way Goldsmith was very much his model.

That Smith admired Goldsmith throughout his adult life is evidenced by the fact that his unpublished novel 'The Wilderness' (1938) has no less than four epigraphs from *The Deserted Village* (Acc. 10426/9).[3] Also, the title-page to *Gowdspink in Reekie* has a drawing by the professional artist Geoffrey Roper of two suited gents, consisting of a monocled Smith facing Goldsmith, both clink-ing each other's glass of wine, while the frontispiece quotes Samuel Johnson as follows: 'Let not his frailties be remembered; he was a very great man'. A closer look at each Section of the poem follows.

The poem begins with an address to Goldsmith as 'gangrel scriever/ Frae the Emerant Isle, a feckless billie, [...]'. This kind of familiarity sets the tone for the entire poem. Smith addresses the 18th century poet more as his equal, as he considered himself as something of a 'gangrel scriever', certainly not part of any literary establishment. As for whether he had anything against 'feckless billies' himself, these subsequent lines make it clear that he did not:

> Aince (as is the happitude o' feckless billies)
> Gied the world and gomerall his dowpmaist thochts
> And wyce cansoteratiouns anent, o' aa things
> Neath the mischancical mune, [...]. (7)

These lines also testify to the Scottish poet's love of word-play; for instance, the colourful 'gomerall' for the much plainer 'blockhead', and 'cansoteratiouns' ap-pears to derive from 'to canse', or 'a pert and saucy style, as displaying a great degree of self-importance', according to Jamieson's *Dictionary of the Scottish Language*. Goldsmith, like many of his Irish compatriots, was undoubtedly a great stylist, but he wasn't quite as inventive with words as some other Augus-tan writers. In fact, Smith did not even mention Goldsmith in an assessment he made of these writers in his essay 'Words of a Feather' (Smith: 1995, 3–5). Here is what he had to say about Swift, whom he evidently admired precisely for his word-play:

> It is interesting, while we are on the 18th century, that in English Litera-ture, at the other end of the room from the formal Augustans, we find a wee gang of word spoofers, playboys of the word, and lo and behold

---

3   The typescript is in the National Library of Scotland: Acc. 10426/9. The epigraphs also include one quote each from Yeats, Freud, and Toller, but the four from Goldsmith take pride of place.

they all, save one, come out of Ireland. There was Jonathan Swift, for instance. In what he called his 'little language' in his *Journal to Stella*, he reproduced the kind of invented language that children and lovers use amongst themselves and which adult or sober writers have lost touch with – natch.

SMITH: 1995, 4

He also mentioned Laurence Sterne, Thomas Sheridan, who 'invented Mrs. Malaprop', and the Scot Tobias Smollett (Smith: 1995, 4).

It was, however, Goldsmith that Smith honoured in his poem-sequence. One recent study of Goldsmith said of him that 'He was a philosophic vagabond and he had been furthering his education in real life', adding that 'The vagabond was to become a celebrated man of letters, one of the best-loved writers of eighteenth-century English literature and firmly associated with London, where he soon settled. Oliver Goldsmith was a journalist, a poet, a novelist and a playwright' (Clarke, 1). While Smith was not quite a vagabond, he was well-travelled, hailing originally from New Zealand, and he adopted Edinburgh as very much his own version of London. As regular art-critic for *The Scotsman*, he could be regarded as a journalist, and of course he was certainly, like Goldsmith, a poet, a novelist and a playwright who wrote *The Wallace* and various radio plays. He wrote only one novel, *Carotid Cornucopius,* but so did Goldsmith, namely *The Vicar of Wakefield*, both very idiosyncratic works. Arguably, therefore, he had much in common with Goldsmith.

Goldsmith was a consistently elegant and occasionally witty writer, but stylistic experimentation and love of word-play were not his forte. What attracted Smith to the Augustan poet, however, was nothing less than his critique of the harmful effects of wealth in 18th century Britain through the medium of his poem *The Deserted Village*. His word-play on Goldsmith's name stretches simile and metaphor in a manner reminiscent of Hugh MacDiarmid:

Gowdsmith, weill and ill-named baith!
For never can the twain bide cosh thegither
But like electricity-conductit fish (O Gowd, O Smith!)
Are curst wi a mutually antimagnetic field. (7)

Goldsmith's name, in short, questions the value of gold, signifying acquisitiveness, and how it disrupts human solidarity.

In the epigraph to *Gowspink in Reekie* Smith quotes the aforementioned lines from *The Deserted Village*: 'Where wealth accumulates and men decay' (6). This is what in the following lines Smith calls 'the banal predicament', and in lines moreover, addressed explicitly to the reader as 'idle lector', which suggest that he identifies with Goldsmith so much that the Augustan poet comes pretty close to being his alter-ego:

> Na, na, my mannie, idle lector, it will never dae
> – As this puir smith and brither bard
> (Thy servant and sobredient varmint
> And brither gangrel, feckless billie tae,
> For the maitter o' yon) kens owre weill
> To jokifie about at this stage
> In our banal predicament. (7)

Smith goes on to point to the incongruity of the 'banal predicament', which has much to do with how poverty affects human relationships. He does so in flamboyant language:

> Never hae I had the bleezin inputence,
> The unconscionable hippocrastitie
> Of Ollie, tae endite a moral leid on *sicna* theme –
> O' aa themes in the zodiac! (8)

Rather than anything to do with 'hypocrisy', Smith's invented word 'hippocrastitie' appears to suggest something grandiloquent, like economic theory. But Smith's target is secular speculations from economists like Goldsmith's contemporary Adam Smith, as refracted through his poem on the causes of poverty.

Smith also plays more directly with the epigraphic quote from *The Deserted Village*, as follows:

> What was't again? I've tint the threid;
> I'm gangin aa agley, led on
> By my ain surcease o' windflaucht verbobesitie...
> – Oh ay, "When wealth accumulates then man decays",
> Or words wi like scantsignifence. (8)

Pretending 'to lose the thread' of his argument, this is very much self-deprecating banter, deliberately misquoting Oliver Goldsmith, but also giving his own twist to the quote, which becomes significant when the poem-sequence has been read in its entirety. Section I ends with a kind of parodic philosophical axiom:

> For then it follows as the nicht the day
> That man is pitten til the door and nae
> Fine moraleesings sweys the bitten hairt
> O' the robber licencee whase porte
> Is ever open til the boskie lieges
> For the sale o' excitipple liquors. (9)

These lines suggest that the thematic focus of the poem lies in what has change in the Old Town, and alludes to *The Deserted Village.* Instead of peasants being evicted from farmland by landlords intent on developing a greater profit from their land, pubs in a way exclude ordinary drinkers in touristy areas through their pricing of drinks. But Smith's serious points are made in a jesting, light-hearted manner; hence the final lines of Section i declare that 'We're in the saddle nou, the fit is on –/ Muse let this be nou my theme!' (9). It's a rollicking ride of a conclusion.

Switching from satirical moralising, Section ii reminds us that 'Auld Ollie' was 'In Reekie aince – why or wharfae's/ No the point the nou (10). The point he does make is 'Ollie' liked

> To tak a daunder through the trollopie toun –
>     The Royal Mile maybe,
> Historic throwgang o' the Modren Athens
> (Yon's a lauch!) [...]. (10)

The rest of Section ii becomes a fantasia describing the two poets exploring the Royal Mile. He asks whether his 'ain perembrodrouthie' or perambulations through 'mine auld romantick toun' led Goldsmith to ask himself the following question:

> Did you find, I ferlie, when your wealth
> Decumulatit hour by fluid hour
> That man was thereby grandified? (10)

The next few lines fantasise about Smith and Goldsmith sharing a 'ghaist trolley-bus route/ Wi the Shennachie Smith as clippie, Gowdspink,/ I can tell ye' (11). This is the first time Smith addresses Goldsmith as 'Gowdspink', taking the Scots version of the 'goldfinch' name very likely from Robert Fergusson's poem 'Gowdspink in Reekie', a small but significant change from the more straightforward 'Gowdsmith' in the 1955 version of the poem. He also changes Goldsmith's nickname from 'Noll' to 'Ollie', possibly because 'Old Noll' was actually Oliver Cromwell's nickname. According to Goldsmith's early biographer, Thomas Percy, who knew him well, there may have been a family connection with Cromwell: 'Although Oliver had evidently his Christian name from his mother's father, yet he used to assert, that it had been introduced into her family by some affinity or connexion with that of the Protector Oliver Cromwell; [...]'. (Percy, 2). Smith was probably aware that there may have been such a connection, but in the later version of the poem decided that he did not after all want 'Ollie' to be associated in any way, and however indirectly, with the odious dictator.

Stanza 3 of Section 11 describes a bibulous jaunt by the two poets at a pub on Castle Hill, 'The Eagle'. But where the pamphlet version differs is that the passing of time becomes more poignant, since 'The Eagle' has become the 'Ensign Stewart', and both on the site of what Smith calls 'auld Mowat's shop', which may have been there further back into the past, so the later version adds two lines in brackets on the 'lacrimae rerum' theme:

> (Gane nou, gane nou, *hélas, mes bons copains, mes*
> *Camarades, hélas, sunt lacrimae rerum,* sae it is...) (11)

The macaronic combination of French, Scots, and Latin adds to the melancholy expressed about the evanescence of things; traditional, old-fashioned Edinburgh 'howffs' meant a lot to Smith. The pub is, or was, near the Assembly Hall, where the Ministers of the (Presbyterian) Church of Scotland meet for the General Assembly once a year. Smith pokes fun at their deliberations, indulging 'theirsels wi a week of blethers/ Anent the evils o' the world o' men', but also giving them an opportunity for a more relaxing time:

> Douce "Eagle", whar the reverent meenister men,
> Far frae the ee o' spouse or Maister Knox neist door,
> Would hae anither Assembly o' their ain
> And tuim their nips and drams as crouse
> As you or me – until alack-a-day –
> The siller's out – and syne decay ... (12)

The reference to 'Maister Knox', whose statue of him delivering an admonitory sermon, is just outside the Assembly Hall is, of course, deliberate, suggesting that the ministers congregate at the pub to escape the rigours of theological and moralistic discussion in favour of convivial drinking and blethering. The final line alludes to the epigraph from Goldsmith, but turned into a light-hearted joke about spending too much on rounds of drinks.

The final stanza clinches Smith's autobiographical link to Goldsmith, namely that both studied medicine at Edinburgh and neither attained a degree in it, although the poet ruefully admits about 'mine Ollie, antient fiere!' that

> [...] ye stuck it langer far nor me!
> A towmond and a hauf and a hauf ye ran
> And me juist twa-three terms, for shame! (12)

In his autobiographical letter to Maurice Lindsay, Smith was even more direct about his reluctance to study medicine, adding some stern self-criticism:

> Despite my pleas to be allowed to study art I followed father's footsteps and entered Edinburgh University as a medical student. Then followed "one crowded *year* of glorious life" and the beginning of that debauchery which, to my pocket's regret, I have continued ever since.
>
> SMITH: 1988, 6–7

Goldsmith's time as a medical student was not dissimilar. Percy had this to say about Goldsmith's time as a medical student in Edinburgh:

> Here for some time he attended the lectures of Monroe, and the other professors in the medical line. But his attention to his studies was by no means regular; and his health was considerably injured, and his pocket frequently drained, by his too often mixing in scenes of dissipation.
>
> PERCY, 21[4]

Smith uses exactly the same word about himself when he refers in the same letter to 'this year of dissipation'.

As the final lines of Section II indicate, Smith thought his strongest bond with Goldsmith was that they both tried to study medicine, but ended up realising that poetry (or writing) was their first love:

> – But ye can see there's a kind o' bund
> Atween us twa, gangrel buddies surely,
> Ay, but bards forbye, I'd hae the world ken – (12)

---

4 Percy continues by observing that '(d)uring that time he is said by some of his contemporaries to have given occasional proofs of his poetical talents'. It is possible, therefore, that Goldsmith, like Smith, became known as a poet in Edinburgh, and that is another link between them, even though the former had not yet published poems at the time.

The above lines continue with a robust note of defiance:

> And if they dinnae, mair's their loss
> No ours, Ollie, for nocht we hae to tine
> (Guid kens) and yon's a fact
> That's incontusaboll at last, at least – or even best. (12)

For Smith his kinship with Goldsmith was incontestable and incontrovertible, and it is in that spirit that the poem has to be read.

The following section presents Smith and Goldsmith on a pub crawl. It begins with a very pictorial evocation in the first stanza of how 'It was snawin as we left the howff ', the falling snow itself described in a vividly metaphorical way: 'celestial hauf-crouns/ And lichtsome florins blawin/ [...] Blawin athort the face like angels' kisses'. It is an image that fuses both the ethereal and the concern in much of the poem with money and the lack of it. The plasticity and inventiveness of Smith's language culminates with the line 'This magnumuni-mondulous expression' (13). It is a Joycean way, also in tune with MacDiarmid, of conveying a sense of wonder, the senses already heightened by drink.

Stanza 2 continues in this vein, and then switches to what Smith calls 'th' Aesthetic Stakes' suggesting to Goldsmith that

> We could likely jyne the Saultear Sociossity
> That hauds its cultural sabbat in the Looinmairkit
> Juist up the causey frae the "Deacon Brodie". (14)

He is referring to the Saltire Society, which at the time was in the Lawnmarket of the High Street and near the 'Deacon Brodie' pub. These lines sound like an in-joke about the Society, which has always promoted Scottish literature, and particularly the Scots language, and writing in Scots. Further down, in stanza 3, he refers to the 'Sadsatiety for the Spukin o' Verse'. Although based in Edinburgh, the 'Scottish Association for the Speaking of Verse' was actually founded by John Masefield in 1924.[5] Such impeccable respectability is undoubtedly what Smith found most amusing, hence possibly the 'sad' in 'Sadsatiety'. His ambivalence about joining such literary/cultural societies is no doubt summed up by the final line of stanza 4: 'But, 'smaitter o' fack, we didnae hae the *time!*/ Juist that'. (15).

---

5  My source is verbal information from Joyce Caplan, the current chairwoman of the Poetry Association of Scotland, which is the direct successor of the Scottish Association for the Speaking of Verse.

The rest of the stanza refers to Burns's friendship with John Richmond, as one of the pubs in the Lawnmarket was actually called the 'Rabbie Burns'. Burns, in fact at one point lodged with Richmond in the Lawnmarket (Crawford: 2010, 242–243). But his focus is more on how Burns was treated by the gentry:

> [...] e'er the Embro gentry lioned him
> And dined and wined but wouldnae gie'm
> The sinecure his bardie ee was on
> > (and richtlie sae)

When Goldsmith lived in Edinburgh as a student, so not yet a famous writer, however, he was nevertheless 'lioned', if in a rather more ambivalent manner. Here is how one Goldsmith biographer put it:

> Goldsmith spent several days at the young Duke of Hamilton's, flattered by the dinner invitations, endeavouring to be the informal companion, naively letting the company into his "circumstances and manner of thinking", only to realize that he was liked "more as a *jester* than a companion" He had been typecast as "the facetious Irish Man", so that he could be patronized and treated with an indulgence bordering on contempt.
>
> DIXON, 12

While Goldsmith's poems and plays, as well as his periodical essays, not to mention his novel *The Vicar of Wakefield*, were widely admired at the time he was never entirely free of not being taken seriously enough by some, even long after his Edinburgh sojourn. His close friend Sir Joshua Reynolds wrote an encomium of Goldsmith after his death, but acknowledged that he was not always admired: 'Dr. Goldsmith's genius is universally acknowledged. All we shall endeavour to show what indeed is self-apparent, that such a genius could not be a fool or such a weak man as many people thought him'. (Wardle, 6).

For Smith, in any case, both Goldsmith and Burns 'had the lauch o'm in the end', thereby linking them in posterity as akin:

> Whareer ye be
> (The twa o' ye's) I'se warand ye're thegither
> > Or God's tint
> His celebrated sense o' justice efter aa. (14)

The same stanza mentions between brackets that the 'Rabbie Burns' pub, apparently in the Lawnmarket has been not '*developed*', but '*Obliteratit*'. This is undoubtedly a protest against the sporadic redevelopment of the High Street. That he felt strongly about Edinburgh Council's insensitive vandalism is confirmed by the poet and memoirist Stanley Roger Green:

> When the High Street and Canongate were sanitized and tarted up for the benefit of tourists, the ancient lands and tenements emptied of their rich, colourful broth of humanity and shunted off to peripheral housing estates, I think Sydney must have died a little.
>
> GREEN: 2007, 37

In the final three stanzas, Smith reverts to, and develops, the conceit that he and Goldsmith are not that dissimilar to Church of Scotland ministers in their comradeship and drinking sessions at the 'Deacon Brodie'; so much so, that the similarities become a matter of theological debate:

> Our god was maybe different (some would hae't)
> Or maybe juist the same – consult
> The scholards on this point
> Maist problemythicale ... (15–16)

The ellipsis, a pause for thought it seems, is there in the poem, but the word 'problemythicale' is most ingenious. The 'god' here may be taken to be Bacchus, but whether one worships Bacchus or the Christian God, it is all a matter of myth, not in the sense that such deities are non-existent, but that we all live within a framework of values embodied by myth, or the stories we tell ourselves. A comment by Iain Crichton Smith is pertinent here: 'Against John Knox he set over Bacchus' (Crichton Smith, 166).

In the final stanza Smith calls Goldsmith 'my menyie' or friend, and praises whatever is the source of the bounty, 'whatna gods there be', by which a pub session of drinking and comradeship is made possible. One such munificent god might be 'Some dumb editor chiel', the 'Benefactor o' the Feast,/ Dispenser o' the precious fauldin stuff [...]' and 'O' fauldin-money, [...]'. The concluding couplet appears to be a direct quote from the bar-man:

> All probonobilutations groatfully imbibed
> In cruse or can – wi thankards and canplenishments.

There is a dazzling fusion of different implications here; 'groatfully', for instance suggesting both the cash nexus and gratitude, and in 'pronobulations', 'pro bono' is a legal term referring to a case taken on for free in order to benefit the community. The gist of meaning in this couplet appears to be about the socially beneficial aspects of pub sessions, both in terms of the economy and personal ones. Above all, the entire section is a glorification of exuberant friendship, even if the friendship Smith celebrates is an entirely imaginary one. It is a paradox, nevertheless, on which *Gowdspink in Reekie* thrives.

In an essay on Smith's 1959 poetry collection *Figs And Thistles*, Sorley Ma-cLean identified this important strand in Smith's poetic oeuvre: '*Figs and Thistles* has much of Smith's romantic and tragic poetry of passion but there is also, as in "To Li Po in the Delectable Mountains of Tien Mu", another authentic Smith, the matchless boon companion whose fun ranged from learned allusive rapier wit to the richest of belly-laughter, [...]'. (MacLean, 78). *Gowdspink in Reekie* is just as good an example, and one which Smith evidently treasured more, as he returned to it nearly twenty years after the earlier version.

Section IV reads like the beating heart of the entire poem-sequence. At a 'howff' in Rose Street, 'The "Abbotsford" maybe or "Daddy Milne's"', the poet describes his vision of 'a lassie frae the mune direct,/ That smiled at me', the second stanza ending with an implicit question:

> And here she was in person, sae it seemed,
> Or maybe 'twas the mirligaes again [...]

Smith's glossary in the *Collected Poems* defines 'mirligae' as a 'spinning wheel', but it can also mean 'dizziness', so the suggestion here is of the poet's head 'spinning' with the vision.

The following section has parallels with his poem 'The Muse of Rose Street'. Although her name is never mentioned, the poem is about Stella Cartwright, a young Edinburgh woman who became legendary for attracting the besotted attention of the poets who frequented Rose Street pubs, particularly Smith himself, Norman MacCaig, Tom Scott and George Mackay Brown.

Both in Section IV of *Gowdspink in Reekie* and 'The Muse in Rose Street', the 'vision' of the woman has elements of the uncanny, in effect an apparition, as in the following lines from 'The Muse in Rose Street':

> Maybe I kent it then, I canna mynd...
>    For there she was afore my een
> A lassie frae the mune, direct –!
>    And smiled at me –
>                It wasna cannie!
> SMITH: 1959, 78

'The Muse in Rose Street' appears to have been written after 'Gowdsmith in Reekie', as it appeared in the April 1956 issue of *Poetry* (*Chicago*), whereas 'Gowdsmith in Reekie' appeared in the autumn 1955 issue of *Saltire Review*. But it certainly describes the same vision as in the later poem and even repeats the final line of the above extract. Arguably, the 'vision' is more effectively de-scribes in the following stanza, identical, save for spelling variations, in both versions of the poem-sequence:

> I said I wasnae feart (she'd smiled, efter all)
> But I felt destruction imminent,
> The haill story clear as in a map
> Writ there in the reik that hung
> Like a haar athort the howff; the end
> Unfleeable, the joy and pain thegither,
> Heaven and Hell, the birth and daith,
> Wealth and decay, the haill catastrophe
> Implicit in conception – it wasnae cannie! (18)

The 'lassie frae the mune direct' seems like a rather apocalyptic apparition, al-most a destructive muse. But the very next stanza pours cold water on this notion:

> Ay, says Ollie the bauld boyo when I tellt him,
> I've heard it all before, and shall again
> Doubtless – and ordered another round. (18)

Goldsmith, or 'Ollie', instead, refers to *his* vision of another woman in *The De-serted Village*. He claims that the ideal woman envisioned by Smith can only be found

> [...] in the country parts where wealth
> Accumulates and men decay, as I wrote once,
> Though now I see I'm wrong – the landward parts
> Are ravished by the townsman's greed
> Of men and treasure both, [...]. (19)

The relevant lines from *The Deserted Village* describe in effect an exploited city prostitute as a simile for the 'luxurious' exploitation of the land by landowners expelling their tenants. At first, her youth makes her attractive:

> As some fair female unadorned and plain,
> Secure to please while youth confirms her reign,
> Slights every borrowed charm that dress supplies,
> Nor shares with art the triumph of her eyes.
> > GOLDSMITH: 1997, 49–62, ll 287–290

But when age makes her less attractive, 'In all the glaring impotence of dress' (l. 294), Goldsmith makes a direct comparison with what happens to the land, which at first seems very grand:

> Thus fares the land, by luxury betrayed,
> In nature's charms at first arrayed,
> But verging to decline, its splendours rise,
> Its vistas strike, its palaces surprize;
> > GOLDSMITH: 1997, ll. 295–298

Such artificial grandeur, however, is at the expense of the peasants, or those who work on the land, hence in this stanza Goldsmith ends with these devastating lines:

> While scourged by famine from the smiling land,
> The mournful peasant leads his humble band;
> And while he sinks without one arm to save,
> The country blooms, a garden, and a grave.
> > GOLDSMITH: 1997, ll. 299–302

But in Smith's poem, 'Ollie' anachronistically takes things further, with this apocalyptic warning about the 20th century, and still applicable to the 21st:

> Natural riches dwindle, die, and men
> Accumulate black wealth on country death
> And build a model factory where all was peace.
> – But, begob, ye'll never change these things
> With T.V., and 3-D, the H-bomb and R.I.P.
> Man gets the just conditions he deserves. (19)

'Begob' in the above lines, even if somewhat stereotypical, signals that this is still Goldsmith as Irishman speaking, yet it merges with Smith's own voice, the voice of a 20th century poet. Within the context of the exchange between these two fantastical drinking-companions, however, Smith switches to talk-ing about their own decay,

> Helping the distillers, brewers, publicans
> And siclike splendid princes o' the earth
> Accumulate our puir ill-gotten wealth – (19)

Throughout the poem-sequence, in fact, Smith reminds us of the epigraph from *The Deserted Village*, but often ironically applying it to the circumstances of their pub-crawl. Section IV ends with 'Ollie' calling the poet 'Theophilus,/ Most pregnant and crackmythical phoolosumphicker'. The name, as it hap-pens, comes from the Gospel of Luke and the Acts of the Apostles, and its Greek derivation means 'friend of God'. Smith addressed as 'Theophilus' seems like an elaborate joke about Smith's philosophical credentials. The entire sec-tion does indeed play with myth in the shape of the poet's vision of 'the Muse of Rose Street', contrasted with Goldsmith's description of an exploited city woman, and extended to apocalyptic warnings about the condition of human-ity in the 20th century. Regarding Stella Cartwright, Stanley Roger Green ob-serves that 'Dante had his Beatrice, Petrarch his Laura, whereas Stella was the lodestar of not one but several infatuated rhymesters, who, like the feminine ideals worshipped by the Renaissance poets, were married and safely out of reach' (Green: 2007, 121). However, according to Maggie Fergusson's biography of George Mackay Brown, she did have a close relationship with the Orkney poet, who also frequented the Rose Street pubs when he lived in Edinburgh, as a mature student. As Allan Massie put it in his review of Fergusson's book: 'Their relationship was chequered. She became an alcoholic and died before she was 50' (Massie, 2006). She also, therefore, had something in common with Goldsmith's unfortunate city woman in his poem. Mackay Brown paid this tribute to Cartwright: 'She wrote nothing herself, but what she truly was, her rare lovely unique essence, is a part of the literature of Scotland' (Fergusson, 259). But while no doubt aware of the ambivalence and discrepancies in his portrait of 'the Muse', it was Smith who did more than any other poet to make Stella Cartwright 'part of the literature of Scotland'.

Section V begins with comments on Einstein and relativity: 'Ay, relativity was pruven richt/ A dozie dizzen times yon famous nicht'. Another perspective on the entire poem-sequence is thereby suggested: it's a reverie in which real-ity keeps shifting. Stanza 2 delves into the kind of meandering conversation, in which 'The wealth o' publicans accumulaitit, ay', that occurs when people drink in pubs:

And as they grew mair stumious ilka hour,
Mair arrogant, dogmatic and opinionate,
Their triviality grew wings and thundert (20)

The word 'stumious' appears to be derived from 'stum', 'a stupid person, or blockhead' according to the Scottish National Dictionary. The conversations, at any rate, deteriorate as follows:

[...] their "points-o'-view"
Recede, diminish til a viewless preen-point
O' coherence, as the hours fled. (20)

And these conversational exchanges deteriorate to such an extent that 'Their fine booze-drawn gyrations in the void/ Nae audience but the speakers' sels enjoyed'. What the poet describes here is not only a matter of relativity, but something more medieval, a Dantesque circle of Hell. It is all redeemed, nevertheless, by the companionship between Smith and Goldsmith, so Section v ends as follows:

For we were nocht exempt, the bard and me,
Gowdie and Smith nae laggarts wi the lave.
– But 'twas a guid excursion nanetheless
As we accumulatit and our wealth decayed. (20)

Here, friendship trumps all, and confirms the truth behind the epigraph from *The Deserted Village*. It is not wealth that matters, but human relationships. Men (or women) decay in their relationships only when making money is given priority, and for Smith having a good time in a drinking-den is the very epitome of cultivating friendship. In the second stanza of Section VI, where he addresses Goldsmith as 'bogus Doc', no doubt for the same reason that neither he nor Goldsmith ever finished their medical studies, the poet declares that

[...] there's maybe
Mair o' gowd in pot-house brabblement
Nor in the earnest hummle-bummle
O' the learnit and michty in their seats – (22)

And in the third stanza, no less than twenty lines are devoted to mocking what he sees as the dominant power-brokers in modern society. His list of these 'larry cretinous', or cretinous fawners, includes 'slee politicos', 'the twisters', 'Company promoters', 'sleekit quacks', etc.

> Whatever 'hell or paradise they seek', he tells us 'they can hae it in per-
> petualfatúitie/ With pleisure and nae prejudice til god nor goat'.

In the fourth and final stanza, however, he admits that 'If I'd accumulate the sacred base doubloons/ I'd neer decay as I dae wantin them!', and:

> Wi ye, auld brither bard, to rant agin wir betters,
> Chack the hand that feeds us, pourin saut
> Intil the skaiths that feel it nocht, [...]. (23)

The 'skaiths' here appear to be about hurts that patrons cannot feel. The whole stanza, in fact, praises the spending of money, however it was acquired, for pleasure, specifically the pleasures of drinking and companionship, rather than for the purpose of wielding power over others. His choice of simile for conveying this is to quote George Stephenson on railway engines:

> – "There is nae limit to the speed
> If the works can be made to stand",
> As Geordie "Rocket" Stephenson aince said
> (Wi a kind o' misfortunate amphibologie, may be). (23)

The 'misfortunate amphibologie' might have something to do with the ambiva-lence involved in the poet's description of spending money to lubricate socia-bility 'In auld Kynd Kittock's snug shebeen', as the poet puts it two lines later. Stanzas 2–4 are an ironic commentary on the epigraph from Goldsmith, and the first stanza not only declares where Smith stands, but also describes the contrast between his poem and Goldsmith's, as follows:

> Na, na, mine Ollie,
> I fear in nae weys could we eer endorse
> Your noble dictum cast in "flawless verse"
> Mair polished, elegant and plat
> Nor my when raggit numbers in your praise. (22)

It is not so much that Smith rejects Goldsmith's 'noble dictum', but he stands it on its head, in that when 'wealth decays', as it does when spending money on drinks, then this benefits human relationships, and indeed friendships. The bond of friendship is strengthened when exchanging rounds of drinks. These lines also describe Goldsmith's reputedly 'flawless verse' as 'mair polished, elegant and plat', where 'plat' probably means 'direct', contrasted with his own 'raggit numbers'.

Goldsmith's Augustan style, however, was at odds, or at least in some tension, with the revival of Scots as the language of poetry in the 18th century, mainly by its greatest practitioners, Allan Ramsay, Robert Fergusson, and Robert Burns. Smith followed this tradition. One critic, David Spooner, pointed out that 'Scottish writers transformed and mocked the Augustans by incorporating ironical echoes in a unique rumbustious poetry', adding 'None more so than Sydney Goodsir Smith'; indeed, he opted for his own version of poetry in Scots, to some extent at least influenced by MacDiarmid and sometimes sounding like a personal idiolect of his own (Spooner, 35).

But despite his own 'raggit numbers', Smith evidently admired Goldsmith's polished Augustan style. Stanley Roger Green observed that in Smith there was a 'disparity between his cultured English accent and his chosen literary language of Lallans' (Green: 2007, 33–34). Perhaps Smith's vivid portrayal of Goldsmith personified his other linguistic identity.

One structural difference between the 1955 and 1974 versions of Smith's poem-sequence is that Section VII in the later version was originally at the end of Section VI. Section VII does, in fact, stand on its own. It is a moving salutation and farewell in three short stanzas to his Augustan companion: 'Here's a final gless til your standless ghaist/ In whatna airt it drees its immortality!' (24). Goldsmith is addressed in the opening stanza as *'mon brave, mon capitaine'*, which echoes how the poet often greeted his friends. As Stanley Roger Green put it:

> It was rare to meet Sydney, who would greet friends with the cry of 'Mon vieux! Mon Brave! Mon Generale!' without feeling that in some way one's daily ordinary life had been somehow transcended, and that at any given company under his careful sifting would sooner or later produce pure gold.
>
> GREEN: 1975, 8

It could be said that by a process of poetic alchemy, Smith's instinctive, voluble sociability produced the 'pure gold' of *Gowdspink in Reekie*.

The second stanza returns to the paradox often mentioned in the poem sequence of applying paradoxical manner the epigraph from Goldsmith as his 'gangrel brither' to more personal, convivial circumstances in which pockets, since 'pooch' means pocket, are emptied.

> I raise my gless, makar,
> To solemnlute ye, gangrel brither,
> Whase wealth in pooch accumulated nane
> But whase rich tresorie o' soul and sang
>     Decay shall never claim. (24)

It is in the final stanza that Smith addresses Goldsmith most directly as 'Gowd-spink, my maik', and the word 'maik' sums up all that Goldsmith meant to him. His own glossary gives three meanings of the word: 'mate, match, peer'. 'Gowd-spink' was, of course, the goldfinch Robert Fergusson wrote about in 'Ode to the Gowdspink', so in a way by alluding to Fergusson, Smith reconciles Gold-smith's Augustan style with Fergusson's traditional 'Scots leid'. Considering that he died less than a year later, the final three lines are very much in tune with the 'lacrimae rerum' motif:

> I'll see ye syne. Guid nicht!
>     – Ye ken.
>     Ay, ye ken indeed!

A reminiscence from the poet Tom Scott shortly after Smith's death is very per-tinent here:

> Just before Christmas 1974 he sent me a copy of the *Gowdspink*, suitably
> inscribed to his "antient comrade" (the comradeship was indeed "former"
> by that time). I replied with a Christmas card of a goldfinch and a joky
> remark that a goldfinch's name, *carduelis,* means "the one who lives on
> thistles" – as poets in Scotland have to do.
>     SCOTT, 4

Tom Scott certainly wrote this in a sombre mood and he may have been too pessimistic. A less sombre comment by the art critic Cordelia Oliver suggests why *Gowdspink in Reekie* has such resonance: '[...] as I found to my delight, the art critic of *The Scotsman* [Smith] was splendid company, not just amusing in himself but also singularly knowledgeable. I remember thinking that to be with him was a bit like going back in time, to the eighteenth century, perhaps' (Oliver, 11).

To end with a reverie, true possibly to both poets in spirit, Alexander Mof-fat's famous 1980 painting 'Poets' Pub', where Hugh MacDiarmid sits at a small table, with Sydney Goodsir Smith across from him, and George Mackay Brown sitting at the same table, while Norman MacCaig stands over his right shoulder could have an imagined 18th century counterpart. It might be titled 'Writers' Coffee-House', set in London rather than Edinburgh, and painted by Sir Joshua Reynolds. It would have Samuel Johnson as the centre of attention, but with Oliver Goldsmith sitting across from him, James Boswell at the same table, and David Garrick, his oldest friend, standing over Dr. Johnson.

## Bibliography

Clarke, Norma, *Brothers of the Quill* (Cambridge, Mass. & London: Harvard University Press, 2016).

Crawford, Robert, *The Bard: Robert Burns, a Biography* (London: Pimlico, 2010).

Crawford, Thomas, 'The Poetry of Sydney Goodsir Smith' in *Studies in Scottish Literature*, Vol. 7 / Issue 1 (1969), pp. 40–59.

Dixon, Peter, *Oliver Goldsmith Revisited* (Boston: Twayne Publishers, 1991).

Eliot, T.S., 'Johnson as Critic and Poet', in *On Poetry and Poets* (London: Faber and Faber Ltd, 1957).

Fergusson, Maggie, *George Mackay Brown: The Life* (London: John Murray, 2006).

Goldsmith, Oliver, 'The Deserted Village', in Robert L. Mack (eds.), *Oliver Goldsmith* (London: Everyman, 1997), pp. 49–62.

Goldsmith, Oliver, 'A Reverie at the Boar's Head Tavern in Eastcheap', in Arthur Friedan (ed.), *Collected Works of Oliver Goldsmith, Vol. III* (London: Oxford University Press, 1966), pp. 97–112.

Green, Stanley Roger, *A Clamjamfray of Poets* (Edinburgh: The Saltire Society, 2007).

Green, Stanley Roger, 'Sydney Goodsir Smith: An Appreciation' in *Scotia Review*, No. 9 (April 1975), pp. 5–8.

Maclean, Sorley, '*Figs and Thistles*' in *For Sydney Goodsir Smith* (Loanhead: M. Macdonald, 1975), pp. 73–78.

Massie, Allan, 'Review of *George Mackay Brown: The Life* by Maggie Fergusson' in *The Daily Telegraph* (30 April 2006).

Oliver, Cordelia, 'Sydney Goodsir Smith', in Ian Begg & Joy Hendry (eds.), *The Drawings of Sydney Goodsir Smith* (Edinburgh: Chapman Publishing for the New Auk Society, 1998), pp. 11–14.

Percy, Thomas, 'The Life of Dr. Oliver Goldsmith', in *The Miscellaneous Works of Oliver Goldsmith, M.B., Vol I* (London: W Otridge & Son, 1812).

Scott, Tom, 'Au 'Voir, Sydney' in *Scotia Review*, No. 9 (April 1975), pp. 2–4.

Smith, Iain Crichton, 'Sydney Goodsir Smith' in *Pembroke Magazine*, No. 7 (1976), pp. 166–172.

Smith, Sydney Goodsir, 'Gowdsmith in Reekie' in *Saltire Review*, Vol. 2 / No. 5 (autumn, 1955), pp. 42–51.

Smith, Sydney Goodsir, *Gowdspink in Reekie* (Loanhead: Macdonald Publishers, 1974).

Smith, Sydney Goodsir, *Kynd Kittock's Land* (Edinburgh: M. Macdonald, 1965).

Smith, Sydney Goodsir, *A Letter Written to Maurice Lindsay in 1947* (Edinburgh: The Saltire Society, 1988).

Smith, Sydney Goodsir, 'The Muse in Rose Street', in Norman MacCaig (ed.), *Honour'd Shade* (Edinburgh & London: W. & R. Chambers Ltd, 1959), pp. 116–117.

Smith, Sydney Goodsir, Typescript of 'The Wilderness' in Acc, 10426/9, Special Collections, National Library of Scotland.

Smith, Sydney Goodsir, 'Words of a Feather', in Neil Mathers (ed.), *The Auk Remembered* (Montrose: The Corbie Press, 1995), pp. 3–5.

Spooner, David, 'Some Propositions on the Great Auk: Sydney Goodsir Smith', in Neil Mathers (ed.), *The Auk Remembered* (Montrose: The Corbie Press, 1995), p. 35.

Wardle, Ralph M., *Oliver Goldsmith* (Lawrence: University of Kansas Press, 1957).

CHAPTER 11

# 'Your maist inebriant savant': A History of Sydney Goodsir Smith's *Carotid Cornucopius*

*Richie McCaffery*

### Abstract

This chapter has a two-fold purpose: to offer the first sustained academic examination of Smith's only published novel, written entirely in a unique form of neologistic and punning wordplay and to give the reader a sense of the history of the development of the novel and its placing in Smith's oeuvre. The only other existing writings on this book, apart from contemporary reviews and passing references in theses are rather uncritical appreciations by Hugh MacDiarmid, who considered it the Edinburgh equivalent of Joyce's Dublin in *Ulysses* and Robert Garioch who praised it in the fest-schrift *For Sydney Goodsir Smith*. This chapter seeks to answer the following question – is this book merely an elaborate *jeu d'esprit* or does it make a deeper point about language?

### Keywords

novel / prose – *Carotid Cornucopius* – postmodernism – modernism – James Joyce – wordplay – *Under the Eildon Tree* – Scottish Literary Renaissance – Thomas Urquhart – Scots language – experimental writing

∴

*Carotid Cornucopius*,[1] Sydney Goodsir Smith's only published novel (1947, rpt. 1964 & 1982), is so much of a *hapax legomenon* of an imaginative utterance that most critics, unsure of how to approach its galaxy of coinages, neologisms, portmanteaus, puns and innuendos, have politely sidestepped it or dealt with it in the broadest of terms as a Joycean 'extravaganza' (Royle, n.d.). Its most vocal champions have been the poet's contemporaries and friends, such as Robert Garioch and Hugh MacDiarmid who both make cameo appearances

---

1  The version of the book used for this chapter is: Goodsir Smith, Sydney, *Carotid Cornucopius* 2nd edition (Edinburgh: M. Macdonald, 1964).

© KONINKLIJKE BRILL NV, LEIDEN, 2020 | DOI:10.1163/9789004426498_013

in the novel and are given unique monikers, 'Rumboat Beerioch' and 'Huwll-and-cry-MacDammit' (35, 37). For Garioch, *Carotid Cornucopius* represented Smith's baptism of fire in the use of Scots as a literary medium (Garioch: 1975, 53). He cited it as an important preparatory work that enabled him to perfect his Scots idiolect and write so effectively in *Under the Eildon Tree*. For instance, our introduction to Carotid (or 'Carroty') in 'Capit Ane' of the book, has a close resemblance to the mock-heroic depiction of the poet as 'Slugabed' in *Under the Eildon Tree*, 'Elegy v' (Smith: 1975, 154–155). The Gaelic poet Sorley MacLean ('Sporley Tak-Quean'), who shared a house with Smith and his wife Marion at 50 Craigmillar Park ('Schloss Schmidt') in Edinburgh during the book's com-position, wrote to Smith shortly after its publication in 1947 to say how he was 'almost shitting [himself] on the train' reading it (Acc. 10281/1).[2] This is an apt description of the comic power and effect of the novel, most of its humour being derived from carnal or coprological sources, leading Smith's second wife Hazel Williamson, to dismiss it as a 'very filthy book' (Thomas, n.d.).

However, the highest estimation placed on this 'monsterpiece' (Hall: 1984, 15) was by Hugh MacDiarmid, who held it up as a work of such scabrous and subversive power that it blazed a trail through the chilly prudery of bourgeois Edinburgh and could proudly stand alongside novels by Lewis Grassic Gibbon, John MacDougall Hay, George Douglas Brown and R.L. Stevenson (MacDiar-mid: 1964, 14). The list of spoof titles by 'Gude Schir Skidderie Smithereens' in the 1964 edition of the book gives us an immediate sense of his desire to both shock Presbyterian primness and entertain: one title is '*A Lust Blawst of the Strumpet Against Chasetity Belts*'. MacDiarmid also cited the novel as the prose triumph of the Scottish Renaissance movement (ibid). *Carotid Cornucopius* is an almost plot-less novel, effectively being one long inventory of things that matter to, or annoy, the author about life in Edinburgh. It resists academic study in traditional thematic and literary or critical ways. For John C. Hall, its wild linguistic medium is its very 'message' (Hall: 1982, 51). As James B. Caird has pointed out: it is 'not a novel in terms of characterisation or narrative, but it is a linguistically inventive, bawdy extravaganza, full of rollicking high spirits and magnificent absurdity, calculated to shock the anaemic and the prudish', such as those looking to explain it in dryly academic terms (Caird, 15). As such, perhaps the only productive method of approach is to look at the history of the development of the novel, where it features in Smith's life and work, the im-pact it had on its contemporary readership and its residual currency today.

---

2   Note: all manuscript sources relate to MS. and Acc. numbers in Special Collections at the National Library of Scotland.

Some contemporary readers were not as effusive as Hugh MacDiarmid and thought that Smith had gone too far in sowing his literary wild oats in the same way the central figure 'Carroty' does. In fact, the very nature of siring illegitimate children through Carroty's nocturnal misadventures is symbolic of the questions of authorial ownership, allusion and intertextuality, of how texts are related to one another and how pastiche, cross-referencing and plagiarism come into play. The book features a long tract on the nature of plagiarism; the same postmodernist questions and ideas of borrowing and citing that are central to *Under the Eildon Tree*. Smith, speaking in character as Carroty, admits that the major progenitors of his novel are 'the Three Mustgethures of Halevilehallow – Prancing Rumbelly [Rabelais], Tommust Furkhard [Thomas Urquhart] and Jape's Joys [James Joyce]' (22). In terms of contemporary critics, one of those who saw Smith as bastardising canonical literature was the older poet, translator and economist attached to the Scottish Renaissance movement, Alexander Gray (1882–1968). Gray wrote to Smith in 1947 to give him advice on his application for a Houghton Mifflin Fellowship: 'I am a little bit sorry you sent them *Carotid Cornucopius*. It is not good for all people to see all things' (see Gray, Acc. 10397). In 1948, after a heated epistolary discussion between Gray and Smith about creative freedom, Gray asserted that 'words are much more sensitive creatures than you young people think. You cannot [...] just do what you like with them' (ibid). However, that was precisely Smith's intention: to have his wicked way with any words of his choosing or invention. This has its precedent in the poem 'Epistle to John Guthrie' from Smith's first 1941 collection *Skail Wind*, where the speaker defends his art against the criticism from his friend that it is written in an artificial language 'which no one speaks':

> We've come intil a gey queer time
>     Whan scrievin Scots is near a crime,
>     "There's no one speaks like that", they fleer,
>     – But wha the deil spoke like King Lear?
>         SMITH: 1975, 13

As such *Carotid Cornucopius* represents something of a Viking raid on language, on Edinburgh pub-life, on the literary canon and on history and the attitudes and values of the time of its composition. While Smith was unsuccessful in his application for a Houghton Mifflin Fellowship, in 1946 he did win an Atlantic Award from the Rockefeller Foundation which enabled him to leave his clerical post in the British Council offices in Edinburgh where he had worked for a year, after a war spent teaching English to Polish refugees and soldiers in Breadalbane and Leven. He never returned to full-time employment.

Work on *Carotid Cornucopius* began in a burst of creativity at the end of the War, in 1945. Although the exact completion date of the book is unknown, it was published by brothers Kenny and Calum Campbell of the Caledonian Press in Glasgow in 1947. The book first appeared in '4 fitts' (four chapters) which is also measured on the cover in potable terms as 'one quart' of the book, in a print run of three hundred copies, priced at the then rather prohibitive sum of one guinea (see Lindsay, Acc. 4791/12).

Garioch has emphasised the 'vastness of the intended design' of *Carotid Cornucopius* – whereas Joyce's *Ulysses* takes place over the course of one day, Smith envisaged that his novel would take place over a year, each chapter being devoted to a separate day (Garioch: 1975, 47). The 1964 revised second edition was extended to comprise eight chapters, which suggests that Smith's grand vision was always doomed to fail. It seems much more likely that this was Smith's affectionate, if impish, attempt to poke fun at his friend Hugh Mac-Diarmid's verbose pronouncements at the time to seek a 'GIANTISM in the arts' (MacDiarmid: 1966, 56). In Smith's own words, the character of Carotid with his grossly drink-swollen carotid artery on his neck is grotesque, a *lusus naturae*, a 'giant-infant like Pantagruel who [is] meant to make you laugh by mentioning the unmentionable in words new-minted for the purpose' (Smith: 1969, 51). There is something to be said about the bestial and intellectual qualities of 'Carroty' – he is a freak of nature but in many ways also an engaging raconteur and literary-minded. He seems to be couched somewhere between Samuel Johnson's observation that 'he who makes a beast of himself gets rid of the pain of being a man' (Johnson, 333) and Gregory Smith's notion of the 'Caledonian Antisyzygy', made up of dualities and contrasts derived from an historical and national splitting of identity and character based on the Union of 1707 (the 'Cheatry of Ruinyon') and the subsequent Anglicisation of Scottish culture and life (Smith: 1919, 4). Certainly the book was a tremendous influence on Smith's thinking, in his own annotated copy of the first edition he has written, dated July 1940, 'the greatest description of the literature yet written'.[3] Setting his novel in the most vernacular pubs and fleshpots of Edinburgh also meant that he was celebrating a life that had at that time largely managed to escape touristic homogenisation and Anglicisation (Riach et al., 140). Arguably it is Roderick Watson, in writing about the novel, who comes closest to striking at the heart of its message as being one based on a Bakhtinian carnival where

---

3    Note: this particular copy, ex-libris Sydney Goodsir Smith, is in the present author's personal collection.

code-switching between high and low registers and topics as well as idioms enables the author, or protagonist, to see themselves in a new or estranged way (Watson, 151).

It is little surprise, then, that in the novel Carroty (the 'Caird of the Cannon Gait') resides in the 'Camera Obscura' cupola of Patrick Geddes's Outlook Tower, which had, by the time the book was written, fallen into disrepair after Geddes' death in 1932. Here Carroty can survey his fiefdom of Edinburgh, while also living in one of the jewels of Geddes's radical and visionary town-planning, thus straddling both the past and the future and belonging in the aspirational and recreational realms of the city equally. Hugh MacDiarmid was very percipient in noticing that Smith's contrasting values, his celebration of high and low culture, basilect and acrolect, is something that naturally finds its home in Edinburgh, a city of heterogeneous architectural styles. For MacDiarmid, Smith was a 'sharawaggian', derived from the architectural term 'sharawaggi' meaning 'the use of irregularity, discordance or incongruity for deliberate, artful, contrastive effect'. He saw that behind the Augustan gentility and Enlightenment intellect of Edinburgh, there was a 'pagan violence' that Smith was able to tap into and unleash, his work accepting the many faces and voices of Edinburgh (MacDiarmid: 1947, 44–47).

Although printed by Caledonian Press, the novel was actually published specifically for the members of the 'Auk Society', the auk being Smith himself, in avian form: an 'extinct bard'. Most autographed copies of the original edition find Smith signing under the guise of 'the Auk', and the copy I used in my research for this chapter is dedicated to George Main, a teacher of languages at Portobello High School: 'For Georgio Main / In the Café, as abusual, the Auk'. The café being Café Royal which is remembered in the book as 'the Carefree Boil', although Smith's preferred hostelry was the nearby Abbotsford ('the Abbotsfork'). The 'Auk Society' was an act of chicanery, because if the book was only privately available, it was not subject to normal commercial censorship rules – exactly the same strategy adopted by the Caledonian Press when they published, in 1947 as well, Hamish Henderson's non-bowdlerised *Ballads of World War II* for members of the 'Lili Marleen Club of Glasgow'. It was also the method used in 1959 by Callum Macdonald to publish Smith's edited selection of Robert Burns's *The Merry Muses of Caledonia* which was again available only to members of the Auk Society. The obscene publications act of 1959 made little concession for literature that might be deemed offensive but was also of artistic merit. The 1964 amendment and slight relaxation of this act helped to bring awareness of the repressiveness of publishing culture in the UK to the reading public. 1964 was also the year the second edition of the novel appeared, lavishly 'luotrated' by artist Rendell Wells. Upon its republication Edwin

Morgan astutely observed that it was 'a pity this wasn't published properly in 1947. It comes rather late now to make much of an impact since the mood is so different, and Joyce has been taken over by the scholars and academics' (Morgan, 131). In 1947, the work of James Joyce would not have been so enshrined and entrenched in academia and exegetical piety and would have been much more the preserve of the more generalised though literary, book-reading public. Richard Ellmann's 1959 literary biography of Joyce is one of the keystone texts to have generated academic interest in his work. That said, sufficient demand remained for *Carotid Cornucopius* to be reprinted for the last time in 1982 by Macdonald Publishers. The third edition is something of a retrograde step in the evolution of the book, as it lacks the quality materials and colours used for the 1964 definitive edition as well as the clear typeface, with its bright, topsy-turvy dustjacket.

*Carotid Cornucopius* is certainly a cult book, though the circle of people who are interested in it and who have read it is likely to be very small. Its cultural, social and political frames of reference are stuck firmly in the 1940s and this means that there are passages that to a modern reader, particularly relating to women and race, might appear at best old-fashioned. Nowadays the novel is more or less forgotten, although there are occasional calls for it, such as those made by the performance poet Harry Giles and Alan Riach who called for its 'thorough annotation and republication' (Riach et al., 140) and Cairns Craig who held it up as one of Smith's 'major achievements' (Craig, 126). Most recently, Patrick Crotty, in his *Times Literary Supplement* centenary reappraisal of the work of Smith, found that 'the testosterone-heavy, beery ethos of post-War Edinburgh vitiates [...] *Carotid Cornucopius*' (Crotty, 15). Crotty's assertion strikes at one of the intrinsic questions raised by the novel: is it merely a *jeu d'esprit*, a literary bagatelle, or is it an experimental, comic novel with serious social and metafictional implications? For Crotty, Smith 'appears to have been torn in life as well as art between the conditions of a gangrel [...] and a privileged rake [...] the tramp and the cad in SGS [...] so sustained their combined assault on respectability that an unresolved quarrel with the values of his brilliant but establishmentarian progenitor may be thought to lie behind his art in its many forms' (ibid.). Although Smith is remembered by many as having a quasi-aristocratic air (he was after all the public-school and Oxford-educated son of a Knight of the Realm and Dean of the Faculty of Medicine at Edinburgh University) his choice of a wife had meant that he was without any income from his father and mother who effectively 'disinherited' him (see MS. 26144/1–11). Most of the 1940s saw Smith living in extremely straitened circumstances, with two young children to support and trying all along to reconcile his desire to be a bohemian poet with domestic responsibility. In a 1946 letter to Kenny Campbell, before Campbell published *Carotid Cornucopius*, Smith admitted that he was so poor he was 'hunting the bawbees like a tripe-hound' (see MS. 2960.16/1). *Carotid Cornucopius* represents a temporary escape from that struggle. It is a retreat into a fantastical realm, where, as Robert Garioch has noted, everyone drinks as much as they like, but no-one becomes incoherently, boorishly drunk (Garioch: 1975, 52). *Under the Eildon Tree* is a much more emotionally nuanced work because it is shot through with an awareness, and indeed a contrition for those who have been hurt. It suggests that Smith cannot go on living a double life as a rake and must in some way accept his responsibilities as a father and husband. In effect, *Carotid Cornucopius* is the preparatory field-work that brought the passionate and dissolute poet to his knees in *Under the Eildon Tree*, trapped in a cycle of self-destruction and one-night-stands.

However, it was not all ennui and gloom. A pawky 1948 article by Smith entitled 'Claret, Oysters and Reels' finds the poet trying to vividly evoke the broiling tavern life of Edinburgh in the 18th century, as well as exploring the nature of his own worshipping of Bacchus (Smith: 1948, n.d.). It is a work of poetic fiction and social history that reveals the depth of Smith's scholarly and sybaritic interests in the Scottish capital. MacDiarmid observed that one of the most eloquent observers and participants in 18th century Edinburgh night-life, the poet Robert Fergusson ('Rairbit Fairgossoon'), 'would be at home' in the midst of the pub denizens of *Carotid Cornucopius* (MacDiarmid: 1947, 44–47). It is clear from the article that Smith is seeking a direct and unhampered line back to this era, an epoch he romanticises as more desirable than the male-dominated one he finds himself in:

> The much more free-and-easy contact between the sexes in the tavern society of 150 years ago was wrecked by Victorian Busybodies, and even to-day the majority of Edinburgh howffs have a grim, separate, and dingy purdah in which females are just tolerated.
>
> SMITH: 1948, n.d.

It seems clear from the above quotation that Smith had little concern for the questions of women's liberation or rights, but rather sought unfettered access to women as sexual beings, or beings of desire, although his early Edinburgh circle of friends in the late 1930s and early 1940s included both sexes in almost equal numbers. In many ways, the novel is used as a stick to beat sections of Edinburgh society of whom Smith disapproves. This is very clear in the enemy and rival figure of 'Duncod', a disagreeable, rich and arrogant character who in Carroty's eyes represents the interests of the City Corporation and big business, at the expense of his own wayward and bohemian lifestyle. Duncod's politics also mark him out as being the 'baddie', in that he is a signed up black-shirt, or Mosleyite, amongst many other things that the author lists with relish: 'The Brattish Bunion of Nitsies, Fashists, Pashists or Bleakshit, blunder the feedershop of Dosewell Boastlie' (64). Throughout Smith's writing, he takes aim at those in a position of institutionalised or political power, rather like MacDiarmid did before when operating in gadfly mode as the 'catfish in the aquarium, stirring up the torpor of the more docile denizens' (Riach: 1992, ix). Take, for instance, Smith's anger at what he saw as the memory of the national bard, Robert Burns being exploited as a money-making enterprise by Edinburgh Council in his 1955 article 'Immortal Mummery' where he warns his readers that Burns should not be allowed to become 'the appendage of a Tourist Drive run by the Chamber of Commerce' (Smith: 1955, 20). As such, *Carotid Cornucopius*, for all of its debauchery and smuttiness, follows the same ethical compass as the rest of Smith's writing, and is not, as John C. Hall has described it, a 'celebration of anarchy', but an eccentric work that follows a deeply individualistic but consistent moral code.

The historical context of *Carotid Cornucopius* is significant. It emerged in print for the first time one year before Smith's poetic masterpiece *Under the Eildon Tree*, which was begun in 1947. There are instances in both books of stylistic and linguistic similarities and both deal with the seamier, earthier aspects of Edinburgh at night, a 'deutero Edinburgh' as Edwin Morgan once described it (Morgan: 1976, 41). In many ways *Carotid Cornucopius* is the dropsical, errant, wayward, evil, though crucially not disowned twin of *Under the Eildon Tree*. It is clear from the exuberance of his long 1947 letter to Maurice Lindsay, published as a Saltire booklet in 1988 that he is in his prime as a writer and poet, with his novel published and *Under the Eildon Tree* on the way from the then newly founded Serif Books of Joe Mardel (Smith, 1988).

Although Smith was not in the habit of keeping a diary in adulthood, he did write some private thoughts in a jotter during the 1949 / 1950 period where he confessed to feeling that he was finished creatively: 'my days for lyric poetry are finished [...] doubt I'll write much poetry of any worth again' and he also attributed much of his worry to having a 'series of meaningless affairs out of sheer bloody mindedness' (see MS. 26156). As such there seems to have been a very narrow window during which Smith felt inspired and driven to write his best work. But even before this low point, in *Carotid Cornucopius* critics such as John Burns detected a 'glimpse of a darker, more serious portrait of the artist, a glimpse which adds just a hint of desperation to the comedy' (Burns, 51). There is a thanatic edge to most of Smith's writing about drinking to excess and seeking the fleeting solace of prostitutes or extra-marital affairs: it is also a major element of *Under the Eildon Tree* where the speaker is seemingly punishing themselves on week-long drinking sprees, which is the fuel behind 'Elegy XIII' where the errant Orphean speaker embarks on a torrid, boozy affair with a girl met in 'The Black Bull o Norroway'. There is certainly a bravado and a jocular gloss placed by Smith on such behaviour (Rum and draucht Bass./– Sheer *hara-kiri!*) but it also shows that he was self-destructive (Smith: 1975, 167–171). What is often overlooked is the fact that in 1945–1947, when both *Under the Eildon Tree* and *Carotid Cornucopius* were written, he was only 30 going on 31, not the older monocled figure we perhaps have in our received image of Smith.

Around the same time, he also met the young teacher Hazel Williamson (1928–2004), who became his wife in 1967 after the death of his first wife Marion in the previous year. He was at the time still married to Marion but had embarked on the affair with Hazel, and his guilt is only now becoming apparent, since we know more about his private life than people will have known while he was still alive, or would have been willing to disclose at the time. In 1951, when Marion was still very much in the picture, he dedicated his short collection of love lyrics *The Aipple and the Hazel* to Williamson: 'To the onlie begetter H. W'. and the closing line from the title poem is used as the epitaph on the grave they share in the Dean Cemetery, Edinburgh: 'And the aipple and the hazel are as ane' (Smith: 1975, 129–130). As such we can see how Smith's personal life and art were intimately connected, if not entangled and he used his writing as a way of making sense of the complex and at times mendacious nature of his existence.

*Carotid Cornucopius* was far from Smith's first and only foray into imaginative prose, but apart from the rather surrealist and stiffly English short story 'At Least We Were Together Until the End' which appeared in *Scotia Review* in 1973 towards the end of his life, it is the only work that made it into print. After a less than illustrious university career at Oriel College, Oxford during the mid-1930s, Smith wrote, on being sent down, the unpublished comic novel *Bottled Peaches* (1936) which owes much to the Evelyn Waugh 'bright young things' university novel of a generation before that of Smith's. The novel survives in typescript in the National Library of Scotland (see MS. 26142). Subtitled 'We Caper into Cul-de-Sacs' it is about a group of feckless but privileged students who spend their time drinking at the expense of studying and at the end of their time at university are confronted with the stark realisation that they are doomed to unemployability and disappointing their parents. In keeping with Smith's proclivity for the novels of Ronald Firbank,[4] *Bottled Peaches* – like *Carotid Cornucopius* – is not held together with a firm or striking plot, but rather a delightfully witty

---

4   See postcard from Moray McLaren to Smith (dated 24/03/1935) discussing the search for Ronald Firbank's grave, in Smith papers Acc. 10397, National Library of Scotland.

meander through irresponsibility, high-living and living beyond one's means. This pattern in Smith's work of seeking escape from adulthood and responsibility and then feeling shackled with contrition for doing so, is intimately connected to Patrick Crotty's observation that Smith lived a dual life as gangrel and gentleman in a sort of 'épater la bourgeoisie' rebellion against his distant yet somehow overbearing father. In *Bottled Peaches* the protagonist Noel Volpane lives in fear of his establishment father 'The Professor' who expects his son to go out into the world and get an exalted job and who does not know that his son has been rusticated by the university for laziness and drinking. This mirrors more or less exactly Smith's own university experience, but the notion of indolence, celebrated in mock-heroic terms in Smith's writing and poetry, is belied by the fact that already, in his early 20s, he had sufficient ambition and diligence to sit down and complete a serviceable and enjoyable novel.

Upon coming down from university, Smith struggled to find his way and drifted to Adelphi in London where he spent a difficult year trying unsuccessfully to carve out his niche as a writer. He grew depressed, began to seriously neglect himself and became very alienated and withdrawn. It was only after his return to Edinburgh in 1938 that he began to write the quasi-autobiographical and philosophical work *The Wilderness* in order to deal with his anguish at what was happening in his private life and in Europe at the time (see Acc. 10426/9). The lead character is, like many of Smith's works, cast as an 'Orpheus manqué'. There is no space to discuss this unpublished work here, but it is worth mentioning because it shows that within a few years, Smith had gone from writing that was Dionysian, epigrammatic and celebratory in nature, to writing something that was deeply psychological, searching and elegiac. Anyone wishing to dismiss Smith's later love poetry as glib, Parnassian or formulaic and *Carotid Cornucopius* as a self-indulgent private joke among friends, needs to understand the vision, ambition and emotional range his work displayed before he was even in his mid-20s, that the ability to have fun and be frivolous was a right he had earned.

The question is, how did Smith's ego as a writer recover sufficiently from the troubled late 1930s, for his voice to come through forcefully and distinctively into print in the mid-1940s? The answer is his discovery of friends and a wife in Edinburgh where he initially returned to recover from illness with his parents and the momentous discovery of the Scottish Literary Renaissance. In a pub one day, the inspirational teacher and Head of English at the Royal High School, Hector MacIver (remembered as 'Erektor MacReiver' in the book) gave the young Smith a copy of Hugh MacDiarmid's 1926 masterwork *A Drunk Man Looks at the Thistle* and Smith's course as a poet seemed to be set – its effect on him was nothing short of numinous (Smith: 2011, 314). In *Pilgrim Souls* MacIver writes that both he and Smith became close friends, often 'setting the Celtic world to rights' in a pub or else supporting each other intellectually through the war by exchanging work and letters (MacIver, 103). We have already seen how Robert Garioch considered *Carotid Cornucopius* to be Smith's major preparatory study enabling him to fully attain his idiolectal Scots voice. The book celebrates conversational language and Edinburgh pub-life because these are the very things that offered Smith a circle of like-minded friends, a support structure, a literary setting and crucially a sense of belonging. These friends included Hector MacIver, Sorley MacLean, Robert Garioch and the artist Denis Peploe, who illustrated Smith's third poetry collection *The Deevil's Waltz*. It is little surprise then, that often it seems like the book is written with his own inner circle in mind as the intended audience.

In spite of this personal nature of the book, it does continue to have a wider application. It not only pushes communication and the novel form to its outer and often most extremely metatextual limits but it is, when taken in the context of Smith's earlier writing in particular, a remarkable achievement. Even the 'Auktor's Buquet', which serves as a foreword to the book, is adorned with a drawing by Rendell Wells which shows the Auk painting the painter who in turn is painting the Auk, thus showing the *mise en abyme* complexity of the thinking behind the book, as well as its many narratives and many source texts. Its debt to James Joyce, although astute readers will notice the passing references to auks and auk eggs in *Ulysses*, is not a predominant feature, as the book makes a vast tissue of allusions to a great number of works and authors, and it is likely that it does not really have much to offer to the Joyce scholar, although it is repeatedly also compared to *Finnegans Wake* in its attempts to capture sounds and cadences of speech. Passages such as the polyphony of voices in the Tolbooth Bar scene in 'Caput Shree' are clearly reminiscent of Joyce's Anna Livia Plurabelle, wife of Humphrey Chimpden Earwicker in *Finnegans Wake* (76–78). Joyce's most abstruse novel is also evoked towards the end of *Carotid Cornucopius* when Colickie Meg, keeper of the Ben Nevis Tavern and Carroty's main love interest, tries to sooth her new born children to sleep with the Lord's Prayer, recast in Edinburgh place-names:

> Our Cramond that Marchmont Newhaven, Holyrood Bruntsfield Grange; thy Colinton Comely-Bank; thy Liberton in Leith, Arthur's Seat Corstorphine; Granton Lasswade our Dalkeith Braids and Forthbrig us our Tollcrosses, as we Fairmilehead then that Grassmarket Cowgate us. Queensferry us not into Tynecastle but Dean Brig us Tron Mayfield, for St Giles Inch the King's Park, the Powderhall, the Gorgie: for Waverley and Waverley.
>
> DUN EDIN. (151)

Colickie Meg is clearly a character similar to Anna Livia Plurabelle because she represents something more than a mortal individual. Meg is seen to represent Mother Earth, and is both nourishing and inspiring, as well as being one of the folkloric holy drinkers like 'Kynd Kittock', who upon her death was given a job as the barmaid at the gates of heaven, to give refreshments to the recently departed (Smith: 1975, 205–215). Anna Livia Plurabelle is the spirit of the River Liffey incarnate. But the prayer above is not the only such Joycean example in the book, there is also a more ribald version, which also shows Smith's debt to Rabelais: 'The Caird is my shoothard, I shole not pant; he meeketh me to ligg doun in agrean rapeutres [...]'. (66). Both examples play on phonetic similarities and puns, which brings the coinages and neologisms of Sir Thomas Urquhart into the equation, but they also show – as Robert Garioch himself observed – that *Carotid Cornucopius* is 'less philologically learned than [...] Joyce' (Garioch: 1975, 51) and for James Caird, Smith's Edinburgh-centric and boozy novel lacked the 'universal implications of *Finnegans Wake*' (Caird, 15).

It is true that Smith wears his learning both loosely and sometimes heavily in the book and at times the writing does feel like a direct parody or pastiche of something else, but this is the nature of Smith's vibrant intertextuality that shimmers through all of his work. *Carotid Cornucopius* anticipates that people will attempt to assess it in soberly critical and academic terms and it does its best to repel such advances by actively commenting in authorial asides and interruptions on not simply the process of composition but the likely ways in which the book will be received and consumed by its audience. It is more a book about the nature of what happens to a text once it has been written, than a typical novel that is wrapped up in its own plot and narrative. It is a book with grand designs that seeks to live and thrive not simply within the confines of its own boards and pages, but also outside of such parameters, like a fantasy character that wants to touch people in the 'real' world. In his 1969 article on the joys of playing with the plasticity of language, Smith claims that 'Concocting new words is an addiction' (Smith: 1969, 50) and we can see *Carotid Cornucopius* as the culmination of that addiction, one of many for man who was 'born excessive' (Smith: 1975, 157). While the book is clearly shot through with an unfastidious lust for life, literature and words as well as giving us glimpses of depression or struggle, it is not simply a comic romp. It marks Smith having come home at last through the war and domestic or psychological difficulty. With this novel, as well as the poem cycle *Under the Eildon Tree*, Smith was able to claim his place as a major performer in the Scottish Renaissance.

## Bibliography

Burns, John, 'Smith's Cornucopia' (a review of the 1982 3rd edn. of *Carotid Cornucopius*) in *Cencrastus*, Issue 14 (autumn 1983), pp. 50–51.

Caird, James B., 'Sydney Goodsir Smith' in *Chapman* Issue 26 (Spring 1980), pp. 14–19.

Craig, Cairns, 'The Literary Tradition' in T.M. Devine & Jenny Wormaid (eds.), *The Oxford Handbook of Modern Scottish History* (Oxford: Oxford University Press, 2012), pp. 99–129.

Crotty, Patrick, 'Doon Canongate: A centenary appreciation of a Scots makar' in *The Times Literary Supplement* (13 Nov 2015), pp. 14–15.

Garioch, Robert, '*Carotid Cornucopius*' in Norman MacCaig (ed.), *For Sydney Goodsir Smith* (Loanhead: M. Macdonald, 1975), pp. 47–54.

Gray, Alexander, Letter to Smith (dated 1947), in Acc. 10397, NLS.

Hall, John C., 'Big Music and Skail Winds: The achievement of Robert Garioch and Sydney Goodsir Smith' in *Lines Review* Issue 88 (1984), pp. 10–19.

Hall, John C., 'The Writings of Sydney Goodsir Smith', a PhD thesis submitted to the University of Aberdeen, September 1982. Accessed online (June 2018): http://ethos .bl.uk/OrderDetails.do?uin=uk.bl.ethos.330725.

Johnson, Samuel, 'Anecdotes of the Revd. Percival Stockdale' in George Birkbeck-Hill (ed.), *Johnsonian Miscellanies* Vol. II (Oxford: Clarendon Press, 1897).

MacDiarmid, Hugh, *The Company I've Kept* (London: Hutchinson, 1966).

MacDiarmid, Hugh, 'Foreword' to Smith, *Carotid Cornucopius* 2nd edn. (Edinburgh: M. Macdonald, 1964), pp. 14–20.

MacDiarmid, Hugh, 'A Scottish Sharawaggian' (review of 1st edn. of Smith's *Carotid Cornucopius*) in *Voice of Scotland* Vol. IV / No. 1 (September 1947), pp. 44–47.

MacIver, Mary & Hector, *Pilgrim Souls* (Aberdeen: Aberdeen University Press, 1990).

McLaren, Moray, Postcard from McLaren to Smith (24 March 1935) in Acc. 10397, NLS.

MacLean, Sorley, Letter to Smith (21 July 1947) in Acc. 10281/1, NLS.

Morgan, Edwin, Letter from Morgan to rare bookseller Kulgin Duval (dated 24 Jan. 1965), in *The Midnight Letterbox: Selected Correspondence 1950–2010* (Manchester: Carcanet Press, 2015), pp. 130–131.

Morgan, Edwin, Review of *For Sydney Goodsir Smith* and *Collected Poems* in *Lines Review* Issue 57 (1976), pp. 40–43.

Riach, Alan & Moffat, Alexander, *Arts of Resistance: Poets, Portraits and Landscapes of Modern Scotland* (Edinburgh: Luath Press, 2009).

Riach, Alan, 'Introduction' in Hugh MacDiarmid *Selected Prose* (Manchester: Carcanet Press, 1992), pp. ix–xxv.

Royle, Trevor, 'More views from auld voyeur with an earthy outlook', (review of 1982 3rd edn. of *Carotid Cornucopius*) in *The Glasgow Herald* (4th Dec. 1982), pagination unknown.

Smith, G. Gregory, *Scottish Literature: Character and Influence* (London: Macmillan & Co., 1919).

Smith, Sydney Goodsir, 'Bottled Peaches' (a novel, unpublished typescript) in MS. 26142, NLS.

Smith, Sydney Goodsir (published under Gude Schir Skidderie Smithereens), *Carotid Cornucopius: The first 4 fitts*, 1st edn. (Glasgow: Caledonian Press, 1947).

Smith, Sydney Goodsir, *Carotid Cornucopius*, 2nd edn. (Edinburgh: M. Macdonald, 1964).

Smith, Sydney Goodsir, 'Claret, Oysters and Reels' in *The Galliard* Issue 1 (1948), unpaginated.

Smith, Sydney Goodsir (Scott, Tom ed.), *Collected Poems 1941–1975* (London: John Calder, 1975).

Smith, Sydney Goodsir, 'Immortal Mummery' in *Saltire Review* Issue 6 (winter 1955), pp. 17–20.

Smith, Sydney Goodsir, Letter from Smith to Hugh MacDiarmid (1 Nov 1941) in John Manson (ed.) *Dear Grieve: Letters to Hugh MacDiarmid (C.M. Grieve)* (Glasgow: Kennedy and Boyd, 2011), p. 314.

Smith, Sydney Goodsir, Personal papers consulted for this chapter: MS. 26144/1–11, MS. 2960.16/1 & MS. 26156, NLS.

Smith, Sydney Goodsir, *Saltire Self-Portraits 3: A letter written to Maurice Lindsay in 1947* (Edinburgh: The Saltire Society, 1988).

Smith, Sydney Goodsir, 'The Wilderness: A Study of a Creeping Disease' (unpublished manuscript) in Acc. 10426 / 9, NLS.

Smith, Sydney Goodsir, 'Words of a Feather' in *Akros* Issue 10 (May 1969), pp. 48–51.

Thomas, Patrick, 'Chronicles of a Misspent Youth: Paxman, Patrick & the Scottish Poets', accessed online (June 2018): www.christchurchcarmarthen.org.uk/?p=1124.

Watson, Roderick, 'Alien Voice from the Street: Demotic Modernisms in Modern Scots Writing' in *The Yearbook of English Studies: Non-Standard Englishes and the New Media Special Number* Vol. 25 (Modern Humanities Research Association, 1995), pp. 141–155.

# CHAPTER 12

# The Merrie Life and Dowie Death of Colickie Meg: An Unpublished Carotidian Drama

*Paul Barnaby*

## Abstract

The comic drama *Colickie Meg* is both an adaptation and a continuation of *Carotid Cornucopius* and is written in the same distinctive idiolect. Although extracts were published in the journals *Lines Review* and *Jabberwock*, it remains both unperformed and unpublished. This chapter examines the five extant manuscripts of *Colickie Meg* held by Edinburgh University Library and the National Library of Scotland. It first traces a compositional history of the play, focusing, in particular, on early drafts that cast significant light on Smith's creative processes and reveal that his most intensive work on *Colickie Meg* occurred earlier (1949–50) than has been appreciated. It next provides a brief summary of the play's action before analysing in depth its relationship to *Carotid Cornucopius*. It shows that the drama downplays the novel's political components and amplifies its mythical subtexts while offering clues as to why Smith did not extend *Carotid Cornucopius* beyond the existing eight 'fitts'. It finally identifies factors – largely connected to its spectacular multimedia nature – that may have prevented *Colickie Meg* from reaching either page or stage.

## Keywords

*Colickie Meg* – *Carotid Cornucopius* – verse drama – comedy – James Joyce – *Finnegans Wake* – Scots language – idiolect

Listed among Smith's 'major works' by Kurt Wittig (293), acclaimed by Thom Nairn as 'a challenging and intriguing work unparalleled in Scottish literature' (175), and trumpeted by the author himself as 'the only successor to the *Three Estates*' (Smith: 1950), the comic drama *Colickie Meg* nonetheless remains unpublished and unperformed. Extracts appeared in *Lines Review* (Smith: 1955) and *Jabberwock* (Smith: 1958), but a projected private printing of the whole text

by the Caledonian Press in 1952 was aborted.[1] Playwright Ronald Duncan dis-
cussed staging the play at Edinburgh's Assembly Hall with Sir Ian Hunter, di-
rector of the Edinburgh International Festival, but the project similarly came
to nothing.[2]

Fortunately, substantial manuscript materials survive at Edinburgh Uni-
versity Library and the National Library of Scotland. The latter, consisting of
two complete typescripts of *Colickie Meg* (MS 26131 and Acc. 11798),[3] have
been studied in unpublished theses by John C. Hall (1982, 338–342) and
Thom Nairn (1991, 170–175), and in an online article by Katja Lenz (2001).[4]
The Edinburgh University Library materials, however, consisting of a manu-
script (Gen 1758) and two much-corrected typescripts (Gen 1762 and Gen
1763), have evaded critical attention.[5] Predating the NLS versions, they cast
significant light on Smith's creative processes and reveal that his most inten-
sive work on *Colickie Meg* occurred somewhat earlier (1949–50) than has
been appreciated.[6] In this chapter, I shall first trace a compositional history
of *Colickie Meg*, focusing, in particular, on the three early drafts held by Edin-
burgh University Library. I shall next provide a brief summary of the play's
action (substantially unchanged in all drafts), before analysing its relation-
ship to *Carotid Cornucopius*, of which it is part-adaptation, part-continuation.
We shall see that the play downplays the political components and amplifies
the mythical subtext of Smith's novel while offering clues as to why Smith
did not extend *Carotid Cornucopius* beyond the existing eight 'fitts'. Finally, I
shall identify factors that may have prevented *Colickie Meg* from reaching
either page or stage.

---

1    There are corrected galley proofs of the Prologue and approximately half of Act I of *Colickie
      Meg* at NLS Acc. 11796. There are references to this abortive publication in a notebook listing
      Smith's forthcoming publications (NLS MS 26157, f. 11) and in a letter from Smith to Hugh
      MacDiarmid, dated 3 October 1953 (EUL MS 2960.16/61).

2    To which Duncan refers in a letter to Smith, dated November 1953, in NLS Acc. 10397. I should
      like to thank Richie McCaffery for drawing my attention to the references to *Colickie Meg* in
      NLS MS 26157 and Acc. 10397.

3    There is also an incomplete carbon copy of MS 26131 at MS 26168.

4    Oddly, none of these authors alludes to the existence of multiple versions of *Colickie Meg*.
      From internal evidence, Hall appears to study NLS MS 26131 and Nairn NLS Acc. 11798. It is
      unclear which TS Lenz examines.

5    Barring a brief description in Barnaby: 2014, 92–93.

6    Hall (309) and Nairn (170) suggest 'around 1951–52' and 'early to mid 1950s' respectively as
      dates of composition.

## 1    Compositional History

None of the extant versions of the play actually bears the title *Colickie Meg*. This, however, is the shorthand title that Smith invariably used in working papers and correspondence, and has been adopted in all existing criticism.[7] Given both the variety and the length of the manuscript titles, we shall employ *Colickie Meg* for the sake of brevity.

### 1.1    *First Version (EUL Gen 1758)*

This manuscript draft in pen covers three notebooks and extends to 82 numbered pages.[8] It bears the relatively brief title *The Carlin Wife*, but the verso of the title page offers a dazzling array of alternative titles: *The Cornucopia of Spring*; *The Cailleach*; *Colickie Meg, the Carlin*; *The Carlin o Ben Nevis*; *The Auld Carlin*; *Carroty & Meg*; *Carroty & the Cailleach*; *The Winter's Tail*; *The Fusstipple of Spring*; *Carrotie's Spring Feast-of-ale*; *The Life and Death of Colickie Meg*; and, finally, *The Merrie Life and Dowie Death of Colickie Meg the Carlin Wife o Ben Nevis*, which will be adopted as the subtitle (with slight variations) of the four following versions. The final page (41) of the MS is dated 'May 23 1949'. Perhaps surprisingly, this draft is in prose and is largely written in the literary Scots of Smith's 1940s verse production rather than the idiolect of *Carotid Cornucopius*.

### 1.2    *Second Version (EUL Gen 1762)*

A bound typescript extending to 75 numbered pages, Gen 1762 bears the title:

THE ROUT OF SPRING
or
THE MERRIE LIFE AND DOWIE DEATH
of
COLICKIE MEG,
The Carlin Wife of Ben Nevis
In
Twa Acts and an Introvale, together with
A Pologue and a Peppibogue

---

7    In addition to works already cited, see, for example, Cuthbertson, 68 and Donald Smith, 128.
8    Notebook 1 contains the Prologue and all of Act I (paginated 1–33, followed by a lengthy insert paginated 23A–23F). Notebook 2 contains most of Act II (paginated 1–30, followed by an insert paginated 11A–11B). Notebook 3 (paginated 31–41) contains the conclusion to Act II and the Epilogue. Notebook 2 also contains pen sketches of possible stage settings.

and including a Full Corpse de Balleyhoo,
A Witches' Saubath, Striptease and
monie ither idle tracasseries, ongauns,
dirrydans, tuimfuilossifeeins,
etc, etc, etc, etc,
    By
GUDE SCHIR SKIDDERIE SMITHEREENS
    Barrelnut.

The TS is not dated but, as it clearly predates EUL Gen 1763, must have been composed in 1949. As might be predicted from the title and from the use of Smith's pseudonym 'Gude Schir Skidderie Smithereens',[9] this draft represents a translation into the Carotidian. The relatively conventional Scots of EUL Gen 1762 is systematically transformed into the 'linguistic riot' (Murison, 28) of neologisms, puns, and portmanteau words that characterise Smith's novel. If *Colickie Meg* is partly a dramatic version of *Carotid Cornucopius*, Smith does not proceed, then, by adapting the *text* of the novel. Smith redeploys characters and situations from the novel, but begins from scratch linguistically, gradually transforming standard Scots into his distinctive idiolect.[10] This second draft remains in prose, albeit of a markedly poetic character. There are extensive corrections and additions in pen, almost all incorporated into the text of Gen 1763.

### 1.3    *Third Version (eul Gen 1763)*

A bound typescript extending to 102 numbered pages, Gen 1763 has the same title (with the same layout) as Gen 1762. There are, however, a number of manuscript amendments in pen on the title-page. Thus 'THE ROUT OF SPRING' becomes 'THE RITE, RIOT, ROUT OR RUTT OF SPRING'. The line 'A Ploy or Diversie-Teazement' is inserted after 'The Carlin Wife o Ben Nevis'. 'Together' and 'including a Full Corpse' become 'thegaither' and 'bencluttering a Fool Corpse', and the line 'The Anerlie Mythifictor' is inserted after 'Barrelnut'. On the penultimate page the TS is dated (in pencil) 'Nov 49–Ap 50 [...] corrected July 50'.

---

9    Which first appears on the title page of *Carotid Cornucopius* (Smith: 1947).

10    Nairn suggests that with *Colickie Meg*, Smith 'made a conscious effort to tone down the linguistic excess of his Carotidian style' (174). It is true that the final version of *Colickie Meg* is much more accessible linguistically than *Carotid Cornucopius*, but a comparison with four earlier MSS of *Colickie Meg* shows, in fact, that it becomes progressively more Carotidian.

The major innovation of Gen 1763 is the transformation of Smith's prose into verse, or perhaps more accurately, its rearrangement into verse lines. As the following example shows, this often involved minimal adaptation of the prose text:[11]

Gen 1762, p. 28 (MS amendments in square brackets, deleted text italicised):

> JOCK: Syne, there was ae muckle michty manitoo o a swaw comes lowpan doun on us, and up gangs the boat and Meg gies a yall I thocht coud be heard in Nova Scotia or eke in Aukland, New Zealand – nae nasturtiums on guid maister Auk naiturally – and, losh me, but the Cailleach's ower the side and [the] boat itsel near sinkan tae. I couldna get my haunds on her and her wallowan aroun[d] like a sea-gaean barrage-balloon, and rairan out abune the tempest and atween great gollops o sea-water "Can ye no get me out o this, Jock Macleerie", says she, "Have ye nae command ower the sea ye bad gomeral?"

Gen 1763, p. 41:

> JOCK: Syne, there was ae muckle michty
> Manitoo o a swaw comes lowpan doun
> Upon us, and up gangs the boat
> And Meg gies a yell coud be heard
> In Nova Scotia wi ease, or eke in
> Auckland, New Zealand – nae nasturtiums on guid maister
> Auk naitureallie – and, losh me!
> But the Cailleach's owre the side
> And the boat itsel near sinkan tae.
> I coudna get my hands on the woman
> She was that bagcumbersoom, wallowan
> Aroun like a sea-gaean barrage-balloon,
> And rairan out abune the tempest
> Atween great gollops o sea-water:
> "Can ye no get me out o this,
> Jock Macleerie", says she, "Have ye nae
> Command ower the sea ye bad gomeral?"

---

11    A later version of this speech is part of the 'Auxtract frae Colickie Meg' published in *Lines Review* (Smith, 1955).

Here and elsewhere in Gen 1763, the coinage of multisyllabic neologisms such as 'bagcumbersoom' corresponds to the demands of metre. Again, there are extensive additions and corrections in pen, leading, in particular, to an expansion in the number and length of stage directions.

### 1.4     *Fourth Version (NLS MS 26131)*

A loose-leaf typescript consisting of 102 numbered folios (plus prefatory material), MS 26131 bears the title *The Rutt of Spring, or, The Merrie Life and Dowie Daith of Colickie Meg, the Carlin Wife o Ben Nevis*. The subtitle begins *A Ploy or Diversi-teaziment in Twa Sack-suctions, thegaither with* [...] then follows the text as amended by pen in EUL Gen 1763. Despite the substitution of 'Sack-suctions' for 'Acts', the terms 'Act I' and 'Act II' are used in the text itself, as they are in all versions of the play.[12] The TS itself is undated, but the suggested date of 1952 in the online NLS Manuscript Catalogue is very probable. This is clearly the TS on which the Caledonian Press galley proofs at NLS Acc. 11796 (dating from 1952 or 1953) are based, for both texts present identical typographical errors, which Smith corrects in the proofs.[13] MS 26131 is essentially a fair copy of the corrected text of EUL Gen 1763. The text presents relatively few new readings, and there are equally few manuscript corrections or additions.

### 1.5     *Fifth Version (NLS Acc. 11798)*

Acc. 11798 is a bound typescript of 112 numbered pages. The title and subtitle are identical to NLS MS 26131, except for the substitution of 'Death' for 'Daith', perhaps reflecting the later Smith's tendency 'to anglicise the spelling of words common to both lingos' (Smith: 1975, xvi).[14] Unlike the previous versions, the dating of Acc. 11798 is problematic. The title page gives Smith's address as '25 Drummond Place', which, in principle, dates the TS to the period 1967–75. The typeface on the title page appears, however, to differ from that of the text proper, and it seems likelier that this version (or, at least, the text on which it is based) dates from the mid-to-late 1950s. It clearly postdates NLS MS 26131, as it includes readings – either in the typescript or added by hand – that appear in the extracts from *Colickie Meg* published in *Lines Review* (1955) and *Jabberwock* (1958) but in no previous manuscript. It shares, in fact, 16 new readings with the *Lines* extract (12 in the original TS, 4 added by hand) and 2 with the

---

12     Only the extract published in *Lines Review* substitutes Scots 'Axts' for 'Acts' (Smith: 1955, 11).

13     The proofs correspond to the first 30 pages of MS 26131.

14     Though it is also the reading present in the first three versions of *Colickie Meg*. In general, NLS MS 26131 is the most faithful to the recommendations of the Style Sheet.

*Jabberwock* text (one in the original TS, one added by hand). As the *Jabberwock* text also includes 5 readings absent from all of the extant manuscripts, we might hypothesise that Acc. 11798 was composed between the appearance of the *Lines* and *Jabberwock* extracts.[15]

The new readings that Acc. 11798 shares with the journal extracts include such freshly coined neologisms as 'trumpest', 'goblips' (p. 46), and 'furorious' (p. 47) where MS 26131 has plain English 'tempest' (p. 43), 'gollops' (p. 43), and 'furious' (p. 43). This shows that Smith is still actively engaged in thickening the Carotidian texture of his language, though the passages selected for journal publication do appear to be the most extensively reworked. In all events, Acc. 11798 is clearly the latest surviving manuscript of *Colickie Meg* and the nearest thing that we have to a definitive text. We shall therefore use it as the source text when discussing the play in general terms.

There is not space here for a detailed comparison of the five MSS, but a sense of Smith's compositional procedure may be obtained by charting the changes in a single passage. In EUL Gen 1758/1, Duncod offers the following aside (p. 18):

> I ken by my secret and black airts that there's the twa o them due, sometime sune and I'm gey near certain Meg'll be the mither o baith on'em. The faithers I kenna. Wad it was me, but I never coud mak ony heidway wi the lecherous auld Meg [Louder] I dout I'm jist no a lady's man & there's the truth o't [sighs].

The text, then, is in relatively standard Scots prose, with none of the linguistic word-play that characterises the Carotidian style.

EUL Gen 1762, however, presents the following (pp. 15–16). Manuscript additions are indicated in square brackets. Text deleted by hand is italicised.

> For I ken,[16] by my sincrete and black airts [and prognostifications] that theres the twa o them due, [ay,] sometime sune, [twa maisteerious mytho-by-inkie babs to bawl,] and I'm gey near certain [by numberologgerummies] that *Meg'll be* [Meg's] the mither o baith on 'em. *The* [Their]

---

15    The readings exclusive to *Jabberwock* are 'for unstanter' (Smith: 1958, 7), 'fley'd for their lifes' (8), 'perglorious viewsion' (9), 'blaast yer een' (10), and 'delectioun', where Acc. 11798 has 'for instanter' (p. 21), 'fley'd out their lifes' (p. 22), 'perglorious sicht' (p. 23), 'blasst yer een' (p. 24) and 'delectatioun' (p. 24). Four of these are conceivably misinterpretations of Smith's submitted text, but 'viewsioun' is clearly an entirely new coinage.

16    As part of Smith's manuscript revisions, 'ken' and 'twa' later in this line are underscored in pen.

faithers I *kenna* [neither ken nor care]. Wad *it* [ane o them] was me! *But*
I never could mak ony heidroads wi the *liquorous auld Meg* [Cailleach].
[Nocht but rebouf and redeukeooll's ban my portion!] Ay, but I'll hae her
dochter [in reversion] (Cackles lewdly and capers), that will I! (Returns to
gathering. Louder) I dout I'm jist no a leddy's man and there's the truth
o't. (Sighs lugubro-ludicrously)

The original TS of Gen 1762, then, remains close to the plain Scots of Gen
1758 and presents few Carotidian neologisms (here only 'sincrete' for 'secret').
Smith's manuscript additions, however, introduce a number of punning port-
manteau terms that will be retained and gradually refined in the following
drafts.

EUL Gen 1763 (p. 24) turns the prose of Gen 1762 into verse:

> For I ken by my sincrete [black airts]
> *Black airts and p*[P]rognostificatiouns, [and ither]
> That there's the *twa* on 'em due, gey sune,
> [*Ay,*] *T*[t]*wa* maisterious mytho-by-inkie
> Babs to bawl; and I'm gey near *certain* [shairtime], tae,
> By souple numbe[e]rio-loggerum*m*[n]ies,
> That Mither Meg's the mither o baith. *Ay.*
> [Ay, baith the twain to be drapt the-nicht
> Yon's my hope-and-yen, onywizard.]
> [Wha may be] *T*[t]heir rumspeaktible faithers *I neither*
> [I neither] *K*[k]en nor care, *nor* rack nor ruin-O!
> Wad ane o them was me, tho.[!] [I greit!
> I grane!] For Meg was aye Duncod's delyte
> [But anerlie, alas, alack in my unmittednegatioun]
> *But* s[S]omehou I *never* could [neer] mak ony
> Heidroads wi the Cailleach, *queyne.*
> Nocht but rebouf and reideukcool
> Has ban Duncod's puirportion! But,
> *But* (Cackles lewdly *and*[,] capers)
> I'll hae her dochter in reversion.
> That will I! (*Returns to table. Louder* [Louder as CC & J return to table])
> I dout it[']s juist
> That I'm no juist a leddy's man[, juist]
> And there's the *truth* [juice and gust] o't sirs. (Sighs lugubroludicrously)

The original TS, then, largely adopts the corrected text of Gen 1762 and ar-
ranges it into verse lines. There are some new neologisms ('rumspeaktible',

'puirportion') while others are refined ('redeukeooll' > 'reideukcool'). Again, though, many more are introduced ('shairtime', 'hope-and-yen', 'onywizard', 'unmittednegatioun') or modified ('numberio-loggerummies > numbeerio-loggerumnies') in Smith's MS corrections. The MS corrections also improve the scansion of Duncod's lines and, through the mock-heroic 'I greit! | I grane!', personify him more vividly, thus avoiding the homogeneity that their uniformly Carotidian language often threatens to impose upon Smith's characters.

NLS MS 26131 (p. 25) comprehensively adopts the corrected text and line settings of EUL Gen 1763. The only amendments are the following:

> Line 1: 'I think' inserted after 'I ken'
> Line 2: 'numbeerio-loggerumnies' > 'numbeario-loggerumnies'
> Line 6: 'the-nicht' > 'the nicht'
> Line 10: 'wha may' > 'wha micht'
> Line 15: 'coud neer' > 'could never'
> Line 21: 'juist' > 'just'
> Line 23: 'lugubroludicrously' > 'lugubroludicrousily'

Of these, perhaps only the expansion of the portmanteau term in line 23 is significant. The choice of Scots or English terms ('micht/may', 'neer/never', 'juist/just') appears to be dictated by the demands of metre, internal rhyme, and assonance rather than any *a priori* lexical stance.

NLS Acc. 11798 (p. 27) introduces four further changes and reverses ones of the amendments made in NLS MS 26131.

> Line 3: on 'em > o'm
> Line 6: 'the nicht' > 'the-nicht'
> Lines 7 and 12: apostrophe inserted after 'o'
> Line 15: comma inserted after 'somehou'

The apostrophe is consistently inserted after 'o' throughout the text of Acc. 11798, and punctuation marks more frequently employed than in the earlier MSS. As can be seen, though, there are few major textual amendments after EUL Gen 1763.

2     Synopsis

Although hardly fast moving, *Colickie Meg* has more of a plot than readers of *Carotid Cornucopius* might anticipate.

### 2.1    *Prologue ('Prelooke')*

Two drinkers, Andra Garioch and Kenny MacCallum,[17] enter the Ben Nevis Bar to escape the March wind. Kenny claims that the wind is raised by the 'Cailleach', or 'Auld Meg of Ben Nevis' (p. 1),[18] to prevent her son Rorie from eloping with his half-sister Biddy, Bride or Bridget. Pressed by the sceptical Andra, he explains that Rorie is Meg's child by Carotid Cornucopius, the 'faither o *aa* men' (3), while Biddy is her daughter by Jock Poseident O'MacLeerie, 'god o the sea' (4). Each year, however, Meg fails to prevent their marriage, and is turned to stone. Rorie and Biddy hold sway through the spring and summer until Meg revives in 'Octonovembro'. Meg then imprisons Biddy inside Ben Nevis until the following spring when 'the hail dirry-dan starts up aince mair'. As Andra and Kenny fall into a drunken sleep, the Auktor enters and introduces himself to the audience. Under his direction, stage hands to arrange the set for the entry of the 'dramantick puirsinners'. The Auktor's entrance signals a transition from the plain Scots of Andra and Kenny to the Carotidian language of the other characters. The latter is thus marked as a dream language spoken by archetypal figures inhabiting the subconscious of the two sleeping drinkers.

### 2.2    *Act I*

The Auktor tells the audience that they are to witness 'ane maist soserious | And tragico[um]farcicomicalitie' (8), featuring Carotid, Meg, Rorie, Biddy, Jock, and Lourd Duncod, 'the wicked vile-yin | O' the peace' (8). Carotid makes his entrance, applauded by a 'mob' that remains present through the play. He is followed by Meg, the 'Improprietricks of the Ben Nevis Bar'. Simultaneously pregnant with Rorie and Biddy, she almost immediately enters labour and retires to bed. In her absence, Jock ('Chief Bottle and Latsman' of the Ben Nevis) and Duncod arrive. As he drinks with Jock and Duncod, Carotid recalls his own miraculous birth (dropping out of the sun onto Edinburgh's Bruntsfield Links), his creation of mankind, and his first meeting with Meg by the Water of Leith. In an aside to the audience, Duncod reveals his plan to carry off Biddy and make her queen of the 'neather regiouns' (27). Meg gives birth to a fully-grown Rorie, who is saluted by a delegation of civic dignitaries. Rorie immediately departs

---

17    In the three EUL versions, the two drinkers are Andra Garioch and Bob Fyffe, a transposition of the names of Smith's friends Robert Garioch and Andrew Fyffe. In the two NLS versions, Bob Fyffe gives way to Kenny MacCallum, a homage to Kenny and Callum Campbell, owners of the Caledonian Press. Who printed the first Four Fitts of *Carotid Cornucopius* and were to print the aborted edition of *Colickie Meg*. Confusingly, the lines spoken by Bob Fyffe in the EUL versions are spoken by Andra Garioch in the NLS versions, while Kenny MacCallum speaks Garioch's original lines.

18    Page references are to NLS Acc. 11798.

in a jeep to fight for the 'Jokiebooties or Jinkaboots' at the 'battle of Presston-pants' (16). To console Meg, Jock takes her to Portobello ('Puertabollockie', 38) to celebrate the Edinburgh Spring Holiday ('Dunedin Spring Hellicat-day', 39). They soon return with the newly born (and fully-grown) Biddy, and Jock tells the tale of her watery birth in the Firth of Forth. Biddy is saluted by the hastily reconvened civic dignitaries and announces her attention to follow Rory to the battlefield. Meg padlocks her behind the bar both to prevent her escape and to protect her from Duncod. Duncod assures Biddy that he will bring his 'mirkie legions' to rescue her (59) but, assisted by the Mob, Meg chases him from the stage. The exhausted Meg falls asleep. At Jock's bidding, Carotid frees Biddy, dismantling the bar in the process. The Auktor reappears, ushers the remaining characters off to bed, and instructs the stage hands to rebuild the bar during the 'Introvale'. He awakens Kenny and Andra, and, with a wave to the audience, accompanies them offstage.

## 2.3    Act II

The Auktor, Kenny, and Andra reappear. The latter resume their seats and promptly fall asleep again as, in the background, do Carotid and Jock. Rorie returns in his jeep, equipped with a ladder to rescue Biddy. The Auktor asks him news of the 'Battle o Presstonpants', warns him of Duncod's plans, and leaves the stage. Rory serenades the sleeping Biddy, while a coven slowly assembles at the other side of the stage. Duncod appears and takes a roll call of seven witches and five warlocks (each accompanied by a familiar). Biddy appears on the balcony and promises to elope with Rory, but, at Duncod's command, the witches capture and bind Rory. Duncod proceeds to oversee the ritual sacrifice of a novice – Biddy's doppelganger and proxy – which will place Biddy in his power. At the last moment, Kenny and Andra awaken and call on Carotid and Jock to intervene. The coven throw Kenny and Andra into the audience, but Jock wakes in time to tell Biddy to deny and forswear the proxy. As she does so, Rory succeeds in knocking Carotid's thunder-dealing staff Oxcalibre against a table leg, causing an explosion, which frees him and temporarily stuns Duncod. Jock draws a chalk circle around Rorie and Biddy. Rorie obtains a rowan branch and red thread from the audience and sends Jock to find a mare's head for extra protection. As Duncod revives, Rorie tries in vain to awaken the still-sleeping Carotid. Taking his destiny into his own hands, Rorie seises Oxcalibre and exchanges curses with an increasingly cowed Duncod. Jock returns with the mare's head, which leaves Duncod 'transfixed, agog, entranced' (93) to the joy of the finally awoken Carotid. Rorie uses his ladder to rescue Biddy, but as they are about to escape, Meg is unexpectedly roused. She uses Oxcalibre to knock Rory from his ladder, hauls Biddy back into the bedroom, and empties a chamber pot over Duncod. She then raises the seven winds to banish both Duncod and Rorie. The personified winds chase the coven and finally Duncod himself offstage. Rorie, however, resists and, as Meg's powers wane and she loses consciousness, he completes the rescue of Biddy. Carotid toasts the young couple but, as Rorie starts up his jeep, the engine backfires, once again awakening Meg. She chases Biddy around stage but collides with Jock and is knocked out, at last descending into her seasonal slumber (her 'dowie death'). Rorie and Biddy finally escape. A dishevelled Duncod reappears, asking for a drink, which Jock serves with 'nae herrit feelings' (106). Almost immediately, though, he is put to flight by the returning Rorie and Biddy. With crowns on their heads, they are accompanied by a procession singing a Song of Spring. After a Ballet of Spring, Carotid and Jock cheer 'the King and Queen o' the May' (109). Exeunt Rorie and Biddy again escorted by the procession.

### 2.4    Epilogue ('Peppibogue')

The Auktor returns to drink with Carotid and Jock who awakens Kenny and Andra. The Auktor bids them dismiss the whole experience as 'a kinna maysimmer magginess' (111). All wish the audience 'guidnicht' and depart the stage arm-in-arm.

### 3    Relationship with *Carotid Cornucopius*

The events portrayed in Act I of *Colickie Meg* largely coincide with Fitts 5–6 of *Carotid Cornucopius*: Meg's double pregnancy and the birth of Rorie (Fitt 5), Rorie's departure for the Battle of 'Passionandpints' (Smith: 1964, 130) and Biddy's birth at 'Pottiebellio-O' (132) (Fitt 6). Act II partly reproduces episodes in Caputs Sevin (Rorie's return and courtship of Biddy) and Ochto, where the 'Wundrous Brothday Feste' (154) for Rorie and Biddy is distantly echoed in the Ballet of Spring. Largely, however, Act II portrays conflicts (Rorie vs Duncod, Rorie vs Meg) that are only foreshadowed in the penultimate paragraph of *Carotid Cornucopius*:

> all that loomed aheid fore them in the doom, tumuldews farture was nocht but straffe and splandour and the feariful strauchle of Rorie and Damcod for the lovand haunts of Bride, and the fierox dustysanctioun battwean Raddleprick and his mither Meg (wha never forgladdened her fastbairn for his primpt and friskest enlarkiment and blackly tuke the pairt of the Sleelock Drouk) for cantroll of his bottlericht, the rich imperium of the Ben Nevis Tap.
>
> SMITH: 1964, 159–160

*Colickie Meg* shares no significant diegetic content, conversely, with Fitts 1–4 of *Carotid Cornucopius* as published in 1947. It would be tempting to surmise that Fitts 5–8, first published in 1964, develop from *Colickie Meg* rather than vice versa. However, early drafts of Fitts 5–6 in Edinburgh University Library (Gen 1761), dated ca. 1945, closely resemble the published versions, and prove that the narrative precedes the dramatic version.[19] There appear, though, to be no surviving narrative treatments of the conflicts dramatised in Act II of *Colickie Meg*. The play is at once, then, an adaptation and a sequel of the novel.

In places, the plots of *Carotid Cornucopius* and *Colickie Meg* diverge. In the novel, Meg is originally Duncod's wife, but when Duncod accepts an English bribe to support the Treaty of Union, she leaves him for Carotid, who patriotically supports 'the heronic Amtrue Flatsure of Saluton or Salt-on' (Smith: 1964, 59). Carotid, however, pines for his deceased mistress Lilithbeth MacBollochie, which partly explains both Meg's infidelity with Jock and Carotid's indifference to being cuckolded. In the play, Carotid and Meg have been partners since the creation of man. Lilithbeth is absent,[20] and Colickie's tolerance of adultery is an aspect of his divine indifference. Duncod lusts after Meg, as in the novel, but there is no suggestion that they were ever married.

In the novel, too, Rorie, becomes an international 'madventurer' (121) after the '45 before returning to Scotland to join a 'rabbelutionary seeksossity' dedicated to establishing an 'Endumpendant Rumpublichouse' (123). Biddy is born during this lengthy absence. In the play, she and Rorie are born on the same night, and Rorie returns immediately after the battle of 'Presstonpants'. Such foreshortening may be unsurprising in a theatrical adaption, but, viewed alongside the elimination of the Union subplot, it suggests that Smith is downplaying the novel's political themes. His nationalist sympathies remain clear in *Colickie Meg*: Duncod is derided as 'ane of thae Ruinionists' or 'Bunionista' (16), but there are no references to historical events more recent than the Jacobite rebellions, and Smith's satire is primarily directed at the 'reprehensitives of Kirk, Law, University, and Armed Forces' (28).

Conversely, the novel's mythical themes are amplified in the play. *Colickie Meg* is a rite of spring, weaving together elements of Celtic and Greco-Roman

---

19    The main difference between the draft and published version is the modernisation of the list of 'sindrie notedbulls' (Smith: 1964, 122) impersonated by Rorie in Fitt 5. Contemporary figures like Dag Hammarskjöld, King Olav of Norway, or Prince Rainier and Princess Grace of Monaco replace wartime names like Prince Paul of Yugoslavia (deposed 1941), Admiral Horthy, Regent of Hungary (deposed 1944), and King Victor Emmanuel III of Italy (abdicated 1946).

20    Though one of Duncod's witches bears a similar name: Bessie MacBallochie (p. 72).

mythology. Meg herself is the Cailleach, the Celtic Queen of winter, who is turned to stone at Beltane. She is both a weather goddess and a maternal creator deity to whose 'ferosofectionate | And perpossuessive allinbrace' (105) the dying return. Carotid is Zeus, Jupiter, or the Dagda, the thunder-wielding 'hail Faither and Brood-Janitor | O' us all' (9). Biddy is both a spring goddess, merging the Celtic Brigid with the Greco-Roman Persephone/Proserpina, and a goddess of love, emerging from the waves like 'Aphrodite Anadyomene' (42). Rorie, as his middle name 'Apollonaris', suggests is Apollo, 'Lord o' the Licht and Luve and Spring | Simmer, Sang, and aa yon kinna thing' (290), whose union with Biddy will 'gie frouth and fatness till the yerth' (105). Duncod is Pluto or Hades, the 'Laird o' Hell' (18) who seeks to carry off Bride/Persephone. Jock is Poseidon or Neptune, god of the sea.

These elements are all present in the novel,[21] but so submerged within Smith's Edinburgh 'pubscape' (Bold, 60) that Carotid may be interpreted as an 'individualistic bohemian' (Hall: 1984, 18) or one of Smith's semi-autobiographical 'gangrel artists' (Burns, 51). In *Colickie Meg*, he is unmistakeably a deity, a celestial master of ceremonies, good-naturedly commenting on or explicating events and appraising the quality of each character's performance of an annual role. In this, he is entirely even-handed. He delights in Meg's summoning of the seven winds, even when it threatens to thwart Rory: 'Ay, Jock, it's a braw deidmanstructioun | This year! The wife's sheerpushan hersel' (97). Similarly, he accepts that even Duncod is indispensable for 'ye wouldna see the bricht licht o' hevin | Gin ye'd nae dark mirk o' hell | To compeer it wi' (110).

The cyclical nature of the mythical events portrayed in *Colickie Meg* suggests, however, a degree of political pessimism. If Rory and Duncod represent light/nationalism and darkness/unionism, then Scotland appears locked in an endless round in which neither party can achieve ultimate victory. Perhaps this provides a clue as to why Smith suspended *Carotid Cornucopius* after the first eight fitts. As published, the novel is finely balanced between an open-ended Rabelaisian and a circular Joycean narrative structure. On one hand, Smith promises us a loosely connected series of adventures, which, like Rabelais' *Pantagruel*, are arbitrarily cut off in midstream. On the other, its mythical subtexts imply eternal recurrence on the model of *Finnegans Wake* with its looping opening and closing lines. From this perspective, Smith's statement that the novel will depict the 'corownansickelisatioun of the funall defeasht of the puirs of daith and wintarry mirk at the hounds of the peers of lufe' (Smith: 1964, 90)

---

21    And are analysed in Hall: 1982, 338–339.

becomes problematic. The cyclical nature of its mythical subtexts dictates that no defeat is final. If Smith had extended *Carotid Cornucopius* by narrating the episodes dramatised in Act II of *Colickie Meg*, as the closing lines of Fitt 8 seems to announce, then the political optimism of the novel would inevitably have been compromised.

• • •

Discomfort with the implied political message of *Colickie Meg*, and fear that it undermined *Carotid Cornucopius*, may partly explain why Smith abandoned efforts to have the play performed or published (particularly after the success of the more overtly nationalistic *The Wallace*). There are, however, other factors that may have prevented it from reaching stage or page. The sheer density of its Carotidian wordplay presents a formidable challenge to both performer and audience. As Smith's friend Iain Cuthbertson (68) wrote, the language is 'difficult to speak and remember':

> as an actor and director of sorts, I never have found yet a way of sustained vocalisation of yon lingo. It is as if each word was a hurdle not to be jumped, but to be dismounted for, inspected, and chortled over. This makes a sentence awfully bumpy to ride. Often, by the time you've got to the end of it, you've forgotten how you've started.

Even if such difficulties could be surmounted, Donald Smith (128) argues that Smith 'moves too far from any existing speech community to be theatrically effective'. However, unlike Joyce's radically polyvalent coinages in *Finnegans Wake*, Smith's Carotidian neologisms almost always have a clear primary meaning. Generally speaking, as John C. Hall (1982, 49) notes, 'the reader can easily supply for himself the word that they are 'replacing' on the commonsense level'. Perhaps, in fact, language is not the chief obstacle to a viable stage production. Thom Nairn identifies two further stumbling blocks. Firstly, Smith pushes his 'prefiguration of postmodernist aesthetics' (173) to 'cacophonic' extremes, particularly in 'the sheer pervasiveness of intrinsic narrative commentary on the ongoing narrative itself'. Secondly, the surrealistic nature of sequences such as the birth of Biddy means that too much of the action happens off-stage and is reported to the audience via necessarily contrived dialogue.

Nairn is certainly right to say that Smith takes postmodernist disruption techniques even further in *Colickie Meg* than in *Carotid Cornucopius*. Smith gleefully demolishes the fourth wall and systematically discourages all suspension of disbelief. The Auktor himself is omnipresent, addressing the audience, haranguing stagehands, serving drinks in the Ben Nevis Bar, repairing damage to the set, and discussing proceedings with the 'dramantick puirsinners'. As befits the enactment of a ritual, the characters themselves possess (and display) foreknowledge of events. Dressed in burlesque costumes, they are prone to disconcerting changes of register. Thus Biddy launches into a 'Tragic Celtic Queen Act' (53), Rory morphs into a Hollywood 'man of action' (90), and Carotid dismisses his own words of wisdom as 'anither profund plastitute | I've just thocht up this mumblement' (110). They are conscious too of their fictional nature: Carotid acknowledges that 'we're aa nocht but craturs | O' the wee Auk's unbrindelt inmaginitatioun' (112), addressing him as 'wee Auktor o my being' (10). They are also aware of the audience's presence. Carotid gestures pityingly to 'aa thae puir misguidit folk' that 'has peyed | Their siller' (45) and waves to the public at the end. Seeking protection against witchcraft, Rorie asks whether anyone in the audience has a rowan-branch and red thread (90). The constant presence of the sleeping Kenny and Andra reminds us, moreover, that the other characters are figments of their dreams.

Nairn also rightly notes that the ceaseless commentary on the action sometimes carries a 'suggestion of ironically recognised discontent on the author's part' (174). When Jock asks the Auktor to 'hot up the unction a buttock' to repair damage to the set, Carotid interjects: 'You mean haud up the inaction' (62). As Jock tries to waken Kenny and Andra at the play's end, Carotid remarks: 'It doesna say muckle | For your bit ploy, maister Auk, | That ye canna keep thae twa sottisheens | Wi their een open' (111). Self-deprecating acknowledgement of the play's slow-moving nature may, however, resemble having one's cake and eating it. In truth, the static quality of *Colickie Meg* is problematic. The main characters spend much of the play seated at the Ben Nevis Bar, and, with alarming regularity, drifting into a drunken slumber. Carotid, in particular, has an exclusively sedentary role and falls asleep no fewer than four times. Meg thrice falls asleep on stage before her final 'dowie death'. Joe and Duncod fall asleep twice each. Twice in Act I and once in Act II, there are four characters asleep on stage at once (Carotid/Joe/Kenny/Andra; Meg/Duncod/Kenny/Andra; Carotid/Joe/Kenny Andra). In the latter instance, there are also two (Meg, Biddy) sleeping offstage. While this is an amusing stratagem on the page, it would be high-risk in performance. The play also suffers from an excess of exposition. In the 'Prelooke', Kenny provides Andra with a plot summary, which the Auktor effectively repeats in his opening speech to the audience. The characters' own running commentary then provides regular reminders of what is to come. Smith may have been understandably anxious about his audience's ability to follow a play written in a dense idiolect and may have calculated too that repeated pointers would free them to enjoy his wordplay. In performance, however, a detailed programme might serve the same purpose.

Nairn's complaint that the main action happens off-stage is truer of Act I (which features the lengthy narration of Biddy's birth). Act II presents quite a different problem, which may have proved the primary obstacle to the production or publication of *Colickie Meg*. Here, the action occurs on-stage but remains awkwardly divorced from the dialogue. As our synopsis above may indicate, the action (Rory's tussles with Duncod and Meg) is essentially physical and, on the page, largely related in detailed stage directions. The plot does not progress via the speech-driven dramatic interaction of Smith's characters, but via the bodily interaction of Rory and a large cast of witches, warlocks, prostitutes, clowns, pseudo-stagehands, and assorted members of the 'Mob'. Its effects are visual rather than verbal. The dialogue essentially comments upon, explains, or simply applauds wordless action. From a production perspective, the script of *Colickie Meg* is incomplete. To be realised on stage, it would require extensive choreography. Even without the 'Ballet of the Seven Winds' and 'Ballet of Spring', the many non-speaking performers would need to be trained dancers. It would also demand a musical score. In addition to the songs contained in the play, the stage directions repeatedly refer to orchestral effects marking the appearance or departure of each character or comically accompanying the physical theatre of Act II. Smith conceived *Colickie Meg* as a multimedia spectacle, necessarily involving the collaboration of a theatrical, musical, and dance company. Clearly, it would also require a capacious performance space with the concomitant financial risk. It is a daunting proposition, then, for the potential producer. Thom Nairn (175) argues that 'given some ruthless editing, a performable version of *Colickie Meg* could be made to work'. A skilled dramaturge could certainly cut some of the more expositional or self-referential dialogue and reduce the number of non-speaking roles, but there is no avoiding the spectacular nature of Act II with its ballets and pageantry. As such, it is perhaps easier to envisage a selective read-through than an abridged adaptation.

The purely physical, visual nature of Act II also, of course, makes *Colickie Meg* unpromising material for a radio play, a genre in which Smith subsequently enjoyed considerable success.[22] It also, however, presents difficulties for a print edition. The thrust of the narrative is contained in stage directions, which, on the page, leave a lot to the imagination. Directions such as the following simply

---

22    There were BBC Radio productions of the following dramas or poetic dialogues: The
      Death of Tristram and Iseult (1947), The Vision of the Prodigal Son (1959), The Wallace
      (1959), The Stick Up, or Full Circle (1961), The Twa Brigs (1964), A Night at Ambrose's
      (1972), Macallister (1973), The Tricky Callant (1974), and Gowdspink in Reekie (1976).

highlight how far the play, in performance, would rely on (unscripted) musical and choreographical accompaniment:[23]

> MEG raises her SEVEN WINDS in succession, by beating a large red-and-white dishclout on the edge of the balcony. The COVEN is progressively dispersed by being chased round the stage by the WINDS appropriately costumed. The Orchestra gives suitable support and the whole scene may be in the form of a Ballet of the SEVEN WINDS, the last gesture of the dying winter. (94)

> Fanfare: RORIE and BIDDY take up positions garlanded on thrones carried in by HANDS and set up on a dais in the centre of the stage. The BALLET OF SPRING is now performed. HANDS distribute garlands and tankards throughout assembled company. (109)

Other directions, conversely, convey all too vivid an impression of clumsy (and often misogynistic) slapstick:

> MEG screeches at BIDDY and grabs at her. BIDDY avoids her. MEG chases BIDDY round stage and RORIE joins in chasing MEG, who is staggering drunkensleepily. JOCK and CC roaring with laughter, cheering them on. CC stumping Oxcalibre on ground in time with Orchestra playing a Galop. HANDS and MOB cheering and shouting encouragement to their favoured runners. (103)

> As CC says this, RORIE clutches MEG's gown and rips it off. She continues her pursuit of BIDDY in her billowing Victorian nightdress [...] Enter JOCK with tray of bottles etc. BIDDY neatly avoids him but MEG crashes full tilt. Both fall with terrific crash, orchestral etc [sic]. RORIE leaps over the prostrate and struggling MEG and JOCK, and grabs BIDDY. (104)

Clearly, Smith aims for a constant alternation of registers, veering back-and-forth between high art and vaudeville, between the sublime and the ridiculous. On the page, though, we can picture the ridiculous but have to take the sublime on trust. In fairness, Smith would doubtless have refined the often rather

---

23    Act I too contains such disconcerting stage directions as 'Maybe a Ballet here' (p. 28) and 'TUMBLERS, JUGGLERS, CLOWNS ETC. Ballet'. (p. 39).

shorthand stage directions for a print edition.[24] It is perhaps significant, though, that the published extracts of *Colickie Meg* are both from Act I, and that the Caledonian Press proofs do not reach Act II, suggesting that Smith was aware of the challenges posed by its visual, spectacular nature and had yet to meet them on the page.

Thom Nairn argues that *Colickie Meg* 'should be published in its existing form as testimony to important if imperfect experimentation' (175). While it certainly merits publication as an extended verse performance in the Carotidian idiom, *Colickie Meg* is less aesthetically 'imperfect' than formally incomplete: the dialogue does not stand on its own. Ideally, a publisher would find a means of suggesting the intended multimedia nature of Smith's conception, perhaps via graphic design. Given Smith's own achievements as an artist,[25] and his friendship with figures like Rendell Wells whose sketches adorn the 1964 *Carotid Cornucopius*, an illustrated edition might well have appealed to the author himself.

### Bibliography

Barnaby, Paul, 'Scottish Theatre Archives at Edinburgh University Library' in *International Journal of Scottish Theatre and Screen* Vol. 6, Issue 2 (2014), pp. 87–99. Accessed online (October 2018): https://ijosts.ubiquitypress.com/articles/abstract/175/.

Bold, Alan, 'Three Post-MacDiarmid Makars: Soutar, Garioch, Smith' in *Akros* Vol. 15, No. 44 (1980), pp. 44–61.

Burns, John, 'Smith's Cornucopia' (a review of the 1982 3rd edn. of *Carotid Cornucopius*) in *Cencrastus* Issue 14 (autumn 1983), pp. 50–51.

Cuthbertson, Iain, 'Sydney and the Plays' in Norman MacCaig (ed.), *For Sydney Goodsir Smith* (Loanhead: M. Macdonald, 1975), pp. 65–71.

Hall, John C., 'The Writings of Sydney Goodsir Smith', a PhD thesis submitted to the University of Aberdeen, September 1982. Accessed online (June 2018): http://ethos .bl.uk/OrderDetails.do?uin=uk.bl.ethos.330725.

Hall, John C., 'Big Music and Skail Winds: The Achievement of Robert Garioch and Sydney Goodsir Smith' in *Lines Review* Issue 88 (1984), pp. 10–19.

---

24  The stage directions in the *Lines Review* extract are in a much livelier idiom than the MS versions (and in Scots rather than English).

25  See Smith: 1998, which includes his own illustrated version of sections of *Under the Eildon Tree*.

Lenz, Katja 'The Use of Obsolete Scots Vocabulary in Modern Scottish Plays' in *International Journal of Scottish Theatre and Screen* Vol. 1, Issue 1 (2000) (unpaginated). Accessed online (October 2018): https://ijosts.ubiquitypress.com/articles/253/.

Murison, David, 'The Language of Sydney Goodsir Smith', in Norman MacCaig (ed.), *For Sydney Goodsir Smith* (Loanhead: M. Macdonald, 1975), pp. 23–29.

Nairn, Thomas, 'A Route Maist Devious: A study of the Works of Sydney Goodsir Smith', a PhD thesis submitted to the University of Edinburgh, 1991. Accessed online (October 2018): http://ethos.bl.uk/OrderDetails.do?uin=uk.bl.ethos.659858.

Smith, Donald, 'The Mid-Century Dramatists', in Ian Brown (ed.), *The Edinburgh Companion to Scottish Drama* (Edinburgh: Edinburgh University Press, 2011), pp. 118–129.

Smith, Sydney Goodsir, *Carotid Cornucopius: The First 4 Fitts*, 1st edn. (Glasgow: Caledonian Press, 1947).

Smith, Sydney Goodsir, *Under the Eildon Tree: A Poem in XXIV Elegies* (Edinburgh: Serif Books, 1948).

Smith, Sydney Goodsir, Letter from Smith to Hugh MacDiarmid (dated 8 August 1950), EUL MS 2960.16/49.

Smith, Sydney Goodsir, 'Auxtract frae Colickie Meg' in *Lines Review* Issue 10 (1955), pp. 11–15.

Smith, Sydney Goodsir, 'Aukstract frae Colickie Meg' in *Jabberwock* Issue 5 (1958), pp. 7–10.

Smith, Sydney Goodsir, *Carotid Cornucopius*, 2nd edn. (Edinburgh: M. Macdonald, 1964).

Smith, Sydney Goodsir, *Collected Poems 1941–1975* (London: John Calder, 1975).

Smith, Sydney Goodsir (Hendry, Joy ed.), *The Drawings of Sydney Goodsir Smith*, collected by Ian Begg (Edinburgh: New Auk Society, 1998).

Wittig, Kurt, *The Scottish Tradition in Literature* (Edinburgh: Oliver and Boyd, 1958).

CHAPTER 13

# Sydney Goodsir Smith's *The Wallace* in Context

*David Robb*

## Abstract

This chapter considers Smith's play *The Wallace* in various contexts. For example, Smith's creative output as a whole; the state of nationalist feeling in Scotland, especially literary Scotland, around the time of the play's writing; Smith's personal life, and his ideas and values and the history of the image of Wallace, as described by Graeme Morton. It will also compare the play with other treatments of the Wallace story, in e.g. Blind Harry, Jane Porter and *Braveheart*.

## Keywords

William Wallace – Scottish nationalism – Scottish independence – Scottish history – verse drama – pageantry – Edinburgh Festival – romanticism

On the 29th December 1959, Christopher Grieve (Hugh MacDiarmid) wrote to Sydney Goodsir Smith, acknowledging and praising his latest book of poems (presumably *Figs and Thistles*, though the title is not specified): 'I think this is your best book – along with "The Eildon Tree" – and on top of the Wallace play a really great achievement. Yet fools say the Lallans Movement has petered out'.[1] No one reading or seeing *The Wallace: A Triumph in Five Acts* can be in any doubt that Smith did indeed conceive it as a significant contribution to the Scottish Renaissance movement, with Grieve as its figurehead, but the great man's comment highlights, however inadvertently, the twin impulses within the play, the result of its place in the changing landscape of Scottish literary life around 1960. It was a moment when, for MacDiarmid's disciples, the post-war phase of his Renaissance still constituted Scotland's literary vanguard, but at the same time less committed observers clearly thought otherwise. The 1960s which were about to unfold would be a decade of strife between the two

---

1   National Library of Scotland (NLS) Acc.10281/1. Hereafter, references to material in the National Library are located in the text.

camps. It is no surprise, therefore, that *The Wallace* reflects tensions which were already in evidence.

Over half a century later, critical estimations of *The Wallace* are tepid at best, and this essay does not attempt to overturn this view substantially, though it seems important to acknowledge the play's place in Smith's work and in the patchy story of twentieth-century Scottish drama. A particularly negative recent account appears in Ian Brown's *History as Theatrical Metaphor: History, Myth and National Identities in Modern Scottish Drama* (Brown, 2016). Brown is dismissive of characters which 'are as wooden and superficial as those of [Robert] Kemp's pageant plays' and sees Smith's 'triumph' as 'a culmination of an approach to Scottish historical material developed over the 1950s [...] the representation of scarcely concealed ideological positions through simplified dramaturgy and windy rhetoric' (Brown, 109–110). He laments the way such plays fail to '[deconstruct] historical myths' and sees *The Wallace* as achieving 'pictorial impact, but little psychological or socio-political effect' (Brown, 220). Along with other plays by Scottish writers of the period, *The Wallace* is compared unfavourably by Brown with *Armstrong's Last Goodnight* by John Arden which (to distil his argument) shows a dramaturgical and linguistic flexibility, an international awareness and an alert, free and nuanced outlook lacking in the plays with which it is juxtaposed. Trevor Royle is more succinct but scarcely less judgemental: it 'owes its strength more to the passion of its author's nationalism than to the play's dramatic structure and sophistication' (Royle, 280). Roderick Watson finds that Smith used 'an entirely stiff and rhetorical Scots for *The Wallace* in 1960, and this tended to make it more of a political pageant than a play' (Watson, 106). Tom Hubbard, however, seems to like the play, but recognises that it divides responses. (Hubbard, 1984). Alan Bold, writing at greater length, is both critical and sympathetic. He notes that it has no dramatic subtlety as its hero, Wallace, 'has no tragic flaw' and is conscious of the artificiality of Smith's poetic rhetoric. It is, he says, 'a piece of special pleading rather than a play' but, despite its 'inexpert execution', it operates on a 'grand scale' and is a 'brave venture [...] a mighty conception' (Bold, 296–298).

The response of newspaper critics at the time of its staging in the Assembly Hall in 1960 was equally mixed. Admittedly, the *Edinburgh Evening News* (23 August) was wholly favourable, welcoming 'the success of this great Scottish contribution to the Festival'. *The Scotsman*'s Ronald Mavor (23 August) also judged that 'the play follows a fine tragic course and there are fine words well spoken': he compared its ending with that of Schiller's *Mary Stuart*, performed at the Festival two years earlier. However, he thought that 'the play has not quite enough interest to hold our closest attention unless it has a hero at its centre' and that Wallace becomes a 'figure of heroic proportions' only in the final confrontation with Edward I. He thought the Chroniclers dramatically ineffective. J.M. Reid, in the *Glasgow Herald* (23 August) thought that the enthusiasm of the first-night audience 'said as much for their patriotic feeling as for the piece itself', a 'triumph' being 'a special kind of masque, a shout of poetic pride'. Smith's play had no 'subtle development of character. The parts were firmly stereotyped'. In Reid's view, 'Mr. Goodsir Smith has made Wallace a rather simple-minded and sometimes almost inhuman hero'. English-based critics were even less likely to be beglamoured by nationalist sentiment. Admittedly, Philip Hope-Wallace in *The Guardian* (24 August) thought that 'the course of the play is strongly propelled and gathers some weight, though it seldom really rushes the imagination', and that, if not finally great, it 'makes an apt and solid contribution to the festival'. Nevertheless, he was conscious of its 'heavy strokes of black and white, villainy and nobleness' and that 'the play is solidly in a tradition of historical drama as it was understood by an earlier generation'. He picked up, however, on 'the play's secondary theme – that of conflicting notions of nationality and patriotism'. The anonymous critic of *The Times* (24 August) was less tolerant, because 'the three hours long chronicle is austerely economical in the matter of drama'. The problem was all talk and no action – we never see Wallace actually doing anything, for the play 'positively prefers to render everything second-hand'. In this critic's view also, the piece came to life only in the encounter between Wallace and Edward who, 'between them might have made a memorable play'. Most dismissive was Irving Wardle in *The Observer* (28 August) who saw it as 'ranting pageantry', 'an arid exercise in black and white nationalism', the 'actionless rhetoric' of which fuelled 'my suspicion that the Lallans movement is yet another plot of the Northern rebels'.

Against all this, Smith received plenty of encouragement and congratulations from friends and other partisan listeners (to the radio production of 1959) and viewers (of the Edinburgh Festival staging in 1960). Prominent Scots, beside MacDiarmid, wrote to him: William MacLellan, Moray McLaren, Robert McLellan, F. Marian McNeill, Robert Kemp, Alastair Dunnett. Albert Mackie wrote enthusiastically to 'Mr Lorimer' (either William Lorimer or his son Robert) after he had seen the script of the play. Many other correspondents, not so prominent in literary circles, also contacted Smith. Among telegrams of good wishes sent on the eve of the Festival production were messages from Robert Kemp, Alexander Reid, Tom Fleming and Iain Cuthbertson, while the radio production of the year before had prompted telegrams and postcards from Hector MacIver, Christopher Grieve, Ronald Stevenson and Helen Cruickshank. Along with these, the National Library of Scotland holds a detailed and appreciative letter from Tyrone Guthrie (3 July 1958) to whom Smith had sent a copy of the play while he was still working on it: Guthrie thought it an 'impressive piece of work' and gave some very precise and trenchant pieces of advice. The American novelist and playwright Thornton Wilder, reading it after the Festival production, was fulsome in his praise.[2]

If one were to generalise from the various comments and communications Smith received about the play, relating to either the 1959 radio production, the Festival production of 1960, or the text on its own, several points emerge. Many correspondents praised what they simply felt was the play's 'nobility'. A senior generation of theatrical commentators (Guthrie, Kemp, McLellan) were thoroughly convinced by Smith's work, not just because of its strident patriotism but also because of what they saw as its theatrical and structural strength. It was the sort of play they liked. Many saw it, too, as a triumphant example of the use of Scots language in a major drama: Smith's Scots was either 'the tongue with which we are all familiar and find intelligible today' (M.A.B. Black: 10281/2) and 'like a blood transfusion to me' (David Stephen: 10281/2) or a welcome hybrid speech which straddled the centuries: Albert Mackie wrote of the 'starkly simple language, English and Scots, reminding me of John Barbour's Bruce. Sydney writes Scots with the ring of truth in it, the authentic accent of both Middle Scots and the popular tongue of the Lowlands today' (10281/2). Many who heard and enjoyed the radio broadcast of 1959 were eager that the play be staged in the following year's Edinburgh Festival but suspicious that it would not be chosen: an aggrieved mistrust of the British cultural establishment, in the form of the Festival authorities, was endemic amongst Renaissance partisans. In fact, its place in the 1960 Festival was made public on 1 December 1959. For Robert McLellan, the play promised a major breakthrough: 'It used to be thought that a Scots dramatist could never break through except via London, and that meant except in English. Successes at the Festival would soon bring Scots into the international scene direct. I am putting my shirt on "The Wallace"' (10397/1).

One can easily see why Smith's play appealed powerfully to patriotic-minded Scots, particularly adherents of the Scottish Renaissance vision. Equally, it is plain why the play's simple moral pattern, with Wallace's strikingly non-complex character, prompted varying degrees of rejection by less aligned critics. The play's nature can be explained to some extent by a number of factors and considerations. For one thing, that word 'pageant', mentioned by a number of critics, highlights Smith's thinking about the kind of literature he wanted to write. In a draft essay on Scottish theatre, he picked up on the complaint that Scottish theatre was harking back, too often, to the past. (There is no clear date

---

2   These pieces of correspondence are in the following manuscript holdings in the National Library of Scotland (hereafter NLS): Acc.10281/1; 10281/2; 10281/3; 10397/1.

to this draft essay, but references to the launch of the first Russian Sputnik and the absence of any comparable American achievement suggest a date of autumn 1957). He takes up the complaint:

> [...] they are right in one thing. Some of the dramatists do hark back to the past.
> To hark back is to return on losing the scent to where it can be picked up again. If the scent has been lost, what could be more sensible?
> The scent, as far as Scottish theatre is concerned, was lost about the time of the Reformation, shortly after the original production of the most famous of our literary curiosities, 'The Three Estates', which aroused such admiration in foreign visitors on its revival at the Edinburgh Festival.
>
> NLS, Acc. 26430/36–41, f. 38

Even without this indication of his thinking, one can infer his consciousness of that greatest and most famous of all Scottish dramatic pageants. In fact, Smith was picking up the scent, with *The Wallace*, in a double sense – back to Sir David Lyndsay's 16th century original, and also back to the epoch-making production by Tyrone Guthrie which so dominated the 1948 Edinburgh Festival. *The Wallace* is the continuation of a Scottish dramatic tradition with two starting points, centuries apart.

The importance to Smith of the Festival production is further suggested by his eagerness to have the approval and guidance of Guthrie himself. Guthrie provided both, generously. The play is 'an impressive piece of work [...] I think the play is romantic – in a robust and noble way'. He was not convinced that the Assembly Hall was the best place for the play, and 'I'd cut [the Chroniclers] *heavily*; using them less as givers of information than as atmosphere – e.g. the names of the siege engines which is real stuff. And be prepared to find them expendable during rehearsal'. He went on:

> I think the *material* of Act IV is more interesting than its treatment. The dullness of the women's parts is rather a pity, & could, I think be dealt with. In effect all they do is say 'Please don't' and 'Don't be so naughty' to the males.
> In general, I think you slightly under-estimate the alertness with which an audience will take up *plot* points, & over-estimate their alertness to matters of philosophy. I think they'll be ahead of you in Act IV and I think, in vague terms, I see a way in which that act could be much more theatrically exciting & say more in terms of England & Scotland. Menteith is nearly, *but not quite*, a magnificent part. He shouldn't fade out in Act V.
>
> NLS, Acc. 10281/2

Smith does not seem to have applied too much of the advice from the re-
nowned director, but his approval would have been important. Smith seems to
have given a number of people his play to read before its first radio outing,
which perhaps suggests some lack of confidence on his part.

It was easy for the play to fall into a pageant-like form because the story of
Wallace was so well established, and the responses of the patriotic audiences
to which he was primarily appealing (whether he fully realised it or not) were
so predictably favourable. Smith had no new vision of Wallace to impart: his
hero was still the centuries-old figure of steadfast Scottish defiance. Smith's
plans involved no innovative subtleties of narrative, no invention of unexpect-
ed depths and complexities – in fact, no deconstruction of historical myths (as
looked for by Ian Brown). Deconstruction would have implied a new perspec-
tive distinct from the traditional understanding of Wallace's tale, but Smith's
Renaissance viewpoint fully accepted that heroic interpretation of Scotland's
ancient defender. No need to deconstruct. The familiar tale has remained stur-
dily constant, though Graeme Morton has explored shifts of emphasis, through
the centuries, of Wallace's story: the hero has been variously fitted into the
unfolding self-perceptions of the Scots and to developing attitudes, north and
south of the border, to the Union (Morton, 2014).[3] The Victorians, for example,
came to regard Wallace as not merely a Scottish hero but a British possession,
a view from which the Scottish nationalists of the 20th century needed to res-
cue him. They largely preferred him over Bruce, despite the victory of Ban-
nockburn. Here, for example, is 'Lewis Grassic Gibbon', seeing Wallace as a
man of the people, and a leader who galvanised the ordinary folk of Scotland:

> The peasants flocked to his standard – suddenly, and for perhaps the first
> time in Scots history, stirred beyond their customary indifference over
> the quarrels of their rulers. Here was something new, a leader who prom-
> ised something new. [...] Presently the Army of the Commons of Scotland
> was being poisoned by the usual aristocratic intrigues, though still the
> troubled peasants and townsmen clung to their faith in the Guardian.

After the nobility's betrayal at Falkirk and Menteith's treachery, Wallace's exe-
cution (in this account) had its effect:

> More serious than Wallace's personal fate, it murdered that fine hope and
> enthusiasm that had stirred the Army of the Scots Commons on the

---

3  Hereafter Morton.

morning of Falkirk. In a kind of despairing hatred, not hope, the Scots people turned to support the rebellions of the various shoddy noble adventurers who now raised the standard against the English. By intrigue, assassination, and some strategical skill one of those nobles, Robert the Brus [...] succeeded in routing the English at the Battle of Bannockburn.

GIBBON, 27–28

Alongside Gibbon's class-consciousness, Smith could also have found the life of Wallace written for young readers by another literary nationalist of MacDiarmid's generation, Lewis Spence. Writing in the immediate aftermath of the Great War, Spence's emphasis in interpreting Wallace was on his patriotism (Spence, 1919). Spence, furthermore, appears to have been drawing, for his biographical outline, on an earlier book by James Paterson, *Wallace: The Hero of Scotland*, of which Smith himself possessed a copy (Paterson, 1900). In all these accounts, the essential tale of Wallace remains constant, whatever emphases (of class-consciousness, patriotism or aristocratic betrayal) individual writers placed upon it. If the final act of his play suggests that Smith did feel the need, after all, to place his own mark on the familiar story, he introduced an innovation that did not finally disrupt the well-established outline.

Edward's offer to make Wallace his principal liegeman in Scotland, effectively ruler of Scotland under the English king, is a *coup de théâtre* dependent upon the familiarity of the rest of the narrative. Why does Smith do it? For its surprise effect, naturally, and also because Smith may have half-realised, with the *Times* critic, that the play's real dramatic potential lay with the interaction of Wallace and the king: something less simple and predictable than Edward's implacable sentence upon Wallace was required. Furthermore, it was Smith's answer to the supreme problem in any dramatisation of the Wallace story: how does one present the patriot's inescapable, dreadful and defeated end as a glorious triumph? Linked to this is the question of how one looks forward from Wallace's fate and implicates it in the triumph of Bruce in 1314. An earlier play, Robert Buchanan's *Wallace: A Tragedy* (1856), for example, has word arriving during Wallace's trial of Bruce's slaying of Comyn and his raising of his standard at Perth. Wallace is able to hear, just before being led off to execution, how the desire of Bruce and the Scots to avenge him has rallied the country, so he knows that his sacrifice is achieving his goal:

O noble Bruce, well hast though kept thy tryste,
Though fortune proved my let. Thou wilt achieve
What Wallace leaves undone. The lot of Heaven
Doth fall on thee, the younger and the worthier.

> And thou, or I misread thy noble nature,
> Wilt justify the call. Methinks from far,
> I catch the cloud-break of thy coming day,
> Bright for thyself, and for thy country, glorious, —
> And, in the blessed foreview, die content.
>
> BUCHANAN, 124

In both plays, it is the example, and the fate, of Wallace which spurs Bruce to a final rebellion against the English king.

And beyond all this, Edward's surprise offer provides Wallace with the drama of a supreme temptation – the chance of ruling Scotland instead of dying a terrible death – which, rejected, raises the incorruptibility of his patriotic idealism to supreme heights. It partly depends, of course, how the situation is played in any given production, but there is scope for suggesting something saintly, even Christ-like, about Wallace here. The sudden temptation perhaps evokes echoes of Christ's temptation in the wilderness (Matthew 4); there may also be a distant recollection of Eliot's Becket, subject to tempters in Part I of *Murder in the Cathedral*. The possibility of the Christ comparison arises, also, at Wallace's final entry earlier in the scene:

> Preceded by a STANDARD-BEARER playing sbandierata with the Bluidie Clout [...] escorted by BLUNT and SEGRAVE, and guarded by four guards, enter, through audience, WALLACE, wearing a laurel crown, his clothes ragged, his hands chained; and, hard at their heels, a rabble of jeering ENGLISH ARTISANS, APPRENTICES, etc.
>
> SMITH: 1960, 145[4]

Even before he witnesses Bruce's flouncing exit from Edward's court, Wallace proclaims, in exalted verse, how his defeat and debasement constitute, paradoxically, his triumph over Edward – like Christ's triumphant victory in degradation. In part, Wallace's (and Smith's) spirit is that of the Spanish Civil War slogan, 'To Resist is To Win!' Paradox is essential in the rhetoric here, while Wallace's intoxicating rhythms and eloquent phraseology ding down Edward's prosaic interjections.

> This is nocht the daith of Wallace, Edward,
> Nor yet the end of Scotland, in your

---

4   All following page references for *The Wallace* relate to: Smith, Sydney Goodsir, *The Wallace: A Triumph in Five Acts* (Edinburgh & London: Oliver & Boyd, 1960).

Menteith-peace, or desert-conquest either,
But the birth-thraws of its glorie and its
Triumph. Scotland has wan, my lord, and you,
Nane ither, gied us victorie....
[Edward: Ha!]
Through this lang war, echt year o' fire and sword
And famine, greit and bluid and daith,
Ye've made a nation, sir. Hammer
O' the Scots indeed! By the Rood,
Ye're richter nor ye ken. Ye've hammerit
A nation intil life, ennobled it,
And held it up like a banner til aa men
For evermair. (168)

As the play moved towards its preordained conclusion, Smith had been developing Wallace as something of a poet-philosopher in preparation for this moment. Before Menteith's fatal entrance in Act IV, Wallace had been musing on what the two women in his life, Ailish Rae and the slain Mirren Braidfute, had meant to him.

And you are luve, Ailie. As Scotland
Is, and freedom tae. Freedom is nae
Place set apairt; like tyrannie
It's neutral. Aa men in chains the day
Are Scots and Scotland the world o' slaves
And prisoners. Juist as you, Ailie lass,
Are luve and freedom huntit in this wuid,
Sae ye are Scotland tae, and Scotland
Freedom – ach, I hae nae words
For what I mean. (123)

As Wallace – and Smith – fumble for words which suggest the supreme desirability of the twin goals which guide him (Scotland's freedom and Ailish herself) and their unity in his life-striving, so there is an echo of an older construction, the feminised vision of Scotland within Victorian Britain (Morton, 127–139). It is an association established earlier in the play, in the aftermath of Mirren's murder.

Ah, Mirren! Here was
The maist beauteous flouer o' the flock,

Here was my luve, here Scotland
Incarnate, the White Rose breathin
In a lassie's form. (43)

The poetic sweep helps conceal one of the unresolved questions of the play: is Wallace's war with Edward's England motivated as much by hatred and revenge as it is by patriotic purity and nationalist feeling?

Edward's offer surprises everyone, both on-stage and off, but it has been insufficiently grounded in our sense of the character. Before this, Edward had been purely villainous, despite Smith's claim, in a review of his own play, that the character is actually quite complex:

> The character, also well drawn in the text, as a man relentless in his determination to dominate the three kingdoms, shrewd in his exploitation of the dissensions among the Scottish nobles, despising treachery even while taking advantage of it, admiring courage and integrity even while crushing them, was presented on radio as a sadistic pervert, without dignity or authority, powerful only in his unwholesome viciousness.
>
> NLS, Acc. 26430, ff. 74–77, f. 75

Act III was Edward's act, where he reveals himself as a sadistic pervert and shows scant admiration for courage and integrity, whatever Smith envisaged. After Wallace's rejection of his offer in Act V, he reverts to type with his demand for the execution to be 'slow, very slow,/ And beautiful' (173). Throughout Act III he is excited and unstable – 'nigh to madness' (100) – and his torture and degradation of the Scots prisoners revolts everyone else on stage. Wallace is up against a psychopath, and Edward's generosity and reasonableness in Act V is lacking in the character we have seen.

Act I has the function of firing Wallace into full-scale armed rebellion. Mirren's death spurs him to vengeance, igniting his low-level guerrilla tactics into patriotic warfare. It also releases him from the act's pervasive domesticity, which she had embodied. One notices how much this act resembles the play which would appear soon after *The Wallace*, namely *The Stick-Up*, a radio play (1961) later turned into an opera by Robin Orr and published in 1969 (Smith: 1969, 1–33). Each presents a central figure who confronts overwhelming and oppressive odds; both decide to fight back, and both reach tragic ends. Wallace and Davie have huge dreams which they strive to realise. In both plays, women embedded in the home are important as they try (and fail) to bring their men to practical, self-preserving but inglorious good sense. Both plays (and heroes) are animated by a sense of justice; both identify Englishness with the prevailing injustice and oppression. Both plays contain imagery of bloodied shirts.

Their heroes finally accept their fates, both having an inherent nobility: Davie's is expressed in his poetic flights of imagination and in his instinct to rebel against the poverty and injustice of the Thirties, while Wallace embodies no-bility throughout    a nobility which is thrown into relief by the unwillingness of the Scots lords to acknowledge it, thanks to his lack of an outward 'noble' status.

The scenes of domesticity at the beginning and end of the play also serve to bring out the essential masculinity of Wallace and his historical role. Guthrie's comment about the dullness of the women's parts is apposite but Mirren and Ailish are not therefore irrelevant. The boldness which Scottish Renaissance adherents found lacking in their 'Anglo-Scots' compatriots is ex-pressed in part by Wallace's willingness to spurn the safety-seeking instincts of his women-folk: the hero's domain is infinitely larger than the home and his nature is the quintessence of manliness. If Scotland is associated with the feminine, as Wallace's more poetic flights imply, then masculinity has to be a central aspect of his heroic energy. But it was possibly typical of the age that Robert McLellan, responding to the play's gender dynamics, could write to Smith in blunt terms: 'I'm just a wee bit worried about the production getting into the hands of a pansy. If it happens please watch that the thing doesn't lose masculinity in movements and gesture [...]' (NLS, Acc. 10397/1). The only 'pansy' Smith has written into the play is the Prince of Wales, whose effemi-nacy had been for centuries part of the narrative of the period and who serves as an inevitable foil to Wallace's magnificent and sturdy patriotic intransigence.

And it is with the endemic Scottish instinct towards peace and accommoda-tion with England that the play is most deeply concerned. The difficulty of the Scots lords in accepting Wallace as their natural superior and leader had al-ways been a prominent element in the Wallace story, but Smith gives it a cen-trality which reminds us how aware, by this stage, MacDiarmid and his adher-ents were of the opposition within Scotland to their programme and ideals. As Robert McLellan put it in his letter of 7 December 1959, following the radio broadcast, 'Menteith put the case for the present Anglo-Scot as plausibly as I've ever known it: we have a tremendous population of Menteiths today' (NLS, Acc. 10397/1). The sense of precariousness – of the outcome of the tussle be-tween the Renaissance vision for Scotland and the 'British' sympathies of the Anglo-Scots – is there from the start. The first point Smith had made in his *A Short Introduction to Scottish Literature* was about Scotland's endemic lack of unity, and instinct for argumentative opposition, throughout the centuries: his focus on the struggle between Scots, rather than the struggle with the English, is at the heart of his play (Smith. 1951, 7). The first words of the Scots Chronicle set the historical scene in terms which begin to lay out the choices: the Scots nobility are struggling for supremacy in a Scotland in which English influence is accepted as playing a part while the 'puir cottar folk' simply want a Scottish peace. For the play's reader, however, the issue lurks even earlier, in the first of the three quotations Smith adds. The famous words of Wallace (as recorded by William Rishanger) before the Battle of Falkirk evoke (even before we realise it) the twin concerns of the play, namely the greatness of Wallace and his achievements, and the responsibility of the Scots to grasp the prize he has brought within reach: 'I have browghte ye to the ryng, hoppe yef ye kunne' (x). If the play is a paean of praise for the heroic Wallace, it is equally an expression of fear that Scotland is perpetually a land of compromisers. That Smith is challenging us with Wallace's glorious and tragic tale is beyond doubt: in his essay on MacDiarmid's *Three Hymns to Lenin*, he writes 'the bard educates the tribe by singing of its ancient glories in order to inspire emulation of its heroes in the present and future' (Smith: 1962, 76). Incitement to emulation is perpetually necessary. Even the final, apparently crassly nationalistic rendition of 'Scots wha hae wi Wallace bled' is a gesture of exhortation rather than of triumphalism.

The threat of Scottish compromise pervades the play, from the attitude of Sir Thomas Braidfute in the opening scene, through Bruce's mix of reasons for inaction and Menteith's refusal to allow Wallace the leadership in Act II. The absence of the Scottish nobility from the field of Falkirk is fatal, of course. In Act III, Edward is able to rejoice that Scotland is divided:

> I need traitors as a sick man physic —
> And, praise be, Scotland's no dearth of them! (84)

At the end of the act, Menteith emerges as the most dangerous and effective traitor of them all, his motives (like Wallace's) a combination of the personal and the patriotic. Just as telling, though, is the rejection of him by the Scots Lords at Edward's court ('*As MENTEITH turns to leave, the SCOTS LORDS turn their backs upon him in silence'* [111]): they disapprove, but they do not act. Wallace is the play's hero not just because of his military success and his heroic end, but also because of his unswerving commitment to the patriotic cause.

Smith's play clearly 'works' in the theatre, in that it is a script which performers can use to put on a show. Even critical commentators acknowledge its visual effect, and a recounting of the Wallace story cannot fail to engage an audience (as *Braveheart* itself demonstrates). Difficulties and limitations arise, however, for audiences and readers not thirled to the cause of the Scottish Renaissance: its issues and concerns are too much of its moment, and of an approach to drama which it is hard not to call naïve. Other difficulties which some have encountered with it – its Scots language (rejoiced in by cultural nationalists but apparently problematic to audiences) and its scarcity of striking stage action (apart from the death of Mirren, the torture of the defenders of Stirling Castle, and the capture of Wallace) – are ultimately lesser issues. Despite Smith's hopes for a career in drama, his most important literary successes lay elsewhere, not in the theatre's address to a wide audience but in the implicit embodiment of his patriotism in verse, a theme explored fully by J. Derrick McClure in his essay in the present volume.

## Bibliography

Bold, Alan, *Modern Scottish Literature* (London & New York: Longman, 1983).

Brown, Ian, *History as Theatrical Metaphor: History, Myth and National Identities in Modern Scottish Drama* (London: Palgrave Macmillan, 2016).

Buchanan, Robert, *Wallace: A Tragedy in Five Acts* in *Tragic Dramas from Scottish History* (Edinburgh: Thomas Constable & Co. and London: Hamilton, Adams, & Co., 1859).

Gibbon, Lewis Grassic, 'The Antique Scene' in Lewis Grassic Gibbon and Hugh MacDiarmid, *Scottish Scene: or The Intelligent Man's Guide to Albyn* (London: Hutchinson, 1934; repr. Bath: Cedric Chivers, 1974), pp. 19–36.

Hubbard, Tom, 'Reintegrated Scots: The Post-MacDiarmid Makars' in Cairns Craig (ed.), *The History of Scottish Literature* IV: *Twentieth Century* (Aberdeen: Aberdeen University Press, 1987), pp. 179–193.

Morton, Graeme, *William Wallace: A National Tale* (Edinburgh: Edinburgh University Press, 2014).

Paterson, James, *Wallace: The Hero of Scotland* (Edinburgh: W.P. Nimmo, Hay & Mitchell, 1900).

Royle, Trevor, *The Macmillan Companion to Scottish Literature* (London: Macmillan Press, 1983).

Smith, Sydney Goodsir, Correspondence and manuscript holdings relating to Goodsir Smith and his work in the National Library of Scotland, used in this chapter: Acc. 10281/1–3, Acc. 10397/1, Acc. 26430 / ff. 36–41 (f. 38) & Acc. 26430/ ff. 47–77 (f. 75).

Smith, Sydney Goodsir, *A Short Introduction to Scottish Literature* (Edinburgh: Serif Books, 1951).

Smith, Sydney Goodsir, *The Stick-Up, or Full Circle*, in *Fifteen Poems and a Play* (Edinburgh: Southside, 1969), pp. 1–33.

Smith, Sydney Goodsir, 'The Three Hymns to Lenin' in Sydney Goodsir Smith & Kulgin Duval (eds.) *Hugh MacDiarmid: A Festschrift* (Edinburgh: K.D. Duval, 1962), pp. 73–86.

Smith, Sydney Goodsir, *The Wallace: A Triumph in Five Acts* (Edinburgh & London: Oliver & Boyd, 1960).

Spence, Lewis, *The Story of William Wallace* (London: Humphrey Milford, Oxford University Press, 1919).

Watson, Roderick, *The Literature of Scotland: The Twentieth Century*, 2nd edition, (London: Palgrave Macmillan, 2007).

CHAPTER 14

# Sydney Goodsir Smith, Artist and Art Critic

*Alan Riach and Alexander Moffat*

## Abstract

This chapter introduces Smith as an artist, ambitious from childhood to paint and draw, identifying three main periods: his satirical drawings in Europe before the Second World War, his drawings and paintings in Scotland after the war, including his illustrations for his major poem-sequence, *Under the Eildon Tree*, and his drawings and paintings from Plockton and the Scottish Highlands. It then presents a selection of his writings as an art critic for *The Scotsman* newspaper, 1960–67, covering such artists as Anne Redpath, William MacTaggart, William Gillies, John Maxwell, Denis Peploe and Joan Eardley, and his criticism and appraisal of the Royal Scottish Academy and the younger artists John Bellany and Alexander Moffat, the Hugh MacDiarmid portrait by R.H. Westwater and exhibitions of new work from Italy and Nigeria, and comes to some conclusions about Smith's predilections and skills as an art critic, and his vision of the interconnectedness of the arts.

## Keywords

painting – drawing – art – art criticism – *The Scotsman* – Anne Redpath – William MacTaggart – William Gillies – John Maxwell – Denis Peploe – Joan Eardley – John Bellany – Alexander Moffat – Royal Scottish Academy – Hugh MacDiarmid – Richard Demarco

## 1 Introduction: Personal and Professional

As a poet, Sydney Goodsir Smith is less well known than many of his contemporaries but he is even less well known as an art critic and artist of some distinction himself.

In 1988, the Saltire Society published a series of 'Saltire Self-Portraits'. Smith's was in the form of a letter written to Maurice Lindsay in 1947. He makes it clear there that his main ambition as a young man was to be a painter, but his parents did not approve. Undaunted, however, he spent a great deal of his life taking every opportunity to draw and paint, amassing a fairly substantial body of work. Denis Peploe's essay on Smith as a painter emphasises this aspect of his artistic production: 'What made Sydney paint? What led a distinguished poet to enter a competitive field in which he had no professional training, and submit his work to critical appraisal? He was certainly no mere dilettante, and although he painted for his own enjoyment, there was dedication and single-mindedness beyond the normal scope of the amateur. His standards were exacting within the restricted range which he set himself' (Peploe, 79).

In the collection made by Ian Begg, *The Drawings of Sydney Goodsir Smith, Poet*, edited by Joy Hendry (Edinburgh: Chapman Publishing, 1998), three distinct periods in Smith's work are revealed.

(1) There is a period in which he is travelling in pre-war Europe, in 1936–37: he moves through Switzerland, Germany, Italy and France and goes to Konstanz; he depicts a portrait of Hitler on a German tavern wall, next to a crucifix and a sign saying 'Dancing Forbidden' with a dancing figure in the foreground and two others sitting at a table, drinking beer. He depicts Fascisti in Florians Café in Venice (where later, in 1971, Hugh MacDiarmid was to meet Ezra Pound); then he presents the Café les Deux Maggots, Paris. His sketches are witty, imaginative, sharp, evidently done while travelling – they show the artist as witness, a cartoonist and a satirist. What comes across is a sense of humour and scorn. Smith clearly chose these subjects to record and make comment on, suggesting both political implication and moral judgement.

(2) In Scotland after the war, Smith is continuing in the same vein, sketching wittily, making sharp observations of his contemporary Scots: a young woman is seen fleeing from a minister, a Scotsman dressed in a kilt is presented in front of a prostitute ('Scotsman facing prostitute with cat'). These lead into drawings accompanying *Under the Eildon Tree* (1948). This is work of a different order, a poet making a series of illustrations to complement the poetry. The artist now is a visionary and the vision is pastoral, the tradition that of the dream poem with an ancient Greek ancestry.

(3) Then there are the drawings and watercolours from Plockton and the Highlands, when he was composing alongside Denis Peploe and Sorley MacLean and to some extent was perhaps working in emulation of William Gillies. In the late 1940s, throughout the 1950s and well into the 1960s, Smith was taking himself more seriously as a committed artist in these works. Norman MacCaig was fishing in the north of Scotland, in Lochinver, while Smith and Peploe were painting watercolours in Plockton. The contemporaneity and continuity of all these activities is important to note: these were all artists engaged with the local habitations of the Highlands and islands, not merely as tourists

but rather as intermittent residents, depicting a community and landscapes insightfully and sympathetically.


## 2    Sydney Goodsir Smith: Art Critic

Sydney Goodsir Smith was art critic of *The Scotsman* from 1960–67.[1] During that period he would write regular weekly reviews of current exhibitions mainly held in Edinburgh. These would include the mundane as well the large and prestigious annual Edinburgh Festival exhibitions, such as those devoted to Delacroix, Modigliani, Corot, Epstein and the Bührle Collection (from Ingres to Picasso).

One of his main tasks was to review the annual Royal Scottish Academy exhibitions, where the leading Scottish moderns held sway. Artists such as William Gillies, John Maxwell, William MacTaggart and Anne Redpath all emerged in the late 1930s, which was the time when Smith himself arrived in Scotland, looking around at the new country with a fresh eye and a keen appetite.

He followed their progress throughout the 1940s and 1950s and as art critic of *The Scotsman*, he was well prepared to write about their work. He conducted a series of twelve interviews, each a 'Portrait of the Artist', where he explores their work in depth and presents a 'state of the art' progress report on Scottish painting and sculpture at that time. In all of the articles he presents independent views and strong positions on the Scottish tradition in paintings and in sculpture, how this tradition might be maintained and re-vitalised.

His views on the RSA exhibitions fluctuate between the critical and the supportive and in 1964 he felt compelled to defend the RSA against increasing criticism (mainly from Alan Bold). Nevertheless, he was strongly in support of the John Bellany and Alexander Moffat 'outdoors' exhibitions, with paintings hung on the railings outside the RSA.

By the mid-1960s, new galleries were beginning to appear in Edinburgh. Richard Demarco's gallery in particular concentrated on the new and fashionable. Smith's views on abstraction were primarily negative, on occasion bordering on the philistine (though perhaps he had his tongue in his cheek) and he was equally critical of fashionable gestures. He certainly relished poking fun

---

1   The material quoted from Sydney Goodsir Smith's articles in *The Scotsman* was made available through the good offices of The Royal Scottish Academy's archives. We are very grateful to Robin Rodger, Documentation Officer and Sandy Wood, Collections Curator for their enthusiastic and helpful responses to all of our queries.

at the absurdities of the so-called 'new' art and this came to a head in his re-
view of contemporary Italian art in 1967.

At this stage there were complaints. Smith's humorous and irreverent atti-
tudes were deemed old-fashioned and out of touch and he was replaced as *The
Scotsman*'s art critic by Edward Gage in the middle of 1967. What follows are

FIGURE 14.1 Sydney Goodsir Smith (2018)
    © ALEXANDER MOFFAT

extracts from Smith's art criticism from *The Scotsman*. Commentary by Alexander Moffat and Alan Riach is presented in italics.

## 3    Part One: Portraits of The Artists

### 3.1    *Anne Redpath*

*Anne Redpath (1895–1965), W.G. Gillies (1898–1973), John Maxwell (1905–1962), William MacTaggart (1903–1981) and Denis Peploe (1914–1993) were leading members of the Edinburgh School, which was the dominant force in Scottish painting after the Second World War. It is notable in the following portrait that Redpath insists that she wishes for no special consideration as a woman but would rather her work be assessed with equal objectivity alongside any male painter.*

#### 3.1.1    Anne Redpath – First Scotswoman to be Elected A.R.A. (*The Scotsman* 13 May 1961)

[...] She tells me she is the first woman artist to be elected to the Royal Academy [London] for sixteen years, the first Scottish woman ever, and the first 'family' woman in the whole history of the Academy. This is distinction indeed. [...]

Although she is naturally proud of the distinctive nature of her recent election, she is rather against the feminist approach to such matters. A painter should be judged as a painter, and for women artists to exhibit together is as silly as would a special exhibition of men over six feet taking size 14 in shoes. I couldn't agree more.

In the same way she resents the terminology used by some critics. A slight, delicate watercolour (say by a man) they will describe as 'sensitive' or some such, but a like piece of work by a woman will be called 'very feminine'. Miss Redpath finds this derogatory, though I don't think it is always meant so. [...]

The increasing formality or abstraction of her work, she thinks, has reached its limit. Influenced by the trend of the times as she is, she would find it easier to paint pure abstracts, but these would not be so' satisfying' to herself nor, indeed, to the spectator.

'I love objects too much to disregard them', she said, 'and I also feel the spectator needs a point of departure, some reference to the familiar start from'. This so echoes my own feelings in the matter that I could not forbear to cheer.

### 3.2    *William MacTaggart*

*In the 'portrait' of William MacTaggart, then President of the RSA, Smith asks a key question: 'Supposing he were Minister of Culture, how would he use the funds*

*at his disposal?' MacTaggart, whose wife was Norwegian, immediately refers to*
*the Finnish example of providing grants and state pensions to artists of all kinds.*

3.2.1      William MacTaggart, President of the Royal Scottish Academy (*The*
              *Scotsman*, 22 April 1961)

William MacTaggart, who was born in Loanhead and studied at the Edinburgh College of Art, is, at the age of 57, at the height of his powers [...]

Though occupying, as President of the Royal Scottish Academy, the highest position in Scottish art life, he can still be regarded as one of 'les jeunes' – the first President, in fact, who belongs unequivocally to what is sometimes loosely described as the modern movement. From the point of view of the future of Scottish painting this is the most admirable circumstance. [...]

He finds the Presidentship irksome only in the matter of time – hours lost from painting – but with experience (he has held the office since 1959) he manages to control the official side of things by refusing to hear about anything until the afternoon – the hours of daylight are sacred.

The purpose of an academy, in his view, is to create a contemporary standard, to encourage and support the best work that is being done – even to the extent of taking risks – in order to recreate the Scottish tradition, not just to continue it.

He considers Scottish painting today to be in an extremely healthy and promising state. 'These things go in cycles for some reason', he remarked, 'and I think just now we may very well be at the beginning of a great period. There is something in the air. Not only in painting'. [...]

Supposing he were Minister of Fine Arts, how would he use funds at his disposal? His reply was unhesitating – providing pensions or state grants to artists of all kinds, as in Finland. He mentioned Sibelius who, gaining one of these while still in his twenties, was enabled to spend his whole long life working as he wanted without the distraction of need. What a gain to Finland!

MacTaggart admitted that it might be difficult to choose the recipients (young and old) but in the Finnish experience the good choices amply paid for the mistakes. In the first Scottish Government I can think of no better such Minister than William MacTaggart. Let us hurry up.

3.3      *William Gillies*

*Gillies admits to liking abstract painting and especially Kandinsky, but confusingly says, 'it's not part of my make-up... I need the contact with nature'. In a similar vein Redpath says, 'I love objects too much to disregard them and I also feel the spectator needs a point of reference'. Smith comments: 'This so echoes my own feelings in the matter that I could not forebear to cheer'.*

3.3.1       W.G. Gillies, Principal of Edinburgh College of Art (*The Scotsman*, 29 April 1961)

William G. Gillies, RSA, was born in Haddington, trained at the Edinburgh College of Art and studied for a while with André Lhote in Paris. He is now principal of his old college and a very spry 62.

He is a gnome or troll character to look at, and one could imagine he would be perfectly at home in the Hall of the Mountain King – a sort of cross between Bertrand Russell and Hugh MacDiarmid – but much quieter. I assure you, less aggressive by far than either of these two dynamos. Which is not to say he does not in his own field, develop an equally powerful charge. [...] Gillies must be one of the most prolific artists in Scotland – or even further afield.

There is a story that he went on holiday with John Maxwell to a little village in the West Highlands and it rained steadily throughout the ten days they were there. But Gillies came home with 35 watercolours, repeat water-colours.

I asked him if this was truth or a coy legend. 'Well', said the maestro, with a complacent twinkle, 'it might not have been quite thirty-five...but' (and the god spake out of the mouth of his creature) 'when I go on a painting holiday, I go on a painting holiday'.

These were watercolours. For his landscapes in oil he does not work directly from nature but builds up his picture in the studio from innumerable drawings and the occasional watercolour sketch.

'A landscape has to be digested. Working from nature, one is distracted by the perpetual change – I get led astray from the original conception. I seek the permanent in nature'.

This is a revealing remark. [...] 'The permanent in the transient' might be a good enough definition of his finest works in landscape.

In Still Life the head is even more in the ascendant. These become almost musical (I am thinking of Bach) in their classical, even mathematical completeness, their wholeness – what is the word I'm looking for – integration? Horrible word.

When I asked him of the influences on his work he spoke enthusiastically of the Edvard Munch show in the SSA in the 1930s. 'They had a great effect on me', he said. [...]

He liked abstract painting and confessed, apologetically it seemed, that he had a hankering to indulge in it, 'but it's not part of my make-up, I'm afraid. My kind of painting comes naturally to me. I need the contact with nature'.

### 3.4    *John Maxwell*

3.4.1       John Maxwell – Painter of Dreams and Fantasies (*The Scotsman*,
            2 May 1961)

John Maxwell was born [in Dalbeattie] in 1905 and will probably be buried
there in 2005 – a creaking door hangs longest, they say, and Maxwell has had,
particularly recently, his fair share of illness, which has occasions prevented
him from accepting commissions for public works, murals and the like.

He studied at the Edinburgh College and then in Paris under Léger and
Ozenfant. Léger was a fine, if rigorous, teacher and Maxwell gained a lot from
him in the way of discipline, but, as anyone can see, the master left no traces of
influence on the pupil's style. These influences have been many and various,
particularly of course those of Chagall and Klee. [...]

He paints very slowly, averaging only a couple of completed works annually
and sometimes spends years on a single canvas. [...]

Personally, he's a very shy chap who hates publicity and likes best to be left
alone to hide away in his own little burrow and brood and work away or listen
to his fine collection of gramophone records or read poetry for his interest in
and love for these sister arts is deep and informed. [...]

Maxwell must surely be one of the most seductive painters alive today –
outside fashion – outside time. We must be grateful, even if he only gives us a
single picture in a year.

*Sadly, Smith's optimism about Maxwell's longevity was misplaced: he died the
following year, 1962.*


### 3.5    *Denis Peploe*

*Smith was particularly close to Denis Peploe, who had illustrated one of Smith's
early books, The Deevil's Waltz (1946). They went on painting trips together, most-
ly to the Western Highlands, with the tiny village of Plockton, a favourite base.
Smith's 'portrait' of Peploe is an affectionate one but it quickly becomes serious
with Smith prompting Peploe to give an assessment of the current state of paint-
ing. The response comes: 'There are two branches today – purely abstract paint-
ing, which has no relation to anything outside the artist's own mind, and abstract-
ed painting, which starts from some aspect of nature or humanity'. We will come
back to this question.*


3.5.1       Denis Peploe – the Atmospheric Quality (*The Scotsman*,
            23 September 1961)

Lugubrious, hilarious, taciturn-fluent, sinister, obsessional, encyclopaedic,
electronic, culinary, serious, enquiring, gaunt, gleg, patriarchal, ancient –

Wolseley-driving, edible-fungophile – in fact, peplovian – Peploe, known in Highland parts as the Admiral of The Paint, Denis Peploe started sucking flake-white from his father S.J. Peploe's brushes along with his mother's milk.

He was born in Edinburgh in 1914 and trained at the local College of Art, whence he went to André Lhote's studio in Paris and thereafter travelled on a scholarship in Yugoslavia, Greece and Italy, where, for a spell, he had a studio in Florence. [...]

He was influenced by Lhote's teachings, though not by his work – 'his theories about linear design and colour design I've thought about ever since'. [...]

When I asked him the usual question about the painters he admired, or who has, in his opinion, in influenced his work, he thought for a bit, searching about maybe, and then came out with, 'One often admires painters who don't really influence one's work at all. I really admire paintings I couldn't or wouldn't want to do myself. Such as the fantastic in art: the Dadaists, the Surrealists, Douanier Rousseau, Soutine, Chirico in his surrealist period'. He did admit to being influenced by Segonzac, though, and then confessed to having always had 'a tremendous admiration for Picasso' – who hadn't really had much direct influence on him at all, he thought. [...]

He went on; 'There are two branches today – purely abstract painting which has no relation to anything outside the artist's own mind, and abstracted painting, which starts from some aspect of nature or humanity, something observed. All art must be related to humanity – after all, it is created by a human hand and a human eye and can only be appreciated by a human eye.

'The ideally pure abstract, unrelated to anything in nature, loses depths that are essential to humanity, such things as harmony, proportion, and will be empty because everything, sign or shape, must have some reference to something in human experience. So purely abstract art must fail'. [...]

His work will probably become increasingly abstracted, but I think we shall never lose this peculiar weathery-geological kind of atmosphere that is his and no one else's. It is probably, when you get down to it, a romantic quality. But it is the classical discipline, 'the hard bounding line' controlling the tumult within that makes for permanence in flux. And this, I think, is exactly what Peploe controls – or maybe what controls him.

### 3.6     Joan Eardley

*In his review of the Joan Eardley Memorial Exhibition, Smith wonders, as many have over the past half century since her death, where she would have gone next. His answer is that one cannot really imagine she would have been long content with Catterline 'once she had subdued it'. Nobody else has ever put it quite like that. The recognition of the affinity with William McTaggart is salutary and the sense that Eardley may well have gone further into unexplored territory is poignant – though of course, the forces Eardley painted in her seascapes of Catterline might never have been subdued. But Smith clearly understands the forces involved. He brings his own experience as an artist into his understanding of the work he is reviewing. He knew he would never himself have 'subdued' Plockton in his own paintings: some landscapes, as Cézanne knew so well, simply call on the artist to return, again and again, to their address and what their meaning is. There is no closure or finality to this.*

3.6.1        Magnificent Eardley (*The Scotsman*, 2 March 1964)
This magnificent show, numbering about 120 works, brings home, especially en masse, how much we lost to the world by Joan Eardley's early death. [...]

The big gallery houses about 30 of her resplendent later landscapes and seascapes painted at Catterline, Kincardineshire, this room is indeed splendid as we follow her progress, a deeper and deeper progress, into an increasingly Turneresque identification with landscape – with the ghost of McTaggart never far away from her stormbound coasts. [...]

[I]t must be loudly cried out that here, in a mere hundred pictures gathered together, is the work of a great painter, a great artist. If she had been spared, I wonder, we must all wonder, where she would have gone next. The jump from her Glasgow slum children, so closely, but not all romantically observed, to the tumultuous romanticism of her Catterline fields and seas, is so violent, or, to curb one's pen, even so abrupt, that one cannot really imagine she would have been long content with Catterline once she had subdued it.

*This question of abstraction in painting, pure and simple, as against a reference point of nature or subject, becomes almost central to Smith's criticism. It is something he returns to in almost every review and 'portrait'. It is part of a bigger debate in the art world, with political and ideological implications. After the Second World War, abstraction in America meant freedom, whereas concrete subject matter was Soviet realism. The Cold War polarised these forms of expression. Smith seems to want to negotiate between them and his reviews come from a middle ground, 'where extremes meet'.*

4        Part Two: Royal Scottish Academy Annual Exhibitions

4.1        *No Outstanding Miracles* (The Scotsman, *21 April 1961*)
The exhibition as a whole is unusual in that there are no tremendously outstanding miracles, but a very much higher level than one has a right to expect in

a come-all-ye market of this nature. The Academy is moving forward rapidly – it has been doing so for some years – and is almost ceasing to be an 'Academy' in the old accepted fuddy-duddy sense of the term. [...]

Portraits, which were once almost the prime interest of an Academy show have long been in a very small minority. Portraiture is evidently a dying art and few there are to practise it. One cannot but regret this: photography is no alternative, and future generations will blame us for our neglect in this regard. Let us deal with the last of the Mohicans first.

Stanley Cursiter presents the Queen Mother bravely trying to hang on to a famous smile. R.H. Westwater has an admirably composed and deeply tanned Lord Boothby, comfortably settled in his robes as Rector of Aberdeen University, a well-modelled alive head, the model of what an official portrait should be. David Donaldson, with 'Sir Hector Hetherington' has attempted something more – or something different – aiming beyond a straightforward likeness maybe. It certainly comes off as a picture.

4.1.1        High Level of Competence (*The Scotsman*, 20 April 1962)

All of which leads us to the pure abstractors, the most fanciful of the lot, and they are all in Room III. Foremost is the inveterate Charles Pulsford with one called uncompromisingly 'Painting, Red' and the other, uncompromisingly, 'Painting, Dark Blue'. The red one is beautiful, I think, drippy and squiggly and splotch straight out of the tube; the blue one dazzling with great intensity of pure colour, deep violet ultramarine.

What on earth would one do with such paintings I know not. I can imagine a series of such panels behind a cocktail bar as poorly decorative slabs of colour, or in a gallery of modern art. To confront one in your sitting room for the rest of your life might become painful. There is certainly no doubt of their impact and power. It seems to me a lot of painting today is like this. Whom is it painted for? C'est magnifique! But is it les beaux arts?

5        Part Three: Challenging the RSA

*At the time of the exhibition John Bellany and Alexander Moffat had on the Castle Terrace railings in 1961, the artists simply thought of Smith then as the art critic for The Scotsman, a pretty establishment role. Then came this review.*

5.1       *John Bellany and Alexander Moffat*

5.1.1        Public Art in Public Places (*The Scotsman*, September 1963)

On the Castle Terrace railings are large and telling decorations by two young painters, Messrs Bellany and Moffat. These two are very much of a 'school' (if one can use such a term about only two people), as, say, Van Gogh and Gauguin were at one period, or Peploe and Fergusson at another.

To the popular fashion of abstract splurging about in the void they oppose the classical discipline of the bounding line of Fernand Léger. Their work is undoubtedly impressive. This is public art, designed to be seen in public places, and I should like to see public commissions coming their way some day.

*The following year, Bellany and Moffat moved their exhibition to the railings outside the Royal Scottish Academy, a much more direct challenge to the institution's authority. Smith responds enthusiastically to this.*

5.1.2     Moral Protest in Paint: Two-man Show on the Railings (*The Scotsman*, 24 August 1964)

Weather permitting, the passer-by can enjoy a popular two-man show of paintings by Alexander Moffat and John Bellany hanging on the railings to the east of the Royal Scottish Academy and the National Gallery. These two painters are declaredly 'committed' (which is why they exhibit their works al fresco), 'political' and 'socialist realist'. They reject the criteria and the social and political implications of the established academies and prefer to exhibit for all to see without let or hindrance or entrance fee.

This is all, maybe, a bit by the way, for the paintings of Moffat and Bellany are of merit – as paintings. Aesthetically, their political message is no less and no more important than the political or social messages of Daumier for Rowlandson.

As a painter, Bellany is a romantic; his protest is similar to that of Delacroix, who is living, for the moment, next door. Bellamy is an artist of talent who has not yet found his direction.

Moffat's efficiently organised picture of a political meeting (H. Wilson on the stand) is an adequate piece of social realism without any political accent and without passion. He has more impact with the general social scene – the pub with the accordionist. Or the sad, Dante's Inferno procession of the bingo queue.

He is no colourist as Bellany is, but his sense of line, and the rhythm of line are, from a decorative or 'public' point of view, strong, active and visually telling – which is what is required for public painting.

*Is it possible that pressure was put on Smith at this time to make a more positive defence of the RSA against the protest of two young artists rattling the cage of the institutional authority? At around the same time, Hamish Henderson and Hugh MacDiarmid were conducting their flyting in the letters pages of The Scotsman, discussing from opposing sides the value and validity of folk song and the popular oral tradition as against literary and intellectual poetry and 'high' art. In any case, the following year saw Smith in support of the RSA, as follows.*

5.1.3      RSA Fulfilling its Task: Case for the Defence (*The Scotsman,*
           24 April 1965)

The Royal Scottish Academy has been under fire in the correspondence col-
umn of *The Scotsman.* 'C'est convenable!' What on earth would we do if there
were no nice big solid institution to attack? Like God, or the Church (to mis-
quote Voltaire) it would have to be invented. Poor old RSA! Attacked by the Left
for being stuffy and by the Right for being bolshie – who can please all of the
people all of the time?

What does one expect from an Academy? The usual RSA show has about 600
exhibits. Obviously most of this will be pretty ordinary stuff. In Utopia, do you
think their academies display 600 masterpieces a year? Academies exist to set
standards; masterpieces are beyond standards, but they usually derive from
them.

The whole point of such exhibitions is to present to the public, in a big mar-
ket place, a general view of the best work submitted, in the opinion of a repre-
sentative body of practising professional artists. If masterpieces only were ad-
mitted, it would be a very small show indeed and would hardly encourage
lesser mortals to continue the long struggle with their 'sullen craft or art'. And
anyway, who is to judge, who is to know a masterpiece (apart from his own, of
course) at first sight? Doctors proverbially disagree: artists have very much
more to disagree about.

Some artists, good and bad, refuse to be associated with, or to accept, or
even to submit to such a judgement, which they regard as incompetent or bi-
ased. Certainly, on the other wing, some young artists refuse to submit pictures
to that body preferring to hang them on public railings in the street – to the
greater gaiety of the Edinburgh scene, in my opinion!

This is not to say that any of those dissidents or malcontents are right or
wrong about the quality of the RSA's judgement. Only time tells that, and even
time's judgements are subject to fashion.

If most of the painting exhibited in these big shows is merely expensive
wallpaper (as it is) – what would you do? Abolish the thing by act of Parlia-
ment? If one dislikes a Government or establishment the thing to do is either
to blow it up or get in there and change it – which is exactly what the senior
members of the present RSA have been doing over the past 30 years or more.
[...]

We judge the past by its greatest achievements the cream has come to the
top. No man can so judge the present, though of course we all think we can.
Although in many respects (in design, for instance) the present age is particu-
larly feeble, the 'general run' of all the arts in most (not all) modern European
periods has been pretty uninspired.

This is not the fault of any academy or establishment – they are merely the products of their own societies, which include rebels as well as conformers. But we cannot do without them.

*Smith would write two separate reviews of the Royal Scottish Academy's Annual Exhibition appearing on consecutive days. In the first he would concentrate on the oil paintings, in the second on sculpture, watercolours and drawings, and architecture.*

6      Part Four: The Rsa: History, Sculpture, Architecture: The Lived Environment

*Smith's 1961 review of the Architecture Room at the RSA contains what is possibly the first public mention of the ill-fated building of St Peter's College, Cardross. By the early 1960s J.A. Coia's architectural practice, Gillespie, Kidd and Coia was led by Andy MacMillan and Isi Metzstein and St Peter's was their masterwork. Now it is in a ruinous state since its abandonment in the 1980s, despite several attempts to convert and re-use the building.*

6.1    *The Royal Scottish Academy Annual Exhibition 1961* (The Scotsman, *22 April 1961*)
The most exciting things in the Architecture Room are J.A. Coia's avant-garde, toy bricks model of St Peter's College, Cardross; John Holt's Victoria Hospital, Kirkcaldy; William Kininmonth's Edinburgh University Student's Hall (not so good inside); Bruce Walker's plan for Derby Street, Dundee; E.V. Collin's proposed developments at Perth and Dunfermline, which have a close family likeness, towers of flats (city of the future stuff) in evidently wooded and lawned countrysides; and two competitive designs by Leslie Graham MacDougall and Andrew Jackson for the Cathedral of Christ the King at Liverpool, both of which are dramatic, expressive and moderately revolutionary.

*Benno Schotz (1891–1984), an Eastern European Jew like Jacob Epstein, who was a major influence upon his work, came to Glasgow in 1912 and was to sculpt portraits of James Maxton and Hugh MacDiarmid. He became Head of Sculpture at Glasgow School of Art. Smith has no doubt about the reasons for Scotland's m eagre sculptural tradition: they are all to do with Scotland's crippling puritanical religious commitments and dispositions. It is also notable that Smith sees sculpture as closely related to architecture, rather than to painting. After the Second World War, there were few images of Bruce in the public domain and the story of William Wallace was also carried by an oral tradition rather in a scholarly or educational context. Smith's play, The Wallace, was a tremendous success at the Edinburgh Festival of 1960, the audience standing at the end of the performance and singing 'Scots Wha Ha'e'. It was published that year and three years later, Pilkington Jackson's bronze statue of Bruce was unveiled at Bannockburn. The plastercast was first seen in 1963, and Smith reviews it positively.*

### 6.2    *The Royal Scottish Academy Annual Exhibition 1963* (The Scotsman, *20 April 1963*)

Mr Pilkington Jackson's monument to 'The Bruce', intended for erection at Bannockburn, will be familiar photographically to many: the full-size plaster model is on view at the RSA this year and forms the gigantic centre-piece in the Sculpture Hall. These confined surroundings are naturally unsuitable for such a large piece of statuary designed to be raised on a high plinth in the open air, but it is good to see it here. The pose is noble – the horse's trappings, equine equivalent of a Roman's toga, being a great aid to the sculptor – and, though designed in what many will regard as an old-fashioned, heroic style with great attention paid to such details as chainmail, decoration on the scabbard and so forth, it will look splendid when in situ.

At the opposite extreme from such high seriousness you may relax with two rather jokey artefacts, both of them pretty hefty in scale. I refer to Benno Schotz's' Alice and the Red Queen' and Thomas Whalen's 'Art Critics'. The latter are three (or was it four?) lugubrious characters of this unhappy race of men in sub-cubist relief, 'available' says the catalogue, in 'stone or cement or bronze'. I should have thought brass would be their proper element – or maybe plastic. This amusing *jeu d'esprit* demands erection in an art college where no disciplinary action would be taken for defacing the said critics' effigies with charcoal moustaches, beards and specs. [...]

Benno Schotz's life-sized 'Alice and the Red Queen', designed for a primary school in Glasgow, presumably the playground, shows that nightmare twain in headlong flight, their arms, legs, skirts, hair, and a supporting tree, forming crossbars, loops, archways and suchlike. I shall not descant on the visual beauties of this work (which are to seek), but I bet it will amuse the bairns – that is, if they are allowed to play on it. Provided it is not fenced off as a precious work of art, it will provide ample opportunities for hide-and-seek, vaulting, swinging, chasing, jumping and even hanging by the neck until dead.

Mr Schotz has the gift of perpetual youth and with it, some would say, the irresponsibility. He has had himself a ball with this large, ungainly construction which aesthetically may be a disaster but which functionally is just the very thing. [...]

There is little to catch the starving eye in the Architecture Section, and this year there are no scale models to conjure our childish delight in little things. No aid to joy, in fact. Exceptions are William Kininmonth's Elgin Town Hall, which looks as if it might be rather fine in its lumpy, blocky way, and Sir Basil Spence's new Crematorium at Mortonhall, Edinburgh, which has a sort of atomic-pile Gothism that is at least ambitious in design though perhaps de-rivative in inspiration. It has obviously been carefully thought about, whereas much of the usual hen-battery stuff (as J.A. Cora's Maternity Hospital at Bellshill, Glasgow, or Sir Basil's Scottish Widow's Building in St Andrew Square, Edinburgh, to Anthony Wheeler's Lochgelly Redevelopment Scheme) seems not to have been thought about at all – at least from the outside – and is as cliché-ridden as any Victorian-Gothic suburban church. The outside appear-ance, especially of large public buildings, does matter.

**6.3    *Historical Reasons for Scotland's Meagre Sculptural Tradition* (The Scotsman, *17 April 1967*)**

Regarding the sculpture, it is a coincidence that some of the best works here are a clutch of almost pocket-sized nudes. The nude is not a subject that has been dealt with much in Scottish art, for obvious historical and psychological (i.e., puritanical-religious) reasons. The fact that this work is very small in scale is a comment on the lack of patronage for sculpture in Scottish public building, which again has historical reasons. Though this prejudice has greatly moder-ated in our era, historically it has meant that no sculptural tradition exists in Scotland. All this applies to other Protestant societies, but I think nowhere so intensely as here.

**7        Part Five: The MacDiarmid Portrait**

*Smith appears to take a lenient position towards the portraiture of the period. Portraits of the Queen and University Vice Chancellors by Cursiter and Westwater respectively are commended, though admitted to be conforming to what would be expected of the academy. This is opposed to John Berger's view of portraiture. In his essay, 'The Changing View of Man in the Portrait' (1967), Berger writes: 'It seems to me unlikely that any important portraits will ever be painted again' (Berger, 98). Surprisingly, Smith approves of Westwater's portrait of Hugh MacDi-armid despite the fact it had been vehemently condemned by the poet's wife, Val-da Grieve.*

**7.1    *The MacDiarmid portrait by R.H. Westwater,* RSA (The Scotsman,**
       *19 April 1963)*

Portrait painting seems to be dying out, like studies of the nude. However, we
have a good trio by the late R.H. Wastewater (the Duke of Montrose, Sir Hector
Thomson and Hugh MacDiarmid).

*John Tonge, in his review of the exhibition for The Press and Journal (21 April
1963), takes a more critical line': Portraits once were more numerous in the R.S.A,
but seldom more deft than David Donaldson's elegant "Young People", Sir William
Hutchison's "Roy Thomson Esq" is very much for the boardroom, the late Peter
Westwater's "Hugh MacDiarmid" does less than justice to the poet.*

*Valda's letter to Westwater (8 August 1962) is ferocity unbound: 'I was against
you painting the portrait from the beginning – as I consider you unsympathetic to
Christopher politically & otherwise.*

> *'What a selfish lousy swine you are Peter –*
> *'Valda Grieve'*

## 8    Part Six: Hamish Henderson

*In 1962, Smith responded to Hamish Henderson's letter in The Scotsman about a
sculpture in that year's RSA exhibition. Clearly, both are enamoured of the sculp-
ture's subject, beyond all disagreements over detail.*

**8.1    *Exchange of Letters with Hamish Henderson* (The Scotsman)**
April 21 1962
    Sir,
    Although I have every sympathy with Sydney Goodsir Smith's desire to bring
on the dancing girls, I must correct him on one small point in his second notice
of the R.S.A. exhibition. 'Pattinatrice', in Italian, means 'skating girl', and if
Mr Smith will treat himself to another eyeful of Emilio Greco's delectable
figure, and let his eye stray every now and then from the nymph's callipygous
contours, he will see for himself that this is exactly what she is!
    I am &c.
    Hamish Henderson
    April 24 1962
    Sir,

In answer to Mr Hamish Henderson, I was aware the 'Pattinatrice' is an Italian skater, but I was not aware in advance (one never is) what photographs of R.S.A exhibits were going to be chosen to illustrate my notice. In the absence of a photograph showing what's what fu' brawlie, to have described this cavorting young lady, who has no clothes on, poor thing, and no skates either, as a 'Skating Girl' might have been a bit misleading to the imagination.

However, I apologise to Mr Henderson and other Italian scholars; let not my terminological inexactitude prevent them from enjoying Signor Greco's fine work.

I am &c.

Sydney Goodsir Smith

9      Part Seven: From Beyond Scotland: Nigeria and Italy

*In the 1960s there were an increasing number of international exhibitions coming to Edinburgh supported by the Scottish Arts Council, the Scottish National Gallery of Modern Art and the Commonwealth Institute. This review is of an exhibition at the Commonwealth Institute, of drawings and pastel work by schoolchildren, organised by David Harding, who had been living and working in Nigeria.*

9.1    *Nigerian Paintings of Innocent Talent* (The Scotsman, 1966)
The interest for many will lie partly in recognising the influence and non-influence of European models on these unsophisticated painters. One seems to see Matisse all over the place for example. There are a number of traditional designs for painted cloth, mostly geometrical patterns as used in the decoration of mud walls in some parts of Africa. Opposed to these are the other paintings of what the west calls genres. In other words, paintings of day-to-day subjects and activities: farming, dancing, street scenes, football, filling stations and so forth. The two categories come together in the form of patterning of the filling up of the pictorial space with a natural child's eye inevitability in almost all the pictures the storytelling purpose of most primitive art is very apparent, innocent and moving as children's paintings are moving.

*This was Smith's final review, perhaps too flippant and critical for the tastes of the readership of The Scotsman, as imagined by the paper's editorial priorities. Smith was replaced as the paper's art critic after this. Flippant it may appear to be but Smith is making a serious point here, insisting that the so-called 'avant-garde' may be simply posturing, with nothing real to say to people. The bold and forthright critic shown here is consistent with everything Smith had been saying throughout the decade. In a position of some influence and authority, he was*

*fearless in the directness of his commentary and understanding his work as an*
*art critic deepens our understanding of his priorities as a poet.*

9.2    *Contemporary Italian Art at Demarco's Edinburgh: Follies in Dotty*
       *Show by Italians* (The Scotsman, March 1967)

The latest enterprise of the ambitious, energetic and sometimes scatty Demarco Gallery (8 Melville Crescent, Edinburgh) is an exhibition of contemporary Italian art – mostly pictures in various media, including flannel – prepared by the National Gallery of Modern Art in Rome. The glory has obviously departed, but, as we all know, empires come and go.

There are 60 works shared amongst 36 artists and most of it (not all) is an awful lot of tosh and exceedingly pretentious tosh at that.

'Uniform Matt Black Metal'. You have to ask specially to see this masterpiece because it is not on show in the main galleries. It is supposed to hang on the wall but it's too heavy, so it lies sadly on the floor in the basement. It is exactly as described – a sheet of absolutely plain, matt black, slightly granulated metal, very slightly concave, measuring about two yards long by one wide. Just that – and the asking price £3000.

The catalogue tells us that Lo Savio's 'conception of space is such that light acquires a structural value of contributing to the definition of surfaces'. So now we know.

In dramatic contrast, upstairs you may enjoy Piero Manzoni's 'Achrome' which is a piece of plain white flannel (or it might be blotting paper, someone else suggested) framed under glass. Nothing else. No mark or tash sullies the purity of this framed piece of pure white flannel. This great work which must have demanded deep thought and careful scissor work on the part of the 'artist' before he finally decided to frame his piece of white flannel, is described in the catalogue as, wait for it – 'intensely experimental'. Let 'em all come!

10     **Conclusion**

Denis Peploe, writing on Smith's understanding of the inter-relationships between all the arts, said this: 'He saw no fundamental distinction between music, prose, poetry, painting and sculpture, although he recognised that the analogies which appear to bring them close serve equally to separate them; one discipline can complement another as long as it does not try to explain it or merely illustrate it' (Peploe, 81).

Looking back over Smith's work as an art critic in the 1960s, it is clear that he helped shape the understanding of what the artists were doing and brought their work into the public imagination. The negotiation between the work of the artists, the role of the newspaper's reporting of art exhibitions, and the engagement and understanding of the public at large are demonstrated here as vital. There was no intellectual posturing, prioritising of jargon or elitist fashion, no question of anything ending up in Private Eye's 'Pseuds' Corner', but there was a contagious appetite for seeing, for trying to empathise and imagine, and for the practice and vision of artists other than himself.

## Bibliography

Berger, John, 'The Changing View of Man in the Portrait', in *John Berger: Selected Essays* (London: Bloomsbury, 2001), pp. 98–102.

Hendry, Joy, ed., *The Drawings of Sydney Goodsir Smith, Poet*, collected by Ian Begg (Edinburgh: Chapman Publications, 1998).

Peploe, Denis, 'Sydney Goodsir Smith, Painter', in *For Sydney Goodsir Smith* (Edinburgh: M. Macdonald, 1975), pp. 79–84.

Smith, Sydney Goodsir, *Saltire Self-Portraits 3* (Edinburgh: The Saltire Society, 1988).

Tonge, John, 'Diversity at the RSA' in *The Press and Journal* (21 April 1963), pagination unknown.

# Selective Glossary of Sydney Goodsir Smith's Scots Words

(Full glossary to be found in *Collected Poems* (John Calder, 1975), pp. 257–269).

| | |
|---|---|
| *abune* | above |
| *ahint* | behind |
| *aiblins* | perhaps |
| *airt* | quarter, direction, district, compass-point |
| *alane* | alone |
| *albeid* | although |
| *antrin /* | rare, occasional |
| *antran* | |
| *ase* | ash |
| *Auld Reekie* | Edinburgh |
| *avizandum* | Scots legal term, taking extra time to consider a case before judgment |
| | |
| *baccy* | tobacco |
| *bairn* | baby / child |
| *ballant* | poem |
| *biggan* | building |
| *blate* | shy |
| *blee* | complexion |
| *blyte* | storm gust |
| *bumbazed* | stunned, dazed |
| *byde / bide* | wait |
| | |
| *cantie* | lively, cheerful |
| *causie* | street |
| *cavaburd* | blizzard |
| *clanjamphrey /* | |
| *clanjamfrie* | mob, rabble, throng |
| *clouts* | clothes, rags; slaps |
| *cod* | pillow |
| *cokkils* | shells |
| *coronach* | lament |
| *couthie* | snug, warm, sociable |

© KONINKLIJKE BRILL NV, LEIDEN, 2020 | DOI:10.1163/9789004426498_017

| | |
|---|---|
| *cramasie* | crimson silk |
| *crottled* | crumble down |
| *crousie* | convivial |
| *crozie* | fawning, whining |
| | |
| *dauds* | dollops, lumps |
| *derns* | secrets |
| *devall* | cease |
| *ding* | strike, beat, attack |
| *doitit* | crazed |
| *dotterel* | idiot |
| *douce* | sedate, respectable |
| *dowilie* | sadly, tearfully |
| *dozie* | dazed |
| *drouth* | thirst |
| *drowie* | musty, humid, wet |
| *dule* | grief, sorrow, anguish |
| *dwaiblan* | stumbling |
| *dwaum* | stupor |
| *dwynit* | declining, wasting away |
| | |
| *een* | eyes |
| *eldritch* | eerie, otherworldly |
| | |
| *fantice* | vision |
| *fash* | worry, bother |
| *fegs* | faith, indeed |
| *ferlie* | marvel |
| *fient a* | not a bit of |
| *fyled* | fouled, defiled |
| *fou* | drunk |
| *fouthless* | infertile |
| *fozie* | fusty, vile |
| | |
| *gallus* | aggressive, bold |
| *gangrel* | vagrant, outcast |
| *gant* | yawn |
| *gean* | cherry-tree |
| *gey* | very |
| *gin* | if, given |

| | |
|---|---|
| *glaizie* | glazed, glittering, sleek |
| *gleid* | fire |
| *goustrous* | frightful |
| *gowdspink* | goldfinch (also Oliver Goldsmith) |
| *grat* | wept |
| *gree* | prize; agree |
| *greit* | cry |
| *guff* | stench |
| *gurlie* | storm-growling |
| *gyte* | mad |
| | |
| *haar / hayr* | hoar-frost, cold |
| *haill* | whole |
| *hairst* | harvest |
| *hamewith* | homewards |
| *has* | halls |
| *haud yir wheesht* | be quiet |
| *Hidderie-hetterie* | hither and thither |
| *hizzie* | jocular / offensive term for a woman, Robert Burns's term for the 'Muse' |
| *Hornie* | Satan |
| *how-dumb-died* | cold dead of night |
| *howe* | hollow |
| *howffs* | pubs |
| *hurdies* | buttocks |
| | |
| *jaggan* | stinging |
| | |
| *laich* | low |
| *langsyne* | long since |
| *lave* | the rest, remainder |
| *laverock* | lark |
| *leid* | language |
| *leman* | lover |
| *leuch* | laughed |
| *ligg* | lie |
| *loosum* | lovable, loving |
| *lowp* | leap |
| *lums* | chimneys |
| *lyft* | sky |

| | |
|---|---|
| *keekin-gless* | mirror |
| *ken* | know |
| *makar* | poet |
| | |
| *mapamound* | globe, atlas |
| *maun* | must |
| *musardrie* | imaginings / musings |
| | |
| *nebstrous* | nostrils |
| *neuk* | corner, nook |
| *nocht* | *nothing* |
| | |
| *oorie / ourie* | dismal, dank, weird |
| *owrehailan* | overwhelming |
| | |
| *quean* | girl |
| | |
| *raff* | abundant |
| *ramsh* | coarse |
| *raucle* | headstrong, passionate |
| *raxed* | reached |
| *reid-biddie* | 'red biddy' – cheap red wine mixed with methylated spirits |
| *reikan* | smoking |
| *retour* | return |
| *rouch* | rough |
| *rouk* | fog |
| *runkelt* | wrinkled |
| | |
| *saikless* | innocent, simple |
| *Sanct* | saint |
| *scelartrie* | crime, infamy |
| *sclimmed* | climbed |
| *scrieve* | write |
| *scrunt* | misshapen dwarf |
| *shennachie* | bard / poet |
| *shilpet* | puny, thin |
| *sic* | such, so |
| *siccar* | certain |
| *siller* | silver |
| *skail* | scatter, disperse, spill |

| *skaith* | hurt, wrong, harm |
| *skalrag* | vagabond |
| *skillie* | gruel |
| *skrcak* | call of bird |
| *skudder* | shudder |
| *skuggie* | shady, shadowy |
| *slee* | sly |
| *slidder* | slither |
| *snell* | keen, piercing cold |
| *sodjer* | soldier |
| *spulyies* | spoils |
| *steek* | shut |
| *stouteran* | staggering |
| *stramash* | clash, fight, conflict |
| *stravaig* | wander |
| *streel* | urine |
| *stots* | stumbles |
| *Suddron* | Southern(er) |
| *sunkots* | something |
| | |
| *tae* | too |
| *tattie-bogles* | scarecrows |
| *thole* | endure |
| *thrave* | 24 sheaves |
| *toom / tuim* | empty |
| *touzie* | dishevelled |
| *treen* | trees |
| *tregallion* | beggar band |
| *tulyie* | broil, affray |
| *tummlin* | tumbling |
| *tumle* | burial barrow |
| | |
| *ugsome* | ugly, horrible |
| *unco* | extraordinary |
| *undeemous* | incomprehensible |
| | |
| *wan* | won, complete |
| *wanhope* | despair |
| *wean* | baby, small child |
| *weirdless* | worthless |

| | |
|---|---|
| *whiddan* | swishing |
| *whilk* | which |
| *widdreme* | nightmare |
| *winnock* | window |
| *wreisted* | tortured |
| *wreiths* | snowdrifts |
| *wynd* | alley, lane |
| | |
| *yestreen* | last evening / night |
| *yill* | ale |
| *yirdit* | buried |
| *yowdendrift* | piled snowdrift |

# Annotated Bibliography of Publications by and about Sydney Goodsir Smith

Please note this bibliography is extensive, but not exhaustive.

### Primary Material

1938

- 'Smith, S. Sydney', Five poems: 'Neuropath'; 'Dive, Plummet-wise, Darling'; 'Powdered lackeys should receive one into disenchantment to lend grace to the wretched business'; 'Once I was adrift on a celestial sea where all the islands I remarked were the same one. They were, of course, all ruled by the Queen'; & 'The Caverned Hand' in John Goodland & Nicholas Moore, eds., *Seven: The New Magazine,* No. 3 (Winter), pp. 12–16.

1941

- COLLECTION: 'Smith, Sydney', *Skail Wind* (Edinburgh: The Chalmers Press, 1941). Note: Smith's first collection, published under Robert Garioch's imprint. Leftover sets of sheets of the first edition were simply stamped 'Second Edition' to give the impression of greater sales (this information according to the late Edward Nairn, bookseller). 80 copies printed, according to friend of Smith and rare book dealer Kulgin Duval. (In a letter dated 26/09/1960 to Alfred T. Cowie regarding the catalogue *First Editions of the Modern Scottish Renaissance,* Kulgin Duval writes that *Skail Wind* is a hard book to track down because 'there were only 80 copies printed'. Letter in present editor's personal collection.).

1943

- One poem, 'Llanto for Garcia Lorca' in John Smith (ed.), *Million: New Left Writing* (Glasgow: William MacLellan), pp. 53–54.
- COLLECTION: *The Wanderer and Other Poems* (Edinburgh: Oliver & Boyd, 1943). Smith's second collection, which according to Smith was met with 'extravagant apathy' (Smith: 1988, 11).

c.1944

- One poem, published as a political leaflet, 'A Ballant for Douglas Young' (Kirkaldy: Arthur Donaldson, Election Agent). Published in support of Douglas Young standing as SNP candidate in Kirkcaldy in February 1944, so the leaflet must date from that point.

1944

- Two poems, 'Manuel (after the Polish of Stefan Borsukiewicz)' & 'Largo' in *Poetry Scotland 1* (Glasgow: MacLellan), pp. 22–23.
- Poem, '1320 – Arbroath – 1944' in *Scots Independent* No. 212 (April), p. 1.
- Poem, 'Nou is the Hert Alane' in *Scottish Art and Letters 1* (Glasgow: MacLellan), p. 39.
- Poem, 'The Pricks' in *Scots Independent* No. 219 (November), p. 3.

1945

- Three poems, 'Hallowe'en, 1943', 'The Mither's Lament' & 'Prometheus' in *Poetry Scotland 2* (Glasgow: MacLellan), pp. 13–15.
- One poem, 'Llanto for F.G. Lorca' (originally published in *Million*) in *Little Reviews Anthology* 1945 (London: Eyre & Spottiswood), p. 101.
- Two poems, 'John Maclean, Martyr' & 'The Scaur', in Hugh MacDiarmid (ed.), *The Voice of Scotland* Vol. II / No. 2 (December), pp. 23–24.

1946

- Poem, 'Weary Faa', in *The New Alliance and Scots Review* Vol. 7 / No. 2, p. 8.
- Extract from *Carotid Cornucopius*, presented as 'Work in Progress', in *The Voice of Scotland* Vol. II / No. 3, pp. 10–13.
- Six poems, 'Loch Leven', 'Largo', 'Ma Moujik Lass', 'Sahara', 'Spleen', & 'Whan the Hert is Laich' in Maurice Lindsay (ed.), *Modern Scottish Poetry: An Anthology of the Scottish Renaissance 1920–1945* (London: Faber & Faber), pp. 104–108.
- Poem, 'Torquemada an the Carapace', in *Scottish Art and Letters 2*, p. 32.
- Three poems, 'Pompeii', 'Loch Leven' & 'Hamewith', in *Poetry Scotland 3*, pp. 13–14.
- Poem, 'Sang', in *The New Alliance and Scots Review* Vol. 7 / No. 7, p. 3.
- Article, 'Synthetic Analysis' (on writing in Lallans), in *The New Alliance & Scots Review* Vol. 7 / No. 9 (December), p. 9.
- Eight poems, 'Luve is a Burn in Spate', 'Say Ye Sae?', 'For Exorcism', 'Weary Faa', 'Blinn', 'Ye Speir Me', 'The Years of the Crocodile', 'The Ninety Days', in *The New Alliance & Scots Review* Vol. 7 / No. 9 (December), p. 10.
- Review of recent Scottish literary periodicals by Smith (*Scots Review*, *Poetry Scotland* etc) in the 'Bookman's Neuk' column of the *Edinburgh Evening Dispatch* (13th December).
- Article, 'A Publisher of the Nineties' (about Leonard Smithers), in John Singer (ed.), *The Holiday Book* (Glasgow: William MacLellan), pp. 219–228.
- COLLECTION: *The Deevil's Waltz* (Glasgow: William MacLellan). Smith's third collection, widely regarded as signalling his maturity as a poet. Inspired by war and Smith's work as a teacher of English to Polish refugees and soldiers in

Scotland. (Note: the poem 'Ye Mongers Aye Need Mask for Cheaterie' appeared in an early, c.1944/45 issue of Norman Macleod's edited American magazine *Briarcliff Quarterly*, issue and pagination unknown, Smith's name appeared as 'Sidney Soodsir Smith'.).

## 1947

- Translation 'frae the French o' Tristan Corbière, 'The Gangrel Rimer and the Absolutioun o Sanct Ann', in *The Voice of Scotland* Vol. III / No. 3 (March), pp. 1–8.
- Poem, 'Marion MacGregor's Lament for Gregor Roy' in *Scottish Art and Letters* 3, pp. 43–44.
- Review, 'The Stein Style', review of Gertrude Stein's *Wars I Have Seen,* in *Scottish Art and Letters 3,* p. 70.
- Poem, 'Tae the Russian Heroes, Oct. 1941', in *The Voice of Scotland* Vol. IV / No. 1 (September), p. 25.
- Poems (titles unknown) in *Poetry: The Australian International Quarterly of Verse* Nos. 23–24 (September), pagination unknown.
- Two poems, 'Money for Old Rope' & 'The Pomp and Circumstance', in *Life and Letters* Vol. 55 / No. 123 (November 1947), pp. 101, 126.
- Article, 'The *Aeneid* of Gawin Douglas', in *Life and Letters* Vol. 55 / No. 123 (November 1947), pp. 112–125.
- One poem, 'Hogmanay Post-War', in *Life and Letters* Vol. 55 / No. 124 (December 1947), p. 233.
- Poem, 'New Year 1947', in *The Voice of Scotland* Vol. IV / No. 2 (December), p. 17.
- One poem, 'Wuid Reik', in *New Athenian Broadsheet* No. 2 (Xmas 1947), unpaginated.
- NOVEL: *Carotid Cornucopius: The First 4 Fitts* (Glasgow: Caledonian Press). 1st edn. of Smith's only published novel, 300 copies printed, for 'Members of the Auk Society' at one guinea each.
- COLLECTION: *Selected Poems: Saltire Modern Poets* (Edinburgh: Oliver & Boyd). A short pamphlet collection of 26 poems, all previously published.

## 1948

- Translation from the Russian of Alexander Blok, 'The Twelve' (later to become 'The Twal'), in *The Voice of Scotland* Vol. IV / No. 3 (March), pp. 1–12.
- Review of William Montgomerie's edited book *Robert Burns: New Judgements* in the 'Bookman's Neuk' column of the *Edinburgh Evening Dispatch* (16th May).
- Five poems, 'Newhaven', 'The Winter o the Hert', 'Leander Stormbunden', 'Frae Exile', 'Alternatives', in *The New Alliance & Scots Review* Vol. 9 / No. 2 (May), p. 30.
- Article, 'In Defence of "Lallans"', in *The New Alliance & Scots Review* Vol. 9 / No. 2 (May), p. 23.

- Review, Robert Garioch's *Chuckies on the Cairn* and the four poet anthology *Fowsom* Reel, in the *Edinburgh Evening Dispatch* (28th July).
- Two poems, 'The Fule o Luve' and 'Luve in Fetters' in *Scottish Periodical 2* (Summer), p. 108.
- One poem and two translations, 'Vox Humana', 'The Bonnie Reidheid (Apollinaire) and 'Open-Air' (Paul Éluard), in *The Voice of Scotland* Vol. v / No. 1 (September), pp. 27–30.
- Humorous article 'Claret, Oysters and Reels' in *The Galliard* No. 1, pp. 39–42. An article celebrating the bibulousness of 18th century Edinburgh and proposing a new drinking club called the 'Hell Fire Club'.
- Poem, 'Bards Hae Sung', in *The Galliard* (Winter), p. 59.
- COLLECTION: *Under the Eildon Tree: A Poem in XXIV Elegies* (Serif Books, Edinburgh, 1948, first fifty copies signed by the author). Widely regarded as Smith's masterpiece. Reprinted in revised, smaller form, red cloth and paperback wraps in 1954.

1949

- Poem, 'The Wraith o Johnnie Calvin' in *The New Alliance and Scots Review* Vol. 9, No. 9 (February), pagination unknown.
- Letter to the editor (23rd May), co-written by Smith & Cedric Thorpe Davie in *The New Alliance and Scots Review Vol. 10 / No. 4* (July) p. 73. Concerns errors made in a review of a radio adaptation of Smith's 'Orpheus and Euridicie'.
- Three poems, 'Apparences', 'The Octopus' and 'The Grace o Gode and the Meths Drinker', in *The Voice of Scotland* Vol. v / No. 3 (June), pp. 20–23.
- Four poems, 'King an Queen o the Fowr Airts', 'Patmos', 'The Royal Drouth' & 'Alane wi the Sun', in *Poetry Scotland 4*, pp. 18–21.
- Poem, 'My World in Under Winter' in *The New Alliance and Scots Review* Vol. 10 / No. 8 (November), p. 139.
- One poem, 'Largo', in John Oliver & J.C. Smith (eds.), *A Scots Anthology* (Edinburgh: Oliver & Boyd), p. 493.

1949–50

- Eight poems, 'The Mandrake Hert', 'Ye Spier Me...' , 'O Soft Embalmer', 'Defeat o The Hert', 'Myth', 'Philomel', 'Belief' and the long poem 'Variorums on a Pint-o-Bass being The Little Odyssey of Ou Tis or A Prayer in Time of Spiritual Peste', in Peter Russell (ed.), *Nine* No. 3 (spring 1949–50), pp. 118–126.

1950

- Poem, 'The Auk's Advice Til a Patriots (efter a visit til the National Museum)', in *The Nationalist and National Weekly* (6th May), pagination unknown.
- Extract from 'The Absent Muse' (a poem sequence), in *The New Alliance and Scots Review* Vol. 11 / No. 4 (July), p. 70.

- Two poems, 'Alane wi the Sun' & 'In Granada, In Granada', in *Scottish Art and Letters 5,* p. 11 & p. 39.
- Article / essay 'Robert Burns and "The Merry Muses of Caledonia"' in John Davenport, Jack Lindsay & Randall Swinger (eds.), *Arena: A Magazine of Modern Literature* Vol. 1 / No. 4.
- Article 'Brother in Misfortune: Robert Fergusson, 1750–1774' in *The New Alliance and Scots Review* Vol. 11 / No. 6 (September), pp. 112, 115.
- Poem, "Gone with the Wind", in *The New Alliance and Scots Review* Vol. 11 /No. 8 (November), p. 146. This issue also contains a review by Smith entitled 'Reekie Robert' of *Stevenson and Edinburgh: A Centenary Study* by Moray Maclaren, p. 155.
- Two poems, 'Hallowe'en 1943' & 'Spleen' in Eric Linklater (ed.), *The Thistle and the Pen: Anthology of Modern Scottish Writers* (Edinburgh: Nelson), pp. 34–36.

## 1951

- Poem, 'The Dowie Croun' from 'The Absent Muse' sequence in *The New Alliance and Scots Review* (February), p. 205.
- Two poems, 'Elegy VIII' & 'Elegy XXI' reprinted from *Under the Eildon Tree* in William Montgomerie (ed.), *Scots Chronicle 1951,* p. 14 & 83.
- Article on Thomas Urquhart: 'The Knight of Cromartie' (based on broadcast for Scottish Home Service) in *The New Alliance and Scots Review* Vol. 12 / No. 3 (June), pp. 43, 47.
- Eight poems, 'Luve is a Burn in Spate', Elegies IX, XI, XXIII, 'The Years of the Crocodile', 'Sub Regno Cynarae', 'Luve's Fule', 'Pole Star' in *The New Alliance and Scots Review* Vol. 12 / No. 4 (August), pp. 73–74.
- LITERARY STUDY: *A Short Introduction to Scottish Literature* (Edinburgh: Serif Books, 1951).
- COLLECTION: *The Aipple and the Hazel* (Glasgow: Caledonian Press, 1951). This pamphlet selection of eight poems is the rarest of all of Smith's publications, only 30 copies printed according to Smith. It is dedicated to 'H.W.' (i.e. Hazel Williamson), who would marry Smith in 1967, after the death in 1966 of Smith's first wife Marion. In a letter from Smith to Alexander Scott, dated 2 March 1951, Smith urges Scott to be discreet about the 'H.W.' dedication, as 'one does not wish to tempt Providence excessively'. (Letter in present author's personal collection of Smith material.) A short extract from the poem 'Song' appears on the gravestone Smith shares with Williamson in the Dean Cemetery, Edinburgh.

## 1952

- Three poems, 'Sappho' (dedicated to Edith Sitwell), 'Credo' & 'Time Be Brief', In *Nine* No. 8 (spring 1952), pp. 269–271.
- Two poems, 'The Aipple and the Hazel' & 'Time be Brief' in *Lines* 1 ('Poetry Edinburgh'), unpaginated. First issue of what became *Lines Review.*

- Review of *The Laughing Philosopher: Being a Life of François Rabelais* by M.P. Willcock, in *Nine* No. 9 (Summer / Autumn), pp. 375–6.
- Six poems 'Luve in Fetters', 'Leander Stormbound', 'Prayer in the Small Hours', 'Wuid-reik', 'The Eldritch Sang', 'The Moment', in Marguerite Caetani (ed.), *Botteghe Oscure IX*, pp. 173–176.
- Seven poems, 'A Birth', 'Letter to the Dolphin', 'Odessa', 'Saagin', 'The Die is Cast', 'The Eldritch Sang', 'The Moment', in *New Scots Poetry* (Edinburgh: Serif Books), pp. 21–27.
- EDITED COLLECTION: *Robert Fergusson: 1750–1774: Essays by Various Hands to Commemorate the Bicentenary of his Birth* (Edinburgh: Thomas Nelson & Sons, 1952). Smith served as editor and also contributes a long introduction and well as copious notes (pp. 11–50).
- Seven poems, 'The Mither's Lament', 'Largo', 'Sahara', 'Ye Mongers aye Need Masks for Cheatrie', 'For My Newborn Son', Elegy VIII, 'The Moment' in Douglas Young (ed.), *Scottish Verse 1851–1951* (Edinburgh: Nelson), pp. 291–294.
- COLLECTION: *So Late into the Night: Fifty Lyrics* (London: Peter Russell, 1952). As early as 1947 Smith was claiming this book to be 'in preparation' by Oliver & Boyd. Peter Russell, editor of *Nine*, stepped into the breach (there had been some talk of Edith Sitwell, who provides an effusive introduction, trying to sell the book to John Lehmann, without success). 500 copies, mostly bought via subscription.

1953

- Two poems, 'Mark Weill' & 'Perpetual Opposition', in *Scottish Journal: The Popular National Monthly* No. 5 (January), p. 9.
- Three poems, 'Gala Water', 'My World in Neather Winter' & 'We Sall Never Want', in *Lines 2* (spring 1953), pp. 11–12.
- *Lines 3* (*Lines Review* from issue 4 onwards) is dedicated to Smith (summer). Contains long poem 'To Li Po in the Delectable Mountains of Tien-Mu' which is 'I.M. Robert Fergusson', pp. 5–8.
- Poem, 'A Bairn Sick', in *New Statesman and Nation* (Vol. 46, Iss. 1174, 5th September), p. 262.
- Four poems, 'Nae Words'; 'Gala Water'; 'Cokkils'; 'First Fall', in *Botteghe Oscure XII*, pp. 124–126.
- Three poems, 'The Aipple and the Hazel', 'Mark Weill' & 'Nec Frustra Vixi' in Robert Conquest, Michael Hamburger & Howard Sergeant (eds.), *New Poems, 1953 (A P.E.N Anthology)* (London: Michael Joseph), pp. 94–96.
- COLLECTION: *Cokkils* (Edinburgh: M. Macdonald, 1953). This short pamphlet collection marks the beginning of Callum Macdonald's professional and personal relationship with Smith. 220 copies, 20 numbered and signed by the author.

– Five poems, 'A Tryst in View', 'The Reid Reid Rose', 'Neer Again, Said I', 'Efter Lang Nicht' & 'Sang: The Bard's Delyte', in *Nine* No. 10 (Winter), pp. 28–31.

## 1954

– Poem, 'Said Heraclitus', in *Lines Review 4* (January), p. 21.
– Poem, 'Vox Humana', in *New Statesman and Nation* Vol. 47 / Iss. 1201, (13th March), p. 320.
– Two poems, 'Queen Murderess' & 'Omens', in *The Saltire Review 1* (April), pp. 20–21.
– Poem, 'Sonnet a l'Hypocrite Lecteur', in *Lines Review 5* (June), p. 18.
– Poem, 'The Eldritch Sang', in *New Statesman and Nation* Vol. 48 / Iss. 1219 (17th July), p. 79.
– Two poems, 'The Aipple and the Hazel' & 'Queen Murderess', in *The Listener* No. 51, p. 306 & 479.
– Review of *The Poems of Robert Fergusson*, Matthew P. McDiarmid (ed.), in *Saltire Review 2* (August), pp. 91–93.
– Poem, ''Tis Late', in *Lines Review* No. 6 (September), p. 23.
– Article, 'Robert Burns and "The Merry Muses of Caledonia"', in *The Hudson Review* Vol. 7 / No. 3 (Autumn), pp. 327–349.
– Five poems, 'Made When Boskie'; 'Said Heraclitus'; 'The Quenchless Gleid'; 'Crime Passionel, or Lothario Surprised'; 'Sonnet a l'Hypocrite Lecteur' in *The Hudson Review* Vol. 7 / No. 3 (autumn), pp. 186–190.
– Preface to Robert Garioch's *The Masque of Edinburgh* (Edinburgh: M. Macdonald), pp. 5–6. Smith is also dedicatee.
– COLLECTION: *Under the Eildon Tree* 'Second Edition Revised' (Edinburgh: Serif Books). According to John C. Hall, the publisher Gordon Wright found unbound sheets for the second edition of *Under the Eildon Tree* and *A Short Introduction to Scottish Literature* in a warehouse once used by Joe Mardel's Serif Books. Wright paid to have these books bound. It is most likely that these copies have marbled boards whereas the original bindings were a light green paperback with wrappers and a red buckram hardcover issue.

## 1955

– Smith serves as editor of *Lines Review* from issue 7 (January) to issue 11/12 (Summer 1956), taking over from Alan Riddell. He remained on the advisory board for a number of issues after he handed over the editorship to Tom Scott.
– Editorial, in *Lines Review* 7 (January), pp. 3–4.
– Poem, 'Neer Again, Said I', in *New Statesman and Nation* Vol. 49 / Iss. 1255, (26th March), p. 442.
– VERSE PLAY: *Orpheus and Eurydice: A Dramatic Poem* (Edinburgh: M. Macdonald). Smith's first published foray into verse drama, interestingly the

pamphlet also lists 'Colickie Meg', Smith's unpublished play of *Carotid Cornu-copius* as 'forthcoming'. 500 copies, 50 numbered and signed with hand-coloured frontispiece by David McClure. Not reprinted in *The Collected Poems* of 1975.

– Editorial, in *Lines Review 8* (May), pp. 4–7. Discusses deaths of Agnes Mure Mackenzie and Lewis Spence as well as the departure of Alan Riddell for Australia, amongst other issues.

– Joint review of *Walter Scott: His Life and Personality* by Hesketh Pearson, and *Robert Burns: The Man, His Work, The Legend* by Maurice Lindsay, in *Saltire Review of Arts, Letters and Life* Vol. 2 / No. 4 (Spring), pp. 72–73.

– Poem, 'The Jungfrau', in *The Voice of Scotland* (Vol. v / No. 4), pp. 16–17.

– Poem, 'Gowdsmith in Reekie', in *Saltire Review* Vol. 2 / No. 5, pp. 42–51. The first outing of this long poem to Oliver Goldsmith which would re-appear in edited, pamphlet form in 1974 as *Gowdspink in Reekie*.

– Article, 'Immortal Mummery', in *Saltire Review* Vol. 2 / No. 6, pp. 17–20. Discusses Burns cult and the co-opting of Burns by city corporations, the rich and powerful – similar in tone to MacDiarmid's *Burns Today and Tomorrow*. See also T.J. Honeyman's reply in *Saltire Review* Vol. 3 / No. 7S (spring 1956), 'Burns – Whose Poet?', pp. 29–32.

– Editorial, in *Lines Review 9* (August), pp. 5–10. Discusses Edinburgh International Festival, Scottish Art and MacDiarmid's *In Memoriam James Joyce*.

– Poem, 'Her Dominion', in *Encounter* (October), p. 23.

– Editorial, in *Lines Review 10* (December), pp. 5–6. Discusses recent cause celebre over publication of Smith's edited version of Burns's *The Merry Muses* as well as Arts Council funding for poetry and drama.

– Extract from unpublished play, 'Auxtraxt Frae Colickie Meg', in *Lines Review 10* (December), pp. 11–15.

– COLLECTION: *Omens* (Edinburgh: M. Macdonald). 300 copies, hand numbered.

1956

– Six poems, 'The Muse in Rose Street', 'Mareeld', 'Granton', 'Cokkils', 'The Jungfrau...', 'The Grace o God [...]', in *Poetry* (*Chicago*) Vol. 88 / No. 1 (April), pp. 28–42.

– Editorial, in *Lines Review 11 & 12* (Summer), pp. 4–8. Concerns a controversy with Dr. T.J. Honeyman at *The Saltire Review* over Honeyman's perceived failure of the Scottish Renaissance. Also contains two Smith poems – 'The Tarantula of Luve' & 'Mareeld' – as 'Botchuments in the Case' (with a nod to Craig's negative review of *Omens*), pp. 55–56.

– Poem 'Runes' & a review entitled 'Burns Beblackened' of *The Russet Coat: A Critical Study of Burns' Poetry and of its Background* by Christina Keith, in *Saltire Review* Vol. 3 / No. 8 (Autumn), pp. 33, 63–4.

1957

- Review of *The Poems of Robert Fergusson: Vol II* ed. by Matthew P. McDiarmid, in *The Saltire Review* Vol. 4 / No. 10, (Spring), pp. 73–74.
- Review of Norman MacCaig's *Sinai Sort* in *The Scotsman* (1 June), pagination unknown.
- Review entirely in Scots of *Poetry Now,* G.S. Fraser (ed., Faber & Faber), in *Lines Review* 13 (Summer), pp. 31–32. Note: this issue also contains a rejoinder by Dr. T.J. Honeyman to Smith's editorial of the previous issue, attacking the Tourism Board's involvement in Burns Festival of 1955, see pp. 28–30.
- Poem, 'To Certain Weill-Wishers', in *Saltire Review* Vol. 4 / No. 11 (Summer), p. 49.
- Article, 'The Last Word: Hugh MacDiarmid's Homage to James Joyce', in *Saltire Review* Vol. 4 / No. 12 (Autumn), pp. 62–66.
- Joint review of *The Silver Bough* Vol. 1 by F. Marian McNeill and *The James Carmichael Collection of Proverbs in Scots*, M.L. Anderson (ed.), in *Saltire Review* 13 (Winter) p. 71.

1958

- Extract from play, 'Aukstract frae Colickie Meg', in *Jabberwock* 5. pp. 7–20.
- Poem, 'In Memoriam Robert Fergusson', in *The Voice of Scotland* Vol. IX / No. 2, pp. 23–24.
- Article 'William Soutar: Poet', in *The Scotsman* (12th April), pagination unknown.
- Article 'In Memoriam James Barke', in *Lines Review* 14 (Spring), p. 3.
- Article / obituary 'James Barke' in *Saltire Review* 15 (Summer), pp. 13–15.
- Poem, 'The Riggins o' Chelsea' in *Gambit: Edinburgh University Review* (Autumn), p. 16 (Note: abbreviated early version of what became a long poem in the 1970s).
- Four poems, 'C.M.G – Perpetual Opposition', 'Twa Mudes o a Makar Manic Depressive', 'Girning Rebukit' & 'Invocation', in *Saltire Review* 16 (Winter), pp. 24–25.
- Review of *Bawdy Burns: The Christian Rebel* by Cyril Pearl, in *Saltire Review* 16 (Winter), pp. 77–79.

1959

- Article on the Burns cult 'Lasting impact on people all over the whole wide world', in *The Scotsman* (22 January), pagination unknown.
- Article on the Burns cult 'Puir Rabbie must be fair birling', in *The Scotsman* (5th February), p. 6.
- Two poems, 'See What I Mean?' and 'Witch of aa Delyte', in *Lines Review* 15 (Summer), pp. 31–32.

– Review of Virgil's *Aeneid* (as translated into Scots by Gawin Douglas, Scottish Text Society edn.), in *Gambit: Edinburgh University Review* (Summer), pp. 29–30.

– Two poems, 'Lines' and 'Sonnet', in *The Poetry Review* Vol. 1 / No. 3 (July – Sept), p. 137.

– Review of Edinburgh Festival performance of Douglas Young's *The Burdies* ('The Greek Burdies of Cloodiegowkburgh'), in *The Scotsman* (12 November), pagination unknown.

– Letter to the editor concerning 'The Wallace', in *The Scotsman* (10 December), pagination unknown.

– Six poems, 'Credo', 'The Muse in Rose Street', 'There is a Tide', 'Vox Humana', 'A Bairn Seick', 'My World in Nether Winter', in Norman MacCaig (ed.), *Honour'd Shade: An Anthology of New Scottish Poetry to Mark the Bicentenary of the Birth of Robert Burns* (Edinburgh: Chambers), pp. 115–121.

– Four poems, 'Saagin', 'The Mandrake Hert', 'Ye Spier Me', 'Defeat o' the Hert', in Dame Edith Sitwell (ed.), *The Atlantic Book of British and American Poetry* Volume 2 (London: Gollancz), pp. 907–908.

– EDITED BOOK: Robert Burns, Smith and James Barke (eds.), *The Merry Muses of Caledonia* (Edinburgh: M. Macdonald, Edinburgh), with some epistolary help by self-taught bawdry scholar Gershon Legman. Barke, the Burns scholar and novelist, died in 1958 before this book was published. The most financially successful of all of Smith's publications, it was reprinted in UK and America in a number of editions and remains in print with Luath Press. Surviving correspondence in National Library of Scotland archives (Acc. 10397/1) show that he quarrelled with Putnam's over royalties (not for himself, but other contributors). This first edition was only available to members of the 'Auk Society', membership was 2 guineas and copies were said to be limited to 1000 (although it is doubtful that this many were in fact produced, a few hundred being much more likely).

– EDITED SELECTION: Smith (ed.) *Gavin Douglas: A Selection from his Poetry* (Edinburgh: Oliver and Boyd for the Saltire Society).

– COLLECTION: *Figs and Thistles* (Edinburgh: Oliver and Boyd). Smith's first substantial collection since 1952's *So Late into the Night*. There was also a limited edition of 100 signed copies, specially bound.

1960

– Letter from Smith to editor concerning David Craig's review of *Honour'd Shade*, in *Spectator* (29 January), p. 136. Smith refers to Craig's review as 'superflannel'.

- The February issue of *Scottish Field* contains a caricature of Smith by Coia as well as the poem 'My World in Nether Winter' and an extract from *The Wallace* (the Great Hall, 23 August 1305 scene), pagination unknown.
- Further letter from Smith to editor concerning David Craig's review of *Honour'd Shade*, in *Spectator* (19 February), p. 25.
- Review of *Barbour: The Bruce, A Selection,* Alexander Kinghorn (ed.), in *Saltire Review 20* (Spring), pp. 71–72.
- LONG POEM: *The Vision of the Prodigal Son* (Edinburgh: M. Macdonald). A long, dramatic poem about Robert Burns, commissioned by the BBC for the Burns Bicentenary (first broadcast 25 January 1959).
- PLAY: *The Wallace: A Triumph in Five Acts* (Edinburgh: Oliver and Boyd). The book of the play. Dustjacket notes say Smith has also written two comic plays – *Colickie Meg* and *King Stobo* (a 'very free translation of Alfred Jarry's *Ubu Roi*) and he is busy working on a tragedy entitled *The Jolly Beggars.*

1961

- Series of reviews of artists / exhibitions ('Portrait of the Artist') by Smith for *The Scotsman* as art critic:
- 'No Outstanding Miracles', a review of the Royal Scottish Academy's Annual Exhibition' (21 & 22 April), pagination unknown.
- 'William MacTaggart, President of the Royal Scottish Academy', p. 7 (22 April).
- 'W.G. Gillies: Principal of the Edinburgh College of Art' (29 April), pagination unknown.
- 'John Maxwell – Painter of Dreams and Fantasies', p. 5 (6 May).
- 'Anne Redpath – the First Scots Woman to be Elected A.R.A', p. 5 (13 May).
- 'Robin Philipson's Strange and Compelling Visions', p. 7 (20 May).
- 'John Houston – A Poet in Paint', p. 7 (27 May).
- 'Joan Eardley – She Just Paints' (16 August).
- 'Alistair Park – Inspired by the Cave Men' (26 August).
- 'Benno Schotz – Nature is his Treasure House', p. 5 (2 September).
- 'Rodick Carmichael – The Picture Grows' (date unknown, but 10th in the series).
- 'Alan Place – Silversmith who Cares for the Craft', p. 5 (16 September).
- 'Denis Peploe – The Atmospheric Quality', p. 5 (23 September).
- Review of *Poems and Songs of Sir Robert Ayton,* Helena Mennie Shire (ed.), in *The New Saltire* 1 (Summer), pp. 83–84.
- Review of Virgil's *Aeneid* as translated by Gawin Douglas and issued by Scottish Text Society, in *Saltire Review 23* (Winter), pp. 78–79.

1962

- EDITED COLLECTION: Co-editor (with Kulgin Duval) of *MacDiarmid: A Fest-schrift* (Edinburgh, K.D. Duval). A collection of essays on MacDiarmid's work, published to celebrate his 70th birthday. Smith also contributes the essay: 'The Three Hymns to Lenin', pp. 73–86.
- Poem, 'The Bells of Hell', in *Lines Review* 18, p. 17.
- Review of Royal Scottish Academy Annual Exhibition, 'High Level of Competence' in *The Scotsman* (20 April), pagination unknown.
- Letter to editor, in exchange with Hamish Henderson concerning sculpture in RSA annual exhibition, in *The Scotsman* (21 April), pagination unknown.
- Article, 'Benno Schotz' in *The Scottish Art Review* Vol. VIII / No. 3, pp. 5–7.
- Review of *John Davidson: Poet of Armageddon* by J. Benjamin Townsend, in *The New Saltire* 4, pp. 76–78.
- Article, as part of a 'Symposium for the occasion of [Hugh MacDiarmid's] 70th birthday' – 'The Bardic Stance' in *Scottish Field* Vol. CIX, No. 716 (August,), p. 37.
- Two poems, 'Tu Fu's View of Fife' and 'Aurora Sluggart', in *Poetry* Vol. 101 / No. 1/2 (Oct-Nov.), p. 122.
- Poem, 'Auld Reekie Blues', in *The New Saltire* No. 6 (Dec), p. 76.

1963

- Review entitled 'Sins of Omission', of *Scottish Books: A Brief Bibliography for Teachers and General Readers* (Saltire Society), in *New Saltire* No. 8 (June), pp. 78–81.
- Article, 'The MacDiarmid portrait by R.H. Westwater', in *The Scotsman* (19 April), pagination unknown.
- Exhibition review of Royal Scottish Academy Annual Exhibition in *The Scotsman* (20 April), pagination unknown.
- Exhibition review – 'Lui Shou Kwan Watercolours at Commonwealth Institute' in *The Scotsman* (27 August). Pagination unknown.
- Exhibition review, John Bellany and Alexander Moffat – 'Public Art in Public Spaces' in *The Scotsman* (Sept), pagination unknown.
- Review of David Craig's *Scottish Literature and The Scottish People 1680–1830*, in *Lines Review* 19 (Winter), pp. 49–50.

1964

- Poem, 'The Secret Isle', in *New Saltire* No. 11 (April), pp. 14–15.
- Article entitled 'Trahison des Clercs, or the Anti-Scottish Lobby in Scottish Letters', in *Studies in Scottish Literature* Vol. 1 / Issue 3, pp. 71–86. Smith's spirited riposte to David Craig's claim (see Craig, 'A National Literature? Recent

Scottish Writing', *SSL* Vol. 1 / Issue 3, pp. 151–169) that contemporary writing in Scots had lost its validity.

– Review of Joan Eardley exhibition, 'Magnificent Eardley' in *The Scotsman* (2nd March), pagination unknown.

– Review of Bellany and Moffat exhibition, 'Moral Protest in Paint: Two-man show on the railings', in *The Scotsman* (24 August), pagination unknown.

– NOVEL: *Carotid Cornucopius* 2nd edn. (Edinburgh: M. Macdonald). An extended version of Smith's comic novel, plus profuse illustrations by Rendell Wells. Standard edition (priced at 35 shillings) and a special leather-bound edition (unknown limitation), signed by both Smith and Wells (priced at 5 guineas).

– EDITED PAMPHLET: Smith (ed.), *Bannockburn: The Story of the Battle and its Place in Scotland's History* (Glasgow: Scots Independent). A collection of writings (historic, academic, poetic, dramatic) on Bannockburn and the importance of Robert the Bruce. Also contains (p. 17) an extract from Smith's *The Wallace.*

## 1965

– Letter from Smith to the editor concerning a recent review of J.H. Egerer's *Bibliography of Robert Burns*, in *Spectator* (12 March), p. 328.

– Smith contributes poems to Ruari McLean's *The Connoisseur: A Magazine for Collectors* (March/April issue). Further details unknown.

– Article, 'Royal Scottish Academy Fulfilling its Task: Case for the Defence', in *The Scotsman* (24 April), pagination unknown.

– One poem, 'Three Men Make a Revolution', in *The Poetry Review* Vol. LVI / No. 3 (autumn), p. 158.

– LONG POEM: *Kynd Kittock's Land* (Edinburgh: M. Macdonald). Long dramatic poem commissioned by the BBC and first televised 28 February 1964.

## 1966

– Two poems, 'Tu Fu's View of Fife' and 'Spring in the Botanic Gardens', in *Akros* Vol. 1 / No. 3 (August), pp. 18–19.

– Eight poems, 'Loch Leven', 'Largo', 'Sahara', 'Spleen', 'We Shall Never Want', 'The Grace of God and the Meth-Drinker', 'To Li Po in the Delectable Mountains of Tien-Mu', and 'Hamewith' in Maurice Lindsay (ed.), *Modern Scottish Poetry: An Anthology of the Scottish Renaissance* 2nd edn. (London: Faber & Faber), pp. 127–135.

– Eight poems, 'Epistle to John Guthrie', 'The Mither's Lament', 'Ye Mongers Aye Need Masks for Cheaterie', 'The Ineffable Don', 'Elegy V' from *Under the Eildon Tree*, 'Leander Stormbound', 'Mandrake Hert', 'Cokkils', in John

MacQueen and Tom Scott eds., *The Oxford Book of Scottish Verse* (Oxford: Oxford University Press), pp. 572–581.

- Smith contributes an 'Introduction' to Robert Garioch's *Selected Poems* (Edinburgh: M. Macdonald), pp. 7–9. Note: in a 12 October 1980 letter from Garioch to Alastair Mackie, reprinted in Robin Fulton's *A Garioch Miscellany*, Garioch wrote: 'There was little notice taken of my poetry till Callum Macdonald published the *Selected*, and that might not have come out if Sydney Smith had not so persistently tried to have it done. Sydney could be practical and business-like: not everyone knows that' (Garioch: 1986, 91).

- Exhibition review, 'Nigerian Paintings of Innocent Talent', in *The Scotsman*, pagination and date unknown.

- EDITED SELECTION: Smith edits *A Choice of Burns's Poems and Songs* (London: Faber & Faber).

## 1967

- Poem, 'Seal Poem', in *Lines Review* 23 (Spring), pp. 19–21. A love poem for Stella Cartwright.

- Exhibition review, 'Contemporary Italian Art at Demarco's Edinburgh: Follies in Dotty Show by Italians', in *The Scotsman* (March), pagination unknown.

- Article, 'Historical reasons for Scotland's meagre sculptural tradition', in *The Scotsman* (17 April), pagination unknown.

- Review of George Mackay Brown's *A Calendar of Love and Other Stories* in *Lines Review* 24 (Summer), pp. 43–44.

- One poem, 'Three Men Make a Revolution' in *English* Vol. xvi / No. 96 (Autumn), p. 239.

- One poem, 'Wale o Ilka Toun', in George Bruce, Maurice Lindsay & Edwin Morgan (eds.), *Scottish Poetry* 2 (Edinburgh: Edinburgh University Press), pp. 113–115.

- Poem, 'C.M.G. – Perpetual Opposition', in Duncan Glen (ed.), *Poems Addressed to Hugh MacDiarmid and Presented to Him on His Seventy-Fifth Birthday* (Preston: Akros), pp. 56–57. Note: poem is also reprinted, plus small expository remark by Smith, in *MacDiarmid: An Illustrated Biography* by Gordon Wright (Edinburgh: Gordon Wright Publishing, 1977), p. 79.

- Poem, Millennial Ode to Hugh MacDiarmid on yet another Birthday Occasion', in *Lines Review* 25 (Winter), 'pp. 20–24.

- Two poems, 'Seal Poem' and 'Serpent of Old Nile', in *Agenda* Vol. 5 / No. 4 – Vol. 6 / No. 1 (Autumn-Winter), pp. 95–97.

## 1968

- Two poems, Elegy vi and xii from *Under the Eildon Tree*, in George Bruce (ed.) *The Scottish Literary Revival: Anthology of Twentieth Century Poetry* (London: MacMillan), pp. 82–89.

– One poem, 'The Bonnie Reidheid' (translation from Apollinaire), in *Scottish International* 4 (Oct / Nov), pp. 45–46.

– One poem, 'The Spirit of Christmas '67', in *Catalyst* Vol. 1 / No. 2, p. 24.

– Two poems, 'Serpent of Old Nile' & 'Christmas Carol 1966', in *Scottish Poetry* 3 (Edinburgh: Edinburgh University Press), pp. 112–113.

1969

– Nine poems, 'Lines', 'Winds', 'Three Men Make a Revolution', 'Late', 'Seal Poem', 'I Saw the Mune', 'Tak Aff Your Dram', 'Winter' & 'The Kenless Strand', in *Akros* No. 10 (May), pp. 29–40.

– Article, 'Words of a Feather', in *Akros* No. 10 (May), pp. 48–51. Extract from a radio broadcast.

– One poem, 'Drifts', in *Scottish International* 7 (September), p. 13.

– COLLECTION: *Fifteen Poems and a Play* (Edinburgh: Southside). Contains Smith's radio play 'The Stick-up, or Full Circle' and accompanying libretto by Robin Orr. 450 copies, available to subscribers (copies 001 to 015 specially bound and numbers 1–50 numbered and signed).

1970

– Poem, 'The Arbroath Declaration, April 6th 1320', in *Scotia* No. 4 (April), p. 2.

– Two poems, 'I Saw the Mune' and 'Winter', in *Scottish Poetry* 5 (Edinburgh: Edinburgh University Press), pp. 83–85.

– Three poems, 'The Mither's Lament', 'Cokkils', Elegy XXIII from *Under the Eildon Tree*, in Tom Scott (ed.), *The Penguin Book of Scottish Verse*, pp. 484–486.

– Six poems, 'Late', 'The Kenless Strand', 'Three', 'Spring in the Botanic Gardens', 'I Saw the Mune', 'Night Before, Morning After', in Norman MacCaig and Alexander Scott (eds.), *Contemporary Scottish Verse* (London: Calder and Boyars), pp. 227–233.

– Eight poems, 'Winds', 'Three', 'Late', 'Seal Poem', 'I Saw the Mune', 'Tak Aff Yer Dram', 'Winter', 'The Kenless Strand', in Duncan Glen (ed.), in *The Akros Anthology of Scottish Poetry 1965–1970* (Preston: Akros), pp. 28–35.

– Three poems, 'Cokkils', 'Elegy XXI' & extract from *Kynd Kittock's Land* in Alan MacGillivray and James Rankin (eds.), *The Ring of Words: An Anthology of Scottish Poetry* (Edinburgh: Oliver & Boyd), pp. 42, 59 & 62.

– 'The Soul at Lairge (Being a specially adapted excerpt from his historical drama *The Wallace*)', in *The Scots Pageant: The Script of the Arbroath Abbey Pageant of the Signing of the Scottish Declaration of Independence* (Arbroath Abbey Pageant Society and Arbroath Independent Trust), pp. 6–30. Note: this is the 'Great Hall / Westminster 1305' scene from the play.

**1971**

- Two poems, 'Auld Reekie Winter Evening' & 'Winds', in *Ariel: A Review of International English Literature* Vol. 2 / No. 3 (July), p. 62.
- Two poems, 'The Deid Tree' and 'Winds', in *Scotia* No. 19 (July), pp. 1 & p. 4.
- Thirteen poems, 'Epistle to John Guthrie', 'The Mither's Lament', 'Lament for R.W.', 'Sahara', 'Largo', Elegy VIII, 'Hamewith', 'King and Queen o the Fowr Airts', 'Cokkils', 'The Grace of God [...]', 'World in Nether Winter', 'Credo', 'The Kenless Strand', in Charles King (ed.), *Twelve Modern Scottish Poets* (London: Lion Library), pp 104–117. (2nd ed. 1976).
- Two poems, 'The Grace of God [...]' and 'Slugabed', in Maurice Lindsay (ed.) *Voices of Our Kind: Anthology of Contemporary Scottish* Verse (Edinburgh: Saltire Society), pp. 33–36.

**1972**

- One poem, 'To the Shade of Yeats', in *Scottish International* Vol. 5 / No. 4 (April), p. 28.
- Article 'MacDiarmid's Three Hymns to Lenin' in Duncan Glen, ed., *Hugh MacDiarmid: A Critical Survey* (Edinburgh: Scottish Academic Press), pp. 141–153.

**1972/73**

- Two poems, 'Spring Cam Yesternicht' and 'The Moon and the Pathetic Fallacy', in *Lines Review* 42–43 (Sept - Feb), pp. 132–134.

**1973**

- One poem, 'The Riggins o' Chelsea or Hame Thochts Frae Abraid', in *Scottish International* Vol. 6 / No. 2 (Feb), pp. 16–19.
- Five poems, The Moon and the Pathetic Fallacy', 'Sunlicht on the Firth', 'The Deid Tree', 'Spring Cam Yesternicht', 'Sang: She Fulls the Hairt', in Eddie Linden (ed.), *Aquarius 6: Scottish* Issue, pp. 26–29 and 35–37.
- Short story 'At least we were together till the end', in *Scotia Review* No. 5 (December), pp. 3–4.

**1974**

- Poem, 'Stormy Day and a Cat, November', in *Akros* Vol. 8 / No. 24 (April), p. 18.
- Extract from *Gowdspink in Reekie*, in *Lines Review* 51 (December), p. 42.
- One poem, 'The Riggins o Chelsea', in *Scottish Poetry 7* (Glasgow: University of Glasgow Press), pp. 74–79.
- One poem, 'Elegy XIII' from *Under the Eildon Tree*, in Maurice Lindsay (ed.), *Scotland: An Anthology* (London: Robert Hale), pp. 405–410.
- Smith contributes an introduction to Robert Garioch and Anne Smith's *Fergusson: A Bicentenary Handsel* (Edinburgh: Reprographia), pp. 5–6.

–     LONG POEM: *Gowdspink in Reekie* (Edinburgh: M. Macdonald). First hundred copies numbered and signed by the author.

**1975**

–     Poem, 'The Years of the Crocodile', in *The Pembroke Magazine* No. 7, p. 165.

–     Poem, 'Stormy Day and a Cat, November', in *Scottish Poetry 8* (Carcanet Press), p. 77.

–     Four poems, 'The Mandrake Hert', 'There is a Tide', 'We Shall Never Want' & 'Wuid Reik', in Antonia Fraser (ed.), *Scottish Love Poems: A Personal Anthology* (Edinburgh: Canongate), pp. 10, 73, 121 & 211. Note: this has been reprinted a number of times, most recently by Canongate in 2002.

–     COLLECTED POEMS: *Collected Poems 1941–1975* by Sydney Goodsir Smith (John Calder, London). Although Smith had been preparing this volume for publication, he died 15 January 1975, so the book was ultimately edited by person(s) unknown. Tom Scott is commonly mistaken as the editor, but he only worked on the 'word leet', or glossary of Scots words. See the two letters to the editor by Alan Bold and Tom Scott in the 21 May 1981 issue of *The Scotsman* for further details about the (mis)editing of the book. The published book is flawed with numerous typographical errors and the layout is odd. See later entries for criticism of this volume.

–     Eight poems, 'Sweit Hairt', 'Rencontre Manqué', 'Never Nae Mair', 'As the Rose', 'Granton Ferry', 'She Fills the Hairt', 'Brooding Rebuked' & 'The Riggins o' Chelsea', in Norman MacCaig (ed.), *For Sydney Goodsir Smith* (Edinburgh: M. Macdonald), pp. 30–41. A posthumous festschrift for Smith.

**1977**

–     Article, '75th Birthday Exhibition for Hugh MacDiarmid', in Gordon Wright's *MacDiarmid: An Illustrated Biography* (Edinburgh: Gordon Wright), p. 136. Note: a reprint of an article that first appeared in *The Scotsman* 17 July 1967.

**1978**

–     Fourteen poems, 'The Scaur', 'Largo', 'Mars and Venus at Hogmanay', 'The Mandrake Hert', 'Ye Spier Me', 'Defeat o the Hert', 'Luve in Fetters', 'A Bairn Seick', 'The Reid, Reid Rose', 'Three', 'Spring in the Botanic Gardens', 'Morning After', 'Sweet Hairt', 'Brooding Rebuked', in Alexander Scott (ed.), *Modern Scots Verse 1922–1977* (Preston: Akros), pp. 70–71, 88–91, 105–106, 135.

**1979**

–     Two poems, 'Aurora Sluggart' and 'Hedonist', in *Chapman* 23 / 24 (Spring), p. 34. Note: this issue also contains elegy ('Aubade') for Smith by William Tait, p. 37.

–     Two poems (song ballads), 'John MacLean Martyr' and 'The Ballant o John MacLean', in *Homage to John MacLean* (Edinburgh University Student

Publications Board). Reprint of collection first printed by John MacLean Society in 1973, pp. 13–14.

**1980**

– Two poems, 'The Grace o God and the Meths Drinker' and 'The Years of the Crocodile', in Edwin Morgan (ed.), *Scottish Satirical Verse: An Anthology* (Manchester: Carcanet), pp. 144–145.

**1981**

– Three poems, 'The Riggins o Chelsea', 'Sappho' & 'Another Version', in Maurice Lindsay (ed.), *Scottish Comic Verse: An Anthology* (London: Robert Hale), pp. 193–198.

**1982**

– Five poems, 'Dialogue at Midnight', 'Mars and Venus at Hogmanay', 'Nicht o Lust', 'Solipsist', 'Weary', in Alexander Scott (ed.), *Scotch Passion: An Anthology of Scottish Erotic Poetry* (London: Robert Hale), pp. 34, 90, 105, 126 & 154.
– One poem, 'Spring in the Botanic Gardens', in Duncan Glen (ed.), *Akros Verse 1965–1982* (Preston: Akros), p. 9.
– NOVEL: *Carotid Cornucopius* 3rd edn. (Edinburgh: Macdonald Publishers). There was talk of John Calder bringing out this edition, having been awarded funds by the Arts Council in the 1973–1974 season, but it never materialised.

**1983**

– Poem, 'A New Ballant of John MacLean', in *Cencrastus* No. 14 (Autumn), p. 16.

**1985**

– PLAY: Paperback reprint of *The Wallace* (London: John Calder).

**1988**

– *Saltire Self Portraits 3: Sydney Goodsir Smith: A Letter Written to Maurice Lindsay in 1947* (Edinburgh: The Saltire Society, Edinburgh). An extremely revealing letter from Smith to Lindsay, providing much important biographical information.
– One poem, 'Largo', in Alistair Lawrie, Helen Matthews, Douglas Ritchie (eds.), *Glimmer of Cold Brine: A Scottish Sea Anthology* (Aberdeen: Aberdeen University Press), p. 206.

**1989**

– A series of pen sketches by Smith (presented by Ian Begg) and elegy XIII from *Under the Eildon Tree,* in *Chapman* 55–6 (Spring), pp. 97–105.

- Two translations, 'The Gangrel Rymour and the Pairdon of Sanct Anne' (Corbière) and 'The Twal' (Blok), in Peter France & Duncan Glen (eds.), *European Poetry in Scotland: An Anthology of Translations* (Edinburgh: Edinburgh University Press), pp. 57–73.

### 1992

- Poem, 'We Sall Never Want', in *Lines Review* 120 (March), p. 8. This is a reprint of a poem that previously appeared in *Lines* 2 in 1953.
- Eight poems, 'Armageddon in Albyn': 'El Alamein', 'Mither's Lament', 'War in Fife', 'The Grace of God [...]', 'Time Be Brief', 'Omens', 'Aa My Life', Elegy v, in Douglas Dunn (ed.), *The Faber Book of Twentieth Century Scottish Poetry* (London: Faber), pp. 147–152. Anthology reprinted multiple times.

### 1995

- 'October 1941', 'A Tink in Reekie', 'xii Orpheus' from *Under the Eildon Tree*, 'Winter Blues', in Roderick Watson (ed.), *The Poetry of Scotland: Gaelic, Scots and English* (Edinburgh: Edinburgh University Press), pp. 624–629.

### 1998

- Poem, 'The Kenless Stand', in Washburn and Major, eds., *World Poetry: An Anthology of Verse from Antiquity to Our Time* (New York: W.W. Norton), p. 1216.
- Poem, 'Slugabed', in Sean O'Brien (ed.), *Firebox: Poetry in Britain and Ireland after 1945* (London: Picador), pp. 36–38.
- Poem, 'The Grace of God [...]', in Simon Armitage & Robert Crawford (eds.), *The Penguin Book of Poetry from Britain and Ireland since 1945* (New York: Viking), pp. 74–75.
- ARTWORK: *The Drawings of Sydney Goodsir Smith,* collected by Ian Begg, edited by Joy Hendry (Edinburgh & East Linton: Chapman Publishing Edinburgh in collaboration with Tuckwell Press). Published on behalf of 'New Auk Society'. Contains many of Smith's pen and pencil sketches as well as his own illustrated version of sections of *Under the Eildon Tree.*

### 1999

- Extract from 'Orpheus' (from *Under the Eildon Tree*), in Geoffrey Miles (ed.), *Classical Mythology in English Literature: A Critical Anthology* (London: Routledge), pp. 153–155.
- Note: John Calder's Calder Publications was due to publish Smith's play *Colickie Meg* as part of Calder's 'Scottish Library' series. Although the book was scheduled and given an ISBN, it was never actually published.

**2000**

- Two poems, from 'Armageddon in Albyn: VII, The War in Fife' and 'The Grace of God [...]', in Robert Crawford & Mick Imlah (eds.), *The New Penguin Book of Scottish Verse* (London: Allen Lane / Penguin Press), pp. 455–457.
- One poem, 'Slugabed' (Elegy V), in Douglas Dunn (ed.), *Twentieth Century Scottish Poems* (London: Faber), pp. 31–32.

**2001**

- Four poems, 'Loch Leven', Elegy XIII, 'Ye Speir Me' and 'Hamewith', in Maurice Lindsay (ed.), *A Book of Scottish Verse* (London: Robert Hale), pp. 419–427.
- One poem, 'Omens', in *Land Lines: An Illustrated Journey through the Landscape and Literature of Scotland* (Scottish Literary Tour Company Ltd), pp. 38–39.

**2002**

- One poem, 'A Ballad for Douglas Young'. Rediscovered in the NLS by John Manson and attributed to Smith, it appears for the first time in *Scots Independent* (March 2002), pagination unknown.
- Two poems, 'Tak aff yer Dram' & 'Song: The Steeple Bar, Perth', in Robin Laing (ed.) *The Whisky Muse: Scotch Whisky in Poem and Song* (Edinburgh: Luath), pp. 128 & 179.
- Eight poems, 'Epistle to John Guthrie', 'Sang: Ma Moujik Lass', 'Largo', *Under the Eildon Tree*, 'Leander Stormbound', 'Cokkils', 'The Grace o God and the Meths Drinker' and 'There is a Tide', in David McCordick (ed.), *Scottish Literature in the Twentieth Century: An Anthology* (Aberdeen: Scottish Cultural Press), pp. 604–647.
- Letter, 'Under the Sign of Scorpio or Venus' – a reprint of Smith's 1947 letter to Maurice Lindsay first printed as a Saltire Self-Portrait in 1988, in George Bruce and P.H. Scott (eds.), *A Scottish Postbag: Eight Centuries of Scottish Letters* (Edinburgh: The Saltire Society), pp. 263–266.

**2004**

- Three poems, 'Hamewith', 'La Cicatrice' & 'Torquemada and the Carapace', in *Markings* Issue 18, pp. 59–61. Accompanied with translations into French by John Manson.
- One poem, 'Epistle to John Guthrie', in Douglas Gifford & Alan Riach (eds.), *Scotlands: Poetry and the Nation* (Manchester & Edinburgh: Carcanet Press & Scottish Poetry Library), p. 155.

– Two poems, 'El Alamein' & 'The Mither's Lament', in Hugh Haughton (ed.), *Second World War Poems* (London: Faber), pp. 269–270.

2005

– One poem, 'For my Newborn Son', in Lizzie MacGregor (ed.), *Handsel: Scottish Poems for Weddings and Naming Babies* (Edinburgh: Scottish Poetry Library / Polygon), p. 26.

– One poem, 'Hamewith', in Lizzie MacGregor (ed.), *Lament: Scottish Poems for Funerals and Consolation* (Edinburgh: Scottish Poetry Library / Polygon), p. 60.

– Excerpts from *The Wallace*, in Lesley Duncan & Elspeth King (eds.), The Wallace Muse: Poems and Artworks Inspired by the Life and Legend of William Wallace (Edinburgh: Luath), pp. 134–137.

– Four poems, Elegy v, 'Ye Mongers [...]', 'Philomel', 'Largo', in Maurice Lindsay and Lesley Duncan (eds.), *Edinburgh Book of Twentieth Century Scottish Poetry* (Edinburgh: Edinburgh University Press), pp. 321–324.

2007

– Extract from *Kynd Kittock's Land*, in Lizzie MacGregor (ed.), *Luckenbooth: An Anthology of Edinburgh Poetry* (Edinburgh: Polygon), pp. 124–125.

2008

– One poem, 'My Luve, My Luve', in Stewart Conn (ed.), *100 Favourite Scottish Love Poems* (Edinburgh: Luath Press), p. 54.

– One poem, 'The Staunan Stanes', in Tom Hubbard & Duncan Glen (eds.), *Fringe of Gold: The Fife Anthology* (Edinburgh: Birlinn), p. 153.

2009

– EDITED COLLECTION: Robert Burns's *The Merry Muses of Caledonia* as edited by Smith in 1959, extended, annotated and introduced by Valentina Bold, who also provides music (Edinburgh: Luath Press).

2013

– One poem 'Stormy Day and a Cat, November', in Hamish Whyte (ed.), *Scottish Cats: An Anthology of Scottish Cat Poems* (Edinburgh: Luath Press).

2014

– Eight poems, El Alamein', 'The Mither's Lament', 'The Convoy', 'The Sodjer's Sang', 'Simmer Lanskip', 'Mars and Venus at Hogmanay', 'The War in Fife' and

'October 1941', in David Goldie & Roderick Watson (eds.), *From the Line: Scottish War Poetry 1914–1945* (Glasgow: ASLS), pp. 173–179.

**2015**

– TRANSLATION INTO FRENCH: *La Vieille Alliance: Pour le centenaire de la naissance de Sydney Goodsir* Smith, by John Manson (Dunning: Fras Publications). 'The Scaur', 'Torquemada and the Carapace', 'Simmer Nichtsang', 'Sang: The Die is Cast', 'Ye Speir Me', 'Luve in Fetters', 'Hamewith', 'Winter Blues', all translated into French (plus Smith's originals) by Manson.

**2017**

– Article / transcript: 'The Auk and the Flaming Terrapin', in *Fras* 27, pp. 4–9. Text of radio talk / obituary on Roy Campbell by Smith (originally broadcast as part of 'Scottish Life and Letters' 18 June 1957). Transcribed and introduced by Richie McCaffery.
– Six poems, 'In Granada, In Granada', 'Prolegomenon', 'King and Queen o the Fowr Airts', 'The Grace of God and the Meths Drinker', 'A Bairn Seick', 'Dido', in J. Derrick McClure (ed.), *A Kist o Skinklan Things: An Anthology of Scots Poetry from the 1st and 2nd Waves of the Scottish Renaissance* (Glasgow: ASLS), pp. 82–89.
– Poem, 'Philomel' appears as 'Poem of the Day', in *The Scotsman* (11 May).

### Secondary Material

**1942**

– Review of *Skail Wind* by G.H.K., in *Scots Independent* No. 178 (March), p. 2.
– Letter to editor concerning *Skail Wind* review by 'The Reviewer', in *The Free Man: Agus Alba Nuadh* Vol. v, No. 11 (August 1st), p. 4.
– Letter to the editor, '*Skail Wind* review: Another point of view' by Hugh MacDiarmid, in *The Free Man: Agus Alba Nuadh* Vol. v, No. 12 (8th August), p. 4.
– Review by 'G.T.' (Geoffrey Taylor?) of *Skail Wind*, in *The Bell* Vol. v / No. 2 (November), pp. 154–157.

**1943**

– Review of *The Wanderer* by 'G.T.' (Geoffrey Taylor?), in *The Bell* Vol vi / No. 4 (July), pp. 351–353.

**1944**

– Review of *Poetry Scotland* by G. M in which close attention is given to Smith's lyrics, in *Scots Independent* No. 212 (April), p. 3.

1945

– Review by J.F. Hendry of *The Wanderer*, in *Poetry Scotland* 2, pp. 70–71.

1946

– Review, by anonymous, of *The Deevil's Waltz*, in The New Alliance and Scots Review Vol. 7 / No. 2, p. 13.

– 'Recent Scots Literature' by Robert Blair Wilkie, in *Scots Independent* No. 239 (July), p. 6. Contains review of *The Deevil's Waltz*.

1947

– Article on Smith's work by Hugh MacDiarmid entitled 'A Scottish Sharawaggian', in *The Voice of Scotland* Vol. IV / No. 1, pp. 44–47. Note: a review / discussion of *Carotid Cornucopius*.

– Review of *The Deevil's Waltz* by 'M.W.P', in *The Dublin Magazine* Vol. XXII / No. 1 (Jan-March), pp. 47–50.

1948

– Article 'Makar Chieftainship' by Norman MacCaig contains discussion of Smith's poetry, in *The Galliard* No. 1, pp. 17–18.

– Review of *Under the Eildon Tree* by Maurice Lindsay ('Books of the Day: Scottish Renaissance'), in *The Scotsman* (11 November), pagination unknown.

– Review of *Under the Eildon Tree* by G.S. Fraser ('Three Scottish Poets'), in *The Times Literary Supplement* (13 November), pagination unknown.

– Editorial by Hugh MacDiarmid 'Direct Poetry and the Scottish Genius', in *The Voice of Scotland* Vol. V. / No. 2 (December), pp. 26–32.

1949

– Review of *Under the Eildon Tree* by Norman MacCaig ('The Galliard's Quair'), in *The Galliard* (autumn), pp. 29 & 56.

– Extended article / review of *Under the Eildon Tree* by Robin Lorimer – 'The Aipple Frae a Tree', in *The New Alliance and Scots Review* (November), pp. 150–152.

1952

– Anonymous review of Smith's *A Short Introduction to Scottish Literature*, in Edinburgh Evening Dispatch (22 February), pagination unknown.

– Anonymous review of Smith's edited book on Robert Fergusson ('Fergusson: Poet of Auld Reekie'), in *The Scotsman* (27 March).

– Anonymous review of Smith's edited book on Robert Fergusson in *Times Literary Supplement* (27 June), pagination unknown.

– Review by 'Jock', in *Jabberwock* (Edinburgh University Review) of Smith's Robert Fergusson book *The Bard and His Master* (Autumn), pp. 31–32.

1953

– Review of *So Late into the Night,* by G.S. Fraser, in *The Times Literary Supplement* (2 January), pagination unknown.

– Short review by Hugh MacDiarmid of *So Late into the Night*, in Scottish Journal: The Popular National Monthly No. 5 (January), p. 13.

– Article / essay on Smith's work by Alexander Scott ('Daylight and the Dark'), in *Lines* 3 (Summer), pp. 9–13. Note: *Lines* 3 was dedicated to the work of Smith.

– Review of *So Late into the Night* by Alastair Thomson, in *Lines* 3 (summer), p. 27.

– Review of *Robert Fergusson, 1750–1774* by anonymous reviewer, in *Robert Burns Chronicle*, pp. 86–88.

– Short review by Peter Russell of *A Short Introduction to Scottish Literature*, in *Lines* No. 10 (Winter), p. 71.

1954

– Short review by James Maclaren of *Cokkils*, in *Scottish Journal: The Popular National Monthly* No. 12 (Jan-April), p. 16.

– Review by W.L. Renwick of *Robert Fergusson, 1750–1774*, in *The Scottish Historical Review* Vol. 33 / No. 115, Part 1 (April), pp. 75–77.

– Anonymous review of *Cokkils* ('Irish and Scottish Voices'), in *The Times Literary Supplement* (7 May), pagination unknown.

– Article / essay on Smith's work – 'The Poetry of Sydney Goodsir Smith' - by Norman MacCaig (then writing as McCaig), in *The Saltire Review 1* (April), pp. 14–19.

1955

– Review by Jackson MacLow of *So Late into the Night* ('A Great Scots Poet'), in *Poetry* Vol. 86 / No. 1 (April), pp. 52–55.

– Short anonymous notice / review of *Orpheus and Eurydice*, in *Saltire Review* Vol. 2 / No. 4 (spring), p. 77.

– Review by A.T. Cunninghame of *Orpheus and Eurydice*, in *The Voice of Scotland* Vol. VI / No. 1 (April), pp. 29–30.

1956

– Poem, by Randolph Snow, 'A Revival of Love', in *Punch* (28 March), p. 350. A parody of Smith's lyrical love poetry.

- Review by David Craig of *Omens*, in *Lines Review* 11 and 12 (Summer), pp. 53–55.
- Review by Edwin Morgan of *Omens*, in *The Saltire Review* Vol. 3 / No. 8 (Autumn), pp. 64–5.

### 1959

- Review, by 'P.T.' of *The Merry Muses of Caledonia* as edited by Smith, in *Gambit: Edinburgh University Review* (Spring), p. 27.
- Review by Norman MacCaig of Smith's *Gavin Douglas: A Selection from his Poetry*, in *Saltire Review* 19 (Autumn), pp. 70–72. Note: there is also a review of Smith's edited version of *The Merry Muses of Caledonia* by an A.R. in this same issue, see pp. 77–79.
- Review / article by Ronald Mavor – 'A Welcome Glimpse of "The Wallace": Important Scottish Play', in *The Scotsman* (2 December), pagination unknown.
- Letter to the editor by Iain MacDowell concerning 'The Wallace', in *The Scotsman* (3 December), pagination unknown.

### 1960

- Review by George Todd of *Figs and Thistles*, in *Sidewalk* Vol. 1 / No. 1, pp. 75–76.
- Review by Maurice Lindsay of *Figs and Thistles*, in *Scottish Field* Vol. CVII / No. 686 (February), p. 50.
- 'A Living Poetry', a review by Norman MacCaig of *Figs and Thistles*, in *Poetry* Vol. 96 / No. 5 (August), pp. 320–322.
- 'Scotland: Wham Bruce has Led', a review of the Edinburgh Festival performance of Smith's *The Wallace*, in *Time Magazine* (5 September), pagination unknown.
- Review by George Todd of *The Wallace*, in *Sidewalk* Vol. 1 / No. 2, p. 57.
- Review by Robert McLellan of *The Wallace*, in *The Saltire Review* Vol. 6 / No. 22 (Autumn), pp. 75–77.
- Review by Eric Linklater of *The Wallace* (as performed at Assembly Hall / Ed. Festival), in *Scottish Field* Vol. CVII, No. 694 (October), p. 58.
- Anonymous review of *The Wallace*, in *Lines Review* 16 (Winter), pp. 42–44.
- Review by Alexander Reid of *The Wallace*, in *Scotland's Magazine* 56, pp. 49–50.

### 1961

- Review by James Fergusson of *The Wallace*, in *The Scottish Historical Review* Vol. 40 / No. 129, Part 1 (April), pp. 80–81.

–  Review by A.D.M. (Albert Mackie) of *The Vision of the Prodigal Son*, in *Lines Review* 17 (Summer), pp. 56–58.

1962

–  Review by Al Alvarez ('Dialect and the dialectic') of (co-edited by Smith) *MacDiarmid: A Festschrift*, in *Observer Weekend Review* (12 August), p. 17.
–  Review by Hamish Henderson of *MacDiarmid: A Festschrift*, in *Lines Review* 18, pp. 45–46.

1963

–  'Critical Relations' – a letter to the editor by David Craig, in *Lines Review* 20 (Summer) concerning Smith's review of Craig's *Scottish Literature and the Scottish People*, p. 50.
–  'Poets Old and Young', Carolyn Kizer reviews *The Wallace*, in *Poetry* (September), p. 397.
–  *Sydney Goodsir Smith* by Hugh MacDiarmid (Edinburgh: Colin Hamilton, 1963). A pamphlet tribute to Smith, written, delivered and published to celebrate Smith's presentation of the Sir Thomas Urquhart Award by the Ed. Uni. Scottish Renaissance Society. A limited edition of 135 copies, subsequently reprinted in MacDiarmid's *The Uncanny Scot* (London: MacGibbon and Kee, 1968), pp. 164–168.

1964

–  Review by G. Ross Roy of *Robert Burns: The Merry Muses of Caledonia* (G.P. Putnam's American edition of 1964), in *Studies in Scottish Literature* Vol. 2 / Issue. 4, pp. 267–270.

1966

–  Review by A. Grommet of *Carotid Cornucopius* (1964 Macdonald reissue), in *Lines Review* 22 (Winter), pp. 42–43.
–  Review by Ian Rodger of *Kynd Kittock's Land*, in *Lines Review* 22 (Winter), pp. 44–45.
–  'Poem for Sydney Goodsir Smith' by Charles Senior in *Selected Poems*, by Charles Senior, M. Macdonald, Edinburgh, 1966, pp. 30–31.

1967

–  Brief review by Robert Fitzhugh of Smith's *Robert Burns: A Choice of Burns's Poems and Songs*, in *Studies in Scottish Literature* Vol. 4 / Issue 4, pp. 257–8.

– Review of *Robert Burns: A Choice of Burns's Poems and Songs* by Douglas Sealy, in *The Dublin Magazine* Vol. 6 / No. 2 (Summer), pp. 99–101.

1969

– Article on Smith's poetry by Thomas Crawford, 'The Poetry of Sydney Goodsir Smith', in *Studies in Scottish Literature* Vol. 7 / Issue 1. pp. 40–59.

– Issue No. 10 of *Akros* was a special 'Sydney Goodsir Smith number' (May), and contains the following items, excluding original Smith poems listed in primary sources above: 'Editorially' by Duncan Glen, pp. 2–5; 'A Redeeming Feature' by Hugh MacDiarmid, pp. 17–20: 'Sydney Goodsir Smith: The Art of Devilment' by Alexander Scott, pp. 21–28: '*Under the Eildon Tree*' by Robert Garioch, pp. 41–47.

– Review of *Fifteen Poems and a Play* by David Buchan, in *Lines Review* 30 (October), pp. 44–48 (see p. 47).

– Review of *Fifteen Poems and a Play* by Robert Garioch, in *Scottish International* 8 (November), pp. 64–65.

– '"The Poetry of Sydney Goodsir Smith" – A Rejoinder' by Alexander Scott, in *Studies in Scottish Literature* Vol. 8 / Issue 1, p. 65.

1972

– Article on poetry of Smith by Duncan Glen 'Poet's Poet: Sydney Goodsir Smith', in *Scotia* No. 25 (January), pp. 1–3.

1975

– Obituary for Smith entitled 'Lyric poet of wynds and howffs', in *The Scotsman* (exact date unknown, certainly mid-to-late January, Smith died 15 Jan), pagination unknown.

– Obituary for Smith 'Sydney Goodsir Smith: Exuberant Scots Poet', in *The Times* (21st Jan), author and pagination unknown.

– 'Sydney Goodsir Smith' obituary / article by George Mackay Brown for *The Orcadian* (23rd Jan). Reprinted in Mackay Brown's 1975 book *Letters from Hamnavoe* (Edinburgh: Gordon Wright), pp. 129–130.

– 'In Memoriam Sydney Goodsir Smith (1915–1975)' by Duncan Glen, published as a separate supplement to *Akros* Vol. 9 / No. 27 (April), 4 pages in total.

– Article on / reminiscences of 'Sydney Goodsir Smith' by Iain Crichton Smith, in *The Pembroke Magazine* No. 7, pp. 166–172. Note: also reproduces 'Elegy XIII' from *Under the Eildon Tree* in its entirety.

– 'Sydney Goodsir Smith: An Appreciation' by Maurice Lindsay, in *The Pembroke Magazine* No. 7, pp. 173–174.

- Issue No. 9 of *Scotia Review* was dedicated to Smith and contains the following articles and creative pieces, as well as photographs: 'Au 'voir, Sydney' by Tom Scott (a personal reflection of his friendship with Smith), pp. 2–4; '"Mon Vieux! Mon Brave!", Sydney Goodsir Smith: An Appreciation' by Stanley Roger Green, pp. 5–6. Two poems for Smith by William J. Tait – 'Adjustan Mysel tae the Situation' and 'Déjà vu', p. 8; Musical 'Lament for Sydney Goodsir Smith' by R.L.C Lorimer, p. 9; Elegy for Smith by Duncan Glen – 'The Dancin Leid', pp. 10–11; '*Carotid Cornucopius*' by Hugh MacDiarmid, a piece praising Smith's only published novel, pp. 11–14; poem 'For SGS' by Alan Bold, pp. 16–18.
- Article 'Sydney Goodsir Smith' by John Guthrie, in *Scotia Review* 10, pp. 2–4.
- A bibliography of Smith's publications, 'Sydney Goodsir Smith, 1915–1975: A Checklist of his Books and Pamphlets' by W.R. Aitken, in *Scotia Review* 10, pp. 5–9.
- Article 'Memories of Two Scottish Poets' by John L. Broom, in *Scotia Review* 10. The two poets are Smith and Charles Senior, pp. 43–44.
- 'In Memoriam Sydney Goodsir Smith' by A.S. (Alexander Scott?), in *Lallans* No. 5 (Mairtinmas), pp. 6–8.
- Review 'Addicted to love' of *Collected Poems* by James Aitchison, in *The Scotsman* (15 November), pagination unknown.
- Review of *Collected Poems* by Stanley Roger Green, in *Scotia Review* No. 11 (December), pp. 38–40.
- FESTSCHRIFT: Norman MacCaig (ed.) *For Sydney Goodsir Smith* (Edinburgh: M. Macdonald). Contains tributes in poetry and prose by Robert Garioch (on *Carotid Cornucopius*), Alexander Scott (on *Under the Eildon Tree*), David Murison (on Smith's use of language and Scots), Hugh MacDiarmid, Iain Cuthbertson (on Smith's plays), Iain Crichton Smith, Sorley MacLean, Denis Peploe (on Smith's art) and a checklist of Smith's work by W.R. Aitken.
- 'In Memoriam' – a review of *For Sydney Goodsir Smith* by Robert Nye, in *The Scotsman* (6 December), pagination unknown.
- *Sydney Goodsir Smith's 'Under the Eildon Tree': An Essay* by Eric Gold (Preston: Akros Publications).

1976

- 'Legacy of a notable poet of the Lallans revival', review of *Collected Poems* by Seumas Stewart, in *The Birmingham Post* (3rd Jan), p. 2 of the 'Saturday Magazine'.
- Joint review of *For Sydney Goodsir Smith* and *Collected Poems* by Edwin Morgan, in *Lines Review* 57 (March), pp. 40–43.
- 'Goodsir Smith: The Auk of the Mandrake Hert', review of *Collected Poems* by Thomas Crawford, in *The Scottish Review: Arts and the Environment* Vol. 1 / No. 2 (Spring), pp. 17–22.

- Review of *Collected Poems* by J.K. Annand, in *Lallans: The Magazine for Writing in Lowland Scots* No. 6 (Whitsunday), p. 35.
- Article 'Sydney Goodsir Smith: Makar Macironical' by Kenneth Buthlay, in *Akros* 31 (August), pp. 46–56.
- Review of *For Sydney Goodsir Smith* in Gaelic by R. MacThomais (Derick Thomson), in *Gairm* 94 (Spring), p. 187.
- Long review of *Collected Poems* by Alexander Scott, in *Scottish Literary Journal* (Supplement 3, Winter), pp. 39–45.

1977
- 'Drinker of Life (In memoriam Sydney Goodsir Smith)', a poem for Smith by William Oxley, in *Scotia Review* 17 (Summer), p. 20.
- 'Letter to the editor' (30th November) by Tom Scott, in *Akros* Vol. 11 / No. 33 (April), p. 124. Note: discusses Scott's role as editor of Smith's *Collected Poems* and denies responsibility for mistakes made.

1978
- 'British Wells', review of *Collected Poems* by Ben Howard, in *Poetry* (February), pp. 297–298.

1979
- Review, 'Sydney Goodsir Smith Reads his Poetry' by Robert Garioch, in *Lines Review* 71, pp. 5–8. Note: concerning a record of Smith reading his poems, called *The Deevil's Waltz*.
- Anecdotal article 'Luve-doitit bard' by Douglas Eadie, in *Radio Times Scotland* (17–23rd November), pagination unknown.

1980
- Article 'Sydney Goodsir Smith', by James B. Caird, in *Chapman* 26 (Spring), pp. 14–19.
- Article 'Three Post-MacDiarmid Makars: Soutar, Garioch, Smith' by Alan Bold, in *Akros* Vol. 15 / No. 44 (August), pp. 44–61.

1981
- Two letters to the editor by Alan Bold and Tom Scott, concerning Scott's supposed editing of *Collected Poems of Sydney Goodsir Smith* for John Calder, in *The Scotsman*, 21 May, pagination unknown.

1982
- Review of *Carotid Cornucopius* (3rd edn.) by Trevor Royle, in *The Glasgow Herald* (4 December), pagination unknown.

1983
- Article, 'Sydney Goodsir Smith' by John C. Hall, in *Books in Scotland* No. 12 (Spring), pp. 8–10.
- Review 'Smith's Cornucopia' by John Burns, in *Cencrastus* No. 14 (autumn) of *Carotid Cornucopius* (3rd edn.), pp. 50–51.

1984
- Article 'Big Music and Skail Winds: The Achievement of Robert Garioch and Sydney Goodsir Smith' by John C. Hall, in *Lines Review* 88 (March), p. 10 and pp. 15–19.
- Poem 'Lament for the Makars' in memory of Smith by Albert Mackie, in *Lines Review* 91 (December), p. 5.

1985
- Article 'Sydney Goodsir Smith: A Poet for all Seasons' by publisher John Calder, in *The Scotsman* (17th August), pagination unknown.
- Programme of the Edinburgh International Festival 1985 for a performance of *The Wallace*, contains a couple of pages of background information on Smith and the play. Unpaginated.
- Review of performance of 'The Wallace' at Assembly Hall 'Spectacular "Wallace"' by Allen Wright, in *The Scotsman* (21 August), pagination unknown.

1986
- Article 'On Sydney Goodsir Smith's Perpetual Opposition and Deviation Tactics' by Edwin Morgan, in *Radical Scotland* (April / May), pp. 38–39. Reprinted in Morgan's *Crossing the Border* in 1990.

1989
- Article 'A Route Maist Devious: Sydney Goodsir Smith and Edinburgh' by Thom Nairn, in *Cencrastus* 33 (Spring), pp. 6–9.
- Short article 'Sydney Goodsir Smith' by Ian Begg, in *Chapman* 55–6 (Spring), p. 96.

1990
- Article / essay 'On Sydney Goodsir Smith's "Perpetual Opposition" and "Deviation Tactics"' by Edwin Morgan, in *Crossing the Border: Essays on Scottish Literature* (Carcanet) pp. 248–250.
- Essay, 'Slugabed and Godless: the Functions of Humour in Sydney Goodsir Smith', in Carla Marengo Vaglio et al, *Le Forne del Comico* (Alessandria: Edizioni dell'Orso), pp. 579–590.

**1991**

– Poem, 'Sydney Goodsir Smith' by Roderick Watson, in Duncan Glen (ed.), *Zed20* No. 1, p. 38.

**1992**

– Article 'Hou Monie Lives Has a Man?' by John Manson, in W.N. Herbert and Richard Price (eds.), *Gairfish: The McAvantGarde*, pp. 90–93.

**1994**

– Article 'Hou Monie Lives Has a Man?' by John Manson, in *Epoch* 5, pp. 12–13.

**1995**

– *The Awk* (sic) *Remembered* Neil Mathers (ed.) Corbie Press. A limited (200) edition anthology published to mark Smith's 80th anniversary of birth and 20th anniversary of his death. Material mostly culled from previous publications.

**1996**

– '3 May 1969' by Alexander Scott, in Neil R. MacCallum (ed.), *Sing Frae the Hert: The Literary Criticism of Alexander Scott* (Aberdeen: Scottish Cultural Press), pp. 50–52.

**1997**

– 'On My Word', Neil R. MacCallum, in *The Scots Independent* (9 August), p. 9.
– Hugh MacDiarmid's 1962 article in tribute to Smith (on winning the Sir Thomas Urquhart Award) is reprinted in Alan Riach (ed.), *Albyn: Shorter Books and Monographs* (of Hugh MacDiarmid) (Manchester: Carcanet Press), pp. 335–338.

**1998**

– Article / review 'A Slice of Edinburgh 1960s History: *The Drawings of Sydney Goodsir Smith, Poet*' by Jack Firth, in *Books in Scotland* No. 60 (Summer), pp. 17–18.

**1999**

– 'Sydney Goodsir Smith (1915–1975)' by Duncan Glen, in *Selected Scottish and other Essays* (Kirkcaldy: Akros), pp. 47–50.

2000

– Poem, 'In Memoriam Sydney Goodsir Smith, 1915–1975' by Neil Mathers, in *Epoch Poetry Review* No. 1, p. 25.

– Essay / chapter by Christopher Whyte ('Corbière, Laforgue et Goodsir Smith') in David Kinloch and Richard Price (eds.), *La Nouvelle Alliance: Influences francophones sur la littérature ecossaise modern* (Grenoble: ELLUG), pp. 61–90.

2004

– Entry for Smith on *Oxford National Dictionary of Biography* by Tom Hubbard: http://www.oxforddnb.com/view/printable/58855.

2005

– Poem, 'The Kiwi Wha Becam the Auk: For Sydney Goodsir Smith' by George Hardie, in *Chapman* 107, pp. 55–56.

2008

– 'SGS: The Gangrel Rymour' – an article by Tom Hubbard on Smith's translations of Tristan Corbière, in *Zed20* No. 23 (spring), pp. 69–71.

2011

– 'Sir Thomas Urquhart's True Legacy: The Influence of Urquhart on contemporary Scottish literature, focussing on the poet Sydney Goodsir Smith (1915–1975)', article by Richie McCaffery given as a conference paper April 2011 and collected in Alexander F. Thomson (ed.), *Sir Thomas Urquhart of Cromarty* (Cromarty Arts Trust), pp. 66–71.

2013

– '"Luve's Arcane Delirium": A Reading of Sydney Goodsir Smith's *Under the Eildon Tree*', Richie McCaffery, in *The Scottish Literary Review* Vol. 5 / No. 1, pp. 31–45.

– 'Photographing Lallans: Alan Daiches, Alexander Scott and Sydney Goodsir Smith's Poems for Television' by John Corbett, in *The Scottish Cultural Review of Language and Literature* (Vol. 20). Note: this also features as a chapter in Eleanor Bell and Linda Gunn's (eds.) *The Scottish Sixties: Reading, Rebellion, Revolution?* (Rodopi, Netherlands, 2013).

2015

– 'Doon Canongate: A Centenary Appreciation of a Scots Makar' by Patrick Crotty, in *The Times Literary Supplement* (13 Nov), pp. 14–15.

–   *Fras 22* was published to mark 40 years since the death of Smith and 100 years since his birth. Of particular interest are three articles: 'Ae Boat Anerlie Nou' by William Hershaw (pp. 13–24) which looks at the poets of the second wave of the Scottish Literary Renaissance (including Smith); 'Sydney Goodsir Smith's *Skail Wind*' (25–32), an article by Richie McCaffery, arguing that this collection was not the failure it is often dismissed as; 'On the Trail of the Extinct Auk' by Richie McCaffery (pp. 4–9).

2018

–   'Sorley MacLean and Sydney Goodsir Smith – poets we need today' by Alan Riach, in *The National* (3rd Sept), online at: http://www.thenational.scot/culture/16683673.sorley-maclean-and-sydney-goodsir-smith-poets-we-need-today/.

## *Material with notable mentions of Smith and his work*

1947

–   Poem 'For Goodsir Smith and Mayakovsky' by Thurso Berwick, in *The Voice of Scotland* Vol. III / No. 4 (June), pp. 15–16.

1954

–   Article, 'Masquing-Gear' by Iain Hamilton, in *The Twentieth Century* (June), pp. 527–539. Note: a very critical survey of the Scottish literary scene and writing in Scots with a focus on Smith.

–   Article, 'Modern Makars Scots and English' by Edwin Morgan, in *The Saltire Review* 2 (August), pp. 75–81.

1955

–   James Kingsley, *Scottish Poetry: A Critical Survey* (London: Cassell), pp. 265–269.

1956

–   Article by Tom Scott, 'Some Poets of the Scottish Renaissance', in *Poetry* Vol. 88 / No. 1 (April), pp. 43–47. See: pp. 46–47.

1957

–   Article, 'Post-War Poetry in Scots' by Walter Keir, in *The Saltire Review* Vol. 4 / No. 10, (Spring), pp. 61–64.

1958

–   *The Scottish Tradition in Literature* by Kurt Wittig (Edinburgh: Oliver and Boyd), see pp. 292–296.

1959

– *Mostly Murder, etc.: An Autobiography* by Sir Sydney Smith (London: George G. Harrap and Co.). Note: Smith's father's account of his international and dramatic life as a high-profile forensic scientist and pathologist. His son is mentioned fleetingly and somewhat grudgingly.

1962

– 'The Beatnik in the Kailyard' by Edwin Morgan, in *New Saltire* 3. Also reprinted in Morgan's *Essays* (Carcanet, 1974), pp. 166–176.

1964

– *Hugh MacDiarmid and the Scottish Renaissance* by Duncan Glen (Edinburgh: W. & R. Chambers Ltd.).

1966

– *The Company I've Kept* by Hugh MacDiarmid (London: Hutchinson).

1970

– 'Scottish Poetry in 1969' by Alexander Scott, in *Studies in Scottish Literature* Vol. VII / No. 4 (April), pp. 211–228, discusses Smith's work of 1969 on p. 225.
– 'To Sydney Goodsir Smith' – an epistolary poem by Burns Singer in Walter Keir (ed.), *The Collected Poems of Burns Singer* (London: Secker & Warburg), pp. 204–206.

1971

– Alexander Scott contributes a chapter, 'Literature', in Duncan Glen's *Whither Scotland? A Prejudiced Look at the Future of a Nation* (London: Gollancz), pp. 187–219. See pp. 191–2.

1972

– *The MacDiarmid Makars: 1923–1972* by Alexander Scott (Preston: Akros Publications), see pp. 14–19. Note: this is the stand-alone publication of a long essay that first appeared in *Akros* Vol. 7 / No. 19 under the same title, pp. 9–33.

1974

– 'Scottish Poets since Stevenson' by Duncan Glen, in *Akros* Vol. 9 / No. 25 (August), pp. 49–70. See pp. 60–61.
– *Contemporary Scottish Poetry: Individuals and Contexts* by Robin Fulton (Edinburgh: Macdonald Publishers), see pp. 173–175.

**1975**

– *Akros* Vol. 10 / No. 28 (August) is of particular interest for three essays (all on separate decades of literary activity). See Maurice Lindsay's 'Scottish Poetry in the Forties' (pp. 36–53); Alexander Scott's 'Scottish Poetry in the Fifties' (pp. 66–89); and Alexander Scott's 'Scottish Poetry in the Seventies' (pp. 105–117).

**1977**

– *MacDiarmid: An Illustrated Biography* by Gordon Wright (Edinburgh: Gordon Wright Publishing).

– John Broom's 'Alcoholic Odyssey', in *The Rhythm of the Glass* edited by Paul Harris (Edinburgh: Paul Harris Publishing), pp. 75–79. See also Broom's 1973 alcoholic memoir *Another Little Drink* (Scotia, published under pseudonym 'Abraham Adams'), pp. 43–4.

**1978**

– 'Scottish Poetry 1974–1976' by Alexander Scott, in *Studies in Scottish Literature* Vol. 13 / Issue 1, pp. 221–249. See pp. 229–235.

– Translation of Elegy XIII from *Under the Eildon Tree* into Esperanto by William Auld: 'El sub la fea arbo', in *Skota Antologio* (Glasgow, Eldonejo Kardo), pp. 248–253.

**1980**

– Alastair Mackie's *Back-Green Odyssey and Other Poems* (Aberdeen: Rainbow Books) contains a long poem sequence entitled 'Orpheus' 'dedicatit to the memory o the late Sidney [sic] Goodsir Smith', pp. 61–74.

– *Collected Poems 1938–1978* of William J. Tait (Edinburgh: Paul Harris) contains an elegy for Smith: 'Aubade' p. 53.

– *Precipitous City: Story of Literary Edinburgh* by Trevor Royle (Edinburgh: Mainstream), see in particular pp. 185–188 and 191–193.

**1981**

– Robert Calder's 'The Direction of the Long Poem', in *Chapman* 30 (Summer) contains references to Smith's *Under the Eildon Tree*, pp. 63–72.

**1982**

– *Chapman* 32 (Spring) contains one poem by Thurso Berwick – 'Brig o Giants' – which is subtitled 'For Goodsir Smith an Mayakovsky', p. 22.

– Translation(s) of unknown poem(s) by Smith into German, in Rolf Blaeser (ed.) *Licht im Nebel: Schottische Dichtung von 13 Jahrhundert bis zur Gegenwart* (Recklinghausen: Buch-Heute-Verlag, 1982).

- Translation by Blažej Belák of Smith's poem 'Largo', as well as translations into Slovak of a selection of poems from *Under the Eildon Tree*, in *Revue Svetorej literatúry*, Issue 18, pp. 93 & 104.

1983

- *Thank You for Having Me* by Maurice Lindsay (London: Robert Hale).

1984

- Roderick Watson's *The Literature of Scotland* (London: MacMillan), pp. 419–422.
- Alan Bold's *The Letters of Hugh MacDiarmid* (London: Hamish Hamilton), see pp. 679–680.
- Cordelia Oliver 'Artists in Scotland, 1959–1983', in Oscar Marzaroli's *One Man's World: Photographs 1955–1984* (Glasgow: Third Eye Centre, Glasgow), pp. 85–89.

1985

- Translation into Italian by Enzo Bonventre of 'Largo', in *Trapani nuova* (29 November), p. 3.
- A. Trevor Tolley's *The Poetry of the Forties* (Manchester: Manchester University Press).

1986

- Robin Fulton, ed., *A Garioch Miscellany* (Edinburgh: Macdonald Publishers), see pp. 32, 36, 37, 56 & 91.
- *Callum Macdonald: Scottish Literary Publisher* (National Library of Scotland). Catalogue for an exhibition dedicated to Macdonald's work, see pp. 19–20.

1987

- Morley Jamieson's 'Recollections of Edwin and Willa Muir', in *Chapman* 49 (summer), pp. 26–31 (see pp. 27–28).
- Translation of Smith poem by William Auld into Esperanto, 'Patrinlamento', in *Omagôl* (Brazil: Fonto), p. 137.
- Cairns Craig, ed., *The History of Scottish Literature: Volume 4: Twentieth Century* (Aberdeen: Aberdeen University Press).

1990

- Mary & Hector MacIver's *Pilgrim Souls* (Aberdeen: Aberdeen University Press), pp. 103, 108, 131.

1992

- *History of Scottish Literature* by Maurice Lindsay (London: Robert Hale), pp. 390–392.

1995

– J. Derrick McClure's *Scots and its Literature* (Amsterdam: John Benjamins Publishing).

1996

– 'Editorial Efterwurd', in *Lallans: The Magazine of Writing in Scots* No. 46 (Whitsuntid), pp. 46–47.

1996

– Margery McNeill, *Norman MacCaig: A Study of His Life and Work* (Edinburgh: Mercat Press).

1997

– George Mackay Brown, *For the Islands I Sing: An Autobiography* (London: John Murray), pp. 122–124.

1998

– 'Editorial Efterwurd', in *Lallans: The Magazine of Writing in Scots* No. 53 (Mairtinmass), pp. 46–47.

1999

– John Corbett, *Written in the Language of the Scottish Nation: A History of Literary Translation into Scots* (Bristol: Multilingual Matters), p. 134.

2000

– J. Derrick McClure, *Language, Poetry and Nationhood: Scots as a Poetic Language from 1878 to the Present* (East Linton: Tuckwell Press), pp. 122–132.
– William Calin, *Minority Literature and Modernisms: Scots, Breton and Occitan, 1920–1990* (Toronto: University of Toronto Press).

2001

– Dorian Grieve, O.D. Edwards & Alan Riach (eds.), *Hugh MacDiarmid: New Selected Letters* (Manchester: Carcanet), pp. 297, 249–250, 429.

2002

– Douglas Gifford, Sarah Dunnigan & Alan MacGillivray (eds.), *Scottish Literature in English and Scots* (Edinburgh: Edinburgh University Press).

2004

– Obituary for Hazel Goodsir Smith by anonymous author in *The Scotsman* (17/05), accessible online: http://www.scotsman.com/news/obituaries/hazel-goodsir-smith-1-531369.

– Christopher Whyte, *Modern Scottish Poetry* (Edinburgh: Edinburgh University Press), pp. 109–116.
– Poem, 'Sydney Goodsir Smith' by Roderick Watson, in *Into the Blue Wavelengths* (Edinburgh: Luath), p. 69.

2005

– Marco Fazzini (ed.), *Alba Literaria: A History of Scottish Literature* (Amos Edizioni), see Christopher Whyte, 'The Poetry of Robert Garioch' pp. 533–551.

2006

– Maggie Fergusson, *George Mackay Brown: The Life* (London: John Murray).

2007

– Poem 'On the Fly-leaf of Sydney Goodsir Smith's *Collected Poems*' by Ken Cockburn, in *Markings* Issue 24, p. 33.
– Poem 'Thochts Ablaw the Eildon Tree: For Sydney Goodsir Smith' by William Hershaw, in *Makars: Poems in Scots* (Kirkcaldy: Akros), p. 9.
– (reprinted 2009): Roderick Watson, 'Death's Proletariat': Scottish Poets of the Second World War', in Tim Kendall (ed.), *The Oxford Handbook of British and Irish Poetry* (Oxford: Oxford University Press), pp. 315–339.
– Roderick Watson, 'Living with the Double Tongue: Modern Poetry in Scots', in Ian Brown, ed., *The Edinburgh History of Scottish Literature* (Edinburgh: Edinburgh University Press), pp. 163–175.
– Stanley Roger Green, *A Clanjamfry of Poets: A Tale of Literary Edinburgh, 1950–1985* (Edinburgh: Saltire Society), pp. 23–38.

2008

– (reprinted 2009) Alexander Moffat, Alan Riach & Linda MacDonald-Lewis, *Arts of Resistance: Poets, Portraits and Landscapes of Modern Scotland* (Edinburgh: Luath), pp. 136–145.

2009

– Margery Palmer McCulloch, *Scottish Modernism and its Contexts 1918–1959: Literature, National Identity and Cultural Exchange* (Edinburgh: Edinburgh University Press), pp. 208–212.
– Robyn Marsack, 'The Seven Poets Generation', in Alan Riach & Ian Brown, *The Edinburgh Companion to 20th Century Scottish Literature* (Edinburgh: Edinburgh University Press), pp. 156–166.

**2010**

- *Correspondence between Hugh MacDiarmid and Sorley MacLean* (Edinburgh: Edinburgh University Press).

**2011**

- Donald Smith, 'The Mid-Century Dramatists', in Ian Brown (ed.), *The Edinburgh Companion to Scottish Drama* (Edinburgh: Edinburgh University Press), pp. 118–129.
- Roderick Watson, 'Scotland and Modernisms', in Emma Dymock & Margery McCulloch (eds.), *Scottish and International Modernism: Relationships and Reconfigurations* (Glasgow: ASLS), pp. 8–19.
- John Manson (ed.), *Dear Grieve: Letters to Hugh MacDiarmid (C.M. Grieve)* (Glasgow: Kennedy & Boyd), pp. 314, 379, 474.

**2012**

- Margery Palmer McCulloch, 'Continuing the Renaissance: Little Magazines and a Late Phrase of Scottish Modernism in the 1940s', in *Etudes ecossaises* 15, pp. 59–73.
- Valentina Bold, 'On Editing *The Merry Muses*', in *Studies in Scottish Literature* Vol. 37 / Issue 1, pp. 95–107.

**2013**

- John Herdman, *Another Country* (Edinburgh: Thirsty Books).

**2015**

- James McGonigal & John Coyle (eds.), *Edwin Morgan: The Midnight Letterbox: Selected Correspondence 1950–2010* (Manchester: Carcanet), pp. 42, 60, 66, 130.

**2017**

- Annalena McAfee, *Hame* (London: Harvill Secker) is a novel about a fictional Scottish poet, but Smith makes a number of appearances alongside Stella Cartwright, and is characterised as a 'degenerate cherub' and womaniser.
- Poem, 'Sydney Goodsir Smith (26 Oct 1915 – 15 Jan 1975)' by Sheena Blackhall, in *Thursdays: Poems and Playlet in Scots and English* (Aberdeenshire: Lochlands), p. 3.
- Special issue of *Poetry Scotland* ('SGS Retro') devoted to poems in tribute to Smith, edited by Sally Evans in Callander (October). Poems by George Hardie, Richie McCaffery, Sally Evans, Robert Calder, William Oxley, Duncan Glen, William J. Tait, Sheena Blackhall, Roderick Watson & Ken Cockburn.

See also: 1967

- *The Poet Speaks: Record 9* (London: Argo Records). Contains recordings of Smith reading from a selection of his work.

1969

- *A Critical Guide to Three Movements in Contemporary Scottish Poetry,* a PhD thesis by Stephen Scobie: University of British Columbia. Part Two of the thesis discusses Smith's work in detail. See: https://open.library.ubc.ca/cIRcle/collections/ubctheses/831/items/1.0104172.

1972

- *No Fellow Travellers,* a short film directed by Oscar Marzaroli to mark Hugh MacDiarmid's 80th birthday. Smith can be seen briefly in the film, in Milnes Bar, seated next to his wife Hazel who is seated next to Alexander and Cath Scott. The only surviving moving footage of Smith with sound.

1982

- *The writings of Sydney Goodsir Smith,* a PhD thesis by John Clifford Hall in 1982: University of Aberdeen. See: http://ethos.bl.uk/OrderDetails.do?uin=uk.bl.ethos.330725.

1994

- 'A route maist devious: A study of the works of Sydney Goodsir Smith', a PhD thesis by Thom Nairn: University of Edinburgh. See: http://ethos.bl.uk/OrderDetails.do?uin=uk.bl.ethos.659858.

2012

- 'Poems chiefly in the Scottish dialectic: Scots poetic translation and the second-generation modern Scottish renaissance (c. 1940–1981)', MPhil (research) thesis by Stewart Sanderson: University of Glasgow.

2016

- 'Our own language: Scots verse translation and the second-generation Scottish renaissance', a PhD thesis by Stewart Sanderson: University of Glasgow. See: http://theses.gla.ac.uk/7541/.

No date

- The biographical entry for Smith on the Scottish Poetry Library website (written by Lizzie MacGregor): http://www.scottishpoetrylibrary.org.uk/poetry/poets/sydney-goodsir-smith.

–   See also the catalogues of Edinburgh University Library - http://www.ed.ac
.uk/information-services/library-museum-gallery/crc/collections/special-
collections/scottish-literature/sgsmith/about and the National Library of
Scotland to get a sense of the wide manuscript holdings for Smith and his
archives. The University of Delaware also holds a substantial amount of
Smith papers: http://www.lib.udel.edu/ud/spec/findaids/smith_sg.htm.

# Index